THE OTHER SIDE OF DEVELOPMENT

The Tribal Story

THE OTHER SIDE OF DEVELOPMENT

The Tribal Story

Edited by

Arun Kumar Ghosh
Ram Dayal Munda

KONARK PUBLISHERS PVT LTD
New Delhi • Seattle

KONARK PUBLISHERS PVT LTD
206, First Floor, Peacock Lane,
Shahpur Jat,
New Delhi-110 049.
Phone: +91-11-41055065, 65254972
e-mail: india@konarkpublishers.com
Website: www.konarkpublishers.com

Konark Publishers International
1507 Western Avenue, #605,
Seattle, WA 98101
Phone: (415) 409-9988
e-mail: us@konarkpublishers.com

Cataloging in Publication Data—DK
Courtesy: D.K. Agencies (P) Ltd. <docinfo@dkagencies.com>

National Seminal on Tribal Issues in the North-Central Sub-region of India (2007 : New Delhi, India)
The other side of development : the tribal story / edited by Arun Kumar Ghosh, Ram Dayal Munda.
p. cm.
Includes bibliographical references and index.
ISBN 8122007988

1. India—Scheduled tribes—Economic conditions—Congresses. 2. Forced migration—India—Congresses. 3. India—Scheduled tribes—Health and hygiene—Congresses. 4. India—Rural conditions—Congresses. 5. India—Scheduled tribes—Government policy—Congresses. I. Ghosh, Arun K. (Arun Kumar) II. Muṇḍā, Rāmadayāla. III. Title

DDC 305.800954 23

Editor: Anna Chandy
Typeset by The Laser Printers, New Delhi, and printed at ASK Advertising Aids Pvt Ltd, New Delhi.

Contents

EDUCATION

HEALTH

ENVIRONMENTAL ISSUES

Preface

In 2001–02, the Council for Social Development undertook a study of the Social Development Profile of Scheduled Castes and Scheduled Tribes in Jharkhand, Bihar and West Bengal. The main objective of the study was to assess the relative socio-economic status of different scheduled castes and scheduled tribes in these states. During the field work we had observed that the problems and issues relating to the livelihood, health and education of the tribals were different from those of other communities. The idea of organising a national seminar focusing on the problems faced by tribes in this region was conceived after the completion of this study. This received whole hearted support from Professor Muchkund Dubey, the President of the Council for Social Development, New Delhi and Dr N.J. Kurian, its former Director.

Accordingly, a two-day National Seminar on Tribal Issues in the North-Central Sub-region of India was organised by the Council for Social Development. It was held at the India International Centre Annexe, New Delhi from 28 to 29 August 2007.

The aim of the seminar was to share the views and research findings of various studies on the subject with a group of experts. The 30 persons who participated in the seminar included scholars and those associated with tribal development programmes from Jharkand and Orissa.

The seminar restricted its ambit to the issues of displacement, livelihood, health, education and environment affecting the tribal people in the North-Central Sub-region. It also covered a discussion on the draft national tribal policy.

The use of the term "North-Central Sub-region" requires an explanation. This sub-region has been classified by some anthropologists as a part of the Central Tribal Region, with a concentration of tribal people covering

Jharkhand, Chhattisgarh, north-western part of Bengal and north Orissa. There may be disagreement over this classification. It has, however, been referred to in this volume as such, since the seminar was organised using this regional identity.

All together 14 papers were presented in the seminar, out of which, we have selected nine papers for this volume. The inaugural address of Mr P.S. Krishnan and the key note address of Prof. Ram Dayal Munda have been converted into papers for this volume. The issues relating to environmental degradation, displacement and rehabilitation were partially covered during oral discussions. A need was felt to include one or two papers on these issues in this volume. Prof. K.B. Saxena contributed two papers on these themes.

The volume is divided into six major themes. There are two papers that cover the themes of Globalisation and Displacement. The subject of Tribal Policy, covered in two papers, is a comment on the Draft National Tribal Policy. The theme of livelihood is covered in three papers. The two papers which address the subject of education, present two opposite view points. The three papers which address the subject of health are over lapping in many respects, but they come out with different strategies to deal with health issues. The paper on environmental aspects deals exclusively with the nature of environmental degradation in the tribal areas and the resultant social injustice to these tribes.

This volume addresses the various conceptual-theoretical and substantive issues related to the livelihood, education, health, environment as well as displacement of the tribal people.

I would like to express my gratitude to the authors who consented to revise their papers and contribute to this volume.

I owe a debt of gratitude to Prof. Muchkund Dubey for his guidance in bringing out the volume in its present form. I am also grateful to Dr N.J. Kurian and Prof. K.B. Saxena for taking a keen interest in the study. Whenever I approached them for their suggestions and comments, they responded kindly and generously.

I extend my sincere thanks to Dr (Ms) M.K. Jabbi, the former Director of the Council for Social Development, for ensuring smooth coordination of the activities undertaken for this project

My thanks extend to Mr R.S. Somi, the former Finance and Administrative Officer for the administrative support provided to me for this project.

I also thankfully acknowledge the constant help I received from Mr A.P. Rai and Mr Suraj Pal Keer during the study.

Finally, I would like to express my sincere appreciation to Ms Tamali Sengupta, Ms Lovely Nagpal and Ms Reeta Khurana for typing the draft of the manuscript.

New Delhi **Arun Kumar Ghosh**

Contributors

K.B. Saxena retired as Secretary to the Government of India and is presently Professor of Social Justice and Governance in the Council for Social Development. His areas of interest include education, health, land reform, environment, displacement and rehabilitation issues. He has several publications to his credit.

P.S. Krishnan retired as Secretary to the Government of India and former Member Secretary of National Commission for Backward Classes. He has decades of experience in handling matters related to the backward classes movement. He also contributed significantly to the preparation of the central government's affidavits in the Indra Sawhney case in 1992, which resulted in the Supreme Court upholding the reservation of government posts for the Other Backward Classes (OBCs).

Again, his presence as Member Secretary of the National Commission for Backward Classes from 1993 to February 2000 has helped ensure that genuinely backward communities that were left out in the first phase of Central lists were brought into the lists.

Vinay Kumar Srivastava is Principal of Hindu College, University of Delhi. He was formerly a Professor of Social Anthropology in the University of Delhi. He did M.Sc in Anthropology and MA in Sociology from the University of Delhi and earned his Ph.D. in social anthropology from King's College, UK. He has published widely in both national and international journals. Some of his important books are: Essays in Social Anthropology (1990, Institute of Social Research and Applied Anthropology, Calcutta); *L' Inde des Tribus Oubliees* (1993, Societe Nouvelle des Editions du Chene, Paris); *Social Anthropology: An Introduction*; in Hindi (1994, Palaka Prakashan, Delhi); *Religious Renunciation of a Pastoral People* (1997, Oxford University Press, Delhi);

He co-edited *Human Ecology in the New Millennium* (2001, Kamla-Raj Enterprises, Delhi); he edited the Volume entitled *Methodology and Fieldwork* (under the series Oxford in India Readings in Sociology and Social Anthropology, 2004, Oxford University Press, Delhi). He was bestowed with the Rashtriya Shiromani Award by the Delhi Telugu Society for his contribution to anthropology. He has delivered the Dr K.S. Mathur Memorial Lecture (2003), Prof. P.K. Bhowmick Memorial Lecture (2005), Platinum Jubilee Lecture, Indian Science Congress (2007), and Prof. N.K. Singhi Memorial Lecture (2008).

Subhadra Mitra Channa is Professor of Social Anthropology in the University of Delhi. She did her M.Sc and Ph.D. in Social Anthropology from the Department of Anthropology, Delhi University. She was a Charles Wallace Visiting Fellow to the Queen's University, UK in 2000, a Fulbright Visiting Lecturer to the Auburn University, USA in 2003 as well as a Visiting Professor to the Maison de Sciences L' Homme in Paris in 2004. She was a Scholar-in-Residence, for the teaching year 2008–09, under the Fulbright program at the University of South Carolina, USA, where she taught, among other courses, Ethnicity and Race. She is at present the Co-Chair of the Commission on the Anthropology of Women, an international body a part of the IUAES (International Union of Anthropological and Ethnological Sciences) along with Prof. Faye Harrison (Chair). She is also a member of the Editorial Board of the Journal of the Royal Anthropological Institute (JRAI) published from London. She has published about 50 papers in many international journals and edited books on these issues.

Harishwar Dayal is a faculty member of the Department of Economics at St. Xavier's College, Ranchi and Director, Eastern Regional Centre of Institute for Human Development. He has done his MA in Economics and M.Phil from JNU, New Delhi and his Ph.D. from Ranchi University. His main areas of interest include: Development Economics, Labour Market, Poverty and the Economic condition of Adivasis. He has written two books, two working papers and contributed 10 research papers on these issues, which have been published in national and international journals. He was a member of the "Expert Group on Prevention of Alienation of Tribal land and its Restoration" formed by the Ministry of Rural Development, Department of Land Resources, Government of India in 2003 under the Chairmanship of Shri B.N. Yugandhar. He was also a member of the technical team for development of "Indicators Relevant for Indigenous Peoples" formed by UNPFII in 2007.

R.P. Mitra is a Lecturer in Social Anthropology in the Department of Anthropology, University of Delhi. He has contributed articles on tribal issues to various journals. He has been appointed by the Madhya Pradesh government to evaluate the conservation cum development programme on the *Bharia*, a Primitive Tribe of the Patalkot area of Madhya Pradesh.

Ravi Kumar teaches at the Department of Sociology, Jamia Millia Islamia University, New Delhi. He has done extensive fieldwork on identity politics, caste based mobilisations, educational inequality and social movements in North India. He worked on "Dynamics of Identity Formation: The Political Economy of Backward Castes in Bihar" for his doctorate and has written over a dozen articles and papers on education, communalism and politics. His publications include *The Politics of Imperialism and Counterstrategies* (co-edited, Delhi: Aakar Books, 2004); *The Crisis of Elementary Education in India* (edited, Sage, 2006), *'lobal Neoliberalism and Education and its Consequences* (Forthcoming, co-edited, New York: Routledge). His specialisation is social movements, identity politics, social theory and sociology of knowledge. He is editor of online journal *Radical Notes*.

B.K. Panda Associate Professor in the National University of Educational Planning and Administration (NUEPA), with a Masters in Social Anthropology and Ph.D. in Educational Anthropology. He has undergone an advanced Training in Educational Planning and Management at UNESCO-IIEP, Paris; He has published a number of articles and books. He is working on issues relating to Educational Planning and Management of Scheduled Tribes and other Disadvantaged Groups, and has conducted a variety of projects and supervised M. Phil/ Ph.D. Scholars in the area of Education of Scheduled Tribes. He has also been continuously involved in conducting training programmes for the Officers and Principals of the Tribal Development Departments of various states.

Sutapa B. Neogi is presently Associate Professor at the Indian Institute of Public Health (IIPH-Delhi), Public Health Foundation of India. She did her specialisation in Community Medicine from the Post Graduate Institute of Medical Education and Research (PGIMER), Chandigarh, a premier Institute of the country. She also holds a degree of DNB (Diplomate of National Board) in Maternal and Child Health (MCH). She has been involved with various national and international agencies in project coordination and implementation and has to her credit a number of publications in journals of repute.

Salil Basu holds MSc degrees in Chemistry and Anthropology and a Ph.D. in Human Genetics. He is a Health Anthropoligist by profession. He started his career as a faculty member of the Department of Anthropology, University of Delhi in 1962. In 1974, Dr Basu joined National Institute of Health and Family Welfare (NIHFW) as Head of the Department of Population, Genetics and Human Development. He took voluntary retirement in 1994 as Professor and Head from NIHFW and joined World Bank as a Consultant and was intermittently associated with the Bank for six years to carry out various health related social assessment projects among tribal communities in various states of India.

During his 20-year tenure at NIHFW, Dr Basu along with his team had carried out several tribal health related projects supported by ICMR, ICSSR, CSIR, NIHFW among various states of India. His total research experience is more than 40 years. He has been guide to 12 Ph.D and five MD students (Genetic Epidemiology) from Delhi University.

Dr Basu was the founder and Executive Director of a NGO "Foundation for Research and Development of Underprivileged Groups", from 1994 to 1999. In 2000, he joined a Consultancy firm, FAITH Healthcare Private Limited, which is involved in Integrated Human Development projects, in areas like health, education, women and children and vulnerable groups, amongst other related areas. Presently, Dr Salil Basu is a Director of FAITH.

P.C. Joshi is a Professor of Social Anthropology in the Department of Anthropology of the University of Delhi. He is the current President of the Society for Indian Medical Anthropology, Mysore and Editor of *SIMA Bulletin*. He has been in the faculty of the HNB Garhwal University, Srinagar, Uttarakhand and the Institute of Human Behaviour and Allied Sciences, New Delhi. He has been a visiting faculty to the University of Heidelberg, Germany and the Global Forum for Health, Geneva. In the recent past he participated in the United Nations Climate Change Conference at Poznan, Poland as a delegate of the European Community. As Asia Coordinator of the multi-country EU framework Integrated Project, he is currently examining micro-level impact of disasters. He has published two books and nearly 60 research articles in various national and international journals.

Introduction

Arun Kumar Ghosh

The greatest challenge that the Government of India has faced since independence is to ensure social justice to the Scheduled Tribes. Along with the Scheduled Castes, and other denotified tribes, they are the weakest sections of the population constituting the matrix of India's poverty. Historically, they have been subjected to the worst form of exploitation. However, the basis of tribal isolation and exclusion is neither caste nor religion, but their ethnicity. Tribals are ethnically different from non-tribal populations due to their distinct culture, language, social organization, and economy.

Since the tribals are ethnically different, tribal issues have received much attention from anthropologists and sociologists. After the publication of Verrier Elwin's '*The Baiga*' in 1939, the development paradigm for the tribals took the course of a debate as to whether the tribals should be left to their own world (*Elwin, 1939*) or whether they should be assimilated in the mainstream (*Ghurye, 1943*). Pandit Jawhar Lal Nehru chose the approach of integration of tribal societies, which lay somewhere between the extreme policies of isolation and assimilation (*Srivastava, 2007*).

The Government of India has been pursuing policies of positive discrimination for the uplift of the Scheduled Tribes ever since independence. Reservation in educational institutions and services as well as introduction of schemes (such as Integrated Tribal Development Projects [ITDPs], Tribal Sub-Plan under Modified Area Development Approach [MADA] and Special Central Assistance) are some of the measures adopted by the Government to ameliorate the condition of the Scheduled Tribes.

However, despite the government's concerted efforts to improve the socio-economic condition of the tribals, the planned development that followed independence, especially the growth of core sectors, displaced a large number of people. During the last five decades since independence, about 30 to 35 million people are estimated to have been displaced due to development projects, including setting up of industries (*Murickan et al, 2003:31*). Only about 25 per cent of the displaced persons have been properly rehabilitated. The majority of the displaced persons are tribals. According to *Cernea*, displacement entails 'impoverishment risk' comprising "landlessness, joblessness, homelessness, marginalization, food security, increased morbidity and mortality, loss of common property assets and social disarticulation" (1999:18) In fact, in the process of development, the tribals have not only lost their livelihoods, but also their own cultural identity. Some scholars look at displacement as one of the manifestations of "development pathologies" (*Oommen, 2006:278*). It was after long persuasion that the forest bill was notified, recognising the land rights of the tribal people.

The North-Central Tribal Sub-region is a part of the Central Tribal Region comprising tribal belts of Jharkhand, Orissa, Madhya Pradesh including Chhattisgarh, Andhra Pradesh and West Bengal (*Ali, 1994*). This region has a high concentration of tribal population spread across Jharkhand, Chhattisgarh, North-Western parts of Bengal, and North Orissa. Of the more than 80 million tribal people in India, about one-fourth belong to these states. This sub-region has a large variety of tribes with their particular geo-climatic and demographic characteristics. The major tribal communities are *Santhal, Oraon, Munda, Ho, Mahali, Bhumij, Sabar, Khond, Gond* and *Kawar*. Some of the most primitive tribes of this sub-region are the *Birhor, Lodha, Mal Paharia, Hill Kharia, Juang, Pauri* and *Bhuiya.*

The Right to Life is enshrined in our Constitution as a Fundamental Right. This implies that people have a right to a livelihood to sustain life. The development process, which was initiated in the country more than 55 years ago has still not ensured livelihood to a considerable section of society. Though the incidence of poverty has declined substantially over this period, more than a quarter of the country's population still lives below the poverty line. The incidence of poverty is much more among the marginalised sections of the society, especially among the Scheduled Tribes. The incidence of poverty among the total Scheduled Tribes population in India was 43.8 per cent in 2003–04 as against 27.5 per cent for the total population (*NSSO, 2004–05*). The incidence of poverty among the Scheduled Tribes population in this region is higher than that of All-India Scheduled Tribes population. In Orissa the incidence of poverty is as high as 75 per cent, followed by Jharkhand and Chhattisgarh with 54 per cent each. In West Bengal, the incidence of poverty among the Scheduled Tribes is closer to the national level as mentioned earlier.

It can be argued that persistence of poverty may be due to the fact that a significant proportion of tribal population is unable to earn even a minimum income to meet their basic requirements. A typical picture of the tribal economy generally revolved around hunting, food gathering, and shifting cultivation, but this is no longer true. Due to the enactment of various laws regarding the use of forests and cultivation in the forest areas, the tribes have suffered the most. In addition, due to the exploitation by moneylenders they have had to sell their assets and other belongings. During 2004–05 more than 61.4 per cent of the tribes were either landless or had land only up to one acre. In West Bengal, landlessness was as high as 81 per cent, followed by Orissa with 53.4 per cent and Jharkhand with 43.5 per cent. In this region the incidence of landlessness was lowest in Chhattisgarh with 31.7 per cent. In this context, it may be mentioned that unfortunately the development process in the recent past has not been labour-absorbing; rather it has been capital intensive, leading to jobless growth. Thus, though there were many tribal plans and sub-plans since independence, their implementation and the ultimate outcome is far from satisfactory.

Tribal culture has its own system of beliefs and practices concerning diseases and has evolved its own system of medicine to cope with them. In tribal culture, "diseases are caused not only due to physical, chemical or biological processes but also due to a number of socially and culturally determined factors" (*Swain, 1994:23*). Religious rites occupy a prominent place among the tribals in the treatment of diseases. The social function of religious rites with regard to diseases and other calamities is to avert these events through magic, omens and taboos. Tribal societies do not associate certain diseases or epidemics with insanitary living conditions of the community. This does not mean that some specific tribal groups do not follow or create clean or sanitary settlements. Tribes like Santhal or Ho maintain a reasonable standard of hygiene.

It is wrong to presume that all tribal groups enjoyed perfect physical and mental health in the past because they lived in the lap of nature in a clean environment. The condition of the various tribes is not uniform. There are areas which are prone to certain diseases. But these diseases are not restricted to tribes only. However, it is true that due to the dependence of the tribes on the forest for their livelihood, their low population combined with a clean environment and the absence of any external intervention, had a positive effect on their health. Over the years, however, gradual infiltration by non-tribal population combined with continuous deforestation and pressure of population on natural resources has led to environmental degradation of the areas where majority of tribal groups live.

As *Singh* (1994) says: "A large number of tribal communities are eclectic in their approach to food which is derived from farm, i.e., agricultural products as well as forest, catering to both plant and animal nutrition. The unfortunate fact today is that there has been depletion of both tribal agricultural land and forest. Despite legal and administrative measures, a sizeable percentage of his land has slipped away from the tribals. Further, it is well known that deforestation after independence has taken place on a big scale, and for this reason and otherwise, there has been large-scale destruction of wild life. Shrinkage of these resources has had devastatingly deleterious effect on availability of food of the tribal" (*Singh, 1994: 44–45).*

The general health problems of the tribal communities in this sub-region are no different from those affecting the rural and other underprivileged sections of our country. These include malnutrition, anaemia, parasitic infections, diarrohoea and respiratory infections. Malaria, leprosy and tuberculosis are also not uncommon among the tribal population. Diseases like goitre and yaws are also present. Tribals also suffer from a deficiency of calcium, vitamin A, riboflavin and animal protein. The poor nutritional status of tribal women directly influences their reproductive health, their survival, growth, and development.

The data on health and nutritional status of women of the National Family Health Survey show that the average Body Mass Index (BMIs) of married tribal women in India was 46.6 per cent which is about 13 per cent higher than that of the general female population of India (*NFHS-3*). It has also been observed that the incidence of anemia is higher among tribal women than the general population in the country indicating a higher prevalence of nutritional deficiency of iron foliate, vitamin B_{12} among other nutrients. According to the *NFHS-3*, the incidence of anemia among the ever-married (*Ever married is referred to a person who got married at any point of time in his or her life time*) tribal women in the age group 15–59 years was 69.2 per cent as compared to 56.2 per cent among this category of women in the general population. A higher prevalence of chronic energy deficiency among Scheduled Tribes in this sub-region has also been observed.

Similarly, the incidence of acute undernutrition and anaemia is considerably higher among tribal children than among the children of the general population As per *NFHS-3*, the incidence of anaemia among the tribal children in the 6–35 months age bracket was 85.1 per cent as against 79.2 per cent in the case of the children of the general population. The incidence of acute respiratory infections (ARI) and diarrohoea are the major causes of illness among tribal infants. In the absence of early diagnosis and treatment, these diseases lead to infant and child mortality.

In the context of increased role of privatisation of health services and the consequent increase in the cost of drugs, one has to think of an alternative system of medicine which would be locally available and cost-effective. Tribal people have developed their indigenous medicine system based on herbs and other items collected from nature and processed locally. They also have their own system of diagnosis and cure of diseases. The wisdom of replacing the traditional health care system of the tribals with the modern health care system has been questioned by many scholars.

Though the National Health Policy, 1983 clearly stated the need for priority attention to primary health coverage to this group, it is reported that primary health services in the tribal areas are far from adequate in terms of the availability of medicine, medical personnel and equipments. Moreover, the health institutions too, are not located in appropriate places in these areas. The National Health Policy, 2002 focused on building up credibility for alternative systems, by encouraging evidence-based research to determine their efficacy, safety and dosage. It also encouraged certification and quality-marking of products to enable a wider popular acceptance of these systems of medicine. However, it did not make any separate policy statement for the tribal population. It, however, emphasised public–private partnership in the sector of health services, where NGOs and other charitable organisations can provide the necessary services.

Though the National Policy of Education (1986) did emphasise the integration of tribal children with a due recognition of tribal cultures for schooling, it failed to address the specific disadvantages characterising the tribal population. The Tribal Welfare Department and the Education Department of the State are both entrusted with responsibility to improve the socio-economic conditions of tribal people. However, an absence of coordination between the two departments in sharing their respective expertise and experiences has stunted educational development among tribals. Though the tribal welfare department is sensitive to the issues of tribals, it lacks adequate expertise. The education department on the other hand, lacks sensitivity to the tribal problems, but it has expertise in educational planning and administration, monitoring and supervision. The infrastructure for education is yet to be developed in tribal areas. Addressing issues of retention of teachers and dropouts among children is necessary for achieving improvement in the educational realisation of this society. The recent NUEPA study significantly focuses on this aspect. *Ashram* school has been viewed as an effective institution to meet the educational needs of tribal children living in the most backward and scattered habitations.

It is to be noted here that the *ashram* schools in many tribal regions are not functioning effectively. Many studies reveal the short comings of the *ashram* schools. There are several inadequacies—lack of appropriate teaching materials, lack of physical infrastructures including adequate number class rooms, library, lack of communication and pedagogic skills of the teachers (*Sharma and Sujatha, 1983*; *Mathur, 1992*; *Nambissan, 2000*; *Nagi, 2000*). Despite the emphasis laid on *ashram* schools, their inability to relate to the tribal situation has come in the way of their spreading education in the tribal areas.

Tribal societies in general have relatively much less gender inequality. They do not have many culturally-discriminatory practices against women. This is reflected in the sex ratio of the tribal population. As per 2001 Census, the sex ratio among the tribals in India is 978 compared to 933 of the general population. The sex ratio is in favour of females in Orissa (1003) and Chhattisgarh (1013), while in Jharkhand it is slightly lower (987), but it is still higher than the all India figure. Though tribal societies have relatively much less gender inequality within themselves, when they come in contact with non-tribals, their women are placed in unequal position in the labour economy. They are discriminated on the ground of gender. Their wages are low, both in agricultural as well as non-agricultural sectors (such as mining). Some tribal women are also sexually exploited. Tribal women are placed in adverse situations in their own ecological setting too, as the women normally go to forests to collect fuel wood and carry it as head-loads, which affects their health condition, particularly during pregnancy and post-partum period. They are already overburdened with other works such as fetching water, cooking, tending to children and agricultural activities. The development projects have affected them more adversely than they have their men.

The gender gap among the tribals can also be found in literacy. As per 2001 Census, the gender gap was 28 percentage points in the state of Orissa, 26.8 in Jharkhand and 25.7 in Chhattisgarh. It was found that a substantially higher proportion of tribal girls were engaged in various household works and allied activities. The non-availability of schools within easy access, also poses a serious impediment to the enrolment of children, particularly girls, for more than half of the predominately tribal habitation.

In spite of various protective legislations enshrined in the Constitution, the process of alienation of tribal land has not stopped. After independence, the tribal areas, particularly in this sub-region, being rich in natural resources, have attracted and continue to attract considerable investment in mines, industries, hydel-power and irrigation projects, leading to direct as well as indirect eviction of different tribal groups. The direct acquisition of land has resulted in considerable displacement and improper rehabilitation has compounded the problem.

In an era of new economic policy of liberalisation and globalisation, needless to say, the entry of the private sector in the arena of development has increased the demand for land leading to more displacement, loss of livelihood and dislocation of lifestyle.

Ram Dayal Munda in his paper entitled "*Globalisation and the Crisis in Tribal Life"* says that the tribals are endowed both with natural and cultural resources and can continue to live without any assistance from the government. They are self-reliant and their development by their own means is sustainable. It is only when outside forces incurse into the tribal areas that the sustainability of natural resources is under threat, resulting in the degradation of the quality of their life. While criticizing the globalisation and liberalisation policies, he says that a new phenomenon of "internal colonialism" has emerged. During the colonial period, the English exploited the tribals but today they are facing severe crisis due to the new economic policy and are increasingly dispossessed of their natural and cultural resources by internal as well as external colonisation. He argues that development for the tribals has no meaning, until and unless it is an inclusive development. This inclusive development would not differentiate between tribals and non-tribals and would ultimately lead to a better society based on equity. He also believes that there are lessons to learn from the tribal way of life which would increase the sustainability of the natural resources of the world at large.

K.B. Saxena in his paper *"Development is War, Underdevelopment is Benign*" has dealt at length and in depth on how the tribals have suffered more than any other social group from displacement caused on account of loss of rights in forest and acquisition of their land from a historical perspective. Originating in the colonial era, the enactment of Indian Forest Act, 1878 and 1927 deprived them of their rights in forest while the Land

Acquisition Act, 1894 displaced them from their own land. The paper deliberates on how these measures had the cumulative effect; of loss of control over natural resources by the tribal communities along with their traditional pattern of livelihood and social organisation. The land acquisition law ignores the constitutional scheme of protection under V Schedule and legal restrictions against alienation of tribal land and the autonomy of self-governance granted to them under Panchayats (Extension to Scheduled Areas) Act, 1996. The dispossession from land combined with the dismal record of their rehabilitation have caused disintegration of tribal society, loss of identity and economic impoverishment. This explains their resistance to acquisition of land, attracting use of coercive power by the state. Saxena further argues that even the much publicised new rehabilitation and resettlement policy, 2007 fails to address their major concerns. It neither assures them alternative land for cultivation nor secure employment in lieu of it. The provisions in the policy on both these aspects are hedged by conditions which fail to create the confidence that either of them would be ensured. Even the entitlements with respect to infrastructure and social amenities in the resettlement colony have been made admissible only where the displacing project satisfies the specified numerical benchmark. The policy also fails to depart from the property centric approach which provides enhanced benefits to land losers, thus leaving the landless tribals ever more vulnerable. The Tribal Development Plan, which forms the basis for rehabilitation in the policy, is conceived as a standardised arrangement for all displaced tribals. It ignores the diversity of social and ecological situations in tribal areas which is evident from different land management practices among tribal groups with varying degrees of community control over natural resources and rights and interests in access to land. The changes proposed in the Land Acquisition Act do not accommodate the concerns of the tribal communities. Thus a bleak future awaits the tribals since land acquisition is getting intensified in the current economic dispensation, with competitive incentives provided by the states to attract capital for industrialisation.

P.S. Krishnan in his paper entitled *"Critical Issues of Tribal Policy"* begins with a comment on the Draft National Tribal Policy, stating therein that it deals with the same problems, the same issues and the same solutions which have been repeatedly discussed over last several decades.

The scheduled tribes need reservation as an affirmative policy for their development. Reservation is one among the many dimensions of the struggle of the Scheduled Tribes for survival and equity. He argues that introduction of "creamy layer" provision in the reservation policy will defeat the goal laid down by the National Policy of Reservation based on constitutional mandate.

He emphasises the need for proper formulation of policy which must be converted into action programme. It requires constitutional amendment, where necessary, legislation, relevant development plans, appropriate machinery for their implementation and more importantly, selection of proper individuals. It is because of wrong selection of individuals, many national commissions set up by the government have turned out to be national omissions. He strongly feels the need for political participation not only at the lowest level of decision making but also at the national level.

He is extremely critical of political leaders who make election promises to a particular community having no tribal characteristics to be included in the list of Scheduled Tribes. The criteria for inclusion of a community in the list of STs should be done purely on socio-anthropological facts. He highlights two other macro issues. The first is the formation of tribal states where the tribals are numerically preponderant and wherever this is not feasible, tribal areas should be constituted into Sixth Schedule Territories with maximum autonomy. He considers that the Fifth Schedule of the Constitution of India is pointless and all the Fifth Schedule Areas should be converted into Sixth Schedule Areas. Along with these two steps, there is also need to take up appropriate measures for enhancing the capabilities of tribal communities so that they can take full charge of their own affairs. He suggests that it is necessary to ensure that the STs/SCs/OBCs get the best of education at all levels so that they are able to get into positions which are comparable to the positions occupied by upper castes and upper classes. Although he appreciates two good steps taken recently, such as Panchayat (Extension to the Scheduled Areas) Act, 1996 and Recognition of Forest Right Act, 2006, but he expresses concerns over their proper and full implementation. Finally, he urges the civil society to assist and guide the people in their struggle to fulfill their genuine needs and aspirations.

Vinay Kumar Srivastava in his paper *"A Critical Reading of the Draft of The National Tribal Policy"* argues that though draft policy claims to strike a balance between protecting tribal cultures on the one hand and integrating the tribals to the mainstream on the other, it has made no attempt to operationalise the concepts of tribe and mainstream. Secondly, he raises the pertinent question as to who would preserve the tribal cultures. Will the non-tribals decide which aspects of tribal cultures need to be preserved? He is of the view that the tribal people themselves are capable of having a critical and introspective look at their culture. This decision of preserving the tribal culture may be left to them. The policies and programmes for the tribal people are formulated by the planners and policy makers who are not very sensitive to tribal cultures and their values. Srivastava feels that sufficient discussions and consultations at various levels involving all sections of people including tribals have not been held while formulating the national tribal policy. Moreover, as the policy document is available only in English, it has not reached a wide section of our population.

Subhadra Channa's paper *"From Equality to Marginalisation: Women of Hunter-food Gathering Tribes"* goes beyond the issue of livelihood. The tribes have not only been deprived of their physical resources but also of their cultural resources as well. Lodha, once considered as a criminal tribe by the colonial administration, have been forcefully evicted from the forest habitats and settled in small hamlets in adverse ecological surroundings. The loss of physical and cultural resources has played havoc with the health of the community's women and has also affected gender relations, which were marked by equality. Channa suggests that any planning for the tribals without empathy and knowledge of their culture will only marginalise them further. The knowledge of environment and use of local resources among tribal women is enormous and in this respect, they are equal to men in their contribution to the household economy.

Harishwar Dayal in his paper on *"Migration as Means of Livelihood for the Tribals of Jharkhand"* says that due to negligible work opportunities in their area, the tribals are forced to migrate to distant and urban centres for better work and wage opportunities. His paper is based on the survey regarding seasonal migration, covering 16 villages. He says that both male and female tribals migrate to work as labourers in brick kilns, agricultural fields, and rice mills as also in the construction sector. Labour contractors (or middle-men) facilitate such migration. As a consequence, the tribals not only get higher incomes but are also exposed to better skills. According to the author, due to such migration, the tribals are becoming aware of the benefits of education and hence are educating their children. He is of the view that migration is certainly beneficial to the tribals and suggests that additional support, both by government and NGOs, is required to facilitate better work opportunities.

R.P. Mitra's paper "*Forest Degradation and its mpact on Livelihood:A Study of a Tribal Village of Chhattisgarh*" examines how the gradual degradation of forests has affected the livelihood of Oraons. Agriculture does not provide adequate support to their livelihood. Forests once played a vital role in their livelihood because they directly depended upon it for secondary sources of income by selling *mahua* flowers, *tendu* leaves, mushroom and various types of seeds and tarmarin. Rapid increase in population has put pressure on natural resources. While the forest department blames the tribals for deforestation, Oraons feel that it is the policy of the government which is responsible for this. Mitra feels that intensive cultivation through the provision of irrigation facilities may improve their livelihood. Also, the recent forest bill recognises the forest rights of tribes and this may help them to solve the issue of their livelihood. Two case studies, one by R.P. Mitra on Oraon tribe in Jeshpur district of Chhattisgarh and the other by Subhadra Channa on the Lodha tribe of Midnapur district of West Bengal, have one thing in common, i.e., increasing marginalisation of these tribes.

Ravi Kumar's paper "*Perisistent Eduycational Marginalisation of Scheduled Tribes: Agruments for an Alternative*" is a critical analysis of educational policies pursued by the Government of India. He argues that educational policies have to be viewed in conjunction with the transition of capitalism from welfare capitalism to neo-liberal capitalism. The tribal communities have been brought within the larger paradigm of the capitalistic framework after adopting the policy of integration with the mainstream. According to Ravi Kumar, the education policies suffered from inherent contradictions right from the beginning—from the Kothari Commission which was constituted in the mid-sixties. Keeping the government/government aided schools in mind, the Commission proposed common schools in order to provide access to equitable schooling to all children across the country. Instead of extending government schools to tribal areas with suitable changes in pedagogy and curricula, the Commission proposed another brand of government schooling (*ashram* schools) for tribal children. At the same time, it remained silent on the issue of private schools. Ravi Kumar feels that the "multi-layer" schooling system has brought about inequality in education. He suggests that an alternative model of schooling within the framework of the common school system may be adopted in the tribal areas, as opposed to what was proposed by the Kothari Commission.

While Ravi Kumar takes a radical theoretical perspective on tribal education, B.K. Panda in his paper "*Education of the Tribes: Role of Ashram Schools in Chhattisgarh and Orissa*" bases his findings on empirical data related to the functioning of *ashram* schools in Orissa and Chhattisgarh. He feels *ashram* schools are most suited for providing educational opportunities to tribal children. He discusses the mechanism as well as constraints of managing *ashram* schools and brings out the different levels of performance in these two states. The efforts made by both state governments and the central government in providing access to schooling in remote and different terrain in the tribal areas have been remarkably effective. *Ashram* schools providing residential facility are considered a critical input for educationally deprived tribal children.

Sutapa Bandyopadhyay Neogi's paper "*Health Issues and Health Seeking Behaviour among Tribals of the North-Central Sub-region of India*" deals with the morbidity pattern and health seeking behaviour of specific tribal groups in this region. Her study is largely based on secondary materials collected from other studies. The findings reveal that not only have communicable diseases continued to persist in tribal areas but some of these diseases like malaria have developed insecticide resistant vectors. Skin infections, infertility and hemoglobinopathies are peculiar to tribal groups. They are now also becoming susceptible to cardiovascular diseases, due to change in life style. She argues that the tribal people resort to some traditional practices because of poor health infrastructure and poor health care delivery services in difficult terrain in the tribal areas. She is of the view that the lack of systematic and periodic documentation of ongoing health care delivery operation, lack of motivation of health workers, shortfall of health personnel in tribal areas, lack of utilisation of health services by the tribal population and lack of adequate finances are some of the reasons for poor performance. She says that an alternative mechanism evolved through public–private partnership has shown promising results in some states. The government has handed over the management of Primary Health Centres (PHCs) and Sub Health Centres to NGOs and corporate bodies. The sustainability of the alternative system of health delivery does not lie in the government withdrawing its responsibility from the social sector. The sustainability depends upon public–private partnership as well as the community itself being a stake holder in the health delivery system.

Salil Basu in this paper "*The Social Dimension of Health and Development in Tribal Communities of the North-Central Sub-region of India*" highlights the need for a holistic approach to issue of health in relation to the tribal community. He says that health is not only the function of medicare variables, but also the function of other variables related to overall development of society. He emphasised the need for adequate data related to health variables like fertility, mortality, morbidity and socio-cultural and socio-biological correlates affecting the health variables for planning effective health care strategies in the tribal areas, information on which are woefully inadequate. Basu examines various health related issues of tribal communities. His findings are based on the available secondary data, supplemented with recent research study. It is a situational analysis with respect to distribution and characteristics, health profile, morbidity and mortality pattern, including health seeking behaviour of the tribal communities of this sub-region. The situation is accentuated by the absence of safe drinking water, proper sanitation and low level of hygiene coupled with primitive health practices.

P.C. Joshi's paper "*Challenges of Health Care in Central Indian Tribal Areas*" examines the public health care delivery and its impact on the tribal population in the state of Jharkhand and Chhattisgarh. Both the states perform quite poorly on development and health indicators. The delivery of health care services and health education has not reached the tribal areas in these two states. There is a huge shortfall of Public Health Centres as well as specialised doctors. Good quality health services are not available for mother and child. Further, even the facilities available in the area are not properly utilised because of the tribals' traditional health seeking behaviour. As a result there is a low percentage of both antenatal checkup and full immunisation among the community. This apart, there is no serious effort to involve the tribal people in the health care programme. The primary level health workers are also de-motivated and do not visit the tribal hamlets regularly. The entire medicinal heritage of the tribal society can also be seen as an alternative system of therapy. There is a need to assess the therapeutic efficacy of tribal medicine and revive it for health promotion, for both preventive and curative purposes. There is also need to bring intellectual property to its rightful custodian.

In the chapter on *"Environmental Degradation and Social Injustice in Tribal Areas: Deficit of Governance and Failure of Democracy"* K.B. Saxena discusses the nature of environmental degradation in tribal areas, the social injustice caused to the tribal people on this account. He argues that the failure of regulatory mechanism to protect the environment and the apathy of democratic institutions to take up the grievances of tribal people in this regard are responsible for worsening their plight. Industrial and mining projects in bio-diversity rich tribal areas by the profit making agencies supported by the government, has not only displaced them from their source of subsistence, but also made the cultivable land in their vicinity infertile. It has polluted water resources and air quality due to which the tribals afflicted with serious life threatening diseases. He writes, "Tourism emerges as a new agenda of environmental degradation and destabilization of tribal society." (*Saxena, 2011*) Ironically, even the approach to conservation of forests is inimical to the tribals because it is guided by market driven plantation selection, depriving them of the multiple benefits of diversity of natural species. The regulatory arrangements to check environmental degradation fail to deliver both on account of the existing provisions of law as well as their implementation. According to author, "the existing laws are ambiguous, loose in formulation, hedged by caveats, lack in clarity and definitiveness in fixing responsibility and seeking compliance." (*Saxena, 2011*) The enforcement is weak and hamstrung, by multiple agencies, with little coordination and clear areas of responsibility. It is also heavily tilted in favour of the industry.

The constitutional mandate for protection of tribal interests is defeated by policies of the government which give primacy to economic growth. The tribals affected by displacement from land and environmental degradation are resisting development projects which cause these externalities. The author is pained to find that the agencies of governance have shown little concern for "horrendous" impact of environmental degradation on the lives of people. This is why the industry violates environmental regulations with impurity. The predicament of the tribal people is worse due to the apathy on the part of political institutions and processes which have failed to exert pressure on the government to protect the environment and the lives and livelihoods dependant upon it. This, in author's view, signifies the failure of democracy.

ENDNOTE

Different scholars have made different estimates on percentage of people living below poverty line. There estimates show higher incidence of poverty than the estimate made by NSSO. According to a government panel set-up under the chairmanship of N.C. Saxena, 50 per cent of Indian population are living below poverty line. Another expert group headed by Suresh Tendulkar estimated 37.2 per cent Indian population are living below poverty line, while the Arjun Sen Gupta's report shows it is as high as 78 per cent.

REFERENCES

Ali, Almas (1994), "Indegenous Health Practices among Tribals: Relationship with Prelevant Diseases" in Salil Basu (ed.): *Tribal Health in India*, Manak Publications Pvt. Ltd. Delhi.

Cernea, Michael, M. (1999), "Development's painful social costs: Introductory Study" in S. Parasuram, *The Development Dilema: Displacement in India*, Macmillan Press Ltd, London.

Ghosh, Arun Kumar (2007), "Tribal Travail, New Economic Policy and the Matrix of Poverty," *The Statesman*, May 18, New Delhi.

Ghurye, G.S. (1943), "The Aborigines—So called their future," Gokhale Institute of Politics and Economics, Poona.

Government of India, National Sample Survey Organisation (2006), "Employment and Unemployment Situation in India, 2004–05," N.S.S. 61st Round Report No. 515, New Delhi.

Government of India, National Sample Survey Organisation (2006), "Land and Pattern of Consumer Expenditure in India 2004–05," N.S.S. 61st Round Report No. 508, New Delhi.

Mathur, P.R.G. (1992), "Tribal Education in Kerala," in Buddhadev Chaudhuri (ed.): Education and Literacy Programme (Vol. IV:54–98), Inter-India Publications, New Delhi.

Murickan, Jose et. al. (2003), "Development—Induced Displacement: Case of Kerala," Rawat Publications, Jaipur.

Nagi, B.S. (2000), "Educating Tribals in India: A study of ashram schools," Kaniskha Publishers, New Delhi.

Nambissan, Geetha B. (2000), "Identity exclusion and the education of tribal communities," in Rekha Wazir (ed.): The Gender Gap in Basic Education: NGOs as Agents of Change (175-224), Sage Publications, New Delhi.

National Family Health Survey, (NFHS-3), 2005–06 IIPS, Mumbai.

National Sample Survey Organisation, (2004-05), National Sample Survey, 61st round.

Oommen, T.K. (2006), "Coping with Development Pathologies: Resistance to Displacement," *Sociological Bulletin*, 55(2), May–August.

Saxena, K.B. (2011), "Environmental Degradation and Social Injustice in Tribal Areas: Deficit of Governance and Failure of Democracy" in Arun Kr Ghosh and Ramdayal Munda (ed.): *The Other Side of Development: Tribal Story*, Konark Publishers Pvt Ltd, New Delhi.

Sharma, G.D. and K. Sujatha. (1983), "Educating tribals: An in-depth analysis of ashram schools," New Delhi: National Institute of Educational Planning and Administration.

Srivastava, Vinay Kumar (2007), Jawaharlal Nehru on Tribes. *Social Science Probings*, 19(2) 135–48.

Singh, Bhupinder (1994), "Factors Influencing Health of Tribal Population Groups," in Salil Basu (ed.): Tribal health India, Manak Publications Pvt. Ltd. Delhi.

Sujatha, K. (1987), "Education of the forgotten children of the forest: A case study of Yemadi tribe," Konark Publishers, New Delhi.

Swain, Saraswati (1994), "Health Disease and Health Seeking Behaviour of Tribal People of India," in Salial Basu (ed.): Tribal health in India, Manak Publications Pvt. Ltd. Delhi.

Verrier, Elwin (1939), "The Baiga," John Murray: London.

GLOBALISATION AND DISPLACEMENT

Globalisation and the Crisis in Tribal life

Ram Dayal Munda

The tribal people had been a self-reliant, reasonably happy and prosperous group of communities. If you look at the history of each tribal community, you will find that the people of each tribal community had seen good days. One reason for this may be that the tribal population in the past was small and they had somehow managed to evolve their own systems that took care of them for centuries. They followed a system of sustainable management of natural resources, which is in crisis today; the forests are receding, the water is getting polluted, there are not many fish left in the ponds. These had never been critical issues in the tribal world earlier, which is probably why they were a happy community once. They not only made efficient use of natural resources but also adhered to a set of cultural resources which provided the moral basis of their existence. Honesty, simplicity and unity are some of the ethical values which are embedded in their culture. These were also the features that made their system sustainable.

In the age of globalisation and liberalisation the "market" is dominating the day-to-day life of a modern man. A family in the metropolitan city is not satisfied with one car; every adult member of the family needs a car each. Such needs make the modern system unsustainable, depleting the natural resources at a fast pace. The tribal people on the other hand, know how to make efficient use of coal and iron. They have used these resources for centuries. The rate at which modern society consumes these resources today, we cannot hope to conserve them even for a the coming hundred years.

Heavy machineries which have come to Jharkhand from Australia have the capacity to destroy hills in a week's time. These are "the white industries" that I have known through my works with the UNO at Geneva. When I narrated stories about these mining industries in our area which are certified by the Australian Government and others, to the Australian aborigines, they were astonished. They told me how the "white industries" were hounded from Australia. These very "white industries" have now come to exploit new opportunities in India and in other Third World countries. The tribal people are untutored in this kind of trade. The prosperity achieved in the past was probably due to availability of local mineral resources like coal, iron, copper and their proper utilisation. How did the Gupta period come to be known as the golden age in the history of India? Perhaps, it is because the people of that period knew how to make use of these natural resources which were available in that area.

The idea has been mooted in several quarters that India will soon become a world power. The crucial issue is not whether India will achieve the status of a world power or not. Surely India will become a world power, because half of these resources like coal, iron and copper are available in India. But more important is the question whether we are to achieve this status by exhausting all our natural resources? Secondly, are we to achieve it by putting the common people of our country in misery and distress? So even though in the eyes of the western world, we will achieve the status of a world power, in our own eyes we will become monsters. The tribal people think that anybody consuming beyond a limit is like a monster that will bring about destruction. If resources are used excessively for consumption purpose, it cannot be sustainable beyond a hundred years. There is a lesson in the past history of the tribal communities, whose happiness came from sustainable management of natural resources as well as from sustainable management of cultural resources which they have evolved over the years.

The principle of cooperation and equality is deeply rooted in tribal culture. It is not only equality between men and women but also among all beings as also between beings and non-beings. In this society when a man goes out hunting, the dog accompanying him also gets an equal share. Their cattle not only have a physical value but also have symbolic value. In the cattle festival they are considered to be sacred and are treated with respect. They eat the same food that tribal people eat. The idea of "mother cow" is deeply embedded in tribal culture. Eating beef is forbidden. The tribal people do not even drink the milk of a cow as they do not wish to deprive the calves of the right to their share of their mother's milk so that they can grow up healthy and help in ploughing of the land. Cattle are considered as companions and family members by the tribal people. Thus human feelings are extended to all animals and plants. It is this way of living that has led to making their lives sustainable. The adoption of scientific methods of increasing the milk of cattle is strange to the tribal mind because it is related to increasing the level of consumption which they know is not a sustainable pattern at all. Their pattern of consumption makes life itself sustainable for much longer than we can ever imagine.

Around 85 per cent of the world's pollution is contributed by the "civilized" people. The life style of the tribal people on the other hand has contributed to making life sustainable and even though their numbers are small, their capacity to survive is much more than that of "civilized" people. They have survived on their own strength. Now, with the introduction of development projects in tribal areas, it is the non-tribals involved in the planning and implementation of these projects who are prospering rather than the tribal people for whose development such projects were conceived of in the first place. Former Prime Minister of India, late Shri Rajiv Gandhi was right when he said that only 15 paise out of a rupee spent on development reaches the beneficiary.

The country is facing an enormous crisis of natural resources. The tribal people are increasingly being dispossessed of their natural and cultural resources through colonisation—both external as well as internal. Recently this process has taken the form of neo-colonisation which has been brought about by globalisation, liberalisation and privatisation. In this scenario global players are directly in touch with the World Bank and negotiate deals directly with the state governments. The extent of exploitation and dispossession of natural resources witnessed in recent years has surpassed that of even the colonial era. In Sundargarh district of Orissa, as many as 37 sponge iron factories have come up and even a white man will turn into a black ghost if the wind does not blow for an hour. In Jharkhand as many as 47 MOUs have been signed with various multinational corporations. The extent of devastation this may cause in this tribal belt can well be imagined. The amount of devastation that has taken place in recent years is much more than what was inflicted during the last one century.

In north Jharkhand, there are areas which have become hopelessly barren due to excavation. Though there are laws which protect the environment through plantation, in this area they do not work as there is hardly any scope for plantation. Leave alone the tribal people, even animals are not ready to wander there. Regarding the resultant displacement, the less said the better. Walter Fernandes, while discussing the issue of displacement, has referred to the tribal population of this region, who were mostly the victims of displacement. Due to displacement, many tribal people have left Jharkhand and have joined the work force in Punjab and Haryana. Delhi is encircled by an outer Ring Road, on the periphery of which about one-third population of this metropolitan city live in unhygienic and sub-human conditions in Jhuggi-Jhopri colonies. Though there are three or four *parshads* (councilors) elected to the Municipal Corporation of Delhi, they only play a very limited role of influencing voting behaviour or supporting their leaders in the general elections. The physical and environmental character of other mega cities like Mumbai, Kolkata, and Bangalore etc., are the same as that of Delhi. There are other mega cities in the world such as Mexico, Tokyo or New York. However, the conditions under which a large majority of people belonging to poorer sections live in these cities are unimaginable.

In the last two or three decades the landscape of Ranchi and Raipur has undergone a significant change. No more do they bear any characteristics of Jharkhand and Chhattisgarh respectively. Multi-storey buildings and commercial complexes have come up so rapidly that the earlier features of these cities are fast fading. All this is happening under aegis of the neo-colonialism brought about by globalisation and liberalisation. What we have read in history books about a clash of civilisations is, not just an ideal concept. We know that Rama and his men feared Ravana and his demons because they thought that they would swallow them up. Likewise the Americans in recent years feared Mao-Tse-tung and his followers because they thought he would reach Hawai through West Coast and conquer them.

This fear was propagated by the Republicans who are backward in their thinking. Yet it is because of this fear that many Americans cast their votes for the Republicans. In a similar fashion many Dalits fear the RSS in India and cast their votes for right wing parties. The English ruled our country for two centuries through the divide and rule policy. However, the earlier character of colonisation has changed and given a birth to neo-colonialism.

The newest form of colonialism that has emerged is not based on fear but on audacity. India has under gone a revolutionary change in Information Technology. Bangalore is in the fore front in this sector. The fat salary packet earned by graduates fresh from the university many a time exceeds the salaries of even senior bureaucrats in the government sector. Yet these young people are working mostly for American companies operating at night in India while it is still day time in America. The American bosses control these companies from that distant continent, while these youngsters cater to their clients who are Americans too!

In India there are big industrialists like Jindals, Mittals who are no less global than their American counter parts. In the wake of the events that unfolded in Singur, West Bengal, it is with regret that we feel that the Tatas who till recently we thought to be our own people also behave like other global players. There is no limit to the profits that can be earned by companies in the corporate sector. Their annual reports show earnings of 100 per cent or 200 per cent. Their profit margins are more than 100 per cent. While it is quite reasonable for any company to earn 5–10 per cent profit for the time and energy devoted by its entrepreneur, it is unethical to earn profits beyond a certain limit. One hears too that many Indian companies are now purchasing foreign companies abroad. These actions are governed by greed rather than by business ethics.

The extensive destruction of natural resources is portended to bring about a terrible disaster on this planet due to which millions of lives will be lost. We are all aware of the many holes in the ozone layers due to the continuous release of pollutants from the earth. We all know that the earth is becoming warmer as a result of which the Mediterranean sea has been rising over the years. Many Scandinavian countries, it is calculated, will sink into the sea. In course of time many other countries like Mexico, Bangladesh, some parts of India like Kerala will also meet with the same fate. The developed nations who are responsible for such devastation probably think that their people will flee to other planets like Mars for their safety because the atmosphere of Mars is congenial to life. Such is their mindset. But even in the face of such calamity it may surprise you to know that the tribal areas like the Gondwana may survive!

A couple of years ago thousands of people died in a Tsunami. The impact of this Tsunami was felt on the Andaman Islands as well as in coastal belt of Andhra Pradesh, Tamil Nadu, and Kerala. In the Andamans, while tribal group like the Jarwas managed to survive, many other people including some army officials died. Not a single Jarwa died in the Tsunami. The Jarwas survived because they had anticipated the Tsunami before it reached their shores and took shelter on hill tops. They have evolved a defence mechanism against these natural calamities. There are many such things we can learn from tribal people provided we are ready to recognise their traditional knowledge which is based on their own life experiences.

The developed nations who are responsible for ecological crisis instead of taking conservation measures themselves are pressurising to undertake them in the developing countries with the responsibility to carry through the policy for conservation. The World Bank is advocating the planting of trees, for which huge amount of funds are being released by them to the developing countries. The irony is that the developed countries are not ready to reduce their level of consumption nor are they ready to compensate the loss of natural resources. The extent of destruction caused by the developed countries can hardly be compensated unless they reduce their level of consumption and this is only possible if they adopt the tribal system of managing natural resources. Thus it would profit the world at large if the policy perspective is aligned along the tribal line of thinking and managing natural resources. In India there are some agencies who are successfully implementing the tribal development programme. It is necessary to identify well meaning people, who are sensitive to the issue of tribal welfare from within the existing system so that their services can be utilised for the betterment of the tribal people.

Pandit Jawaharlal Nehru in his foreword to *Philosophy for NEFA* advocated the idea of an Adivasi Panchsheel and said "Let them develop according to their own genius". There are plenty of geniuses among the tribal people. They are not only concerned with human beings but also with animals, plants, the sun, the moon and everything in the universe. In other words, they are concerned with the creation as a whole. Today in a market dominated world, a new concept of inclusive development has emerged in order to bring all sections of people in the process of development. This may be a new concept for the modern man but it is not something new in the tribal world. The tribal society has remained inclusive from the beginning. It is not that everything in the tribal society is relevant and needs to be emulated. There are some irrelevant things which need to be discarded. Drinking is associated with tribal way of life and cannot be discarded easily. However, discipline and restraint is called for where there is over indulgence. The tribal families who are leading a disciplined life are healthy and it is not uncommon among the tribals that they can see the rising sun for a 100 years. Many a time a wrong image has been projected about the tribal people. The so called "civilized" people feel that they are against modernity. That they do not need water, electricity or any such modern amenities of life which can bring about a change in the quality of their life. This is because society at large has never interacted with the tribal people closely.

While on the one hand a number of development projects are being initiated in tribal areas, on the other hand this has led to large scale displacement of the tribal people. The tribals are thus victims of liberalisation and privatisation. Their livelihoods have been severely affected. The growing realisation of their plight has led private parties to negotiate a better deal with the tribal people. Today the United Nations are advocating the idea of equal partnership in any deal with them. But the ground reality is that there is nothing open and transparent about these deals. Most of the people occupying the positions in the Ministry of Tribal Affairs or Department of Welfare in the state have no sensitivity for the tribes. Nothing good can be expected from them. They should be replaced with honest and sensitive people who are willing to work for the cause of the tribal people.

The solution would be to set up a well-equipped Tribal Academy to draw in the brilliant minds from within the tribal society itself. The academy should not be set up on the pattern of University Grant Commission (UGC) as it will only create another "creamy" layer of tribal people who will neither belong to their own people nor be part of the mainstream. This Academy should ideally comprise not only tribal people but also those who have devoted the lives to the cause of tribal people!

REFERENCES

Elwin Verrier (1959), *A Philosophy of NEFA*, Government Publications, Shillong.

Fernandes, Walter (1998), "Development-induced Displacement of Eastern India" in S.C. Dube (ed) *Antiquity to Modernity in Tribal India: Continuity and Change Among the Tribals*, Inter-India Publications, New Delhi.

Development is War; Underdevelopment is Benign: Political Economy of Tribal Displacement in India

K.B. Saxena

Focus on Displacement

Development, for most people of the country as also elsewhere in the world, is perceived in positive terms as something inherently good, natural, beneficial, desirable and even inevitable (Chew and Denemark, 2001). Though this thinking is essentially rooted in the European enlightenment, it became a dominant theme of political discourse in the post-war period, particularly in nations liberated from the colonial rule. These nations were hugely attracted by the standard of living conditions in countries of Europe and America which they accepted as the goal towards which they should move. Emulating their conditions was characterised as development. The road to realise this goal lay in replicating their model and strategies. This generated a great deal of theorisation on how this could be done. Economic aid and training of policy makers and academia prepared the intellectual foundation for firmly grounding the western conception of development as the ruling ideology. The development discourse and practice unmistakably reflect this thinking. This paradigm of development has, however, generated numerous distortions and conflicts with regard to its distributional effects and engendered conditions of persistent impoverishment of certain communities and regions. These effects were attributed by protagonists either to the social and cultural inadequacies labelled as "backwardness" of groups and the geography of the regions or to the organisational arrangements and the delivery system in effectuating this goal. The nature of development itself was never questioned. The result is a considerable hostility to "development" in the groups/communities who have continued to suffer its disastrous effects. Tribals in India are the foremost among such groups. Far from perceiving this "development" in positive terms, they have come to characterise it as a declaration of war against them and consider their "underdevelopment" (absence of such development) as benign in comparison.

One of the issues which has brought to the fore this antipathy to development is the forcible acquisition of their land for various development and regulatory projects leading to their large scale displacement from land, habitat, livelihood, and environment. This displacement has resulted in the loss of livelihood, multiple impoverishments, disintegration of their social and cultural organisation, and exposed them to the processes of exploitation more intense than they have experienced ever before. The development induced displacement adversely affects other sections of the poor too but there are reasons why it causes much lesser damage to them than it does to the tribals. This explains the intense resistance that has surfaced against it in several places and the reason why this paper focuses on the displacement of tribals.

Tribals and Displacement

Among factors which distinguish the displaced tribals from the other displaced persons in terms of the intensity and the multi-dimensionality of the adverse effects suffered, the foremost relates to their disproportionate share in this outcome. While reliable official estimation of the magnitude of displacement and its distribution among various social groups has been lacking, the non-official sources based on several research studies have quantified that since independence, nearly 60 million people have been displaced due to the development projects till 2000 of which more than 40 per cent are tribals (Fernandes, 2006)[a]. The report of the Expert Group on Prevention of Alienation of Tribal Land and its Restoration places this figure at 47 per cent (MoRD-2004). Yet, there is a general lack of awareness in the decision makers and the country at large about the enormity of the problem and the suffering of the tribals specifically. Constituting around 8 per cent of the total population of the country, the displacement has been particularly cruel to them as it affects nearly 20 per cent of their population. The situation is traumatic because only a small percentage of the displaced persons (around 25 per cent) have received some sort of rehabilitation of which the displaced tribals would be even less. This implies that more than

75 per cent of the affected displaced tribals have been just left to fend for themselves (*Fernandes, 1991, 1998*; Planning Commission, 2003). With regard to those who are considered to have been rehabilitated, research studies have brought out the insensitivity, ineptitude, incompetence and bias in the efforts (*Kothari, 1996*). What is revealed is not merely inadequate planning but the very absence of planning (*Fernandes, 1998*; *Mathur, 1995*).

Secondly, there is a concentration of development projects which cause displacement in tribal areas because the development strategy is based on maximising the productivity of natural resources of the country for economic growth. The tribals happen to inhabit areas which have a concentration of natural resources for such development—mines, forests, water etc., and consequently a great deal of potential for industrialisation. The scale of exploitation of natural resources has been considerably accelerated and its pace intensified with the onset of new economic policies and the integration of the national economy with global finance, investments, and trade. This has attracted large scale foreign investment for this purpose: The state governments are competing with each other in doling out incentives for attracting such investment. The number of MOUs signed with the foreign/ national investors by the state governments of Orissa, Jharkhand and Chhattisgarh involving thousands of acres of land held by the tribals would indicate the enormity of the ongoing and the likely future displacement (Perspectives, 2007). But the tribals may also suffer displacement on account of their powerlessness. This happens when the projects originally selected for location in the non-tribal areas are shifted to the tribal areas on account of opposition to them from the local people in the former who command greater clout in decision making as, for example, in the case of transfer of army firing range to Jharkhand from Bihar (*Fernandes, 2008*)*. The site selection is not always a dispassionate and technically driven decision in other situations too and politics often mediates in this process (*Balagopal, 2007*)[a].

The paradigm of conservation pursued by the government is also accentuating this process and is, in fact, another facet of the development ideology. The approach to conservation is premised on the antagonism between humans and nature. Forests, wildlife and other forms of bio-diversity, environmentalists believe, can only be conserved if they are not interfered with by human presence. This requires removal of the existing

* This was stated in an address by Walter, Fernandes on the occasion of release of Social Development Report (2008) at the Council for Social Development (New Delhi) on 18th September, 2008.

habitations from areas where such bio-diversity exists and their relocation elsewhere. The inherent conflict between nature and humans constitutes the essence of this paradigm. The tribals are overwhelmingly affected by this approach to conservation since they have been residing in and around the forests traditionally, and are dependent upon its resources overwhelmingly for their survival and, therefore, targeted for relocation. Ironically, the tribals are also victims of environmental degradation caused by development. But the conservation ideology does not focus on this dimension. They thus end up suffering consequences of both development and conservation. The latter is intertwined with the former in their perception and experience.

The third factor due to which the tribals face extensive displacement is what has been termed as the process of sequential exhaustion in the context of forests. (*Gadgil, 1989*). This process involves, in the first place, exploitation of forests which constituted the lifeline for the tribals living in the vicinity by contractors for commercial and industrial use. These agencies first exploit the forests which are the nearest to the villages and after exhausting the more accessible areas, proceed to exploit the more interior forests for this purpose thereby progressively denuding them of the material used by the tribal communities. This occurs through stages beginning with the process of closure followed by cutting down of natural forest and replacing it with commercial plantations. A similar process has been witnessed in respect of the construction of dams which, in the early phase, were taken up nearer the habitations of areas of developed agriculture dominated by the non-tribals. After exhausting such sites, the efforts shifted to the hilly areas which are inhabited by the tribes (*Fernandes, 1991*). The latter dams are also bigger in size, involve larger displacement and benefit those not displaced. This is because land owned by the non-tribals in the plains gets the facility of irrigation while the tribals occupying upland are uprooted.

The tribal areas also become the easy and preferred target for acquisition of land for another reason. Land held by the tribals is not transferable due to legal restrictions on its alienation. The market in respect of tribal land is, therefore, not developed due to which the cost of acquisition is very low in terms of the outgo on compensation. There has also little obligation to rehabilitate the displaced persons. This is the reason why much more land is acquired than is actually needed and later lavishly utilised by project agencies for housing, township and institutional needs unrelated to the project. No sustained protest against or opposition to such acquisition is encountered from the tribal land holders due to their low level of awareness and capacity, political marginalisation and lack of empathy for their suffering in the larger society. For these very reasons, protest where resorted to is also easily subdued by the local officials with the threat of detention and use of force. Similar level and scale of displacement in the non-tribal areas would encounter stiff resistance and invite political intervention.

The tribals also suffer the brunt of displacement due to the multiplier effect of development. Once a tribal area is chosen for the location of an industry, numerous other industries follow. Some of these are ancillary to the main industry while others are attracted by the infrastructure development resulting from the setting up of industry. More areas are acquired for their needs. Major projects also get expanded over time, extending the boundaries of their land by additional acquisition. Supportive services quickly follow these industries to cater to the varied requirements which enlarge the area of acquisition and the scale of displacement. Huge influx of manpower takes place in the area for supply of labour and services which pushes the magnitude of displacement far beyond the level caused by the formal land acquisition. The tribals, overwhelmed by these forces, become an easy prey to this expansion due to their social fragility against the dominant groups and powerlessness in the polity.

Tribal Displacement—Colonial Roots

Involuntary displacement is an example par excellence of the conflict between the state and the tribes since it is the state action which is responsible for the dispossession of tribals from their land, consequent multiple impoverishments and even social disintegration. The process can be traced to the colonial period when the British Government initiated three major policies which were detrimental to the tribal interests and showed total lack of sensitivity to their implications for them. The first related to the restructuring of the agrarian structure with a view to increasing revenue which imposed intermediaries over the tribal peasantry for collection of taxes and levies. This introduced the upper caste non-tribals as superior land owners over the autonomous tribal communities which had traditionally exercised control over the natural resources in their territories and managed them for the benefit of their members. This measure led to numerous processes of exploitation by these intermediaries and their staff engaged for collection of taxes and several non-tribal cultivators brought in by them to enhance revenue through higher productivity from land under their control. Through devious ways, these outsiders dispossessed the tribals from their land. The second policy related to the colonial state's assumption of control over natural resources—land, water, forests, which were managed by the local communities for individual and collective use, for commercial exploitation. This was effected through legal instruments which recognised the sole right of the sovereign to such resources. Any other claim to use these resources was considered valid if accompanied by an authorisation by the state. The policy had the effect of extinguishing/derecognising rights and interests in such resources based on customary laws, traditions and practices which were not interfered with by the preceding rulers. The enforcement of this measure deprived the tribals of their numerous life supporting benefits including livelihood derived from the use of these resources. The third policy lay in extending the "state system" to the tribal areas which had autonomous self-governing communities. The "state system" manifested in the imposition of an alien legal system involving recognition of rights, adjudication of disputes, paradigm of crime and punishment and a conception of property totally beyond the comprehension of tribals and conflictive of their traditional pattern of governance. It also introduced regulatory administration consisting of civil and police functionaries to enforce laws and government policies who replaced the functions of the head of the community operating through a collective mode of decision making. These arrangements also brought in a number of outsiders (non-tribals from the plains) as officials to run the "state system" in contact with the tribals who were ignorant of and totally insensitive to the social organisation, culture and values of the tribes and carried with them a baggage of biases, values and interests which hurt their self confidence and esteem. Faced with the multi-faceted exploitation and a total sense of helplessness, the tribals spontaneously rebelled against the state at several places. These revolts were suppressed with the use of massive force. The experience, however, forced a slight change in the British policy towards the end of the 19th century recognising the distinctiveness of the tribal communities and their fragility against the dominant larger community from the plains and, therefore, the need for their protection against the latter. This understanding was translated into protective legislation in respect of their land and a degree of autonomy given to them in the management of their affairs. The areas of tribal concentration were demarcated where special safeguards were introduced to minimise their contact with the outsiders.

After independence, much of this protective architecture has been retained and some more measures have been added to it. These arrangements have also been incorporated in the Constitution with a view to making the protection of the tribes a responsibility of the government. Besides provisions relating to the fundamental Rights and the Directives of Principles of State Policy which provide entitlements to all citizens, Articles 244, 244A, 275(A), 342, 338(A) and 339 deal exclusively with the tribals. These include, among others, reservation of seats in legislature, public services and educational institutions. The erstwhile "excluded" areas and "partially excluded areas" have been re-designated as "Sixth" and "Fifth" schedule areas. The Governor of the state, who has special responsibility in respect of these areas, has powers to stop, amend or modify the operation of any central or state law in the Fifth Schedule areas. He is required to send a report in respect of this schedule every year to the President. Article 238(2) authorises him to make regulations for peace and good governance of the scheduled areas. This power can be used to restrict transfer of land by or among the members of the Scheduled Tribes, regulate allotment of land and money lending. There is a provision for constitution of a Tribes Advisory Council in the Fifth Schedule areas which the Governor is required to consult in discharge of his responsibility for the welfare of the tribes. Similarly, the Sixth schedule contains provisions for the administration of tribal areas relating to the specified states included in it. The laws enacted by the state governments to prevent alienation of the tribal land to the non-tribals continue to operate. Panchayats (Extension to Scheduled Areas) Act, 1996 (PESA) has extended Panchayati Raj Institutions to scheduled areas under which *Gram Sabha* has been granted special powers relating to the land acquisition, grant of prospecting license and mining lease, minor forest produce and protection against alienation of land. This law recognises village community's competence to manage natural resources in scheduled areas and consultation with *Gram Sabha* mandatory in respect of matters relating to these subjects. The Supreme Court, in a significant judgment (Samtha Vs State of Andhra Pradesh), has prohibited transfer/leasing of tribal land to the non-tribals or private industries in scheduled areas. (*Balagopal, 2007*)[b]. Reservation of seats for STs in *Panchayats* and chairpersons of *Panchayats* has also been mandated.

Notwithstanding these provisions and other institutional arrangements for protection of the tribals, they have been progressively displaced from their territory, land and livelihood and subjected to numerous processes of exploitation far exceeding those witnessed in the colonial times. This has happened through twin processes of unequal social interface with the larger non-tribal society and the state action. Both have worked at tandem and neatly converge to nullify the protective architecture. The first has come through large scale expansion of the state machinery, regulatory and development infrastructure and diverse range of economic activities. This has led to a massive intrusion of the non-tribals into the tribal areas, overwhelming the tribals with unequal social relations, capture of their land through devious ways, control over their labour, iniquitous exchange in respect of marketable produce and cultural hegemony. The other has resulted from the increasing acquisition of their land by the government for development and regulatory projects. The consequent loss of land and livelihood, separation from their territory and environment and disruption of their kin relationship and social networks have subjected them not only to multiple impoverishments and lower quality of life but have disintegrated their social organisation, eroded their cultural values and self confidence. The tribes also lose their identity as they are forced to migrate in search of work to various parts of the country where they do not get recognition as Scheduled Tribes. Theirs is a classic case which demonstrates that the legal and policy architecture is insufficient to protect the tribal interests unless the government is adequately sensitive to their plight and is strongly determined to neutralise the dominance of the larger community and its interests in governance and social relations and undo the devastating effects of its own action.

The roots of tribals' displacement lie in the unequal power relations in Indian society (*Kothari, 1996*) where the decision making of the government is concentrated in a small privileged class representing the dominant social and economic groups. The laws and policies enacted by the government reflect their perceptions and interests. Their power is derived from their control over resources—economic, human, intellectual and cultural, access to economic assets, knowledge creation avenues and opportunities for advancement. The tribals, on the other hand, are denied this control, access and opportunities through a wide range of discriminatory and exclusionary practices. Laws, policies and programmes represent manifestation of this power. The conceptualisation of "development", "progress" and articulation of "national interest" emanates from this position of power. As the interests of the dominant sections are quite often in conflict with those of the tribals, the decisions taken by them severely hurt the tribals who neither participate in the decision making on the project that displaces them nor reap its benefits (*Fernandes, 1991*). Still the decisions are justified as necessary and in national interest. The affected tribals are required to make sacrifices for this overarching good. Over the past six decades, the composition of groups that wield power and dominance of interests in its exercise have not radically changed. The change of political regimes has not resulted in bridging the gap created by this inequality of power. The tribals are not able to transform these unequal power relations in their favour and influence decision making on issues which affect them vitally. This is because they are numerically small (only 8 per cent of the population) and not adequately socialised in the institutional processes of politics to exert effective pressure. They are also weak in knowledge, resources and capacity to articulate their interests and to skillfully use their limited strength to protect them.

Distinguishing Aspects of Tribal Displacement

While involuntary displacement adversely affects other sections of the poor too, there are weighty reasons why its impact on the tribals is more severe and irredeemable than in the case of others. This acute vulnerability arises from the characteristics which define tribal identity, social and economic systems and cultural values. Some scholars have challenged the portrayal of the tribal society as undifferentiated mass of simple cultivators exploited by the non-tribals and ethnically isolated from the larger society and deny that it is different from the non-tribal jati society (*Corebridge, 2004*). Notwithstanding that some degree of differentiation has also emerged in the tribal society as a result of its integration with the economy and the process of development, still, as a group, the tribals retain their relative homogeneity and cultural ethos reflected in their life as a community and their social relations with non-tribal outsiders which constitute their defining features. Of these, only those which have a bearing on their problems in the context of displacement would be referred to here.

The foremost among these characteristics is the perception of land in the psyche of a tribal. While land for the tribes is undoubtedly the primary and the most important source of their subsistence whether in the case of settled agriculture, shifting cultivation or mixed farming system, its value for them is much more than a productive asset for livelihood activities. Land, for them, is closely tied to the territory which is related to their ethnicity and, therefore, the rationale of their very existence. It has almost a spiritual connotation for them. Without land, they lose their identity and cultural distinctiveness as can be seen from the plight of tribal immigrant labourers in the tea gardens of Assam. Even the provision of alternative land would fail to fill up the vacuum created by the loss of land associated with their clan. This explains why the loss of land has more disastrous consequences for the tribals than for other vulnerable groups. Secondly, unlike any other community, the tribals are overwhelmingly dependent on forest. This dependence includes forest as a source of food not less than 50 per cent in the form of shifting cultivation, fruits and flowers, animals/livestock and undergrowth (tubers etc.), medicines, fodder, house building, raw material for craft activities, implements for ploughing etc., and monetary income by selling firewood, grass, seeds, leaves, fruits, processing of liquor (*Fernandes, 1993*). As a result of displacement, the access to forest is lost. This loss and its value in the household economy of the tribal is neither captured in the definition of land nor in the scheme of compensation when the land is acquired. The access to forest is also not replicated by provision of suitable forest land in the resettlement arrangement. Besides, the access to forest is enjoyed not merely by those who have land but also those without land. This would underline the devastating impact of displacement on the tribals resulting from acquisition of their land, habitat and environment as it breaks their symbiotic relationship with forest. Thirdly, the tribal economy is still characterised substantially by barter arrangement despite their increasing exposure to money market. Their contact with the market is infrequent as their needs are few and level of purchasing power low. Therefore, their capacity to comprehend the mechanism of economy dominated by the money market and cash transactions is limited and they are not able to cope with its exploitative forces and manipulative devices when exposed to the intrusive market economy, money transactions, individualization of dealings and commercialisation of relations (*Fernandes, 1991*; *Mahapatra, 1999*). One has only to go to a village *haat* (market) in the tribal areas to see how they are cheated in multiple ways in every transaction as buyers and sellers. Displacement would throw them into the vortex of this market completely, where they would be more vulnerable than before. Fourthly, the tribals are a kin centered society and their social organisation is closely knit together through ancestry of clan having no social relations outside it (*Pathy, 1992b*). They consequently feel uncomfortable and virtually scared when they interface diverse sets of persons with no bond of trust and understanding. They are unable to build new social networks in place of the traditional ones they have lost. Displacement, therefore, leaves them with no social support.

The tribals are also adversely affected by a discriminatory and dualistic paradigm of property rights which is anchored to the legal recognition of access to and use of land. The access to land which is in conformity with tenancy laws and reflected in land records is termed as ownership and carries with it the ingredients of property rights—the rights of use, transfer mortgage, exchange etc. Usually, individual occupation of cultivating plots backed by authentic documents is considered as valid ownership. But the access to forest as also to other common property resources is governed by customary rights traditionally enjoyed by people living in the vicinity which may not be entered in the land records. These are use rights or facilities which do not bear the characteristics of property. Displacement deprives the tribals of compensation when land, forest and other common property resources over which they enjoy customary rights are acquired. Due to their much higher dependence on resources which are custom governed, the loss of access to them and denial of compensation in lieu of it has much greater impoverishing effect on them than in the case of others. This aspect is more striking in the case of shifting cultivation areas or even settled agriculture on high slopes where the lands in occupation of tribal groups were usually not surveyed and therefore their rights were not recorded. The land in such areas was treated as government property and the use of land by the tribals was perceived as illegal (as explained in detail later in the paper). (*Roy Burman (n.g.)*; *Pathy, 1992*[b]; *Mahapatra, 1998*).

The tribal social organizations are closely interwoven around the principle of "community" reflected in the deep community consciousness (Viegas, 1991). They are characterised as informal economic and political structures as against the predominantly individual based formal systems of the non-tribal society (Fernandes, 1993). It is this institution of community and the bonding it creates that protects and regulates the use of land and other natural resources besides safeguarding its cultural ethos (*Viegas, 1991*). Individual patches of land may be cultivated by households but subject to the sanction of the community (*Gadgil, 1989*). This is, in fact, the pre-colonial structure of land ownership where property in land had a dual meaning. It belonged simultaneously to the community and to the individual household/family with the former accepting individual use of the latter on patches cultivated by it. The jurisdiction of the community extended to the common property resources too. The rights of the community, therefore, were considered primary (*Hidayatullah, 1983*) and individual use emerges from its sanction. Right to use by a household operated in a structure of communal ownership (*Mahapatra, 1993*). The Colonial government introduced individual ownership of land supported by a formal/legal document, thereby separating the individual from the community and forging relationship directly with the state. This weakened the collective organisation of the tribals as a social group to withstand the onslaught of the hostile and exploitative non-tribals they came in contact with. Still, the community continued to function as a decision making institution on diverse matters including those of land and other natural resources within the limited space available to it in the changed dispensation. But the loss of land and the consequent displacement from territory destroys even this fragile remnant of the community and exposes the individual tribals to numerous processes of exploitation in the absence of its collective strength.

Tribals also have very little exposure to the outside world. Their dealings with the outsiders are limited to the local commodity market and the government officials when they visit the villages. The exchanges in the local market are few and transactions are confined to limited commodities in small quantities and largely non-monetised. Cash is now replacing barter arrangement. Where the tribals are forced to migrate in search of work, they are also exposed to the labour market. The contact with the government officials is rarely on their initiative. The experiences in respect of contact with both the market and officials make them extremely vulnerable to diverse kinds of exploitative mechanisms and hegemonic behaviour of the non-tribals.

The protective provisions for the tribals prohibit transfer of their land to the non-tribals. Due to the non-marketability of their land, they have little idea of its actual value in monetary terms. The value of money itself as an instrument of exchange is beyond their comprehension due to their inadequate exposure to transactions based on it. Also, when their land is acquired, they get very little compensation due to the absence of sale deeds or their insufficient number on account of the above restrictions on transfer of land to the non-tribals (*Mahapatra, 1998*). Even information on production expenditure and productivity of land required to assess net annual profit/income from such land which could constitute the basis of are alternative method of computing market value is not available. The lack of knowledge, resources and capacity to represent and protect their interests before the competent authority compounds the problem. In addition, they are not able to contest its fairness in the reference court. They are also cheated by the government officials and intermediaries in the payment of compensation. The overwhelming dependence on land for subsistence provides them with little opportunity for obtaining cash income. They have, therefore, little experience in handling large sums of cash and appreciating its value. As a result, they fail to invest it in purchasing alternative land and squander away the cash award in buying things of little value cajoled by traders.

The other important feature of tribal society is that it is rooted in the oral tradition, where word of mouth governs social transactions and behavioural practices and trust is the bedrock on which inter-personal relations operate. The tribals are not socialised in the written word or documentary proof or evidentiary support as the basis of truth. This has been the primary reason why they are not able to take advantage of the laws to protect their land and become easy victims of the non-tribal encroachers who usurp their land by obtaining manipulated documents in their favour even when land remains in their possession. Their commitment to the truth and trust in the word of mouth act to their severe disadvantage since the entire judicial system is embedded in the superiority of written document against the oral one. They lose their case in the court of law despite the soundness of their claim. A word of mouth is insufficient evidence against a document or written proof which contradicts it.

The acute vulnerability of the tribes when faced with involuntary displacement also arises from their very low position in the matrix of human development. Educational attainment is important in this context as it is instrumental in acquiring necessary knowledge and capacity to protect interests. Tribals come out poorly on this count. The level of literacy among them is the lowest among all social groups. In the circumstances, they depend upon others to obtain the needed information and guidance and become victims of misinformation, motivated advice and unethical pressures. Due to the lack of awareness regarding the provisions of acquisition law, they are unable to participate in the legal space available to protect their entitlements unless helped by empathetic social activists, NGOs or other supportive organisations.

Yet another contributing factor to their inability to adjust to the situation caused by dislocation from their traditional support system is their limited skill base for livelihood activities. The tribals are primarily agriculturists (some groups are not even exposed to settled agriculture). They are overwhelmingly dependent upon land and forest resources for subsistence and their economy is predominantly based on cultivation of land and collection of minor forest produce. They, therefore, do not have any other skills to eak out a livelihood. The acquisition of their land and physical displacement from agriculture/forest based occupations have particularly disastrous effects on them as they find it difficult to take up any other livelihood activity. As no land is usually provided in compensation for the land lost to acquisition, their inability to take to any skilled vocation forces them to take up unskilled manual labour of various types which subjects them to even greater exploitation and distress. Their vulnerability gets compounded when they find that the government officials dealing with the resettlement planning are not even sensitive to their problems and most unhelpful in addressing them.

There is a wide agreement that where involuntary displacement takes place, the poorer sections among the affected persons suffer the most. The tribals constitute the bottom layer of even the poorer sections. Though the dalits (Scheduled Castes) also share this vulnerability, sufficient exposure to the outside world, diversity of skill base and occupations, socialisation in the market economy and greater ability to engage with the non-dalits place them in a relatively better position than the tribals. The displacement also lowers the level of their human development still further. Their literacy levels are 47.10 per cent as against all India level of 65.38 (2001). The female literacy is 34.76 per cent which is lower by approximately 20 per cent from that of the general population. The dropout level of ST children from school is also the highest. The infant mortality rate in the tribes is 84.2 per cent per 1000 as against 60 per cent for the general population, under 5 mortality rate is 126.6 per cent against 82 per cent in respect of others. The percentage of under nutrition in the tribes is 55.9 per cent as against 41.1 for the general population. The tribals seeking medical treatment for sickness is a measly 9.4 per cent of their population on an average. Even in this small number, only 34.3 per cent had access to the government health services. The incidence of poverty among the Scheduled Tribes at 45.86 per cent (rural) and 34.75 per cent (urban) in the year 1999-2000 is substantially higher than the national average, while the rate of poverty reduction in them is the lowest among all social groups (MTA, 2005). In respect of access to drinking water, sanitation, credit and skill development, the tribals are at the bottom of the heap. Landlessness which was relatively lower in their case at the time of independence is spreading faster than in the case of other communities. The tribes have the second largest share of landless persons in the country (*Rath, 2006*). In matters of hunger and starvation, they are the worst affected among all social groups. They also are bracketed in the lowest segment (Rs.387.69 for rural areas) of the monthly per-capita expenditure which is even worse than that of SCs with Rs.418.51 (*Rath, 2006*). The low performance in terms of development indices is an indication of how the entire system tends to treat them. It is this sense of exclusion and their inability to counteract it which puts them at much greater risk when their only source of survival, i.e., land is taken away from them.

Antipathy of Tribals to Development

Involuntary displacement is carried out to pursue "development" which is labeled as "public purpose" for acquisition of land. This displacement is unique in as much as it is effected through the process of law. But there are also other laws which have the objective of promoting development specific to the vulnerable groups. In the case of the tribals, for example, the strategy of development is built around the protection of their existing land against alienation by non-tribals in order that they are not displaced from their territory, land, habitat and environment. The law of acquisition is in direct conflict with these protective laws and has the effect of overriding them which results in displacement. Ironically, this displacement is even justified in the interest of the tribal people themselves and executed by the very Government which is constitutionally bound to protect their interests. Thus, the logic of development is presented in a manner which papers over the acute contradiction in the actions of the state. It is, therefore, necessary to unravel this paradigm of development to comprehend its nature and processes and lay bare its implications for the tribals.

Development is conceptualized as a necessary, desirable and even inevitable phenomenon. It is thought of as a public good about which there is little possibility of any contest since it is perceived to benefit larger number of persons. Implicit in this understanding is its supposedly neutral character which confers on it an inherent rationality. It is also intertwined with national progress and pride and, therefore, emerges as an overarching aspiration of every citizen which should supercede all other considerations questioning its assumptions. The social reality in respect of the tribals briefly outlined above would suffice to establish that development is not a neutral phenomenon at all. It is a widely contested notion with sharply antagonistic meanings given to it depending upon the position one is defining it from. It does not have uniformly beneficial implications for all persons. Development activities have dissimilar effects on different social groups. Some may gain from them while others may lose on account of its adverse impacts. The history of development in India certainly indicates that the tribals have all along been on the losing side. That is why they tend to view this development as a war unleashed on them and consider their "underdevelopment" in comparison as a benign phenomenon. Obviously, then, the paradigm of development pursued in India reflects the perception of the dominant social and economic groups and serves their interest (*Shah and Sah, 1998*). For the tribals, this development has meant deprivation of the means of production, access to livelihood and life supporting environmental resources. The effects it generates are, therefore, negative for them.

The reason why "development" is negative for the tribals lies in its nature and processes. Shorn of its theoretical sophistication, development is perceived in terms of modernization, higher per-capita income, improved standard of living and industrial progress. This vision, it is argued, can be achieved only through the growth of GNP which would generate other beneficial effects. The strategy was articulated in the early five year plans which fixed maximization of productivity of country's industrial, mineral resources, irrigation and power potential as the goal to be pursued (*Fernandes, 1998*). This route to development obviously requires huge capital investment and use of advanced technology. Its visible manifestations are viewed in terms of large infrastructural and manufacturing projects. Since these projects cannot be executed without large areas of land, compulsory acquisition of such land becomes necessary and, therefore, inevitable. The tribals get most affected by this model of development since they live in areas which are rich in natural resources such as minerals, forest and water. The physical displacement, therefore, emerges as the logical consequence of this development. The development is projected as beneficial to the local people and even the adversely affected tribals because it is assumed to provide productive employment opportunities to them and generate increase in their income. The social reality that has emerged from such projects is that the assumed benefits to the tribals never materialize. Rather, the development processes unleashed by these big projects produced a sinister phenomenon described as "internal colonialism". Its effects on the tribals were wholly negative. This feature has arisen on account of their dispossession from land both through the process of acquisition by the Government as well as alienation by the incoming immigrants and loss of livelihood besides disempowerment from the status of dignified self-employed farmers to the ranks of cheap labour for industry and construction. The multiple impoverishments generated by these effects led to their destitution. In these situations, the tribals lose their identity as well. Overwhelmed by the influx of outsiders into their area, they get reduced to a minority in the very location of their concentration. In addition, the forced migration in search of work results in shrinkage of their population, disintegration of their social organization, deprivation of the protective safeguards as a consequence of non-recognition of their ST identity and, worse, loss of confidence and self-esteem. The cultural impact of displacement gets manifested in social disarticulation, extinction of their traditional political institutions and destruction of their values. On the other hand, outsiders who came to the area both for executing the projects as well as for numerous supportive activities gain enormously in terms of access to the productive resources, jobs, higher income and improvement in the quality of life. These benefits also give them social status and political power in the area. The contradictory distributional consequences of this development lead to the subjugation of tribals by sections benefiting from it and their consequent social degradation. The new forces which the tribals are confronted with treat them with contempt, create divisions and tension among them and break their solidarity. Lacking in strength to withstand the aggressive onslaught of these social forces, they lose control over their lives. This process by which a highly developed, urbanized and modernized territorial enclave dominated by the non-tribal beneficiaries emerges in contrast with the increasing destitution of the rural periphery inhabited by the tribes is conceptually termed as "internal colonization". (*Areeparampil, 1989*; *Roy, 1982*).

Additionally, this phenomenon of development also hurts the tribals through its adverse ecological impact since the environment is subordinated to the economic growth and the nature gets repudiated for generation of wealth, goods and services. The negative externalities get manifested in the use of land not in harmony with nature, pollution of water resources, degradation of the quality of air and irreversible damage to the bio-diversity. Since the tribals are dependent upon these environmental resources for their subsistence and dignified survival, they get doubly victimized—firstly by deprivation of their productive and environmental resources which causes loss of livelihood and other life supporting benefits and, secondly, by environmental degradation. The latter diminishes the productive potential of their soil, pollutes the water bodies, reduces the beneficial nature of the bio-diversity, and lowers the quality of life exposing them to new diseases unknown to the area. This agenda of development is incompatible with the attainment of social justice and commitment to human rights enshrined in the Constitution and international declarations (*Bakshi, 1989*).

The approach to conservation is also an integral part of this overarching paradigm of development. It is articulated by the very elites who determine the nature of development. Having degraded nature in pursuit of development activities, they now wish to preserve pockets of nature for their benefits. Thus emerges a programme of conservation which focuses on ecological restoration through enclosure of forest, protection of wildlife in an isolated environment and demarcating areas of rich bio-diversity to protect them from human interface. This paradigm of conservation serves the interests of the elites in two ways: moulding biodiversity in terms of their tastes and earmarking spaces for their pleasure and relaxation as retreat from their stressed life and, at the same time, harnessing it for economic growth through the medium of national and international tourism. The strategy of conservation is essentially embedded in the inherent incompatibility between nature and humans. Any human contact with biodiversity is perceived as a threat to its preservation. Therefore, the only way to protect it is to remove all human interference from it. With this objective, massive projects of physical dislocation of the tribal communities, living for centuries in forest areas, are undertaken. The age old harmony these communities had with the nature and wild life is disregarded. On the contrary, the existing degradation of environment is attributed to the dependence of tribals on forest rather than the development activities pursued by the government. This logic conveniently covers up commercial exploitation of forest resources which is responsible for ecological degradation and resultant social injustice as well. The commercial exploitation can be observed in the massive mining and industrial projects taken up in the bio-diversity rich areas, replacement of the existing natural forest species by commercial plantation to cater to the needs of urban consumers, assignment of the huge areas of forest land for growing raw material for the industry and promotion of international tourism. The tribals emerge as the greatest and the most pronounced losers of this model of conservation in the same manner as they have suffered the maximum from the conceptual frame of development. They get physically shifted from their habitat and territory rooted in their identity, deprived of the access to land and forest resources on which they entirely depended for survival and even denied compensation for this vital loss since they do not posses "property" rights over these resources. This model of conservation is spearheaded by the forest bureaucracy, industrial bourgeoisie, investment capital, urban middle class and the elite conservationists combine. The enormous power and clout which these sections command in the policy process is evident from the way they have used not only the executive and the legislature for serving their class interests. Even Judicial decisions on the subject reinforce this conservation paradigm. This is best exemplified by legislations on forest closure and ever increasing restrictions on access to forests such as the Forest Conservation Act, 1980, Wildlife (Protection) Act, 1972, non-adherence to the provisions of laws relating to recognition of existing use of forest land by the tribals, prosecution and eviction of the tribals from their cultivating land and habitat in forests, and relocation of tribals outside the forests by expanding area of wild life sanctuaries and national parks. The Judicial sanction to this approach comes from the Godavarman case which has enormously expanded the ambit of forest governance and denial of tribal rights.

Instrumentality of Law

This mechanism of alienation of tribal land to the corporate and other non-tribal interests is carried out by the government through the instrumentality of law. With the rationale provided by the paradigms of conservation and development, the deprivation of the tribals of their land is carried out through two legal instruments. One defined the rights and interests in land de-linked from the traditional pattern of land holding and use and the other enabled the compulsory acquisition of land for public purpose by the state. The first instrument concerns the forest related policies of the colonial government culminating in the Indian Forest Act, 1878 which was later replaced by the Indian Forest Act, 1927. The colonial capture of forest was guided by commercial considerations embedded in the ideology which served the function of "mastering, exploiting, transforming and commoditizing" nature (*Pouchepadass, 2001*). This was effected through techniques, tools and a system of government control which extinguished/ circumscribed access of the local communities to their traditional resource bases. Tribal communities which overwhelmingly depended upon forest resource base for their existence were the worst affected by this arrangement. Besides, with their bias for settled agriculture, the colonial government considered the practice of shifting cultivation as wasteful and its consequent attempts to stop this pattern of farming. This had even more deleterious effect on the tribes who practiced this form of cultivation. The incentive to clear the forests in the early phase of their rule emerged from two policy interventions. One related to the imposition of the permanent settlement which increased the avarice of zamindars to bring forest land under cultivation for maximization of rent and the other was introduction of contractors in the working of forest for extracting timber required for laying out railway network. Both led to extensive deforestation which disrupted the lives of the tribal communities and destroyed their relation with natural environment. State control over forest was also designed to transform natural forest into a domesticated, rationalized and optimized form of forest reflected in the plantations (*Pouchepadass, 2001*). After independence, the government carried on with the same approach towards forest. The later laws i.e., the revised Forest Act, the Wild Life Protection Act, 1972, the Forest Conservation Act, 1980, the Tree Prevention Acts of different states and the Forest Policy, 1988 have followed this ideological lead. The Forest Act not merely converted forest into state property but also empowered the government to extinguish/circumscribe customary rights of use of forest resources by the local population. The Wild Life (Protection) Act, 1972 considers any human habitation and movement within the jurisdiction of wildlife habitat as a threat to their survival and, therefore, provides the rationale for removal. The tribal communities living in these areas get evicted and relocated. The process of declaration and demarcation of such wildlife areas is undertaken unilaterally by the government without even consultation with the affected communities. The Forest Conservation Act, 1980 prohibits the use of forest land for non-forest purposes and delegitimises habitations and rights of cultivation and other uses of people living in these areas. The Supreme Court has struck a further blow to the interests of the tribals by expanding the definition of "forest" to conform to its dictionary meaning, notwithstanding the condition on the ground and the nature of their ownership and classification in land records. This order had the effect of including even those lands in the definition of forest on which pattas were issued to the tribals by the revenue department of the state governments on the basis of their status in land records. As a result, lakhs of tribals who have been living in and occupying for a long time—land in these areas became encroachers overnight. Many of them have been cultivating these lands before they were even declared as "forest". No efforts were made by the forest bureaucracy to transparently determine the pre-existing rights of the affected tribal communities as required by the law. The Tree Preservation Acts even disallowed felling of any tree on self-owned land without the prior order of the competent authority. The Forest Policy, 1988, while conceding the need to meet the domestic requirement of fuel-wood, fodder and minor forest produce, introduced Joint Forest Management by the communities residing in and around the forest and the forest department for protection of forest and benefit sharing. This method of involvement of the local communities undermined the traditional community management system, brought the forest under state control through the back door and encouraged commercial species for plantation. It had little to show by way of tangible and substantive benefits for the communities participating in the arrangement and contributing voluntary labour. (*Perspectives, 2007*).

The other instrument relates to the compulsory acquisition of privately owned land by the government under the Land Acquisition Act, 1894. While there are a large number of laws for compulsory acquisition of land, Central and state, the Land Acquisition Act, 1894 is the oldest and the most widely used. The conceptual frame of acquisition laws is provided by an overarching rationality for decisive state control over private (rayati) land. The juridical base for these laws is embedded in the doctrine of Eminent Domain while "public purpose" lends moral defense to it. This mode of deprivation of the tribals of their lands is the most distressing form of alienation because no legal remedies are available against it unlike the alienation of tribal land by non-state actors. It is also sought to be justified on the ground that it is in the interests of the very people who are devastated by it. Through this action, the government become the very agency to deplete the land resource base of the Scheduled Tribes which has the constitutional responsibility to prevent this from happening and to protect them against measures which threaten their dignified survival. The design of the Land Acquisition Act, 1894 is anti-thetical to the traditions of the tribal communities and the rights and interests in land based on them. This is the reason why the acquisition of land hurts the tribals more than any other process by which they are dispossessed from their land.

Design of the Land Acquisition Act: Overriding Protective Laws

The acquisition law places itself in a pre-eminent position vis-à-vis other laws because it supersedes them when it is applied. The constitution provides a number of protective measures for the STs. Certain areas with concentration of the STs have been carved out as scheduled areas where restrictions have been placed on land use and transactions which may have the effect of disturbing the existing control of the tribals over this resource and displacing them from it as a result. Laws have been enacted in various states to protect land held by the tribals from being alienated to the non-tribals. Special dispensation has been created for reinforcing the control of the tribal communities over natural resources in their respective jurisdiction in these scheduled areas. PESA, 1996 represents the most explicit measure of such empowerment recognizing thereby a governance structure for the tribes at grassroots different from other areas. When the LA Act is used to acquire land belonging to the STs located in these areas, these protective arrangements simply get ignored. The LA Act assumes primacy, priority and overriding character. It becomes a superior law. (*Ramanathan, 1996*; *Parasuraman, 1999*). This is justified legally on the ground that the LA Act is a central law while protective legislations are state laws (state laws on acquisition of land, where existing, also operate in the same manner) and morally on the ground that "public purpose" supersedes "individual" or "group" purpose in laws enacted for the tribes. The inherent inequality is evident in this arrangement because such laws may still apply to the non-tribal individuals/organisations but the government gets exempted because of its superior power and political legitimacy. The whole ideology of protection and differential treatment accorded to the STs based on the above referred instruments gets nullified by the dominant law of acquisition. The tribes have to be content like the non-tribes with a mere claim for compensation. They cannot invoke protective provisions.

Conceptual Frame

The overarching conceptual frame of the Land Acquisition Act is embedded in the juristic doctrine of "Eminent Domain" which lends justification to the compulsory acquisition of privately owned land as an exercise of sovereign power. The ethical rationality of the exercise of this power is bestowed by the expression "public purpose". The Eminent Domain gives unfettered powers to the state to acquire any private land subject only to the observance of the required procedure and the payment of compensation. The affected citizen has no choice in the matter except to part with his/her land. "Public purpose" juxtaposes an affected land loser against others who may benefit from the project involving acquisition of land in the "larger welfare" that may be achieved. The use of both concepts hurt the interests of the tribes more than they do of the other affected citizens. They negate the protection available to them under laws and the constitution, ironically, by the action of the government itself. Worse, this action of the government is immune to any contest or challenge in the courts. Still worse, this alienation of tribal land by the government is absolute in character, large scale in nature, against the consent of the affected tribals and without any obligation for its replacement by alternative land which bestows commensurate benefits. The law does not even contemplate a notional continuity of their association with the land with which they have an emotional bond linked in their memory to their identity and existence through provision of a partial transfer on lease rather than an outright loss of ownership. The legal frame does not even place any limits to such alienation or insist on exploring alternatives to avoid it altogether or restricting it to the most minimum. It also fails to take into account the alienation of tribal land in the vicinity of the acquired land due to the pressures unleashed by development activities pursuant to the acquisition of land and make provision to prevent it.

The conceptual frame of law militates against the architecture of protection laid down in the Constitution in other ways too. While taking away land from the tribals which is absolutely central to their dignified existence, it does not even mandate comprehensive rehabilitation and resettlement of the displaced tribals within their traditional homeland so as to maintain cultural and social contiguity with the territory from which they have been ousted. The law does not obligate the government to undertake relocation of the displaced tribals to an alternative site with transparency and sensitivity and in terms of a design of resettlement which has their informed consent and participation, and helps to rebuild their shattered lives. The blueprint of such a scheme would necessarily have provision of alternative land for cultivation and other livelihood activities, comparable access to forests and other common property resources, dignified habitat, social facilities and physical infrastructure as per their aspirations, affirmative state action which ensures legal protection applicable to the schedule of their area and other rights. The law is entirely one-sided in giving sanctity to the action of the government depriving tribals of their life supporting resources and causing their physical displacement but imposes no commensurate duty on it to undertake measures to recreate their social and cultural organisation, regenerate their lost livelihoods and recreate their social networks and communitarian existence. Rather, the law leaves the tribals to fend for themselves. The meager compensation tribals receive for their loss of land causes insult to their injury. The injustice to the tribals resulting from displacement is, therefore, more severe than in the case of others.

Land

The design of the Act is against the interests of the tribals in several ways. One relates to the understanding of the expression "Land" used in the Act and the perception of its value. The land in the Act is conceived as a piece of earth with an economic value, i.e., a productive asset capable of generating income. It is a commodity which can be traded in the market place the value of which is concretized only in terms of the money it fetches in sale. Its loss, therefore, can be compensated by payment of cash of equal value. For the tribals, the perception of land goes for beyond its material value. It carries cultural and even spiritual significance and cannot be traded for money. It sustains and rejuvenates the power of life in those who are attached to it and lends its holder dignity and status. That is why its loss is perceived as an obliteration of their existence, their very being (*Roy Burman, 1992*). The second feature of the difference in perception emerges from the rights and interests attached to the land. The law conditions rights and interests to a valid ownership which alone entitles its loser award of compensation.

The cultural traditions of the tribals relate rights and interests to their use sanctified by the community not conditioned by State validation. The law does not permit payment of compensation for loss of rights in land which are embedded in its use not supported by title nor it recognises community as a valid authority to sanctify use of land by an individual member. This wide gap in understanding and the dual categorisation of land it has introduced create a social divide in the community between the two categories of land losers. There is a third category of land holders who have legitimate claim to the use of land in terms of existing provision of law or policy which remains non-regularised or validated despite its eligibility. They also do not receive any compensation for loss of land on this account.

Conception of Rights

The law also has the propensity to restrict rights and interests in land to individuals and entirely ignores, if not derecognises, the existence of "community" in this discourse. This is typically conveyed by the definition of the expression "person interested" which refers to one who is entitled to file a claim for compensation. Such persons also enjoy the privilege to participate in the land acquisition proceedings. This colonial construct of rights is based on the notion *res nullius* which means something which has a legal owner or holder. When applied to land, it implies that if a land does not have an owner or holder, it carries no rights. By implication, such a land accrues to the state. The conceptualisation does not take into account the social and cultural systems of the tribes within which rights and interests in land accrued to the tribal users. In the tribes, access to land accrued to individual households as members of their community and the usufructory rights occurred subject to its regulation (*Pathy, 1992*)[a]. The kinship ties which form the basis of tribal social organization are central to the tribal existence. The colonial articulation of rights focused on the centrality of the individual holder tends to fragment communities into individuals and thereby undermines the tradition of community control over natural resources which constitutes the essence of tribal cultural identity and governing arrangements. The tribal community is more than a sum total of the tribal individuals but has a personality, structure of authority, interests and a role which cannot be discharged by the individual members. This has two effects; one, the community rights in land and management of eco-system get no recognition and, therefore, their loss carries no entitlement to compensation. Two, the regulatory, adjudicatory and developmental role of the community is destroyed. Certain deleterious consequence for the tribals follow from these effects. First, the phenomenon of "displacement" also focuses on the individual tribal land loser which is counter-productive to any scheme of their rehabilitation and resettlement (*Prabhu, 2007*). Second, the tribals become increasingly vulnerable to exploitation when they are resettled since the community support gets eroded.

The anchoring of protection of individual rights to legal recognition has also ended up doing great injustice to the tribal right holders. This happens in two ways. One, the ambit of loss of rights is considerably narrowed to the land considered *raiyyati* under the relevant tenancy law (under individual occupation as per the land records). But rights accruing to the tribal households with the sanction of the community which preceded this individualisation do not get recognised either in payment of compensation or in rehabilitation and resttlement. Such rights are varied and extensive. They cover the entire gamut of community property resources where no individual household has exclusive usufructory rights but all households have free access to them irrespective of whether they own land or not. The common property resources which include common lands, water bodies and forests contribute substantially to the income generation and life supporting facilities are entered as government property in the account of a particular department such as revenue, PWD, irrigation in the land records. When such resources are acquired under the Land Acquisition Act, the government becomes entitled to compensation. The modalities of payment are settled by the government depending upon the nature of requiring agency. When a government department requires the land (Schedule 1), usually, it does not involve payment of its cost by the agency as the government continues to be the overall owner of property. It therefore takes the form of notional transfer of land from one agency to another. Where a private agency requires the land (Schedule 2), the compensation accrues to the government. In both cases, the government is the direct or indirect beneficiary (*Prabhu, 2007*). No compensation accrues to the affected tribals (or others, if any). The government does not take into account the loss suffered by the tribals in respect of these lands for computation of compensation even though it is well aware of their dependence on such land and their customary use of it.

The other loss resulting from "individualisation" approach to rights lies in ignoring the existence of the community centered and controlled land management systems such as the shifting cultivation areas and cultivation of agriculture on high slopes bulk of which remained unsurveyed and unsettled. The practice of survey and settlement operations in the colonial period, by and large, focused on areas of settled agriculture as legally entitled basis for articulation of rights and their recognition since lands under it were a source of revenue to the government. Shifting cultivation by definition is not a stable arrangement of agriculture as a piece of land is not tied to a user on a permanent basis. The user rotates its cultivation among different plots in a specified area each year while leaving the uncultivated plots free for natural regeneration. The system operates with the sanction of the community. When such areas were taken up for survey and settlement in the post colonial period, the method of preparing land records deprived users of their rights in respect of such lands. The plane table method used for surveying land did not go beyond 9^0 slope while the tribals used lands at a much higher elevation. The result was that the lands cultivated by them beyond 9° slope were assumed to be barren and waste with no individual claim and thus recorded in the account of the government. (*Roy Burman (n.g.)*; *Pathy, 1992*[a]; *Mahapatra, 1998*) The affected tribals cultivating those lands on higher slopes whether in settled or shifting agriculture segments, therefore, became totally invisible in land records. Their use of such land is now officially treated as encroachment. As their traditional usufructory and cultivating rights over those lands do not get recorded, the acquisition of such lands neither entitles the affected tribals to any compensation or its replacement with provision of alternative land nor rehabilitation which accrues to only the recognised land holders. Even in areas coming within 9° slope, authentic information is not available on how land records classified land under shifting cultivation since in the absence of identified individual plots, land users had no recognisable evidence of their rights. This failure to record rights happens due to the ignorance of officials about the management practices in respect of such lands which are at variance with the pattern of individuals land holdings in settled agriculture. These are the areas where the primitive tribes usually reside. They are the most vulnerable groups when their lands are acquired. In the absence of a proper rehabilitation and resettlement suited to their cultural requirement, the affected members do not have the strength to withstand the sudden pressure of adjustment to a new situation forcing them to eke out their livelihood by working as wage labourers. The severe trauma resulting from such pressure may shorten their life span. If the group involved is very small, it may even hasten its their extinction.

Basis of Entitlement

The expression "person interested" forms the basis for entitlements under the Act. The payment of compensation for acquisition of land is the key entitlement. The definition itself anchors the expression to those who claim an interest in compensation. But what constitutes an "interest", how it is to be determined and who has such an interest have not been explained. However, the practice of acquisition has related it to only the owners/title holders of land. It does not include the holders of other interests which are based on use derived from customary practices, bilateral arrangements and oral contracts and are unrecorded. The loss of these interests resulting from the acquisition of land does not get compensated. The displaced tribals are the most adversely affected by this definition of "interest" since their rights in forest and other common property resources, as mentioned earlier, are not backed by any legal document or proof and may be unrecorded. Besides, in certain states (Jharkhand, for example), tenancy laws governing the tribal groups have a provision which permits reclamation of wasteland for cultivation (Korkar) and entitles the individual who has made the land cultivable to get a patta if eligibility conditions are satisfied. The claims for getting such occupancies regularised, when filed by the concerned tribals, do not get disposed of due to the inaction of the revenue bureaucracy. These interests, therefore, get ignored for payment of compensation on account of the interpretation of the term "person interested".

The framework of entitlement is embedded in the loss of land only and that too is entirely anchored to ownership of land as reflected in the land records. These documents enter the names of owners and exclude a whole lot of users of land owned by others. Those without land who lose livelihood based on the acquired land are not compensated. This leaves out the landless tribals engaged in cultivation as tenants or agricultural labourers or artisans who draw resources from acquired land for their Income generating activities from the benefit of compensation.

The approach to compensation entitlement is pronouncedly individualistic in identifying interests. It is not sensitive to the value of community as an institution in the social organization of land (*Mahapatra, 1998*). It, therefore, does not get recognised as a "person interested" and, on this basis, as a claimant for compensation. This ignores the social reality of the role of community in the management of land and other natural resources in the tribal social organisation.

Compensatory Arrangements

The most striking example of how the tribals suffer from the existing provisions of law is particularly evident in the design of the compensatory arrangement for loss of land. The structure of compensation scheme is iniquitous to the tribals in the following ways.

Firstly, the compensation is conceived in terms of money as an equivalent of the value of the asset lost rather than replacement or restitution of the asset. Equating the value of land to be acquired with the specified quantum of cash does the greatest violence to the tribals' conception of land and its value for them. The land can never be matched by anything else other than land itself and land associated with their "territory" cannot be the same as land elsewhere. It is not a commodity exchangeable with money. The monetary equivalent of the land is doubly unfair to them because of their inadequate exposure to the market economy and consequent inability to appreciate the value of cash as its replacement. This is not the situation with the non-tribals.

The second feature lies in the manner in which compensation is determined. The law anchors this determination to the notional market value at the site of displacement. It does not provide any guidelines on how this market value is to be assessed. The authorities dealing with the acquisition of land usually derive market value from the purchase and sale transactions in the vicinity of the land to be acquired by taking an average of the rates at which these transactions were effected in the preceding three years. This procedure of assessment is most unsuitable in the case of tribal land since the laws in most states prohibit transfer of tribal land to the non-tribals. Therefore, there are no valid transactions in respect of such land except where both parties are tribals (*Mahapatra, 1998*). Such cases are very few since the tribals do not part with their land except in cases of extreme adversity and helplessness. There is, however, great likelihood of benami transactions being registered by the non-tribals. The few valid transactions that may have been registered would not present a situation of a willing buyer and a willing seller of equal strength. The unequal status of parties and unequal circumstances of the deal have a bearing on the money value recorded in such transactions. The tribals also lack confidence and capacity to bargain so as to derive an optimum value from these transactions. This is true when they sell their agriculture and minor forest produce as well. Their routine market transactions in other goods and services are largely through barter arrangements. The law does not take cognizance of this feature. Some state governments have adopted alternative modes of assessment taking into account the capitalised value of land derived from the value of produce or the net profit earned from cultivation for a specified period. These methods are also unsatisfactory for a variety of reasons.

The third feature of compensation scheme is reflected in the mode of its payment. Since the market value of land is assessed in terms of the notional price it would fetch, the payment is made in cash. This is most disastrous for the tribals because they have no experience of handling the large amount of cash they receive compared to the small cash they handle while trading in goods and services in the village market. The result is that the cash is squeezed by the cunning non-tribals (traders, liquor venders, middlemen) in exchange of commodities of little value (*Mahapatra, 1998*). The law does not even enjoin the acquisition authority to procure alternative land for them from this amount so as to avoid this hazard.

The fourth feature is that the notional market value which the tribals receive as compensation is inadequate to purchase alternative land of equivalent productive potential near the resettlement site (*Mahapatra, 1998*). The result is that the tribal land holders losing land become landless since the cash is squandered and no replacement of land is made. The whole compensation, arrangement turns them into paupers and destitute.

The fifth feature of compensation scheme lies in the ambit of what it covers. The ambit of compensation is confined to the loss of land. It does not include social losses such as the fragmentation of the community and consequent loss of its support in adversity, breakdown of kinship networks, disintegration of local structures relating to credit and marketing, increased susceptibility to exploitation, social disarticulation and emotional trauma etc. In short, compensation never makes up for the immisserisation and traumatisation of the tribals resulting from the land acquisition and consequent displacement. It provides no safety to them but destroys several protective shields in their existing life (*Prabhu, 2007*).

Damages to Un-acquired Land

There have been several instances where project activities have damaged productive potential of land in the vicinity of the acquired land (*Sastry, 1992*). The environmental effects of these activities cause deprivation of land which may also lead to displacement of the holder (*Paranjpye and Kewatramani, 1997*). The persons so affected get no relief from the project authorities for this loss of productive asset. There is no provision in the law to either mandate compulsory acquisition of such land or to compensate the landholder for the irreparable damage caused to the land/water bodies/vegetation. This may be because the damage is caused long after the acquisition of land has been accomplished. The damage occurs particularly where industrial, mining and power projects are taken up. The tribals are the worst victims of this type of damage to their assets because the polluting projects are concentrated in areas where they inhabit. They are also weak and unorganised to hold the polluting authorities accountable for this loss. The project authorities assume no responsibility for this damage and refuse to address the problem either by paying compensation or making technological intervention to restore the soil/water body. The government also fails to take any action.

Profligacy in Acquisition

Another feature of the law of land acquisition relevant to the tribal areas is the area of land acquired for different projects. There is no provision in the law which lays down norms in terms of a reasonable area required for acquisition of land for a specific project. This is left to the discretion of the government which relies on the assessment of the project agency/requiring body. The law does not even mention that the acquisition of land should be minimum and as economical as possible in view of its social cost. Since the land is acquired for diverse range of projects, central government should have laid down some norms for different sectoral projects. Neither the central nor the state governments have prescribed the required standards. This has resulted in such distortions as the widely varying area of land acquired for similar projects in two different locations and the land acquired much in excess of the need currently and foreseeable (*Asif, 1999*). The apex court has imposed no such obligation on the Government to provide the rationale for the area of land acquired in every project. The assessment made by the requiring body is accepted as valid for this purpose. The acquisition authority undertakes no scrutiny of the proposal received from the requiring agency for this purpose. This has led to an excessive area being acquired which cannot be utilised for the project and is, therefore, diverted for purposes other than the one declared at the time of acquisition besides making lavish use of it for housing of officials, township and such other non-essential uses. The Expert Group on Prevention of Alienation of Tribal Land and its Restoration found that the mining companies, particularly coal companies, were acquiring land far in excess of their requirements. It came across extensive townships whose opulence was seriously questionable. The Group also castigated mining practices which waste land and lack good intentions and recommended that these should be curbed (*MoRD, 2004*). The profligacy shown in the assessment of land for acquisition is particularly biased against the tribals because their land carries very low rates of compensation on account of restrictions on its transfer to the non-tribal individuals and agencies. Land markets are under-developed and the price of tribal land is depressed (*Prabhu, 2007; MoRD, 2004*). The tribals also lack knowledge, resources, capacity and clout to challenge the proposal and influence the decision making on the issue. They are also the most powerless with no articulate spokesman of their interests and the least politically mobilised group to agitate the matter and get support from the mainstream political parties. The larger non-tribal community unaffected by acquisition is indifferent to their plight. In fact, the local people among them are strongly supportive of development projects because of the benefits they expect to derive from them.

The Practice of Acquisition: Manipulative Transfers

There is another phenomenon associated with the land acquisition which afflicts the tribals in a major way. This relates to the manipulative and induced transfers of land as soon as it becomes public knowledge that the land may be acquired for a project (*Mahapatra, 1998*). Persons with resources and power exert pressure on the poorer landholders, particularly the tribals, to sell the land to be acquired. They frighten them with disinformation that their land is going to be expropriated by the government and they should better transfer it quickly to at least get some money from its sale. Their sole motive is to purchase their land cheaply, get it mutated in their name and later claim enhanced compensation by using their resources and capacity and, where required, by taking the matter to the reference court. Their intention is also to obtain the benefits of employment, business contracts etc., as a displaced person. The law has no provision to prevent this mischief by freezing such transfers before the process of acquisition is initiated. There is also no proactive action on the part of the district collector to prevent this from happening. The tribals being very gullible become easy victims of this exploitation.

Rehabilitation and Resettlement: Evolution of Policy

Displacement, until recently, remained a non-issue and the displacement of tribals was treated with even greater indifference. That is why there was neither a law nor a policy or even a firm commitment to address the numerous problems created by displacement. The approach of the Government in the matter had been "minimal" and "residual" (*Marsden, 1998*). It was limited to payment of compensation and construction of houses with the barest amenities for relocating the affected persons to the new site. The interventions in the matter were pronouncedly ad-hoc and project-specific. This resulted in discriminatory treatment meted out to the affected displaced persons including the tribals in different places and at different times. There was also no uniformity in the rehabilitation package extended to the displaced tribals in central and state funded projects. From the early 1980s, some concern was shown for the displaced tribals which was reflected in the issuance of specific guidelines for their rehabilitation. For example, in 1980, the central government Department of Irrigation, directed the project agencies to allot wasteland in the command area or arrange to have land taken from the larger land holders for allotment to the tribals in addition to the payment of compensation. The guidelines issued by the Ministry of Home Affairs in 1982 made more comprehensive recommendations which included checking extensive land acquisition, payment of full compensation before eviction, taking up land based rehabilitation with community centric design of resettlement and allotment of land to one member of the land losing family. A committee of central ministers in 1982 reiterated the need for allotment of land to the tribals in the command area of the project, if necessary, by taking a portion of the land from the larger land holders besides making provision for residential land, necessary civic amenities, employment etc. The Bureau of Public Enterprises in 1986, among other things, stressed on providing vocational training at the cost of the project and mandatory consultation by the Ministry concerned with the tribal welfare while preparing the rehabilitation scheme. In 1984, a more comprehensive policy for rehabilitation of the displaced tribals was recommended by a committee constituted by the central government which laid emphasis on participation of the tribals in its design and execution and suggested a constitutional amendment to enable the central and the state governments to enact laws for this purpose. It was specifically stated that special care should be taken for the rehabilitation of food gatherers, hunters, collectors of forest produce, cultivators of forest land, shifting cultivators and tribal artisans dependent on the forest raw materials. A standing committee was constituted in 1986 to monitor the speedy rehabilitation of the displaced tribals by the Ministry of Social and Womens' Welfare. In the 1990s, the resettlement policies for the displaced persons were brought out by the Coal India and the National Thermal Power Corporation (*Pandey, 1998*).

It is evident from the brief evolution of the rehabilitation policy for the displaced tribals that the sectoral ministries issued guidelines specific to their projects and there was no national policy which applied to all development projects taken up by the central government or its organisations. Almost a similar situation existed at the state level though the state governments came out with laws and/or policies in this regard much earlier than the central government did. But the enactment of laws, or declaration of policies or issuance of guidelines did not translate into tangible benefits for the displaced persons including the tribals. The laws were also too weak to be of any assistance to the affected persons (*Mathur, 2006*)[a]. They were poorly conceived and lacked participative structure and accountability of implementing officials to the affected persons (*Ramesh and Joseph, 2006*; *Ramesh and Guntipally, 1997*). Introduced largely under the pressure of international funding agencies, these instruments suffered from infirmities and inadequacies. There were too many defects and lacunae, (*Bhuskute, 1997*). Besides, inconsistencies, vague definitions, selective application and difficulties of implementation further compounded the problem (*Banerjee, 1997*). Even where clear norms were laid down, as for example in the tribunal award for the oustees of the Narmada project, the affected persons are getting a short shrift due to the apathy of the concerned states towards its implementation. The Apex court has also failed to intervene in the matter of rehabilitation of the displaced persons barring an odd case here and there. The government's approach in the matter till recently was pronouncedly manifested in "avoidance" of commitment and flight from commitment already made which has taken multiple and insidious forms at the state and local level (*Cernea, 1999*)[b].

Resettlement and Rehabilitation has been elaborately conceptualised in the international literature. This is basically seen as a management issue which involves prolonged administrative action to mitigate adverse effects described as "risks" which a displacee faces. The resettlement management, at its core, is the management of these risks which involves constantly balancing risks with counter-risk measures for which risk identification and analysis is the very first task (*Mathur, 2006*[b]; *Cernea, 2006*) These risks have been identified in terms of eight basic impoverishment processes arising from social and economic deprivation, i.e., landlessness, joblessness, homelessness, marginalisation, increased morbidity and mortality, food insecurity, loss of access to common property resources and social disarticulation (*Cernea, 1996, 1997, 1998*). To this list, the ninth deprivation identified as the loss of schooling (*Mahapatra, 1999*) and tenth one, as the loss of access to public service ahead of displacement (*Mathur, 1998*) have been added. These risks have differential effects on different categories of people. The affected tribals experience most severe effects from these risks for reasons outlined earlier. The task of rehabilitation and resettlement involves planning for their mitigation by identifying and managing counter risk actions for each of them. This counter-risk action involves reconstruction from landlessness to land-based settlement, from joblessness to re-employment or provision of employment, from homelessness to house construction, from marginalisation to social inclusion, from increased morbidity and mortality to better health care and adequate nutrition, from food insecurity to availability of food and provision of purchasing power to avail of it, from loss of access to common property resources to restoration of such assets at the resettlement site, from social disarticulation to community reconstruction, from educational loss to educational restitution, and from loss of access to public services ahead of displacement to continue these services until physical dislocation has been effected. (*Mahapatra, 1999*; *Cernea, 1997*). This task requires a comprehensive resettlement policy with statutory obligation covering public and private sector, high degree of political commitment, systematic planning, efficient implementation with participation of the beneficiaries at all stages. It should be a continuous process and not a one-time activity until the displacees have recovered from the multi-faceted impoverishment. (*Cernea, 1997*; *Mathur, 1998, 2006*)[a] Indian researchers and activists have also stressed on these aspects for rehabilitation of the displaced persons particularly tribals. (*Fernandes and Paranjpye, 1997*; *Mahapatra, 1999*; *Mathur, 2006*)[a,b]. The framework presented by Cernea has been substantially incorporated in the World Bank funded projects as also those financed by other donor organizations in their projects. The performance of the concerned governments has been extremely tardy (*Cernea, 1999*)[a]. Even in the World Bank funded projects, despite training of personnel carrying out rehabilitation and liberal financial provisioning, rehabilitation carried out suffered from serious deficiencies (*Delhi Forum, 2008*). Only one or two of the ten risks outlined above were addressed (*Joseph, 2006*; *Garg, 2006*). Far from mitigating various risks, problems were even encountered in identification of people at risk due to skewed power distribution among social groups (*Aggarwal, 1998*). In respect of other projects, several evaluation reports have brought out the wide range of negatives in this regard. These include narrow construction of displacement leaving out many eligible persons, absence of preparedness, counseling and participation, predominance of economic bias to the neglect of social rehabilitation (*Mahapatra, 1999*), landlessness and joblessness, increased morbidity, fragmentation of village, food insecurity, non-availability of even basic infrastructure (*Agnihotri, 1998*) and inadequate planning and institutional weaknesses in implementation (*Kothari, 1996*). The deficiencies also related to policy formulation, financing, methodology of assessing risks, mechanism for grievance redressal (*Joseph, 1998*). The deficit in this regard is even more glaring in the case of the displaced tribals as the efforts made for their rehabilitation failed to take into account the social, cultural and psychological aspects of tribal groups, the need to protect laws and institutions which safeguard their interests and the priority of keeping intact the "community" in tribal resettlement. Besides inadequacies of efforts covering these aspects, the implementation has also lacked sensitivity about human aspects of it and requisite motivation to administer its various components. These negatives could not be neutralized due to the absence of supportive structures. (*Mahapatra, 1998, 1999*; *Pandey, 1998*; *Agnihotri, 1998*).

Impact of Displacement on Tribals

The tribals have been among the earliest victims of involuntary displacement induced by the development projects. The impact of such displacement and industrialisation following it has, therefore, been the subject of considerable anthropological and sociological investigation, particularly in the eastern India. The studies in the sixties and seventies uniformly highlighted its multifaceted adverse effects on them (*Sachidananda, 1965*; *Sengupta, 1979*; *Roy Burman 1961*; *Das and Banerjee, 1962*; *Vidhyarthi, 1970*). Their findings brought out disturbing negative effects ranging from infiltration of undesirable cultural influences and dispossession from land to discrimination in labour market and social relations, sexual exploitation of the tribal women etc. The later studies also brought out in their findings the iniquitous regime of compensation in terms of methods of determination of the market value of land, delay in disbursement (*Pandey, 1998*), administrative corruption (*Mathur, 2006*)[a] and other ways of cheating the tribals of their dues in its payment, exploitation by money lenders, lawyers, traders, middlemen, local intermediaries and even land acquisition officials on its receipt (*Jaamdar, 2006*), besides profound socio-cultural disruption in their lives experienced by them (*CSE, 1985*). The resettlement provided to them showed that even the minimum facilities were not created at the site. The implementation was marked by lack of understanding and appreciation of the tribal society, poor delivery system, absence of monitoring and failure to consult the tribals in designing the rehabilitation and resettlement scheme (*Mahapatra, 1998*). The substance of these studies indicated how the development projects led to the loss of control over resources which the tribals commanded within their eco-system and how they were forced to shift to a pattern of economy to which they had neither any exposure nor capacity to deal with (*Mahapatra, 1999*). The projects were heavily loaded against them.

The social and cultural impact of industrialization in some of the later studies pointed to a more disturbing trend. Culturally, the displaced tribals were devastated. The intrusion of the non-tribals pertaining to different social categories into the area disintegrated the tribal community organisations and their value system. The loss of social control led to the increase in tension and a variety of social problems such as alcoholism, delinquency and suicide (*Vidyarthi, 1970*; *Sengupta, 1979*; *Fernandes and Thukral, 1989*). The affected tribals internalised many traits and practices of the non-tribal society such as smoking, drinking, gambling, use of cosmetics by women. They were completely alienated from their surroundings and faced total exclusion in the new society. They soon became victims of even more sinister forms of exploitation like immoral trafficking in women and entanglement of youth in urban oriented crimes. Economically, their suffering was irreparable as they were transformed from self-employed farmers to invisible proletariat in the destitute urban labour market. Their agricultural practices were basically geared to subsistence and self-consumption. The displacement ruthlessly exposed them to wage and the market economy. They found themselves placed in a new set of relations in which they were unequal and, therefore, experienced newer exploitations not known to them earlier. More than the economic suffering, the loss of agricultural vocation was emotionally shattering and psychologically devastating. They were unable to obtain alternative dignified employment since they lacked necessary education, skills and experience of other vocations. Besides, they were deprived of the numerous life supporting benefits which they derived from the land and specially the forests and other common property resources. They faced ruthless employers as wage labourers and fell into indebtedness, bondage and contract work in coal mines (*Sengupta, 1979*; *Pandey, 1998*). Some of them failed to get even the meager compensation for their land while others, who received it, were squeezed of it through devious ways (*Ekka, 2004*; *Mahapatra, 1998*; *Mathur, 2006*)[a]. Trapped in the vicious cycle of increasing destitution, they suffered from food insecurity, chronic malnutrition and increased morbidity (*Agnihotri, 1998*). The political impact of these changes were manifested in their total marginalisation, loss of identity, disruption of social network and lack of control over their lives (*Pandey, 1998*). In many places, the affected tribals also faced discrimination in the job market and the level of wages received (*Fernandes, 1997*). They were also confronted with the hostility of the original inhabitants of the area where they were relocated because of the competition in access to labour market, grazing land, drinking water facilities etc. (*Perspectives, 2007*). The negative social environment transformed their social behavior which was observed in deviant traits in tribal men such as alcoholism, crime, suicide, delinquency, wife beating, polygamy etc. (*Fernandes, 1997*). This had an adverse effect on their health making them susceptible to new diseases (*Thukral, 1989*; *Mahapatra, 1998*) and even emotional disorders. These experiences led to the loss of self-esteem resulting from the declining self confidence and devaluation of their social identity (*Pandey, 1998*). The arrogance of the dominant community contributed a great deal towards this feeling. The totality of impact relegated them to a sub-human level of existence (*Vidyarthi, 1970*; *Sengupta, 1979*; *Areeparampil, 1989*; *Thukral, 1989*).

The tribal women emerged as greater victims within their society. They were marginalised both within the family and outside (*Thukral, 1996*). Their work load increased but status deteriorated (*Fernandes, 1991*). This happened because the change of vocation and social environment (*Agnihotri, 1998*) and in the means of production from shifting to settled agriculture or from agriculture to wage driven vocations (*Menon, 1993*) alienated them from decision making processes within the family and downgraded their status as productive workers in the economy. They were either confined to homes or resorted to home based activities or took up wage labour activities in the market where they faced discrimination both with regard to the nature of work and the level of wages in addition to the sexual exploitation. Most of them became domestic aids and help. The low level of literacy and the hostile non-tribal world contributed to this situation. Additional work load, insecurity in food supply and emotional tensions led to the deterioration of health in women and children. Tribal women also suffered from loss of dignity and autonomy within the family due to internalization of non-tribal traits by the tribal male members and graduated from economic independence to social and economic subordination. They were doubly disempowered*. The experiences can be summed up in the acute feeling of their psychological marginalisation.

Rehabilitation policies also suffered from gender disparity. Women

* Fernandes has an explanation for this phenomenon. Tribal women were alienated from the natural resources which formed the basis of economic importance, social status and cultural freedom. Their relatively higher status in traditional environment

members of the family (adult unmarried daughters, widows, deserted, divorcees) were not treated as a separate family. Concerns of widows and single women were not addressed and no specific provisions were made in them addressing their specific concerns like employment, protection, sanitation facilities, security etc. Pronounced inequality of knowledge was practiced where even access to information on displacement and norms of compensation and other entitlements were denied to them both by the displacing agency and the male members of the family (*Basu, 2006*). Women were also emotionally traumatized when in the absence of land as the mainstay of joint family, nuclearisation of family took place and social disintegration started. There was no counteracting strategy to neutralize these adverse impacts.

Resistance Movements

The tribal communities have had a long history of resistance against the introduction of policies and governance system which have the effect of destroying their social and cultural institutions and subjecting them to exploitation and subjugation. The numerous tribal revolts against the government during the colonial period are well documented. But the resistance movements against acquisition of land after independence have rarely been documented and researched. This is because resistance has been localised and easily subdued by the government due to the powerlessness of the tribals in the society and the polity. But stronger and more widespread resistance has emerged in recent times in view of the extensive level of acquisition of land. The qualitative difference in the current phase of resistance compared to the earlier one lies in the political visibility that the issue of displacement has lately acquired. This is largely because the land owners in developed agricultural areas are also affected besides the tribal

---

emanated from the control they exercised over common property resources. Deprivation of this resource causes not only economic impoverishment but also loss of social support. This is because of the clear division in the tribal society between family affairs and social spheres. The man represents the household in social deliberations while the woman manages the family and its economy and production system. This is particularly true in the shifting cultivation. In settled agriculture, man emerges as the main decision maker. The loss of traditional resource base turns the woman into a house wife in the absence of a comparable vocation and deprives her of making any contribution to the economy of family. This leads to transfer of power to man. Displacement, therefore, weakens tribal society and degrades the status of women. (Fernandes, 2006b).

peasantry. This visibility can be seen in the widespread criticism of the existing law on acquisition of land and the rehabilitation policy for persons displaced as a result of it. The visibility can also be attributed to the numerous civil society groups advocating the cause of displaced peasantry, particularly the tribals, who have also produced literature on the desired changes in the Land Acquisition Act, 1894 and the design of a new rehabilitation policy to address their concerns. Three major official documents lately have also deliberated on this issue. These include: Report of Expert Group on Alienation of Tribal Land and its Restoration (*MoRD, 2004*), Report of Standing Committee on Tribal Development (*MTA, 2007*) and Draft National Tribal Policy (*MTA, 2006*). This has forced the Central government to announce the revision of both these instruments to assuage the peasantry. The National Rehabilitation Policy, 2007 has been notified by the Ministry of Rural Development (*MoRD, 2007*) and the Rehabilitation and Resettlement Bill, 2007 was introduced in the Lok Sabha to provide statutory support to it (*Lok Sabha, 2007*). Simultaneously, the Ministry has introduced the Land Acquisition (Amendment) Bill, 2007 in the Lok Sabha (*Lok Sabha, 2007*). The relevant issue now is whether these initiatives reverse the past experience with regard to the land acquisition and rehabilitation and address the concerns of the agitating tribals and the advocacy groups representing their interests.

Suggested Changes in the Law

Since the law on acquisition of land is central to their concern, the suggested changes would be taken up first for scrutiny. The most critical issue in this regard relates to the sanctity of the constitutional scheme of protection for the Scheduled Tribes. This protection extends to placing restrictions on alienation of their land, governance of scheduled areas, management of natural resources within their territory, preservation of their identity etc. The existing land acquisition laws have ignored this dimension in the process of land acquisition. But the suggested changes in the acquisition law, now before the Parliament, make no attempt to undo this wrong. No restriction has been incorporated with regard to the acquisition of tribal land thereby nullifying the effect of laws relating to the alienation of tribal land. The revised draft of the acquisition law continues to ignore PESA, 1996 and does not take note of the need for consultation with *Gram Sabha* of the concerned village in the matter relating to the acquisition of land as required in it. It has thus repudiated the ethos of self-governance and management of natural resources conferred on the tribal communities in the scheduled areas by PESA, 1996. The proposed Bill continues to violate the directions of the Supreme Court in the matter of utilisation of land in the scheduled areas emerging from the judgment in the *Samtha* case. The acquisition of tribal land would continue to displace members of the tribes from their existing habitat, environment and land thereby exposing them to the loss of cultural identity besides numerous other adversities. No safeguards have been built in the amended provisions to mitigate this situation. Evidently, therefore, the acquisition of land by the government would continue to take precedence over the constitutional scheme of protection for the tribals and, therefore, rob the protective provisions of their utility. When the government which is charged with the responsibility of enforcing these protective provisions itself renders them valueless, such a government would invoke little faith and confidence in its ability to protect the tribals against alienation of their land from non-government agencies as well. The government has also declined to relax its reliance on the notion of Eminent Domain for assuming absolute power to acquire privately owned land irrespective of the communities involved. This would negate as before the essential differentiation which has been recognised between the tribal communities and other social groups in the Constitution. The government has failed even to minimise the impact of land acquisition on the tribal communities by mandating that the acquisition of tribal land should be avoided wherever possible by exploring non-displacing options and, even when unavoidable after exhausting this exercise, it should be minimised by working out the least displacing alternatives. No such provision has been built into the draft of the revised land acquisition law to demonstrate some degree of sensitivity to their problems. The National Rehabilitation Policy, 2007 does require that the objective of exploring non-displacing and least displacing alternatives to be explored generally but not in the context of the tribal land specifically. In fact, the Policy in the Preamble has stressed the need to minimise the acquisition of agricultural land for non-agricultural use but the same concern has not been extended to the tribal land.

The dominant concern for the tribals facing acquisition of their land is to get some respite from acquisition by curtailing the scale of acquisition currently in process and likely to be taken up in future. The amendments in the law have proposed to remove the acquisition of land for companies from the purview of the Act with the intention of reducing the level of compulsory acquisition of land by the government. But this change is illusory because the definition of "public purpose" has been so widened as to include the requirement of land for companies in it. This is on account of the wide range of activities included in "infrastructure projects" for which land can be acquired under the label "public purpose". These activities would, in most cases, be executed by national and international companies. The tribals, therefore, would get no relief from this provision. The requirement of land for companies can also be accommodated under another component of "public purpose" which extends to "any activities useful to the general public". In such cases, the land for companies to the extent of 30 per cent of their total demand would be acquired by the Government if the remaining 70 per cent has been procured by companies directly. These two provisions camouflage the requirement of land for companies and use the provision of compulsory acquisition through the backdoor. Besides, leaving companies to directly procure land from the land owners through market transactions would be of no help to the tribals. This externalisation of acquisition would have pronouncedly negative implications for them. This is because the scale of displacement would not get reduced, only the mode would becomes different. The tribal land owners would also not have the strength to resist private procurement of land, despite their unwillingness to sell it, due to the coercion exerted by companies, given their resources, clout and propensity to use muscle power. This mode of acquisition would, in fact, be worse for them. This is corroborated by experience of tribals in the cases of private acquisition by companies. With poor bargaining capacity, they would be pitted against unequal buyers. Such transactions would lack transparency and accountability. Still worse, the displacees of private procurement would be deprived of the benefits of rehabilitation and resettlement which would be available only to those whose lands are acquired by the government. Thus, the alternatives suggested in the Bill to leave 70 per cent of acquisition of land for companies to direct procurement is worse than the compulsory acquisition by the government.

The tribals would have benefited if the suggested changes had incorporated a provision for transfer of tribal land on lease to the requiring agencies rather than outright transfer of its ownership. This would have enabled them to get premium as well as annual rent from the transferee and enabled them to retain ownership of land. The periodical renewal of lease would have given them the benefit of appreciated value of their land through revision of premium and annual rent at the time of renewal. This alternative which was strongly advocated by some civil society groups, particularly for tribal land holders, has been completely ignored.

The definition of land in the existing law which in official usage is interpreted to mean privately owned land remains untouched. No change has been made to enlarge its meaning by incorporating other categories of land. The narrow meaning given to it in the practice of acquisition would, therefore, continue to exclude government/public/panchayat/forest land and other community property resources. The rights subsisting on such lands in the case of its acquisition would remain unrecognised for payment of compensation. Some concession has been made to the Scheduled Tribes and other traditional forest dwellers in this regard by recognising their rights in relation to forest for computation of compensation in view of the recently enacted law on the subject*. But this recognition of forest rights does not extend to other lands mentioned above. The lands managed by the community outside the forest area which carries no individual rights of ownership but only of use with the sanction of the community would continue to be excluded from compensation entitlement. Many areas containing such lands have not been surveyed or surveyed only up to 9° slope. No records of user practices with regard to such areas may exist as the un-surveyed land would have been recorded as "government land". Such users would be disregarded for compensation. More importantly, the revised proposal continues to view land as a commodity and acquisition of land as an economic loss to its owner. The proposed changes make no attempt to incorporate the tribal view of land encompassing its social, cultural and spiritual dimensions and, consequently, fail to provide for an alternative compensatory scheme commensurate with this perception for its loss. The amendments do expand the definition of "person interested" so as to enlarge the circle of those who are entitled to claim compensation for loss of their land. The tribals who enjoy rights in forest land would now be recognised as "persons interested" for this purpose in view of the recently enacted law mentioned above as also those having tenancy rights under the relevant state laws or interest in easement affecting the land. But the tribal occupants of government/panchayat land would continue to be excluded from its purview. The "primitive" tribal groups in shifting cultivation areas whose lands have not been surveyed or wrongly recorded as "government land" but not characterized as "forest" would also be excluded. The suggested changes continue to disregard the existence of the "community" as a collective entity in the definition of "person interested". This has particularly adverse implications for the tribal areas, more so in the context of PESA, 1996 where the predominant role of the community in the expression *Gram Sabha* has been recognised in the management of land and other natural resources.

* The Scheduled Tribes and Other Traditional Forest Dwellers (Recognition of Forest Rights) Act, 2006.

The revised definition of "public purpose" does not accommodate the concerns of the Scheduled Tribes. Far from restricting the area of acquisition, the revised definition enlarges its scope by inclusion of strategic purpose, infrastructure projects and any other purpose useful to the general public where 70 per cent of the required land has been purchased through negotiations. The wide scope for acquisition created by the new formulation would fail to reduce the scale of compulsory acquisition and even acquisition for the need of companies. The retrogressive aspect of the proposed definition is that the welfare activities focused on the poor which existed in the earlier formulation have been omitted. From the view point of the tribals, this is crucial since the acquisition of land for purposes of rehabilitation including allocation of land to the displaced persons is not included in the definition. The revised proposal, therefore, forecloses the option of providing replacement of land as compensation to the tribals in the case of acquisition of their land. The scheme of compensation in the suggested amendments continues to ignore the loss of livelihood and retains its ownership centric bias. This would continue to deprive the landless tribals from any compensatory benefits thereby creating the social divide within the tribal community. The spiral of impoverishments resulting from displacement is worse for them as they have nothing to fall back upon to start an alternative livelihood.

The compensation scheme continues to be anchored to the "market value" for its determination with no basic departure from the existing law and its practice. This mode of determination has already proved most inadequate in the case of tribals due to the restrictions on the sale and purchase of tribal land. The provision now proposed to correct this situation requires the state government to specify the floor price per unit area of land. This would, however, make no significant difference in the accrual of compensation amount since this floor price would be calculated on the basis of land transactions in the adjoining areas or vicinity. This method of reassessment would also fail to elicit the real market value of land much less the value as perceived by the tribals. The government has disregarded the most favoured alternative for compensating the tribals by substituting replacement value in place of "market value" as its determinant in order to enable the land loser to obtain alternative land of the same productive potential as the one lost. The "market value" determined by land transactions is flawed due to the numerous distortions in the land market. These transactions are neither transparent nor fair or neutral in terms of status, circumstances and bargaining capacity of the parties involved.

On the mode of payment of compensation, the Bill makes no change in the existing practice of cash payment which is highly detrimental to the affected tribals. No special protection has been built into the proposal by way of Government intermediation in procuring alternative land with cash compensation or its safe parking to ward off pressures from the vested interests to squeeze it from the tribal recipients. But the most disappointing aspect of the revised proposal is the rejection by the Government to provide compensation in the form of alternative land for the tribals which alone could protect them, to some extent, from the disaster they face on account of displacement.

The suggested provision for mandatory social impact assessment in the case of acquisition of land for the purpose of preparing a rehabilitation and resettlement plan is a welcome initiative to realistically asses the social cost of the proposal. But the good intention has also been seriously compromised by restricting it to areas involving a specified size of physical displacement. In the case of scheduled areas, this would be applicable where 200 or more families *en masse* get displaced. Its importance has also been diluted because the provision has not been linked to the process of acquisition so as to influence the decision on the desirability of acquisition itself on the basis of its findings. Even for the purpose of rehabilitation and resettlement, the specification of a numerical benchmark for the applicability of this provision has diminished its utility as it would end up excluding a large number of projects from this obligation. This is particularly so because tribal settlements are usually small in size and dispersed in hilly terrain over a large area. The positive aspect of the provision is further minimised by excluding the requirement of land for national security involving emergency acquisition of a minimum area. Considering that the defense establishment is the agency responsible for the largest displacement of the tribals (*MoRD, 2004*), the restrictive application as suggested would further hurt the interests of the tribes. In such cases, the task of providing institutional safeguards for protecting the interests of the affected families has been left to the agencies requiring land who may not be adequately sensitive to the concerns of the affected tribals. The conception of social impact assessment itself is flawed as it focuses entirely on the impact of the project on infrastructure, public facilities and institutions and ignores the impact on people in general and their economic, social and cultural conditions in particular. In this view of the matter, the exercise of social impact assessment would fail to bring out the traumatic effects of displacement on the tribes and address them appropriately in the rehabilitation and resettlement plan.

The draft of the revised law makes no improvement in creating conditions for effective participation of the affected persons in the acquisition proceedings. The methods of conveying information about the acquisition of land continue to be irrelevant to the tribal areas. The affected tribals are likely to be largely illiterate. The newspaper circulation in tribal areas does not extend beyond the district towns. The gazette notifications are not accessible even to the educated persons let alone the ordinary tribals. The information contained in the preliminary notification is too inadequate to enable the concerned tribals to express their views on the proposal. The time within which objections have to be raised is insufficient. These provisions have not been suitably changed so as to adopt user-friendly methods of conveying information. More important, the *Gram Sabha* has not been involved in this exercise nor provision made for supply of adequate information and necessary facilities despite the requirement of consultation with this body in PESA, 1996. While a provision for such consultation has been incorporated in the National Rehabilitation and Resettlement Policy, 2007 and the Rehabilitation and Resettlement Bill, 2007, no such requirement has been incorporated in the Land Acquisition (Amendment) Bill, 2007 where it was most necessary.

The Bill has introduced a provision to disallow any transactions in respect of land under acquisition after issue of notification under section 4(1) of the Land Acquisition Act with a view to checking unscrupulous transfers of land. This is intended to protect the tribals, among others, who are the greatest victims of such transfers. But this provision would fail to stop such transactions because they usually precede the initiation of acquisition proceedings with issue of notification under section 4(1). There is no proposal to empower the collector to take preventive action to stop these transactions before issue of notification under section 4(1) by sending necessary directives to the revenue officials and involving the *Gram Sabhas/Panchayats* to caution people against giving credence to disinformation which induces such transfers.

The suggested changes in the provisions relating to reference for adjudication on compensation amount do not take any corrective action in respect of the situations where the illiterate and poorer land owners like the tribals are pressured to accept the award and are, on this basis, debarred from making an application for referring their case to the court. Similarly, no changes have been effected in the provision regarding re-determination of the compensation where a higher amount has been awarded by a reference court. The tribals and such other vulnerable groups fail to file a written application for such redetermination as they do not get to know the decision of the reference court in time. The Bill fails to obligate the collector to act *suo moto* in such cases with a view to benefiting the eligible persons.

The amendment proposals have introduced certain restrictions regarding transfer of acquired land which remains unutilized. One such restriction relates to the reversion of land to the government if the requiring agency fails to utilise it within a period of five years. But the provision would only benefit the government since, on reversion of such land, no obligation to restore the unutilised land to the erstwhile land owners has been incorporated. Even the alternative option of paying additional compensation to the land losers in lieu of restoration so as to mitigate their suffering on this account has not been accepted.

The proposed changes do contain a commitment for the rehabilitation and resettlement of persons who are involuntarily displaced due to the acquisition of land. This was a much sought after provision and is, therefore, welcome. But its disquieting feature lies in the specification of norms for the admissibility of this benefit contained in the National Rehabilitation and Resettlement Policy, 2007 and the corresponding Bill introduced in the Lok Sabha. In the case of tribals, this provision is applicable where 200 or more families en masse are displaced. This implies that where the level of displacement is lower than this numerical bench mark, the displaced persons would fail to get the benefit. The intended exclusion is neither rational nor defensible and considerably diminishes the utility of this provision. The magnitude of exclusion on this account would be particularly large in the case of the affected tribals.

Rehabilitation and Resettlement Policy

The Policy for rehabilitation and resettlement of the displaced persons covers all projects where involuntary displacement takes place. One of its objectives is to minimise displacement and to promote, as far as possible, non-displacing or least displacing alternatives. It also strives to provide a better standard of living to the displaced persons by making concerted efforts for enabling accrual of sustainable income to the affected families. Within the project area, the Policy extends benefits to not merely land owners but also to those losing livelihood. It incorporates requirement for social impact assessment and creates a dedicated administrative arrangement for preparation and implementation of the rehabilitation and resettlement plan in consultation with the affected persons. The admissible set of entitlements include provision of house sites, allotment of agricultural land, preference in access to employment in the project and training for employability outside, financial grant for construction of house, cattle-shed for agriculturists, work-shed for rural artisans and subsistence allowance to all the displaced persons for a specified period. The core amenities and social infrastructure needed for the resettlement colony have also been broadly indicated. An elaborate institutional arrangement for monitoring and grievance redressal has been laid down. The additional measures for the Scheduled Tribes require preparation of a Tribal Development Plan which involve settlement of pending land rights, restoration of alienated land and a programme for development of alternative fuel, fodder and non-timber forest produce on non-forest lands within a period of five years where the affected tribals are denied access to forest. The tribals have also been promised preference in allotment of land if the government land is available in the resettlement area and additional financial assistance for loss of customary rights or usages of forest produce. The displaced tribal families shall, if possible, be settled in the scheduled area in a compact block and, where settled out of the district, they would receive 25 per cent higher rehabilitation and resettlement benefits in monetary terms in respect of the specified items. They shall also get allotment of land for community and religious gatherings. It has also been mandated that the *Gram Sabha* or the *Panchayat* in the Schedule V areas and the councils in the Schedule VI areas would be consulted in accordance with the provisions of the PESA, 1996 and the other relevant laws in all cases of land acquisition before issue of notification under the LA Act, 1894. The tribals, who were in possession of forest land prior to December, 2005, would be eligible for the benefit of the Policy.

But the Policy does not address the major problems which agitate the affected tribals. The most important of them is that the government should avoid the spectre of displacement and, if that cannot be done, to scale down its level. The Policy makes no concession for the scheduled areas or to the Scheduled Tribes in respect of the acquisition of land. It does not even contain an assurance that the acquisition of tribal land would be avoided unless absolutely necessary and minimised, if unavoidable. The promised exercise enshrined in the objectives of the Policy to minimise displacement and explore non-displacing and least displacing alternatives does not specifically contextualise it in respect of land held by the STs. Even as an exhortation of a general nature irrespective of the affected groups, it lacks sincerity and commitment. The displaced persons are not associated with this exercise which has been entrusted to the Administrator in charge of the rehabilitation and resettlement in consultation with the concerned project agency. Even this limited objective with its non-transparent process is not incorporated in the Land Acquisition (Amendment) Bill, 2007 where it was most required so as to influence the decision on the proposed acquisition. The Policy has been made applicable to the projects in future and has ignored the huge number of displaced persons from earlier projects who have remained unrehabilitated. The displaced tribals are the largest group among such persons. Besides, the numerical benchmark specified for its applicability makes it evident that even in respect of the future projects, the Policy would not be applicable to all of them. This benchmark, although lower in respect of the tribal, hilly, desert areas than in respect of other areas is irrational and arbitrary and would exclude a large number of the affected tribals from even the meager benefits that the policy offers. The Policy creates doubts about its universal coverage for rehabilitation and resettlement even in the areas of its applicability due to lack of sufficient clarity in the definition of the "affected family" and the caveats attached to it. It also fails to include persons who suffer secondary displacement on account of the project activities though their land is not acquired. The tribals are among the major victims of this displacement which is neither recognised nor addressed.

As for the entitlement of benefits, the approach in the policy continues to be property-centric since the loss of livelihood and access to the common property resources is not covered by any compensatory arrangements. Only a provision has been made for development of fuel, fodder and non-timber resources on non-forest lands where the tribals are denied access to forest. The discrimination in the entitlement of individual benefits to the affected persons such as the allotment of land and the provision of employment between those who lose land and others who do not own land but lose livelihood is also implicit. On the issue of allotment of land which concerns the tribals most, the policy offers no concrete assurance at all. There is no commitment to provide land for land whether in the case of irrigation/hydel projects or other projects. The provision of land mentioned in the policy has been made conditional to the availability of the "government land"/ "wasteland" in the resettlement area. This condition is most unlikely to be satisfied. The option to acquire private land for such distribution has been specifically disregarded. The provision of employment to one person from each affected nuclear family lacks positiveness and credibility. It has been subjected to the availability of vacancies and the eligibility of the displaced job seekers. In the current paradigm of economy, development projects create very meager employment opportunities and, that too, in the skilled category, by and large. Due to the low literacy levels and lack of skills, the tribals would not be able to satisfy the requirements for such jobs even if available.

With regard to the infrastructure and amenities, an invidious distinction has been introduced in the range of entitlements admissible between the projects which satisfy the specified numerical benchmark and those which do not do so. As the concerned state government has been authorised to determine the civic amenities and social facilities, the provision would lend itself to arbitrary decisions depending upon the clout which displacees command in different situations.

The gender bias is also reflected in the policy since the definition of "family" has failed to recognise every unmarried adult daughter as an independent unit deserving separate rehabilitation. The women headed households do not attract attention in the policy. The concerns of women in general have been ignored since neither the baseline survey and census collect information relating to them nor the rehabilitation and resettlement scheme incorporates affirmative action for them. The displaced tribals would suffer additionally if intra-family distribution of land has not been entered in land records since even the adult sons would not be entitled to separate units of rehabilitation and resettlement. The requirement for a Tribal Development Plan in the Policy suffers from serious inadequacies. It is characterised by a uniform and standardised approach and fails to reflect the diversity of the social and ecological situations in the tribal areas. The land management practices differ widely in the tribal areas with varying degrees of community control over natural resources. The shifting cultivation areas where the tribals use land on hilltops by rotation are inhabited usually by the "primitive tribes". The survey and settlement operations have not mapped out all such areas and individual uses of land particularly on slopes beyond 9° have not been recorded either because of the nature of cultivation (shifting in place of plough) practiced in that terrain or the lack of familiarity of concerned officials with the land use and management pattern. In the schedule VI areas, the pattern of land holding is communal, the land records do not exist and the tribes are opposed to their preparation. There is an extensive variety of rights and interests in access to land resources covered by customary laws. In addition, there are some hunter and food gathering tribes entirely dependent on forest with no fixed habitat as they move from area to area in search of food. The Tribal Development Plan, therefore, cannot be neatly standardised and based on a homogenised model applicable to the non-tribal communities which the Policy seems to do. The conceptual and structural frame for the rehabilitation and resettlement of the displaced tribals, therefore, needed to be designed taking into account their specific socio-ecological situations and ethnic characteristics. This is particularly important for the tribes in remote areas, least exposed to the outside world. This complexity in planning has not been recognised let alone accommodated in the policy. Besides, the Policy makes no provision for addressing the negative cultural and emotional, psychological externalities, social disarticulation, devaluation of culture, emotional trauma experienced by the displaced tribals resulting from the sudden break with their kinship networks, exposure to the hostile larger society and intrusion of the incompatible adverse cultural and social norms from immigrant non-tribals in the area. Also, some risks among the ten associated with displacement identified in international literature fail to get even recognised let alone mitigated in the framework of the policy. Overall, the policy offers a faltering and limited commitment in respect of the fundamental concerns of the tribals. There is neither right based entitlement or concrete assurance in respect of land and employment nor a guarantee of congenial and culturally compatible relocation with replacement of the facilities and amenities, if not better, enjoyed by them prior to their displacement.

Prospects: Hope or Despair

The foregoing analysis makes it evident that there would be no respite for the tribals from displacement and little hope of getting dignified rehabilitation and resettlement. They are pitted against an ideology of development and a vision of national aspiration articulated by the ruling classes which in all its dimensions presents a theatre of war to them. It brings in its fold displacement, disruption, impoverishment, misery and uncertainty with no mitigating features to cheer them up. They are powerless to change either its nature or its intensity, scale and speed. They have little clout in the larger society or support from the mainstream political forces even to get the desired accommodation in the rehabilitation and resettlement. With their back to the wall, they are fighting a last ditch battle with their peaceful resistance to the projects to save their land as also the way of life which they are most likely to lose. Progressive proletarianisation, aggressive incorporation in the lowest rung of the Indian society and decimation of their identity are the prospects which await the displaced tribals. The grand architecture of protection and the "vibrant" democracy flaunted with self assurance by the ruling elite provides no comfort to them in the bleak future which stares at their face.

REFERENCES

Aggarwal, Dinesh (1998): 'Preventing Impoverishment from Displacement. The NTPC experience' in Mathur and Marsden (ed), Oxford University Press, New Delhi.

Agnihotri, Anita (1998): 'Poverty Alleviation concerns in Orissa State Policy on Resettlement', in Mathur and Marsden (eds), Oxford University Press, New Delhi.

Areeparampil, Mathew (1989): 'Industries, Mines and Displacement of Indigenous People: The case of Chhotanagpur', in Fernandes and Thukral (eds), ISI, New Delhi.

Asif Mohammed (1999): 'Land Acquisition Act: Need for an Alternative Paradigm', *Economic and Political Weekly*, June 19.

Baxi, Upendra (1989): 'Notes on Constitutional and Legal aspects of Rehabilitation and Displacement', in Fernandes and Thukral (eds), ISI, New Delhi.

Balagopal, K (2007)[a]: 'Impact of Grants to Industries', *Economic and Political Weekly*, September 29, 2007.

Balagopal, K (2007)[b]: 'Illegal Acquisition in Tribal Areas', *Economic and Political Weekly*, October, 6, 2007.

Banerjee, Rahul 1997: 'A Critique of Madhya Pradesh Resettlement Act', in Fernandes and Paranjpye (eds), ISI, New Delhi.

Basu, Malika (2006): 'Gender Focus in Resettlement Planning', in Mathur (ed), Oxford, New Delhi.

Bhuskute, R.V. (1997): 'The Maharashtra Rehabilitation Act, 1989', in Fernandes and Paranjpye (eds), ISI, New Delhi.

Centre for Science and Environment (1985): Second Citizen's Report on State of India's Environment, Centre for Science and Environment, New Delhi.

Cernea, Michael M. (1996): 'The Risks and Reconstruction Model for Resettling Displaced Population', Keynote address at International Conference on Reconstructing livelihoods, Oxford University.

Cernia, Michael M. (1997): 'The Risks and Reconstruction Model for Resettling Displaced Population', *World Development*, Vol. (25) No 10.

Cernea, Michael M. (1998), 'Impoverishment or Social Justice? A model for Planning Resettlement' in Mathur and Marsden (eds), Vikash, New Delhi.

Cernea Michael M (1999) Development's Painful Social Costs, Introductory Study in S .Parasuraman.

Cernea, Michael M. (1999)[a]: 'Forward: The Power of Synthesis', in Mahapatra (1999).

Cernea, Michael. M. (1999)[b]: Introduction, in Parasuraman S. (1999):

Cernea, Michael M. (2006): 'Resettlement Management, Denying or Confronting Risks' in Mathur (ed), Oxford University Press, New Delhi.

Chaudhuri, Buddhadeb (ed) 1992: Tribal Transformation in India, Vol. III. Inter-India, New Delhi.

Chew, Sing C and Denemark, Robert A (eds) 2001: The Underdevelopment of Development, Sage, New Delhi.

Chew, Sing C. and D. Denemark, Robert, A. (2001): 'On Development and Underdevelopment' in Chew and Denemark (eds), Sage, New Delhi.

Commission, Planning (2003): The Tenth Five Year Plan, Government of India, New Delhi.

Corbridge, Stuart, Jewitt, Sarah, Kumar Sanjay (2004): Jharkhand:, Environment, Development and Ethnicity, Oxford, New Delhi.

Corbridge, Stuart (2004): 'The Ideology of Tribal Economy and Society', in Corbridge, Jewitt and Kumar, Oxford University Press, New Delhi.

Das, A.K. and Banerjee, S.K. (1966): 'Impact of industrialization on the life of Tribals in West Bengal', Tribal Welfare Department, Calcutta.

Delhi Forum (2008): Displacement Juggernaut, case studies from states, New Delhi (For private circulation).

Dube, S.C. (ed) 1998: Antiquity to Modernity in Tribal India, Vol.1 continuity and change among Indian Tribes, Inter-India, New Delhi.

Ekka, Alex (2004): Sources of displacement, paper presented at an orientation programme for personnel involved in resettlement and rehabilitation programme for displaced persons, India International Centre, New Delhi, June 28-30, 2004.

Fernandes, Walter and Thukral, Enakshi Ganguly (eds) 1989: Development, Displacement and Rehabilitation ISI, New Delhi.

Fernandes, Walter (1991): 'Power and Powerlessness: Development Projects and Displacement of Tribals', *Social Action*, Vol. 41, No. 3 (July-September).

Fernandes, Walter (1993): 'Forests and Tribals: Informal Economy, Dependence and Management Traditions' in Miri (ed), IAAS, Shimla.

Fernandes, Walter and Paranjpye, Vijay (eds) 1997: Rehabilitation Policy and Law in India: A Right to Livelihood, ISI, New Delhi.

Fernandes, Walter (1998): 'Development Induced Displacement in Eastern India', in Dube (ed), Inter India, New Delhi.

Fernandes, Walter (2006)[a]: 'Liberalisation and Development induced displacement', *Social Change*, Vol. 36, March.

Fernandes Walter (2006)[b], 'Development—induced Displaced and Tribal Women', in Rath, (ed), Sage, New Delhi.

Gadgil, Madhav (1989): 'Forest Management, Deforestation and Peoples' Impoverishment', *Social Action*, Vol. 39, No. 4, Oct-Dec.

Hidayatullah, M. (1983): Right to Property and Indian Constitution. Arnold Heineman, New Delhi.

Jaamdar, S.M. (2006): 'Upper Krishna Project: Recent Improvements but Resettlement still Elusive', in Mathur (ed), Oxford University Press, New Delhi.

Joseph, Johny (1998): 'Retrofit Economic Rehabilitation Using Impoverishment Risk Analysis: The Maharashtra Experience', in Mathur and Marsden (eds), Oxford, New Delhi.

Kothari, Smithu (1996): 'Whose Nation: The Displaced as Victims of Development', *Economic and Political Weekly*, June 15.

Lok Sabha (2007): The Land Acquisition (Amendment) Bill, 2007, Bill No. 97 of 2007.

Lok Sabha (2007): The Rehabilitation and Resettlement Bill, 2007, Bill No. 98 of 2007.

Mahapatra, L.K. (1993): 'Customary Rights in Law and Forests and the State', in Miri (ed), IAAS, Shimla.

Mahapatra L.K. (1998): 'Good Intentions or Policies are not Enough: Reducing

Impoverishment Risks for Tribal Oustees', in Mathur and Marsden (eds), Oxford University Press, New Delhi.

Mahapatra, L.K. (1999): Resettlement, Impoverishment and Reconstruction in India, Vikas, New Delhi.

Marsden, David (1998): 'Resettlement and Rehabilitation in India', in Mathur and Marsden (eds), Oxford University Press, New Delhi.

Mathur, H.M. (1995): 'The Resettlement of People Displaced by Development, Projects: Issues and Approaches, in Mathur (ed), Vikas, New Delhi.

Mathur, H.M. (ed) 1995: Development, Displacement and Resettlement: Focus on Asian Experiences, Vikas Publishing House, New Delhi.

Mathur, H.M. (1998): 'The Improvement Risk Model and its Use as a Planning tool', in Mathur and Marsden (eds), Oxford University Press, New Delhi.

Mathur and Marsden (eds) 1998: Development Projects and Impoverishment Risks, Oxford New Delhi.

Mathur, Hari Mohan (2006)[a]: 'Resettling People Displaced by Development Projects: Some Critical Management Issues', *Social Change*, Vol. 36, No. 1, March.

Mathur, H.M. (2006)[b]: 'Introduction and Overview', in Mathur (ed), Oxford, New Delhi.

Mathur, H.M. (ed) (2006)[b]: Managing Resettlement in India, Oxford, New Delhi.

Menon, Geeta (1993): 'Tribal Women: The Ignored Sector in the Development Debate', in Miri (ed), IAAS, Shimla.

Ministry of Rural Development (MoRD) (2004): Report of Expert Group on Prevention of Alienation of Tribal Land and its Restoration, Government of India, New Delhi.

Ministry of Rural Development (2007): The National Rehabilitation and Resettlement Policy, 2007, Government of India, New Delhi.

Ministry of Tribal Affairs (MTA) (2005): Interim Report of the Standing Committee on Inter-Sectoral Issues relating to Tribal Development, October, 2005, Government of India, New Delhi.

Ministry of Tribal Affairs (2006): Draft National Tribal Policy, Government of India, New Delhi.

Ministry of Tribal Affairs (2007): Second Interim Report of the Standing Committee on Inter-Sectoral Issues relating to Tribal Development on Displacement, Resettlement and Rehabilitation of Scheduled Tribes, Government of India, New Delhi.

Miri, Mrinal (ed) 1993: Continuity and Change in Tribal Society, IAAS, Shimla.

Pandey, Balaji (1998): Depriving the Underprivileged for Development, ISED, Bhubaneshwar.

Paranjpye, Vijay and Kewatramani, Lolita (1997): 'Swamped by NTPC Fly Ash: A Review of the Rehabilitation Policy', in Fernandes and Paranjpye (eds), ISI, New Delhi.

Parasuraman. S. (1999): Development Dilemma, ISS, Netherlands.

Pathy, Jaganath (1992)[a]: 'Tribal and Indigenous Peoples of the World', in Chaudhuri (ed), Inter India, New Delhi.

Pathy, Jaganath (1992)[b]: 'The idea of a tribe and the Indian Scene', in Chaudhuri' (ed), Inter India, New Delhi.

Perspectives (2007): Abandoned: Development and Displacement, The Perspectives Team, New Delhi

Pouchepadass, Jacques (2001): 'Colonialism and Environment in India: A comparative perspective', in Thorner (ed), Tulika, New Delhi.

Prabhu Pradip (2007): Development and Displacement in Tribal India, Annexure VI to MTA (2007), Government of India, New Delhi.

Ramanathan, Usha (1996): 'Displacement and the Law', *Economic and Political Weekly*, No.31 (Nov.24-June 15)

Ramesh, M.K. and Guntipilly, Francis (1997): 'A critique of the Karnataka Resettlement of Project Displaced persons Act, 1987', in Fernandes and Paranjpye (eds), ISI, New Delhi.

Ramesh, M.K. and Joseph, Francis. A. (2006): 'The Karnataka Resettlement of Project Displaced Persons Act, 1987: A critical perspective', in Mathur (eds), Oxford, New Delhi.

Rath, Govind Chandra (ed), 2006, Tribal Development in India—Introduction, Sage, New Delhi.

Roy, A.K. (1982): Jharkhand: Internal Colonialism, Frontier, Calcutta, April 17 and 24, 1982.

Roy Burman, B.K. (1961): Social Processes in the Industrialization of Rourkela, Census of India, cited in Pandey (1998), ISED, Bhubaneshwar.

Roy Burman, B.K. (1992): 'Indigenous People and their quest for Justice', in Chaudhuri (ed), Inter India, New Delhi.

Roy Burman (n.g.): Historical Ecology of Land Survey and Settlement in Tribal Areas and Challenges of Development, Council for Social Development, New Delhi.

S. Parasuraman(1999): The Development Dilemma: Displacement in India, Macmillan Press, New Delhi.

Sachidananda (1965): "Impact of Industrialization on Bihar Tribes" Cultural Forum, Nos. 1&2, Vol. 7.

Sastry, VNVK (1992): 'Displacement and New Dimensions of the Unrest in Tribal Areas of Andhra Pradesh', in Chaudhuri (ed), Inter India, New Delhi.

Sengupta, Nirmal (1979): Destitutes and Development: A Study of Bauri Community in Bokaro, Concept, New Delhi.

Shah, Ghanshyam and Sah, D.C. (1998): 'Development and Resettlement of Tribals: Sardar Sarovar in Gujarat', in Dube (ed), Inter India, New Delhi.

Singh, Chhatrapati (1989): 'Rehabilitation and Right to Property', in Fernandes and Thukral (eds), ISI, New Delhi.

Thorner, Alice (Ed) (2001): Daniel Thorner Memorial Lectures, Tulika, New Delhi.

Thukral, Enakshi Ganguly (1989): 'Dams for whose Development', in Fernandes and Thukral (eds), ISI, New Delhi.

Thukral, Enakshi Ganguly (1996): 'Development, Displacement and Rehabilitation—Locating Gender', *Economic and Political Weekly* (June 15).

Vidyarthi, L.P. (1970): Socio-Cultural implications of Industrialization in India, Planning Commission, New Delhi.

Viegas, Phillip (1991): Encroached and Enslaved: Alienation of Tribal Lands and its Dynamics, ISI, New Delhi.

TRIBAL POLICY

Critical Issues of Tribal Policy

P.S. Krishnan

The draft Tribal Policy circulated in July 2006 deals with the same problems, the same issues and the same solutions that have been discussed over the last several decades. The only difference between then and now is the diminished sensitivity of "civil society" to the deprived categories and the increased complexity of the socio-economic environment.

It is also observed that there is a danger in general of trying to impose solutions in the issues relating to Scheduled Tribes, which are out of context. For example. in scheduling and non-scheduling or de-scheduling of tribes, there is a reference to the "creamy layer". This reference apparently arises from the anxiety to see that different Scheduled Tribes at different levels of backwardness are able to get their share of the benefits from the reservation policy. Educated middle class society is conscious of reservation because candidates for posts and services under the State belong to this class. But reservation is only one of the issues of dimensions of the tribal struggle for survival and equality. There are many other dimensions to the struggle of Scheduled Tribes for survival and equality, apart from reservation, like prevention of loss of their lands, restoration of their lands which have passed on to others, development of their lands, access to high quality education from school level to highest level and consequent creation of access to opportunities of employment at all levels in modern society, and preservation of their traditional rights to forest produce.

However, coming to the issue of "creamy layer", the present situation is that both the "creamy layer" and "non-creamy layer" among the Scheduled Castes and Scheduled Tribes, taken together are not able to occupy even half, in the case of Scheduled Castes, and less than half in the case of Scheduled Tribes, of the seats reserved for them, even in courses of general education, even in the Delhi University. The situation is even more bleak in professional and technological institutions. Given these circumstances, if the notion of "creamy layer" is imported in the context of Scheduled Castes and Scheduled Tribes, it would lead to further depleting whatever limited and very inadequate numbers of Scheduled Castes and Scheduled Tribes in these courses and the unfilled seats will revert to the general category and to that extent will defeat the goal laid down by the national policy of reservation, based on constitutional mandate.

The concept of "creamy layer" was laid down by the Supreme Court in its judgement of 1992 in the Mandal case (**Indra Sahney vs Union of India**) in the context of the socially and educationally backward classes. While laying this down, the Supreme Court specifically laid down the caveat that this concept has no relevance to the Scheduled Castes and Scheduled Tribes. In fact, the correct name for this concept of "creamy layer" would be "Socially Advanced Persons/Sections of the castes identified as Socially and Educationally Backward". While the anxiety that every Scheduled Tribe should get its due share and the concern that many of the tribes among the Scheduled Tribes are being left out from the benefit of reservation are both serious concerns, one should not forget the total tribal context in proposing solutions for this problem.

Proper formulation of any policy is an important first step. The next step is to see how to convert it into an action programme. An action programme would consist of constitutional amendment, where necessary, legislations, relevant developmental plans, establishment of appropriate machinery for their implementation and proper selection of individuals to man the machinery. The last step is important because it is possible to destroy any policy, any programme, any institution by selecting the wrong individuals to implement and administer them. Dr Ambedkar, in two of his important addresses on 4.11.1948 and 25.11.1949 to the Constituent Assembly, set up after Independence to frame our Constitution, warned that a good Constitution can be sabotaged very constitutionally by putting it into the hands of wrong individuals. Today we see this happening in various ministries, departments and commissions. Many of our national commissions, to a substantial extent, have become national omissions as appointments to these are not always made on the basis of their understanding of the issues and ability to take uncompromising, honest and correct positions on them.

Political participation at different levels is crucial for improving the status of Scheduled Tribes. Panchayats are the lowest level of decision-making and a very important body in the day-to-day life of the Scheduled Tribes. But at the national level, the highest level of decision—the Scheduled Tribes have only a limited participation. At the sub-national level, too where it is possible for them to have a better representation, they have been either deliberately or by accident of history, divided, with one piece of tribal territory attached to West Bengal, another until recently, tagged on to Bihar; a third piece was, until recently, existing as a part of the Central Provinces/ Madhya Pradesh and another piece in Andhra Pradesh. Other tribal areas are attached to Maharashtra and Gujarat; and a small bit is in Kerala. At the time of Independence, the Scheduled Tribes had no State of their own —not even in the North East. They had to go through a lot of struggle to get their own States in that region. During their struggle they were misunderstood and treated as secessionists. Then, with belated wisdom, the states of Meghalaya, Mizoram and Nagaland were carved out, all states with preponderant populations of Scheduled Tribes. However, this process covered only a small part of India and is yet to work out in the major areas of India where the majority of India's Scheduled Tribe population lives.

The demand for Jharkhand was given a short shrift by the States Reorganisation Commission in 1955. It was just summarily dismissed without even a paragraph devoted to it. After Jharkhand was infiltrated by non-tribals, the truncated State of Jharkhand was created since it was created out of only the tribal region of Bihar, leaving out the adjoining tribal territories of West Bengal and Orissa. In the present truncated Jharkhand, Scheduled Tribes form only 32 per cent of the total population. This is really not a tribal State; it only has a tribal as its Chief Minister. This is true of Chhattisgarh also. As such there is still considerable scope for creation of States with total or near total populations of Scheduled Tribes. There is scope for at least four to five such States in the Central Indian belt—a larger Jharkhand, North Dandakaranya, South Dandakaranya or Gondwana in the place including Chhattisgarh and Bhil-land in Western India, across northern Gujarat, southern Rajasthan and southwestern Madhya Pradesh,. The names may be different, but the logic is that Scheduled Tribes should be the majority population in as large an area as possible and in as many territories as possible, minimizing the non-tribal population percentage in these areas. Only then can there be a possibility of the tribal people of ruling themselves and taking legislative and executive decisions in accordance with the constitutional scheme. It has to be appreciated that a state in India has got an autonomous status in our Constitution and while this benefit of State-level autonomy has become available to different major linguistic populations in the country, it has till now eluded the Scheduled Tribes except in the small North-Eastern region. It would thus be appropriate of the Indian state to create state-level status for the Scheduled Tribes to the maximum extent possible and this is something the Scheduled Tribes and their friends should actively demand this and undertake democratic mobilization in support of this demand.

Another crucial area to which the Scheduled Tribes themselves have not paid enough attention, is the manner in which a number of communities which are not tribes are trying/or have succeeded, to get themselves included in the Schedule Tribes list. Though almost all the entries in the Schedule Tribes lists for different states fulfill the necessary criteria, but even if there are a few included in the list, who do not fulfill the criteria, it will jeopardize the legitimate opportunities that should be available to the genuine Scheduled Tribes. In fact, this is already happening. Though the leaders representing genuine Scheduled Tribes have expressed their resentment to such unprincipled additions and efforts, they have not pursued the matter, they are lacking in constant vigilance over the matter and as such, they are not able to take steps in time to thwart such moves by the government and some interested non-tribal communities. There was an instance of one of our former prime ministers who on a visit to Assam, promised a certain backward community that they would be declared a scheduled tribe. Such promises should be formally included in the list of corrupt practices under the Representation of Peoples Act, 1951.

There is a set of criteria on the basis of which alone can a community be listed as a Scheduled Tribe. A community cannot be listed as such unless it is a tribe. This should only be determined on the basis of socio-anthropological facts. There should be no promises in this regard either during the elections or before them. Going back to the incident regarding one such promise made in Assam and the unconstitutional moves to fulfill that promise, it is nothing but *Rajakiya Vyabhichar* or political profligacies. As a consequence of the wrong promise made the community was duly removed from the list of Socially and Educationally Backward Classes (SEdBCs/OBCs/BCs) which in reality it fell within and, simultaneously, an ordinance was issued including it in the list of Scheduled Tribes for Assam.

Ordinance-making is an extra-ordinary measure to be resorted to only rarely and when it is unavoidable, but to use this measure for purposes such as the one mentioned above is abominable. In the instant case, neither the government which made the ordinance nor the succeeding government could go beyond the ordinance and move a Bill in the Parliament. As a result that community fell between two stools, ceasing to be in the list of SEdBCs and not gaining the status of a Scheduled Tribe. It should be against such instances that the genuine Scheduled Tribes raise their voice and take firm steps to prevent such wrong inclusions. A campaign for incorporating a provision in the Representation of Peoples Act declaring pre-election vote-oriented promises regarding inclusion of a community in the list of Scheduled Tribes, or for that matter even in the list of SCs or BCs, to be an act of corruption under that Act, would be in order. In fact no individual, including the Prime Minister, is in any position to make such a promise given that there is a set procedure for inclusion in the list of Scheduled Tribes. In the case of Scheduled Castes and Scheduled Tribes, the procedure requires careful and unbiased study and recommendation by the state government and by the anthropological wing of the organisation of the Census Commissioner. This is an age-old procedure and after the amendment of Article 338, it is also mandatory to consult the National Commission for Schedule Castes and the National Commission for Scheduled Tribes for their views in each case. In the case of SEdBCs the procedure laid down by the Supreme Court and by the National Commission for Backward Classes Act and similar State Acts/State Executive Orders mandates an examination of Requests for Inclusion by the National Commission for Backward Classes in respect of inclusion in Central lists and the respective State Commissions with regard to State lists. Inclusion in these lists is based on the Constitutional concept behind them and on the social realities underlying the Constitutional provisions and has to be combined with objective criteria and unbiased examination. This is not a matter of patronage.

If a community is in the list of Scheduled Castes or Backward Classes and is not able to get its due share of the benefits of reservation provided for all communities in its list, that can not be a ground, for its inclusion in the list of Scheduled Tribes, or for it to demand such inclusion.

Notwithstanding this, there have been a few, rare instances, where such efforts have succeeded in the past. This has had and continues to have detrimental effects on genuine Scheduled Tribes. More such efforts are afoot. A typical example is the recent agitation of the Gujjar community of Rajasthan for inclusion in the list of Scheduled Tribes. They are a hard-working genuinely backward class in Rajasthan, though in Kashmir they are a genuine Scheduled Tribe rightly included in the Scheduled Tribe list for Jammu and Kashmir State. The same community can be at different stages of development, progress or backwardness, in different parts of the country. According to my study and analysis recorded in the advice of the

NCBC in respect of certain cases of the borderland between Maharashtra and Gujarat, the Patels of Gujarat, a very advanced community, were originally Gujjars and the state derived its name from them. In the socio-economic environment of Gujarat, historically they have made great progress and become one of the most advanced communities not only of Gujarat but of the country. In other states, which they inhabit like Rajasthan, Haryana, Uttar Pradesh etc., they have ceased to be a tribe in the historical past and become a caste which is still socially and educationally backward. This community nurses the grievance that as a backward class caste, it is not able to get its due share.

The remedy for such imbalances within the same category is to sub-categorise the communities in each list based on their varying levels of backwardness and ability to compete, with appropriate sub-quotas for each such sub-category, within the total quota for that category. This method of sub-categorisation of SEdBCs though widely used in the peninsular states and rarely followed in the north Indian states. As in all matters pertaining to the SedBC, the Centre still trails behind the peninsular states. Where this method has been adopted it has resulted in the better spread of the benefits of reservation and reduction in the level of justified discontent. In the landmark judgement in the Mandal case, the Supreme Court upheld the Constitutional validity of such sub-categorisation in respect of SEdBC. It is to be considered whether this approach can be adopted in the case of Scheduled Tribes and if so how? To my knowledge, there is only a rare and single instance of sub-categorisation of Scheduled Tribes in one State. This is virtually unknown to anybody. This matter needs to be examined further so that a mechanism which will enable the vast majority of the Scheduled Tribes population comprised in the large tribes of Central India like the Gond, Santhal, Munda, Oraon, Bhil, Koya etc., are able to get their due share of the benefits of reservation at the national level, and so that intra-State disparities can be addressed. This should be done in a harmonious manner by internal consultation and discussion among the Scheduled Tribes and a formula should be adopted on the basis of unanimity and consensus and without mutual bitterness. On no account should it be allowed to become an electoral exercise or adventure.

There is a need here to highlight two other macro issues. First is to reiterate the importance of formation of states, which are really tribal with preponderant tribal population. The maximum number of such states should be formed. Secondly, wherever statehood is not possible at all or where it is yet to become a reality, tribal areas should be constituted into Sixth Schedule territories and should have maximum autonomy. In the Constitution, the Sixth Schedule is provided at present only for the North-East. A simple Constitutional amendment can extend it to all other states. The Fifth Schedule which is provided for tribal areas in states in regions other than the North East is, in my opinion, pointless. All Fifth Schedule areas should be converted into Sixth Schedule tribal areas. There is a ten-year old recommendation to this effect by a Committee called the Bhuria Committee.

Along with these two steps, there is also need to take up measures for enhancing the capabilities of tribal communities so that they can take full charge of their own affairs, whether in separate states and or in fully autonomous Sixth Schedule areas. This will help them to throw up leaders, who will conduct themselves with maturity, responsibility, integrity and respect for law and which reflects the real tribal culture of sharing and concern for the larger society. These features of tribal society are of great relevance to India, and Scheduled Tribes should not allow the real characteristics of their culture to sink without a trace in the process of politicization and modernisation.

The biggest disadvantage for the Scheduled Tribes is that, in the country as a whole, they are only a small a proportion of the total population. At present they constitute only 8.17 per cent of the Indian population. If the two or three communities which are included in the list of Schedule Tribes, though they do not fulfill the criteria are excluded from this computation, the percentage of Scheduled Tribes would be still less. But in the areas where they have the strength of numbers they can fulfill their aspirations in different ways discussed earlier—first statehood; second sub-statehood; third Sixth Schedule Areas; and finally maximum autonomy. One of the good steps taken recently is the Panchayats (Extension to the Scheduled Areas) Act, 1996 and the other is the recognition of the rights of Scheduled Tribes and other forest dwellers in forests and forest produce by the Scheduled Tribes and Other Traditional Forest Dwellers (Recognition of Forest Rights) Act, 2006. But their proper and complete implementation remains a problem. This requires deep thought on the part of the Scheduled Tribes and their friends. We have full knowledge of what has gone wrong in India. There is no problem which we are not aware of. There is no solution which we do not already know. But the crux of the issue is that known solutions are not adopted in a holistic manner and put into effect comprehensively except in certain areas and to a limited extent. It is happening in certain areas because of good tribal leadership, good representatives, good officers and sensitive non-tribal people. But, such instances are occurring more by accident or chance than by design.

Besides these major concerns, there are also other issues. Whenever an ST person rises a little higher the civil society of advanced classes become suspicious. They do not want educated Scheduled Tribes, they do not want educated Scheduled Castes they do not want educated backward classes. This is upper class hegemony, common to all the upper classes be it the Hindus who constitute the vast majority of the upper classes of India, the Muslims, the Christians or the Sikhs. They want this upper class hegemony to continue. In India, it must be kept in mind that the upper classes are drawn from the upper castes or advanced castes, though all those belonging to the upper or advanced castes are not part of the upper classes. It is this mindset and attitude which should be changed. We must ensure that the Scheduled Tribes are enabled to get the best of education at all levels so that they are able to get into positions which are comparable to the positions occupied by upper castes and upper classes. It is for this purpose that reservation and its proper implementation becomes relevant. Instead, in the case of Scheduled Tribes, reservation has become straitjacketed, with the same percentage of reservation for all areas of the country, not matching the demographic pattern of Scheduled Tribes, who are bunched together densely in some areas and are sparsely distributed in other areas. Scheduled Castes and Backward Classes are rather more evenly spread out throughout the country, but in the case of Scheduled Tribes the same percentage nationally would result in inadequate benefits in areas of their concentration and therefore in the national totality.

The latest surveys of the NSSO and their analysis show that the country has reached a critical stage, with about 80 per cent of the people who are poor and vulnerable. They see no hope for their future. Achievement and wealth is confined to the top 4 per cent while another 18 per cent constituting the middle class have some resources, access to education and room for hope in the future. Sensitivity to these 80 per cent is getting lost. The achievers and the hopeful aspirants and their classes and castes are only interested in pursuing their own self-interest in a narrow manner And the concept of sharing and of assigning a fair share for all in development, progress and prosperity is not acceptable to them. Just as in the *Mahabharata*, when Krishna negotiated with the Kauravas on behalf of the Pandavas, he urges them to give half of the Kuru kingdom and territory to their Pandava cousins, when this was rejected he pleaded that they be given at least 5 villages. To this the Kauravas arrogantly replied that they would not give the Pandavas even the space required for planting even the five pins. It is in the same manner that every long-denied right offered to the Scheduled Tribes, Schedule Castes and backward castes by the state, as bound by the

Constitutional mandate, is opposed by the upper classes. The strategy seems to be to first to weaken the backward castes then the Scheduled Castes and finally the Scheduled Tribes. They fondly dream of a country where only Manu of the past prevails and there is no Ambedkar, no Mandal and no reservation. This has also, unfortunately been the dream nurtured by some of the greatest scholars and intellectuals in this country. From the middle of the 19th century the British nurtured the present upper classes from the upper castes and modelled them into the modern elite of today, thus compounding the advantages they had already secured in the centuries before the British. The British did not classify any of them as the "creamy layer" and eliminate any of them as they belonged to the "creamy layer". Thus they have risen, without any impediment, to their present levels of eminence. Now it is the turn of the Scheduled Tribes, to whom every opportunity should be allowed to rise to levels of eminence. All support should be extended to those who are coming up from among the Scheduled Tribes, Schedule Castes, backward classes as well as backward minorities. These issues are interrelated. Generally we tend to focus on issues of Scheduled Tribes in certain specific areas where largest numbers of Scheduled Tribes live. There is, however, also a need to focus on specific tribal issues even in those areas where they do not have such advantage of numbers. For example, in Kerala the Scheduled Tribes do not constitute even one per cent of population. In Kerala and similar states the problems of the Scheduled Tribes are far more difficult. It is not possible for them to have a proper voice even in the Panchayats. The question of how to support the Scheduled Tribes for survival and progress in states like Kerala also deserves thought.

To conclude, it may be said that it is necessary that civil society should actively assist and guide the tribal people in their struggle to fulfill their genuine needs and aspirations. Failure will have its adverse consequences for the country. The Naxalite movement is growing and spreading across states. It is no use to merely to proclaim them as violent. We do not want violence. We do not believe in violence. But it is only if the Constitution is properly and fully implemented in the interest of people, then alone can we efficiently counter violence. But if we do not allow democratic solutions to come about, if we do not facilitate democratic solutions, where and to whom will the Scheduled Tribes go?

The issues of Scheduled Tribes are an important aspect of the problems faced by India. India can compete with China only if it takes its people forward, in their entirety. Unless all sections of people are able to experience their due share in the fruits of e progress and in all opportunities, the shining India that we dream of will turn out to be a mirage.

A Critical Reading of the Draft of the National Tribal Policy

Vinay Kumar Srivastava

The Draft of the National Policy on Tribals was released in February 2004, during the tenure of the NDA government.[1] It began with the following observation: "For the first time after the country became independent, the Government of India is preparing the formulation of a National Policy on Scheduled Tribes". From almost the late 1930s, especially after the publication of Verrier Elwin's *The Baiga* (*1939*), we have been discussing the approaches to solving tribal problems, and how they can be put into practice. We have also been analyzing (and referring to), at least for the last 50 years, the findings and suggestions of various commissions, committees, and task forces, appointed from time to time to look into the state of affairs and the problems of the tribal communities in India.

What we did not have was an overarching policy that could guide our efforts. In the past, many a time, the need of a tribal policy was felt, and some efforts were definitely made to formulate one, but a properly formed policy document could never emerge. In fact, many thought that Pt Jawaharlal Nehru's five-point *Foreword* to the second edition of *Verrier Elwin's A Philosophy for NEFA* (*1959*) was nothing short of a policy document, or had at least laid down the foundation of a policy, and it is a well known[2] fact that it is widely quoted in almost every anthropological publication on tribes. Nevertheless, there was always a felt need for a national policy. Against this background, it was heartening to come across the circulated copy of the Draft of National Policy on Tribals in 2004.

Contrary to our expectations, it was hardly discussed in the press. A seminar to discuss it threadbare was planned by the National Institute of

Rural Development (NIRD) in Hyderabad, and the Prime Minister was expected to inaugurate it, however no such thing materialised. The Indian Anthropological Association, during the course of its seminar, devoted one of its sessions (on 26 March 2004) to a discussion of the Draft, and later circulated a summary of its proceedings.[3] In other words, the Draft of National Policy on Tribals went largely unnoticed.

Thereafter, in July 2006, under the direction of the UPA government, another Draft was circulated. It was called the Draft of National Tribal Policy (a Policy for the Scheduled Tribes of India). The Draft was available on the Internet and in the accompanying letter, the Joint Secretary of the Ministry of Tribal Affairs requested the readers of the policy document for their critical observations and comments. In comparison to its predecessor, the second Draft evinced larger interest. Unofficially, I learnt that almost two thousand five hundred responses to it have come in so far. Some university academics have lectured on the Draft.[4] The A.N. Sinha Institute of Social Studies in Patna also organised a one-day seminar to discuss it, but so far its proceedings have not been published.[5]

We are not aware of the kind of responses which have so far been received by the government regarding the Draft, since this information is not available to the public. Many concerned tribal organisations and other research institutes claim to have sent their comments to the Ministry of Tribal Affairs, but to what extent they refer to the Draft is not known. Since these are not in the public domain, one does not really know the kind of criticisms that have been submitted by various agencies and non-governmental organisations (NGOs). Barring one short article by B.K. Roy Burman, which appeared in the *Economic and Political Weekly* (26 August 2006), there are virtually no comments available on the Draft, although it has been in circulation for some time now.[6]

Perhaps it was not accessible to a vast majority of the people who are concerned with it. Firstly, as it was available on the Internet, and not all (particularly people from tribal and peasant areas) have an access to the Internet. Its copies were not sent out to libraries or to departments dealing with tribal studies, nor made available to the larger public. Secondly, the Draft was in English language and not translated in any other language recognised by the Eighth Schedule of the Constitution of India. A document of such great importance should have been widely circulated. It should have been printed in national newspapers, or in Government of India publications (such as the *Employment News, Yojna and Kurukshetra*). It should have been translated into other Indian languages, since, of all responses to it, the most important response would have been of the tribal communities for whom it was prepared. It should have been translated into tribal languages, especially those that have scripts. The Draft should have been made an object of discourse, particularly in areas of tribal concentration. It certainly was not a mammoth task and could have been done at the local level with the intervention of government machinery and NGOs. For instance, an NGO should have been given the task of calling the tribal leaders at the local level and sharing with them the salient points of the Draft, advising them to discuss those in their own hamlets, villages and neighbourhoods, and the other areas of influence. In this way, a discourse would have been initiated leading, not only to its critical evaluation, but refinement as well. In the Patna seminar, where the Draft was the subject, most of the speakers from tribal areas principally spoke not about the Draft but of their problems, as perceived by members of their communities; so the focus was on the *panchayat* (council) elections not taking place in tribal areas, PESA (The Provisions of the Panchayats [Extension to the Scheduled Areas] Act, 1996) not being implemented, tribal women being enticed to come to cities to work as maids or being engulfed in the flesh trade, regarding the acute malnutrition in tribal areas and the extremely high infant mortality rate, about schools not having teachers and hospitals not having doctors, the high figures of unemployment, the evil effects of displacement, etc. In other words, the seminar was converted into a forum where tribal problems, in general were spelt out. The speeches of tribal participants, and the deliberations that followed were insightful, but the aim of the seminar, which was to discuss and improve upon the tribal policy, was lost. I think one of the pivotal reasons for this was the non-availability of the Draft in a language that the people understood. Had it been available to them and the opportunity given to them to read it closely, the tenor and content of their presentation would have been different and to the point. As tribes are marginal communities in India, so also the Draft of their Policy Document.

Against this background, it may be surmised here that of the more than two thousand and five hundred comments which are believed to have been received by the Ministry of Tribal Affairs, many may well have been statements of tribal problems in general (or concerning specific areas) rather than perceptive comments on the Draft. Unless the non-tribals take an interest in tribal issues, tribals will always remain on the periphery, at the mercy of the state. What is urgently required is the "centring of tribal problems" so that more and more people (tribals and non-tribals, insiders and outsiders, foreigners and Indians) take active interest in tribal issues, contributing positively to the debate regarding their progress. The Draft has the potential to do this because it brings in a capsule form all the major issues pertaining to tribal societies. Through this article, I urge upon the state to make it an object of discussion, involving people from different walks of life. The Draft should not meet the fate of any other government document, lost to oblivion as soon as it is released.

2

Important differences exist between the two versions of the Draft, released at different points of time by different central governments. The first one was considerably short and did not cover all the areas of importance to tribal societies; for instance, the forced migration of tribal people to non-tribal areas, or violence in pockets of tribal concentration. Throughout the text, it is submitted that the aim of the government is to bring the tribes into the mainstream of Indian society, but in the end, in a section titled "assimilation", the steps in which integration could be achieved are delineated. The approach of "assimilation", usually associated with the work of A.V. Thakkar, G.S. Ghurye, and other social workers, which argued that the tribes should "melt" in the "mainstream", in lasting relations of interdependence with other communities, was debunked long time back. Assimilation was neither ethically right nor empirically possible. Therefore, when anthropologists, and others familiar with the approaches to tribal problems, saw the Draft of the Policy mischievously ending with "assimilation", they were taken aback. Perhaps, the authors of the Draft committed a *faux pas* by using the term "assimilation", though they certainly did not think in terms of "dissolving" the tribal identity with that of the outsiders. I do not believe that today any serious student of tribal studies, which may be referred to as "tribalology", would ever argue in favour of "assimilation" (or "forcible assimilation" or "de-tribalization"). That each culture has the right to survive and each community of people has the right to decide how it wishes to live is an undisputed fact; it is *de facto* the spirit of the age where the world is envisaged as a "garden of differently coloured flowers, each having its own gene pool, but synergistically existing with the other." This analogy is intellectually captured in the concepts of multiplicity, diversity, pluralism, and multiculturalism.

The second Draft, impressively written, is at least five times longer than the first. It examines the issues in detail, takes care not to leave out any matter of importance to tribes, and suggests some points of methodological importance that could be adopted for further study. If the first Draft meted out perfunctory treatment to tribal problems, sometimes displaying its insensitivity, the second is far more sensitive and responsible. It is concerned with the theme of inclusive and holistic development, i.e., all sections of society should participate in the programme of development and benefit equally from it. The backwardness of even a single community will slacken the over-all economic and social growth of the country. The second Draft of the Policy is a "text" worthy of study, initiating a debate, and this is an additional reason for its translation into Indian languages and its wider circulation.[7]

Running into 23 downloaded pages, the Draft is divided into 23 sections, each further broken down into points. One of my preliminary observations is that its repetitiousness at places reduces its readability; for instance, the characteristics of tribes as identified by the Lokur Committee figure on pages 2 and 21. Needless to say, a point should be spelt out at one place, and at other places it may be referred to, rather than repeated verbatim. My other observation is that some of its sections should come in the beginning (for example, 1.3, 1.4, 20.1 and 20.2). The ideas contained in the policy can be presented in many ways, in a detailed manner or succinctly. However, assuming that its existing 23 sections remain as they are, and their intra-repetitiousness is carefully pruned, they still need to be classified properly, so that the Draft grows logically. One of the exercises I conducted was to cut the different sections of the Draft and rearrange them in the following order, and then, I read it keeping in mind the main headings under which different sections had been classified. Through this exercise, I could get a better sense of the underlying aims and philosophy of the Draft than the earlier. The rearrangement of the different sections of the Draft was like this:

Opening Statements of the Policy

1. Preamble
2. Need for the Policy
3. Guiding Principles of the Policy
4. Objectives of the Policy
5. Strategies

Location of Problems

1. Alienation of Tribal Land: Tenurial Insecurity
2. Tribal-Forest Interface

3. Displacement, Rehabilitation and Resettlement
4. Violent Manifestations

Areas to be Strengthened: Aims, Solutions, and Strategies

1. Enhancement of Human Development Index
2. Creation of Critical Infrastructure
3. Administration of Tribal Areas
4. The Regulatory and Protective Regime
5. Adoption of the Tribal Sub-Plan Strategy
6. Gender Equity
7. Communication Strategy
8. Empowerment
9. Enlisting Support of Non-Governmental Organizations (NGOs)

Attention to Specific Domains

1. Conservation and Development of Particularly Vulnerable Tribal Groups (PTGs)
2. Tribal Culture and Traditional Knowledge
3. Research and Training
4. Monitoring, Evaluation and Review Mechanisms
5. Scheduling and De-scheduling of Tribes

This does not, however, imply that I approve of the existing titles of the sub-sections, for, better (and less value-loaded) captions can always be devised. For instance, in the context of the PTGs, the use of the word "conservation" implies "status quo", also reminding one of the biological meaning of this term which is "preserving the things (or their protection) as they are"; on the contrary, what is desired here is the "salubrious survival" of certain groups which have a near-constant or declining population. The groups survive not in their pristine forms; they do not remain as they are—museum pieces and curios—but develop in the direction of rest of the country. Against this background, this section may be titled "Survival and Development of Particularly Vulnerable Tribal Groups (PTGs)".

3

One of the major problems in tribal studies today, and this is clear from the Draft as well, pertains to the "definition" of the social formation known as "tribe". Many of us think that since we are concerned with the communities of people classified as Scheduled Tribes, and there is less ambiguity about this term, although some communities classified so may not deserve the appellation of "tribe", not much will be gained by bogging down into the ever-polemical and inconclusive issues of the definition. As per this argument, our concern is with the "Scheduled Tribes", and not with "tribes"; the former category includes about seven hundred communities, according to the Draft, which, notwithstanding their inter-cultural differences, share the same relation of deprivation with respect to non-tribal people.[8] Within themselves, the tribes have a lot of economic variation—some are affluent, some are poverty-stricken, some tribes have their members in civil services, some are unemployed for years—but in comparison to non-tribes, they have a low human development index. Therefore, the issue is to plan out the operational programmes of development for those who are already classified as members of the Scheduled Tribes. In other words, our job is not to classify people in one or the other category; this is the duty of the government and its various departments to determine whether people deserve inclusion in a pre-designated category. Our job is to think about the welfare of those who are already listed as Scheduled Tribes.

The other view is that in India the continuities between tribes and castes are so much that it often becomes difficult to distinguish (or separate) one from the other. Not only is this the experience of the contemporary students of tribal societies, but was also of the census enumerators in the late 19th century.[9] Often, the communities were arbitrarily listed as "tribes" (or "castes"), and this decision was left to the perception of the local community by the individual enumerator. There have been cases of communities classified as tribes in one state and castes in the other. These anomalies have often been brought to our attention.

The presence of the continuities between tribes and castes did not imply that there were no differences between them. The differences existed, and there were "real communities" that approximated (and in some cases were the ideal types of) the textbook definition of tribe. However, a large number of communities, classified as "tribal", dwelt in close proximity to "caste" communities, having long-standing relations of exchange. These relations have obviously contributed towards a myriad of similarities between them, thus bringing castes and tribes closer, leading to a deviation of both the social formations from their ideal definitions. The important point, however, is that notwithstanding these similarities, the tribes have tried to maintain their respective identities, as have the castes. The conclusion from this observation is that it is not entirely a worthless exercise to think in terms of the social and cultural indices that constitute a tribe as different from caste. A blurring of the social categories does not imply their complete merging. That tribes and castes have constituted the two types of social formation is still a relevant point of departure to understand certain aspects of contemporary India, and therefore the matter of definition should not be skirted.

The Draft notes that the criteria evolved by the Lokur Committee for declaring a particular community as a Scheduled Tribe are: an ensemble of primitive traits, distinctive culture, geographical isolation, shyness of contact with the outside world, and backwardness. Immediately after delineating them, the Draft notices that "even all these broad criteria are not applicable to Scheduled Tribes today" (p. 2). On page 21, it says: "The criteria laid down by the Lokur Committee are hardly relevant today. For instance, very few tribes can today be said to possess 'primitive traits'."

Two questions emerge at this juncture: first, which of the above criteria are relevant today for defining a tribal community, and which of them have become defunct? Second, what is meant by "primitive traits"? In other words, how will this concept be operationalised? Which characteristics of a community deserve to be designated as "primitive"? For instance, is "honour killing" or "polyandry" a "primitive trait"? Many of the traits that are found in the so-called "primitive" societies, because of which they are also called "primitive", may also be found among the contemporary affluent and patriarchal societies. Ironically, when these characteristics are found among the latter, they are not called "primitive". The point is that in the context of definitional issues, we need to use concepts that have an operational value, i.e., they are given an empirical content, and with their help, we are able to classify societies as objectively as possible.

The word "primitive" used for certain kind of societies, came into vogue in the latter half of the 19th century during the colonial era, in which reigned the ideology of evolutionism. The Victorian scholars were interested in tracing the stages through which human society had passed, before it reached its then extant state. It was also thought that the non-western societies (of Africa, Asia, Oceania, Latin America) of that time were the "remains", "survivals", and "vestiges" of the pre-historic ages, and the intensive study of which would illuminate the past of the Victorian society. Unsurprisingly, one of the foremost evolutionists of the 19th century, Sir Edward B. Tylor, called these societies "social fossils", the "palaeontological" evidences of the early type of social formations. This implies that the term "primitive" was used in a temporal sense.

One expected that with a decline of the 19th century evolutionism, the word "primitive" would not be used for non-western, simple and pre-literate societies; that in the era of post-evolutionism, they would not be viewed as remnants of the past, but rather as contemporaries of the western world. The fact that they practiced foraging, were pre-literate, had a small population and a simple technology (that could easily be learnt and transmitted), and changed less in comparison to the wider world, was because of their isolation and a homeostatic equation they maintained with their habitats, and not because they were survivals of the past ages. It is obvious that a relatively isolated community in harmony with its ecosystem would have a larger continuation of its characteristics over time, than one exposed greatly to the outside world, changing briskly and frequently. Using the word "primitive" for our contemporaries was paradoxical, and it justly deserved elimination from our vocabulary as term used for simple, preliterate societies.

Alas! This did not happen. Classical evolutionism was debunked but certain terms it popularized (such as "primitive", "savage", "uncivilized") continued to be used for simple societies. It does not surprise one, against this backdrop, that the Lokur Committee defined a tribe in terms of the "primitive traits", without realizing that the term "primitive" is wrongly used for contemporary simple communities. The Draft notes that words—like "primitive", "backward", "savage"—used for describing tribal communities are pejorative. I have seen many educated tribal men and women reacting sharply and vehemently to the description of their respective communities as having characteristics that are labeled "primitive". The Draft, at one place, notes that the value-loaded and disparaging terms used for defining tribes "need to be replaced with terms that are not derogatory" (p.2). At another place, it notes that since the criteria that the Lokur Committee has put forward have lost their relevance today, there is a need to identify other "accurate criteria" (p.21). One expected that the Draft would give some suggestions in this regard, but it leaves it to the future deliberations on this subject. However, in the beginning, it tries to offer a definitional perspective on tribal communities, which deserves a few comments.

4

It notes that tribal communities:

> are known to dwell in compact areas, follow a community way of life, in harmony with nature, and have a uniqueness of culture, distinctive customs, traditions and beliefs which are simple, direct and non-acquisitive by nature (p. 2).

Anthropological writings, popular articles, and coffee-table books on tribes reinforce certain images in which they wish to see them. These writings and pictures earnestly wish to captivate the readers' attention, thereby promoting their sale. To this end, their efforts would meet with success only if they portray the "bizarreness" of tribes, showing them as "head-hunters", "tattooed", "cannibals", practicing some of the strangest forms of marriage and family and cooking, as well as rituals for disposing of their dead; depicted as wearing more of jewelry than clothes, and living in "compact" pockets, with the least communication with the outside world. These are the images in which non-tribals wish to see their tribal brethren. Therefore, notwithstanding the changes of vast scale and magnitude that the tribal society is experiencing all over the world, where their local systems are constantly being affected (and bombarded) by changes occurring outside, the irony is that the writers on the tribes (and their photographers) wish to keep them "frozen", in the representation of "oddities", as "romantically different and bewitching" as they could be. Verrier Elwin's idea of a "national park" for tribes, which might have been rejected long time back, continues to linger in our imagination, as a result of which we do not want to renounce certain conceptions about tribes. Apart from this, we have also come across cases where tribal leaders and entrepreneurs try to preserve certain aspects of their traditional culture (calling them "pristine"), for it has a roaring marketable value. Cultures are showcased for the market. It is clear from this that human beings ubiquitously want to see (and preserve) diversity, rather than be in a world of uninteresting similarities.

The above definition from the Draft is another example of a frozen picture of tribes. Contrary to this, empirical studies point out that no more do tribal communities dwell in "compact areas". The "community way of living" has also broken down. Tribal families are moving out of their areas in search of jobs, and sometimes they have to travel for thousands of miles to reach a suitable location, where their never-ending struggle for survival begins. The hold of their respective communities over their lives has weakened, for it is unable to protect their interests and promise them a life of dignity. Tribal territories now have residents from various shades of life and strata, who not only make fun of tribal customs and practices, but also take advantage of their powerlessness and gullibility. It is well known that for giving way to several development projects, almost forty per cent of the persons permanently displaced from their native habitats are tribal, who are now dispersed in different parts of the country, painfully searching for opportunities to get two square meals.

The Draft notices, as do the other official publications on tribes, that tribes are scattered "over all the States/Union Territories, except Punjab, Haryana, Delhi, and the Union Territories of Pondicherry and Chandigarh" (p. 2). While these three States and two Union Territories do not have the native communities scheduled as tribes, a large number of tribespersons from other parts of the country have moved to these metropolises where they work as domestic and shop servants, rickshaw-pullers, loaders and coolies, vendors of newspapers and magazines at traffic red-lights, and many of them have ended on the breadline, as beggars, destitute, sex-workers, organ-sellers, and even petty deviants and criminals. The harrowing experiences of these people—of underpayment, receiving ridicules and scourges of dehumanisation, the constant beatings and abuses they receive from their employers and law-enforcing agencies, the sexual exploitation their women and children undergo—have yet to be ethnographically captured.

The tribal migrants are permanent. No economic and social resources are left in their native places to which they can hopefully return for survival. What reigns there is poverty, but the cities to which they have migrated would at least guarantee their basic survival, at least they would not die of hunger, albeit the episodes of oppression, torture, and exploitation regularly occurring in their lives. The Draft should have thought about these people, whose number in the metropolises is multiplying every year, but no census is available on them, since their native areas are either being sacrificed at the altar of development or have become almost irrevocably impoverished because of ceaseless crop failures and unfavourable ecological factors. It is unwise to assume that tribal habitations and their habitats would remain as they were in the past. In the name of "development for national interests", the tribes have been the biggest—and the most muted—losers. Today, when like the bright light attracting moths, the cities (metro- and megapolises) are swelling with the unremitting streams of tribal migrants, who would not like to return to their native places, it becomes all the more important that the interests of these people are vouchsafed forever. This would only be possible when the tribal world is viewed as perpetually in dynamism rather than as a closed, stable, and frozen entity, and special schemes and laws are devised and implemented for safeguarding its interests.

Tribal culture today cannot be described as "unique". Half a century ago, one could still speak a little authoritatively of the culture of a tribal community, in contrast to the culture of its neighbours. The anthropological monographs produced during the first half of the 20th century were a good example of the description of tribal exoticism, where it was clear that a tribal community could be studied without referring to the outside world. The skein of thought running through these studies was of anthropological holism—a tribal society was a "complete society" (or "whole society"), and not "part-society with part-culture" as was a peasant society, and therefore, it could be studied in isolation from the wider world with which it hardly had any networks and linkages.

Although this was the typical anthropological practice, I am quite skeptical of the view that when anthropologists explored the tribal world, it was complete in its isolation. Even then, it had relations of reciprocity, or of raiding and attack, with other communities in their neighbourhood. Elsewhere I have argued (1994) that the relations between the Nuer and the Dinka were almost like "international relations", for each one of them was an independent political entity, and negotiated the ties among them in accordance with the established practice. An understanding of their relationship was thus essential to understanding either of them. The pattern observed in the Sudanese communities existed in a number of Indian tribal communities.

However, as these communities dwelling in the same space were of the same scale and followed a by and large similar economy, the differences between them were not as pronounced as were those between them and the fully settled agricultural communities or the townspeople. Changes in the ways of living were surely surfacing because of their relations with their neighbours. Innovations made in one were being carried to the other, where they were modified and adapted to the local reality. Cultures were always porous, but the changes were so minor, and only minutely visible, that they were almost relegated to the backseat. Against this backdrop emerged the perspective of anthropological holism and the structural-functional approach, yielding certain notions about tribes, which were far from being true.

Similarly, tribal traditions and beliefs are neither as "simple" nor as "direct", as the Draft says. Tribal cosmologies are highly complex, requiring an intensive anthropological study. They are embedded in the "unconscious" mind of their creators to such an extent that for their understanding, they require a detailed study, as Claude Lévi-Strauss and other structuralists have done from time to time, uncovering each of its layers one by one till one reached the basic principles of their organisation. It seems to me that those who have characterised tribal beliefs as "simple" have at the back of their minds the evolutionary ideas—that the tribal societies are "simple" and in course of time, become "complex". They are the "juveniles" of an evolving human society; hence, everything they have (technology, material culture, ideology, beliefs and practices) is simple and direct. The stereotypes about which I spoke earlier are further reinforced by the terms and expressions we have uncritically used for them.

5

One of the greatest services we may render to a proper and realistic understanding of tribal society is to refrain from using value-loaded assumptions, irrespective of whether they are positive or negative, such as the ones found in the Draft: tribal way of life is "woven around harmony with and preservation of nature" (p.3); tribespersons have "innate skills" (p.12); they have "innate communitarianism, the ethos of caring for, and sharing with others" (p.13); they have "egalitarianism, concern for the environment" (p.20). What is being submitted here is that various institutions may be built on the basis of these characteristics which are regarded as "innate" to tribespersons; for example, the institution of tribal co-operatives and the credit system may be constructed on the values of community-living, caring for others, and sharing the gains with co-villagers (p.13).

Here, it may be pointed out that these traits generally attributed to the "collective personality" of tribals have also been given to non-tribal, peasant and rural people. How do they become the diacritical characteristics of tribespersons is stated nowhere? Do we ascribe these properties in general terms to traditional societies, and since tribals happen to be one of its examples, they also possess them? In that sense, these characteristics certainly do not become the diagnostic traits of tribal societies.

Moreover, they are not more than a set of assumptions about tribes transmitted with each generation of anthropological writings. We have always thought in terms of dichotomies: what tribals have the non-tribals lack. So, if tribals (as a type of traditional society) have "community living", the people on the opposite pole are "individualistic"; if tribals conserve their environment, their polar opposite indulges in wanton destruction; if tribals respect their elders, the non-tribals reject them as "unwanted species"; if tribals have subsistence economy, the non-tribals have market-oriented economy. This mode of dualistic thinking has damaged our understanding, since it does not take into cognizance the fact that the characteristics attributed to a society falling in proximity to one pole in juxtaposition to the other, may in fact be present in the other. Each society is a fair mix of a variety of characteristics, of which some are accentuated at a particular time because of its habitat, available opportunities, interaction with other societies, the role of the externally-situated political state, and the ideology of integrating societies or leaving them as they are. If tribes did not have the concept of money at one time, it was because they did not need it, and also they were not a part of the monetised economy, but once they became, they have learnt the principles of its operation and value. To label contemporary tribal societies as "unmonetized", as some economic anthropologists continue to do so even now, is grossly wrong. Such conceptions widen the gap between "what used to be" and "what is".

Tribes had internal feuds, raids, plundering, institution of slavery and public killing of slaves, body mutilations, repressive laws, harsh punishments, lack of individual freedom, destruction of property, and all those practices that would make one think *de novo* about the image of tribal folks as "noble savages". Neither did they lack competitive spirit nor were they egalitarian. Many spatial movements of the sections of tribes owed their genesis to internal differences and persisting conflicts between them. By colonising newer territories, sub-tribes of a tribe became autonomous tribes, with different names, although in cultural terms, they continued to share several similarities with the parent tribe. My submission is that the contemporary tribal reality is different from what the Draft tries to present by taking an easy recourse to the stereotypes that anthropological and popular writings have time and again reinforced. Its suggestion is that for defining the tribal society, "more accurate criteria need to be fixed", but I think this will be possible only when we think anew, transcending the popular discourse and images about tribes. I do not think that contemporary tribes want to see themselves in the mould in which anthropologists have depicted them from the colonial times. Unfortunately, although anthropologists have tried their best, they have not been able to dissociate the concept of tribe from the lurking "primitivism" associated with them, and which, as a matter of fact, is the focus of attention, having great commercial and market potential. Oddities sell; being peculiar and bizarre brings money.

The Draft notes the diversity of Scheduled Tribes and their increasing number over time. That each tribe has a set of specific needs, requiring a specific programme for its development, is undisputed, but then, there are also certain needs that all tribes have, and therefore, they must be incorporated in every programme for tribal development; for instance, the alleviation of poverty, restoration of cultivable land to them, safeguarding of their rights in forests, protecting them from exploitation and oppression by usurpers of their land, moneylenders, liquor vendors, etc.

However, certain tribes are victims of problems, which are peculiar to them, emerging out of their historically conditioned existence and leading to a stigma being associated with them. Such problems require special schemes and a change in mindsets of people. We have here in mind the examples of de-notified communities, and nomadic and semi-nomadic tribes. I think that most writers on tribal issues (as does the Draft) forget about de-notified communities. Their sufferings and episodes of de-humanization are heart-rending. Being victims of the "stigma of criminality", their community suffers as a whole, for such prohibited deeds, in case committed, by one of their members, or even when the deed was not committed by any one of them. The so-called "nomadic" and "semi-nomadic" communities suffer from the same stigmas. The erstwhile relations of synergism the nomadic and semi-nomadic pastoralists had with peasant and farming communities have now become one of hostility and antagonism. The agriculturists want to drive them out of their areas the moment they see them. No more are they considered useful depositors of animal manure, but a nuisance to the germinating or standing fields. The result is that each year conflicts—often bloodied—take place between peregrinating pastoralists and peasants, and the intensity of these conflicts is becoming more and more serious with the passage of time.

The Draft, under Section 20 titled "Scheduling and De-scheduling of Tribes", inserts two points (20.8 and 20.9) on nomadic tribes. The observation that they occupy the "lowest position" in society is not correct. In fact, they are placed at the middle levels of caste hierarchy, and in some parts of India, are quite respected for their occupation as well as demeanor.

For instance, the Rabari of Gujarat are considered to be the "trustworthy confidants" of Rajputs (*Srivastava, 1997*). They have the same image in Rajasthan, although they are not included in the list of Scheduled Tribes. While it is true that many of them do not own or possess land rights or house titles, it is not quite right to say that they are "constantly on move" and do not have "any single place or state of domicile." The usual pattern among them is to return to their permanent abodes (located in one or the other states of India) after the grazing expedition, just before the onset of monsoon rains, and after the harvest, usually after the festival of lights (Diwali) they resume it. The popular image of these people as "constantly on move" is not supported empirically. Each of these communities belongs to a village, where it has its cluster of dwellings. It may also be noted that among these communities, not everyone moves: women, old, infirm, and diseased people, and children continue to live in their permanent habitations. Even when these graziers do not return to their villages with their animals, which are too large in number to be herded back, and so they continue to move around for the entire year in the grazing lands, their relations with their villages remain intact. Herdsmen are periodically replaced; some return to their villages for an errand or for agricultural work. Furthermore, as conflicts between pastoralists and agricultural communities are intensifying, more and more able-bodied men are being entrusted with the tasks of managing the migratory herds. Women are being increasingly withdrawn from these migratory groups.

When revised, the Draft should take up the problems of the de-notified and nomadic and semi-nomadic communities in separate sections, rather than including all of them under a common section, as it has done now, where they do not deserve to be placed. One of the main purposes should be to focus on the interests of the communities which are marginalized among the tribes in general.[10]

6

Section 12 of the Draft deals with the Primitive Tribes or Primitive Tribal Groups (PTGs), a list of 75 Scheduled Tribes, created in 1973, which are supposed to be more "backward" than the others.[11] The following criteria have generally been used for their classification, viz. pre-agricultural level; dwelling isolated and remote habitations; small number; near-constant or declining population; low levels of literacy; and economic and social backwardness. Recent data on their population does not seem to be available, which is why both the Draft and the Planning Commission's Tenth Five-Year Plan (2002–07) document refer to their figures of the Census of India—1991, when they were 1.32 million people, distributed among 15 states and union territories. Regarding the criteria for their identification, the Draft notes that they "suffer from lack of specificity". Should this be redressed, and an attempt made to evolve specific and operational criteria?

With respect to this question, the Draft submits that there is no need to undertake this attempt, since presently there is no proposal to add any more communities to the list of Primitive Tribes. But, if tomorrow, a need does arise to identify some more primitive tribes, then we should have with us the criteria ready for our task. Whether or not the need exists now, the concepts in currency must be properly defined, as, even when they first came into existence they were not defined properly and the criteria by which they were defined were not remotely specific. One of our expectations from the Draft was that it would offer working definitions of the concepts used in understanding tribal communities rather than just admitting that the criteria used so far lacked specificity and operational value.

Setting aside the issue of evolving criteria for identifying the primitive tribes, the Draft suggests that since the word "primitive" has "derogatory overtones", it must be changed. Retaining the same acronym, PTGs, it suggests that these communities may be called "Particularly Vulnerable Tribal Groups", although it also submits, for reasons not given, that this change in name "may be merely cosmetic" (p. 15). Does it mean that in spite of this change in name, the same image continues? Does it mean that in the same manner that even the fairest cream cannot permanently make dark skin white, so also a change in nomenclature will not exorcise the prejudices forever? In a one-day seminar that the Indian Anthropological Association had organized on 24 April 2006, three months before the Draft of the Tribal Policy was publicly circulated, B.K. Roy Burman had proposed that because of its pejorative connotation, the term Primitive Tribes should be changed to Vulnerable Tribes.[12] Reacting to his proposal, my submission was that vulnerability is a relativistic condition. Each community is vulnerable to internal as well as external forces; however its strength to withstand them varies. Moreover, we lack universal criteria to measure the degree of vulnerability. Rather, it can only be intuitively inferred.

The main idea behind the list of primitive tribes is that these communities demand special attention from the state because they lag far behind the other Scheduled Tribes in the indices of development. They are "more vulnerable to hunger, starvation, malnutrition, and ill health."[13] One may refer here to the analogical (or, rather euphemistic) distinction that *Bhupinder Singh* (*1990*) has made between the two types of tribal communities: first, those that demand the "first-aid treatment" (which means "little help"); and second, those which require "hospitalization" (i.e., proper intensive care). The primitive tribes, he thinks, fall in the second category. Incidentally, he also proposes that they may be called the "Primary Tribes." I think the idea behind the nomenclature is far more important than the name itself. Unfortunately, when we discard one term, we look for an alternative of an equivalent length—so, the acronym PTGs would remain, whether the words are changed, as the Draft has proposed, or the term Primitive Tribes is replaced by Primary Tribes. All terms have limitations. Concepts are not vacuous, which means that each one of them projects a particular image (and also, carries a set of stereotypes); whether we use the term "Particularly Vulnerable Tribal Groups", or "Primary Tribes", or think of any other equivalent, the images behind them remain the same.

In addition, we should also note that the "words" that replace those which presumably have "derogatory overtones" in course of time come to acquire their own sets of stereotypes and disparaging notions, and thus become equally laden with derogation. For instance, when the word "tribe" replaced the earlier words such as "primitive" or "savage", it was thought that the former was value-neutral and free from prejudices; but with the passage of time, it has also acquired its own images, some of them in continuity with those that were associated with the earlier terms. Ask a layperson about the images that come in his or her mind when the word "tribe" is used; the answer would of "people living in hills, mountains, forests and deserts, far away from the "maddening crowds", who are pre-literate, wear feather hoods and bead and shell jewellery, tattoo their bodies, are scantily clothed, hold bows and arrows, javelins and spears, speak an incomprehensible dialect, live in flimsy huts, are suspicious of outsiders, etc."

The same images would surface in the minds of people when they are questioned about the earlier terms used for tribes such as "primitive", "savage", "rude", or "non-civilized". And, these images may continue even when we replace the word "tribe" with words like "simple" and "small" society, or certain local words such as *janjati, adivasi, jana, adimjati*. Some words used in India for tribes—like *vanvasi, vanyajati, girijan*—are already tainted for they point towards their forest and mountainous existence, and thus all those stereotypes that are associated with forest and mountainous living are also associated with tribes. That is why, whichever word replaces "tribe" will in course of time come to acquire a set of stereotypes and prejudiced images. So, whether we call them "Primitive Tribes" or "Particularly Vulnerable Tribes" will not make much difference, since the images associated with them will scarcely be dismantled. Perhaps, K.S. Singh's suggestion (*cited in Béteille, 2000: 169*) to call "tribes" (or Scheduled Tribes) not "tribes" but by a value-neutral term "community" (*samudaya*), a term that can also be used for the Scheduled Castes or any other social category having some kind of a collective living, is worth considering, for this word is free from the load of pre-conceived images, except that of sharing collective sentiments.

My suggestion here is that we should definitely drop the word "primitive", since it is a condition, with a temporal meaning, but not replace it by any other term, because of the likelihood of its acquiring the same derogatory images over time. Rather, we may call the existing list of Primitive Tribes, or more tribes that may perhaps be added to it tomorrow, simply as one of "Tribes Requiring Urgent Attention from the State". I think this is the basic idea behind the concept and the list of Primitive Tribes.

The Draft divides the existing primitive tribes into two categories, depending upon their respective degrees of isolation (p. 15). This attempt is made to draw attention to their specific needs so that culturally-rooted and holistic programmes may be devised for them. In the first category are those which are "insulated from the surrounding populations and are placed in isolated ecological environments". Its examples are the Jarawa, Sentinelese, Shompen, Cholanaicken, etc. The second category includes those tribes (such as the Birhor, Chenchu, Jenu Kuruba) which are "located on the fringes of "mainstream" population and have some contact with them."

The first category of the PTGs is termed the "heritage group". No such succinct term has been improvised for the second category. Although captivating, the term "heritage group" should be avoided, for it points towards their evolutionary status, as if they are the remnants of the first kind of humans who inhabited the earth. In biological terms it also implies that they are the carriers of the primordial (and uncontaminated) genetic stock. It should not be forgotten that the image the term "heritage group" conjures, would inspire both anthropologists and geneticists to invade their areas for researching the evidences of pristine traits.

Moreover, it is utopian to imagine that the so-called "heritage groups" are insulated from the outside world; they certainly are not an "island unto themselves". Studies show that communities such as of the Jarawa and Cholanaicken have come in contact with their neighbouring populations, and gradually these contacts are increasing. Often, the Jarawa come out of their forests onto the Andaman Trunk Road, demanding tobacco and items of food from the travelers. Though contacts of the type which have been established with the Jarawa have not yet come into existence with the Sentinelese and Shompen, they are definitely aware of the external world and have been periodically receiving gifts from visitors to their islands, who happen to be from the administrative services and research organizations. Untiring efforts are being made to bring these hitherto insulated communities out of their cocoons. Against this backdrop, how far would it be justified to regard these communities as "cut off" from the extraneous world?

As mentioned earlier, the two categories of the PTGs that the Draft creates have an implication for their respective development programmes.

For the PTGs of the first category, a group-oriented approach, which would include the conservation of their habitats, lifestyles, and traditional skills is proposed. For the second category, a mix of the approaches of group-orientation and area-development is proposed. In other words, it would lay emphasis on economic programmes. Undoubtedly, the problems of more isolated communities are different from those relatively less isolated, but this difference is basically a matter of degree. The communities are placed on a continuum—more isolated communities become less isolated over time. Therefore, we need to evolve a single approach that combines the issues of the development of the group with that of the area, rather than separating them as has been done in the Draft. For this task, we need to engage the expertise of medical scientists and physical anthropologists, which would look at the aspects of health and illness, and genetically transmitted diseases, of these communities.

The Draft rightly notes that data on the PTGs are "inadequate". Leaving it to the respective states to compile these will not be enough. The Anthropological Survey of India should take up the challenge of collecting and analyzing the intensive data on each of the PTGs. Funding agencies (like ICSSR, UGC, ICMR) should give grants for working on these communities, and also promote the publication of unpublished research reports on these subject that may be lying in libraries and research organizations. In addition, university anthropology departments should give priority to the study of the PTGs. Collectively, we would be able to generate data required for formulating plans for the survival and development of these communities.

The Draft observes that the alienation of land is the "single most important cause of pauperization of tribals" (p. 6). With resources dwindl-ing, as a result of mass exploitation, tribal economies have already become highly precarious, lengthening the periods of low production and hunger among them, and once their land is taken away, forcibly or with persuasion in name of the national interest, their condition is irreparably worsened. The Draft has used the right word—"pauperization"—to describe their condition. Once they part with their land, in the absence of alternative sources of survival, the tribals reach the brink of destitution, beggary, vagrancy, hopelessness, and dehumanization. In this context, I recall what an anthropologist working among the tribal populations of Chotanagpur said in a seminar more than 20 years ago. He narrated how when he asked a Santal why he was a Jharkhandi, a member of the Jharkhand movement. To which tribesman's reply was that: "You give my land back to me, and I shall stop being a Jharkhandi." The answer speaks a lot about the condition of tribal persons: they have lost their land, not only to the moneylenders and usurpers who came from outside, but also to the state for institutions of development. Of greater concern is the fact that the land that they lost was the most productive, and what they received in return, if at all the compensation was in terms of land, was situated far away from the place of their rehabilitation, and was of poor quality, most vulnerable to the vagaries of the weather, yielding low productivity and thus creating every possible opportunity for them to leave it and move to multi-caste villages and towns, looking for jobs that would scarcely sustain them.

The Draft also rightly notes that the migration of non-tribals into tribal areas has been of great disadvantage to the local people. The outsiders have not only usurped the land, but also subjected the tribals to all kinds of exploitation that they, hitherto being the masters of their land and resources, were least aware of. Against this backdrop, two steps need to be taken urgently. First, the illegal transfer of tribal land should be stringently checked; and second, the alienated land should be restored to tribes. This would require an in-depth study of the anti-alienation land laws (and their amendments) that different states have enacted from time to time, and how the outsiders have succeeded in circumventing them. The Draft says, the nodal ministry (the Ministry of Tribal Affairs) of the government will quickly undertake a study of the loopholes and shortcomings in the various state laws, and come out with a model legislation, serving both the steps stated above. What is not said in the Draft is when this work would be conducted and when we could expect the legislation. The issue of land alienation requires to be dealt with urgency, not only because it has jeopardized the lifeline of tribes, making them live perpetually on the doles that the governments and NGOs give them, but also because it is the prime cause of several violent manifestations of tribal interests in different parts of the country.

In this context too, the anthropologists can play a significant role by providing empirical studies of land alienation from different parts of the country. Unfortunately, despite the fact that a large number of tribes in India have remained unstudied, no organization is making a concerted effort to promote an intensive, field based study on the subject. Moreover, anthropologists should give more importance to the study of issues that are pauperising (and proletarianising) tribal communities. They should also take up critical studies of various legislations and their effectiveness. We sadly note that due to the virtual non-development of what may be called "legal anthropology", we have not carried out the studies of laws and their role in initiating changes in society. We need studies of how land alienation actually takes place, for this will also throw light on the relations the tribespersons have with the others. The Draft, in other words, should explicitly emphasize the role that the anthropologists, the Anthropological Survey of India, the various tribal research centers, and the concerned NGOs can play, in order to generate data on which the legislations and policies may be based. The help of these agencies may also be sought for updating and computerizing land records.

The Draft is gender sensitive. It, for instance, suggests methods to check high drop out among girl students. It recommends special provisions for every girl joining the school at the primary level. Here, in the context of land alienation, it suggests that the land distributed to tribals, or the one restored to them, will be registered in the "joint names of both the spouses, or in the name of the woman alone" (p. 6). This is a good suggestion, considering the fact that there is a gender dimension to land alienation. The outsider "men" cajole, sweet-talk, coax, pressurise, and threaten "tribesmen", also playing upon their simplicity, gentility, and credulity, thus forcing them to part with their land. Gifts of liquor (tobacco and other intoxicants) to "tribesmen" have also played a significant role in these illegal transactions. The fact that the extra-domestic domain is usually male-oriented in all societies, including the matrilineal, also implies that most of the inward migration is of males who develop their ties with the local tribal men. These relations eventually lead to the alienation of tribal land. The inward migrants, though in some cases do succeed in sexually exploiting tribal women, are unable to establish the same kind of relations with the women folk that they are able to establish with tribal men. They may cajole a man to part with his land but not so with the women, who are singularly concerned with the welfare of their household and children. And, then, there are no outsider women who migrate and establish similar relations with local women, like the relations their men forge with the local men that can lead to the tribal women being deprived of their land. Land alienation has been entirely a male-job, and can be effectively checked by registering land in the name of women.

Then there is the state-sponsored development which also causes alienation of tribal land. The Draft offers a number of suggestions, of which the most important is the principle of least displacement. People should only be subjected to the trauma of displacement when it is absolutely necessary in the name of "public purpose" *sensu stricto*. Surely, communities must sacrifice their individual interests for the nation, but which interests are truly "public" and "national", and which are not, needs to be discussed fully. There should not be any relativism with respect to it, for what may be considered "public" might turn out to be "not really public", but rather serving the interests of some vested groups, as seen from the point of view of the community earmarked for displacement. This has caused a lot of discontent among the communities that have been targeted for displacement, often leading to the episodes of violence, since they think that their displacement from their traditional habitats in fact serves the interests of some affluent, politically well-connected, communities. I have often heard tribesmen saying that the poor among them become the "sacrificial lambs" (*bali ka bakra*) in all the displacement programmes.

One agrees with the Draft that the entire process of displacement (if it is absolutely mandatory and there is no alternative) should be made "more humane" (p. 9), but how this will actually be done, what kinds of attitudinal change would be introduced among the officials working in tribal areas, who often look down upon the tribespersons, and how the participation of people would be ensured in the development project, needs to be discussed not only theoretically but demonstrated in practical terms as well. As the PESA Act provides, displacement would take place after obligatory consultation with the community. Undoubtedly, this is a suggestion with which none would disagree. The paradigm of development all over the world is in favour of what development practitioners have called "interactive participation", where people are involved right from the inception of the project to its completion.[14] Their voice does not go unheard, though if there is a difference of opinion between them and the project officials (the financers, development specialists), it is sorted out through what is called the "dialogic approach." The aim is to arrive at consensus, since it is essential for the success of a development programme.

The concept of community has acquired a central place in the discourse dealing with the issues of determining pressing needs of people, the course of development, displacement, and resettlement, and scheduling and de-scheduling of communities.[15] Here, the assumption is that the community is homogeneous and reaching consensus is not difficult. The reality, however, is far different. Each community is differentiated and stratified. The male view is different from the female; the old people have different things to say as opposed to the young; the vocal sections of society would say different things than the relatively reticent ones; and each of its layers (strata, whether caste or class) holds a different point of view. In other words, a community comprises contesting perspectives on reality. The larger is the community, the more varied are the views. And, therefore, certain questions become extremely important: With whom in the community will we hold consultations regarding the issues of development? How would we arrive at a consensus? What is the meaning of the term "community"? What we have to avoid is the point of view of the dominant and/or vocal sections of the community. The definition of community and how a particular community defines itself (its boundary-maintaining mechanisms) is all the more important because the Draft proposes that in industrial enterprises (except small ventures) established in the Scheduled Areas, the community displaced would be made a "partner" in the industry or a certain percentage of the profit would be used for its development. If community is of such vital importance, it must be properly defined, both from a theoretical perspective and how "members of a collectivity" define themselves.

8

The Draft notices a "deep sense of exclusion and alienation" that the Scheduled Tribes have started feeling over a period of time. (p. 15). They believe that they have been mercilessly deprived of what is rightfully theirs, and what should have justly reached them is not really reaching them. They also feel that whenever they have legitimately protested, they have been hauled up as "offenders" and "criminals". Against this background, they view the state as their "exploiter and enemy." On the other hand, the unscrupulous elements, invariably from outside, posing as the messiahs and problem-solvers of tribespersons, are playing upon the gullibility of tribals, and spreading among them the culture of violence. The scenario in some states is so bad that all development programmes have virtually halted.

Although the Draft draws our attention to the violent manifestations in tribal areas, its analysis of the situation is conservative. It is possible that the tribals may be initially attracted to the outsider groups (identified variously as Left Rebels, Red Army, Maoists, Naxalites, Extremists) as they appear to be their "protectors and friends", but soon, it is the fear and violence perpetrated by them that makes tribals succumb to their wishes. Empirical studies of the relations between Maoists/Naxalites (or any other insurgent group) and tribal people have not been done, mainly because of the problems in carrying out fieldwork in these areas, but whatever little information we have, tells us that tribals are quite disillusioned with the tall claims that the outsiders induce them with, and instead exploit them for their own political goals and interests. Nevertheless, they cannot wriggle out of the situation because of the local conditions and the threatening fear. The situation of tribal (as well as non-tribal peasant) communities is alarming because of their exploitation by the "perpetrators of violence" on the one hand, and their interrogation by law-enforcing agencies, on the other. The truth is that the tribals are confused about whom to believe: the rebels who claim that they are waging a war against the state on their behalf so that their rights and resources are restored to them, or the state that says that it is trying to protect the tribal people from the mindless violence that the rebel outsiders commit.

The Draft observes that the violent eruptions in tribal areas should not be treated as a law and order problem to be "tackled through policing", or the local people are armed to fight the outsider groups, as is being done in certain parts of the country (p. 15). Although not mentioned, it is clear that the Draft has in mind the case of Salwa Judum. Money being spent to fight the rebels should instead be diverted to tribal development. Rights of tribals over natural and financial resources should be restored. Issues of economic deprivation need to be addressed.

Take the case of the states that are in the grip of violence. The tribal areas of Chhattisgarh lack the basic civic amenities, such as roads, health centers, and educational institutions. The area that witnesses the maximum episodes of violence is beyond the reach of the police. Productivity from the land is extremely poor. A pall of gloom and hunger prevails over these tribal areas. Almost ninety per cent of the state of Jharkhand is without irrigation facility; and 80 per cent of tribal villages are without electricity, roads, drinking water, and health centers. Obviously, against the background of this economic and social reality of the famishing masses, it is unsurprising that people should fall prey to even a flicker of hope that the rebels offer. Once the conditions improve, there will be less likelihood of people being susceptible to glib and utopian talks of the rebels. Endogenous and all-round development of tribal communities is the panacea that would last.

It should not be forgotten that it would take a long time to achieve this ideal, of empowering people economically as well as socially, when the anti-socials make no impact on them, but it would only be possible when they are freed from the impending fear of the rebels. Tribes surrender to them out of fear, and not out of respect for their mission. One is really doubtful if people are sympathetic to them. Under the garb of working for the people's problems, the rebels in fact fulfill their own interests. Tribal communities in rebel-infested areas know about it, but they cannot openly say this because of the fear amidst which they live. That is why it is imperative that the rebels are flushed out of tribal and rural areas. Development requires freedom, an ability to think independently and creatively, and perform experiments to bring out the best. The zealousness that development projects desire is trampled under the jackboots of fear. That is why massive police action is the first imperative step before the programmes of endogenous development begin.

In comparison to the human development indicators in India as a whole, those of the Scheduled Tribes are much lower. The Draft notes that tribes in general suffer from geographical and cultural isolation, the features of which are not reflected in the human development index. The shyness that the Lokur Commission attributes to tribespersons may be an outcome of their persistent isolation. Against this background, they are unable to take decisions and make choices. This would be possible only when their capability grows and they are empowered. Education plays a significant role in accomplishing these goals (of empowering people and building their capacity), besides, of course, many others, such as of upward social mobility, expanding one's rational understanding, and saving one from the wicked designs of moneylenders and usurpers of their land.

The Draft reiterates many well-known suggestions to improve upon the educational standards among tribal communities. One of them pertains to the nature of teachers in schools in tribal areas. The Draft notes that most of the teachers happen to be non-tribal, who besides being unsympathetic to tribal problems and ignorant of these, look down upon local cultural practices and regard tribal persons as inferior to them.[16] The negative effect of this is the high drop rate of tribal children due to the alienation they experience in schools. Having noted this, however, the Draft moves on to the aspects of changing the curriculum for tribal children, instead of suggesting measures to deal with the issue of teachers.

The problem of lack of professionals affects both schools as well as dispensaries and primary health centers. Tribal areas suffer from both teacher and physician (doctor) absenteeism. The Draft proposes the need to devise an "appropriate personnel policy" to ensure that various functionaries are present in tribal areas, including the remote and far-flung areas (p. 6); however, what such policy would be is not discussed anywhere. It may be recalled how Pt Jawaharlal Nehru used to take an active interest in selecting government functionaries for tribal areas.[17] He tried his best to dispel the myth that a posting to tribal territories was a kind of punishment. The enthusiastic, challenge-accepting, government officials were expected to inspire the same level of confidence among the lower staff. Nehru was of the view that in order to work with the tribals, we needed committed officers of a special temperament.

Within the model of endogenous development, it is suggested that tribal men and women may be trained to take up the role of teachers and doctors, and then they be sent back to work, in their own home territories, with some additional material incentives. This would certainly reduce the problem of teacher and doctor absenteeism and apathy in tribal areas. Such professionals would not only feel at home in familiar surroundings, but would also have the challenge to ameliorate the condition of their own people. The inducement to be potential leaders of their respective communities would hopefully be miraculous, and keep tribal professionals entrenched to their areas. However, till the time this dream becomes a reality, we would have to inspire non-tribal teachers and doctors to work wholeheartedly in tribal areas. For this, both moral and material incentives are generously required, so that the tribal posting is not seen as punitive, besides of course, inculcating among them a sympathetic understanding of the tribal way of life and its strength.[18]

What is required is a centering of tribal values and lifestyles, and also their contemporary problems, in our discourse created through any media. What non-tribal people can learn from tribes should be brought to the centre of our intellectual discourse; it should be the intention to awaken awareness among non-tribals as to how the bulwarks of our civilisation are built on the values (and attitudes to life) that tribals created, nursed, and lived by. The state governments should finance the publication and wider dissemination of this literature (p.22). Correspondence courses on tribal life and culture should also be started in a number of universities, similar to the one that the Arunachal University has recently started.

Books and the other educational material prepared for tribal students should be, the Draft notes (p.10), in their respective languages. This suggestion, though not new, is laudable, but it poses a plethora of problems. Many tribal dialects lack scripts; many of them have disappeared or exist in a vestigial form; and many tribes have almost fully adopted and internalized the languages of their non-tribal neighbours, and these languages are no more treated as alien. Moreover, many tribespersons would like to receive their education in a language (including English) that guarantees their future employment. On many occasions, while on fieldwork in tribal areas, I have been told that the local people want teachers good in English so that their children learn the language which would further their chances in the national and international job markets. Therefore, to think that tribes are a conservative lot—and they want their traditional practices and dialects to continue—is nothing but myopic.

The books prepared for tribal students, in their languages, the Draft says, should acknowledge the "role of tribal leaders and tribal people in the struggle for Indian independence" (p.10). Here, it may be recalled that not every tribe participated in the freedom movement. Some tribes were located in such far-off and inaccessible areas that the news of the national movement rarely reached them. So, these chapters may also highlight the other achievements and glorious feats of tribal people. While this is a good thought with a view for generating interest among tribal students in studies, as their books will have chapters on them, their culture, and their contributions to the nation, but this suggestion is jaundiced in case it does not think beyond tribal societies. One of my submissions is that we should have a larger participation of people of all strata in tribal issues and problems; in other words, tribal issues and problems should be centred rather than remaining at the margins. Against this setting, it is imperative that we think of introducing chapters on tribal life in all school and college books so that the non-tribals also come to know that their country has a large tribal population. The Draft should think in terms of transcending ghettoisation (i.e., something meant for tribals only) and focus on increasing sensitivity among all sections of society for tribal communities.[19]

9

One of the areas which has received inadequate attention is the subject of sports among tribal societies. The Draft attends to this issue, suggesting that the participation of tribals in sport events at all levels, including the international, should be increased (p. 5, 11). It also assumes here that the tribals have "inherent talent" (p.5). Whilst it may be acceptable to so praise tribal people and their characteristics heartily, in emotional, larger-than-size, and hyperbolic terms, these "adjectival praises" are subjective and should be avoided. Who is not "inherently talented" is a moot question. Is there an objective way of ascertaining an "inherently talented" community of people from one which is not?

Besides increasing the participation of tribals in sport events, it is equally essential that the traditional tribal sports are studied and encouraged. And, as the little tradition is carried forward and systematised to become the great tradition, in the same way, tribal sports should be developed to become the national sports. Similarly, tribal handicrafts, arts, and organic and ethnic products are promoted and developed commercially, but in all cases, the benefits should come to the communities which are its true inventors and preservers. This also applies to their ethno-medical and ethno-veterinary practices, which are in the process of being recorded and properly understood both by field anthropologists and the NGOs. The oft-heard suggestion is that tribal medicine (herbal, animal, and naturopathic, but not supernatural) should be incorporated in the official health-care system, so that its benefits are enjoyed by all. Before this is done, however, certain issues need to be resolved: for instance, of patenting, the authorship of medicine, benefits going to the people, safeguarding the habitat of people so that its exploitation (and overexploitation) does not cause irreparable damage, involving local people in the marketing of medicine, and respecting customs and taboos regarding the preparation and use of medicine. It should always be kept in mind that medicine is a part of their social and cultural system, and therefore, before it is researched with an aim to make it public, its context should be properly studied and respected.

The "indigenous (or local) knowledge" of people should be documented, as fast as possible before it is lost. For this task, the research funding agencies of the government should announce special schemes, scholarship, and publication grants. The idea of establishing an Adivasi Bhawan in Delhi, which would "showcase" tribal material and non-material culture, is laudable (p.18), but instead of having just one in the country, there should be one in each state having tribal population, for this will enable us keep a record of a large number of tribal cultures than what would be possible in one such institution. Moreover, the existing "tribal museums", governmental as well as private, such as the Museum of Mankind (in Bhopal), should be given funds to accomplish this goal. These museums, however, should be dynamic; in other words, they should keep pace with the changing tribal reality, since one of the criticisms about it is that they "freeze" reality, thus becoming conservative and maintaining *status quo*.

The Draft hopes to create awareness among tribespersons about the nefarious practices they have (such as addiction to liquor and drugs, witchcraft) and to help eradicate them (p. 5, 17). In the context of money lending, it notes the consumption needs of tribes that constrain them to enter into a vicious circle of never ending debt-bondage (p. 14). In the areas of health, hygiene, and sanitation, the awareness of tribals needs to be increased (p. 12). Then, they should also know about the perils to which they are exposed because of migration (p. 14). Although not mentioned, the tribespersons should also be aware of the high vulnerability of their communities (particularly of those situated close to highway routes) to HIV/AIDS. Voluntary action should be supported in "service deficient far flung areas" (p. 6). The question here is: Who will take up the job of diffusing awareness among them?

It is the NGOs which come to our mind as the first candidates. In addition, the anthropologists can play a remarkable role. It would be apt to promote the idea of "resident anthropologists", those who are stationed in tribal communities and allotted the work of introducing ideational changes among people. With their multi-method and "do-it-yourself" approach, and the ability to spend long, untiring, hours with communities, anthropologists have the potential to blossom into "advocates", "activists", "change-leaders", and "grass-root workers." Since they are taught to be humble learners of other cultures, they are modest, patient, respectful, empathetic, sensitive, and conscientious; they are the best choice to start a dialogue with people regarding the correct path they should take, in order to change for the better. The Draft should explicitly identify the roles the anthropologists can play in tribal development.[20] Not only are the anthropologists the right professionals for this task, their public recognition will give them and their work a tremendous boost. Otherwise, as an insider, it would not be wrong to state that they would feel left out of the process and would feel that what they could have done for the tribal people in a proper manner, is assigned to inept persons, whose approach to the tribals is of paternalism, bossism, and imposition. Tribespersons would thus reject the innovations and plans because these are not correctly explained to them and also since their social and cultural values are not kept in mind while introducing these changes. The expertise of anthropologists lies in their familiarity with the tribal people and their neighbours, their knowledge of the tribals" social and cultural systems, and of what they want from the outsiders, the state and the development agencies.

Anthropological opinion is imperative on all issues confronting tribes. For instance, in case of health (pp.11–2), one of the suggestions is we shall promote a synthesis of the Indian medical system (such as Ayurveda, Siddha) with tribal and modern medicine. *Prima facie* this suggestion seems to deserve recommendation, for it intends to combine the best of each of these medical systems into one, which then can be promoted among tribal communities (as also, among others). However, on closer examination, it is found that each system has its own theory of how a disease is caused, which guides the regime of prophylactic, curative, and therapeutic treatment it furthers. To achieve a synthesis of the different systems may not be possible in reality; it may, in fact, be contrary to the spirit of medical pluralism.

What is required is an intensive comparative study of tribal medical systems from different parts of the country. Then, a further study of the pharmacological properties of their herbal and animal medicine is undertaken in scientific laboratories, and if found to be efficacious, they deserve promotion in tribal areas as well as in other parts of the country, keeping in mind the commercial and ethical issues mentioned earlier. Needless to say, tribals should not be deprived of benefits that follow in the wake of its commercialization, since they are the inventers of the medicine and have been using it from the days of yore. Thus we allow people to have the option of choosing from different medical systems. What is important is that the functional health care systems are available to them; in other words, doctors, nurses, pharmacists, hospital beds, and infrastructures must be available, irrespective of the system that is locally promoted. The Draft should therefore be as practical in its approach as possible.

The Draft notices that the condition of tribal women is better than their counterparts in non-tribal societies. Like human society in general, tribes also recognise gender differences, but the types of disadvantages which women are subjected to in non-tribal societies are largely non-existent in tribal communities. This may be inferred from many indices, including sex ratio among them. Here, the Draft rightly notes that as they are "mainstreaming" (becoming a part of the mainstream), many negative practices (of the outside communities) are finding a place among them (p.17). The path followed by the tribes towards Hinduisation, and then, sanskritisation, produces adverse effects for their women. As tribes sanskritise, they withdraw their women from working in the fields, or carrying out other economic tasks, like women among the higher castes. Gradually, they become "unproductive" and become only "consuming" members of the community, thus declining in status. Once they lose economic independence, they become vulnerable to many other upper caste Hindu practices, such as the demand for dowry, losing rights in family property, ill treatment of female children, female infanticide and are deprived of basic rights, etc. The Draft notes that already the female to male sex ratio in children, among tribes, has declined from 985 per thousand males in 1991 to 972 in 2001.

Changes affecting the supposed "gender equality" among tribes need to be studied in detail. All those practices that unfavourably affect women must be eliminated through legal and social interventions. Certain ideological strands have to be changed, one among them being the belief that tribes hold about black magic and witchcraft. A cursory survey of news about tribal societies from eastern India (for instance, published in *The Telegraph*) would inform us that a significant proportion of them deal with the cases of witchcraft and the horrendous punishments meted out to the witches. The NGOs should take up the task of weeding out such obnoxious beliefs from tribal societies. Some thought should also be given to reserving jobs for tribal women.

The Draft submits that the migration of tribal women to cities to take up menial and domestic jobs would be discouraged by "providing an enabling regulatory/policy framework" (p. 17). Whilst the first part is understandable, and a good step, the second does not make it clear as to what the alternatives would be. Migration of tribespersons to towns and cities is directly proportional to the degradation of their habitats, virtual starvation, and displacement from their traditional territories. In alien contexts, they are forced to do any job in the tertiary sector of the economy, since they lack the marketable skills that the urban areas require. In other words, the problems of tribal women cannot be solved in isolation from this dominant scenario. But, the rights of the tribes in the towns and cities to which they have migrated must be protected, and for this a regulatory/ policy framework is expected. It is utopian to think that we would be able to check tribal migration by making people well entrenched to their habitats when there is virtually nothing available there. Everybody perceives towns and cities to be places of opportunity, where one can carry out any occupation—"caste-free" and "class-free"—and without being a victim of any social criticism. Against this backdrop, it may not be possible to curb migration, but the rights of migrants are to be protected. Tribal migrant women have to be saved from exploitation, ill treatment, and non-payment (or less payment) of their wages.

10

The Draft states that in order to have the expected changes take place in tribal areas, the level of administration "has to be raised expeditiously" (p.19). Discussing both the Fifth and the Sixth Schedules of the Constitution, the Draft is favourably inclined towards the former. It says that the full potential of the Fifth Schedule has yet not been realised (p.19), and then suggests the steps that could be adopted for this purpose. Regarding this, Roy Burman (2006: 3645) writes:

> The Seventh Five-Year Working Group for Tribes in its report observed that while the fifth schedule was paternalistic in its thrust, the sixth schedule contains the germs of self-management.

Further, he says (p. 3647) that in a workshop of 20 May 2006, attended by sixty tribal leaders, including Giridhar Gomang (former Chief Minister of Orissa), one of the declarations was to replace the Fifth Schedule by the Sixth Schedule covering all areas with preponderance of tribals, with the positive aspects of PESA. Roy Burman (pp. 3645–6) also rebuts the charge of the Draft that in the Sixth Schedule, there is no democratic set-up below the district level. He shows that the Para 4 (a) of the Sixth Schedule permits the Regional or the District Council, with the permission of the Governor, to formulate rules regarding the constitution of the Village Councils and the powers exercised by them. In other words, alternative structures exist in the Sixth Schedule for self-management. The aim of the tribal administration should be to give as much power as possible to the people for governing themselves, and deciding about their affairs, and therefore, the merits (both manifest and latent) of the Sixth Schedule should be objectively examined. The suggestion of the Draft to reinstate the "single line of administration" in tribal areas (p.5) is not acceptable, since it would lead to a concentration of power in district officials. On the contrary, the aim should be to achieve decentralisation at the grass-root level. This is essential for achieving the participatory approach towards tribal development.

The highlight of the Draft is an explicit recognition of the idea of de-scheduling of the tribes. Point 3 in Section 20 states that the "uniqueness" of the Indian system is that the communities are included as well as excluded from the list of the Scheduled Tribes. The Draft says that it is an "ongoing process" (p.21). While this sounds good theoretically, to the best of my knowledge, there has not been a single case of a Scheduled Tribe being excluded from the list. The reason behind this is not only the political pressure that the communities exercise on the government to remain scheduled and receive benefits for all times to come, but it is also true that no tribal community (including of those which are most represented in civil services, bank jobs, other gazetted and non-gazetted jobs) has achieved that level of affluence which would disqualify them from being on the list of Scheduled Tribes. In each community, there are families that have moved upward in economic and social terms, and there are also lowly placed families desperately needing the policy of compensatory discrimination for their betterment. That is why even when some people from a reserved community have done well, it cannot be de-scheduled, for this would also negate the chances of the most deserving ones from seeking benefits.[21]

At the same time, the Draft notes that if more communities continue to be added to the list of Scheduled Tribes—and K.S. Singh had estimated in 1993 that more than 1000 cases from different communities were pending before the government—then the benefits that go to the existing communities would be reduced; so only those communities deserve to be added to the list, about whose status there is no iota of doubt. The Draft recognises the existence of stratification among the tribes, which seems to have occurred because a small section of the Scheduled Tribes has "cornered" most of the benefits (p. 21), and since they continue to receive them, they further consolidate their position. The aim of the policy of compensatory discrimination is to help the underprivileged; therefore, the Draft boldly proposes a system of sub-categorisation of tribes, which would imply that we identify the different economic strata within a tribe, and seek to exclude from the benefits those which have "caught up with the general population" (p. 22).

Against this background, the Draft suggests that we give serious thought to the idea of excluding the "creamy layer" among the Scheduled Tribes from the benefits of the policy of positive discrimination as well as to the process of de-scheduling communities that have come at par with the general population. The Draft also suggests that vigorous steps should be taken to improve upon the quality of education imparted to tribespersons so that they are empowered and are able to compete on their own strengths with the general population. Once this is done, perhaps they would not require any reservation for their uplift. I think this is what the Draft means when it talks in terms of exploring "alternative affirmative actions". To make people independent of the grants they receive from the state would be a reality only when they are empowered in educational, economic, and legal terms. Three months after the Draft came into circulation, the Honorable Supreme Court's verdict sought to exclude the "creamy layer" among the Scheduled Castes and the Scheduled Tribes from the purview of reservation (*The Hindu*, 24 October 2006).[22]

In fact, we have been feeling for a long time that excessive gaps are surfacing between tribal families as a consequence of reservation. While some are able to take full advantage of the policy, others lag behind. The purpose of preferential discrimination will only be fulfilled when it reaches the deserving rather than those who are at an advantage and compete on their own with the other strata of society. As pointed out earlier, each tribal community comprises layers within it; some of these are better placed, whereas the others continue to be in a state of abject poverty. It is the latter, undoubtedly, which need more care and development policies than the former. Issues pertaining to the subjects of "excluding creamy layers" and de-scheduling are sensitive, and their reception, approval or disapproval, depends upon the community to which the respondent belongs. The Draft has already initiated a nation-wide debate on these issues. Against the background of these ideas, it may be hypothesised that the paradigm of reservation has started shifting from the communities towards families. It seems that the individual is becoming increasingly more important than what he is, in the existing system of reservation—it is his welfare that is gradually becoming the concern of the state and the developmental work. In the present system, an individual receives benefits because of his ascribed status, rather than his individual merits and demerits. The pendulum is swinging in the direction of the individual. Whether it finally stays there will be the story of the future.

Although Section 21 is titled "Research and Training", it has hardly anything to offer about "training". The questions remain: Who will be trained? What would the curriculum for training be? Who would the trainers be? What will the trainees do? It rightly states that the tribal way of life is under threat in a "liberalised and globalised economy" (p. 22). But, it may be kept in mind here that globalisation does not forcibly change the way of life; what it does is that it provides a set of alternatives to people. Whether they change or not is entirely their discretion. However, the alternative ways of living it puts forth are so alluring that communities do not remain untouched. Globalisation does not uproot cultures; on the contrary, it provides highly effective technological mechanisms to reinforce and spread them. The Draft proposes that intensive and concurrent research should be carried out at the micro and macro levels, not only with the academic interest of learning about the changing tribal reality, but also in order to have the base-line data that would guide our planning and development programmes.

Earlier, I had observed that tribal studies needed to be encouraged. Financial support should be made available on priority to fieldworkers and students who intend to work in tribal areas. Day by day first hand fieldwork in certain parts of the country is becoming a difficult proposition as tribal areas are reeling under the episodes of violent manifestations. Studies in these areas, whether done through the content analysis of news reports, or by interviewing people formerly associated with these movements, should be given priority. Researchers planning to study tribal communities which so far have not been studied should be encouraged. Furthermore, a number of dissertations and theses on tribal communities, lodged in university and college libraries, need to be published; in case they cannot be published in full, due to academic reasons, at least, their abstracts should be published, so that we know which communities and which of their aspects have so far been studied. The Draft observes that the Tribal Research Institutes (TRIs) shall be strengthened, both in terms of their research activities and in their interaction with the outside academic world. In addition, there is a suggestion to set up at the central level a National Institute for Tribal Affairs. However, its functions (whether it would undertake research or coordinate the activities of the TRIs) are not spelt out.

11

This brings us to the evaluation of the tribal policy document. The goals of the tribal policy document are: to improve the quality of life of tribal people; to see that the benefits of development reach them and all tribes develop equally, so that there is no hierarchy among them; and in spite of these massive changes taking place among them, the tribal culture should remain intact, so that a balance is attained between development and culture; and finally, the part (the tribe) should be integrated to the "whole" (the mainstream, the total society).

A policy is holistic; it is a total document, covering all aspects of the lives of people. Irrespective of the social sector to which it concerns, a policy provides a "road-map" to development and delineates the guidelines for work. Being a model for action, it is a formal declaration of intent; that is why it must be written down so that it is a constant reminder, and it also sanctions that one does not deviate from the goals collectively agreed upon. Embodying the values of society, although charted out by the government, it is for the other institutions (and their personnel) to implement it. They have to develop sensitivity to tribes and the work to be carried out among them. Unless the policy is translated into action, it will be nothing but a "sheet of paper", an academic and literary exercise, and an end in itself.

The Draft begins, as we noted earlier, with a dilemma, which is to strike the right balance between protecting tribal culture, values, and identity, on the one hand, and to ensure their integration with the mainstream, on the other. But which concept of the mainstream the authors of the Draft have in mind, is not stated anywhere. It is well known that the mainstream is a concept with various nuances, and its empirical connotation differs from one community to another.[23] Or, is the term "mainstream" used to mean the modern institutions, such as the educational system, health-care system, income-generational practices, secular and democratic systems? Moreover, the areas where the tribes are in majority, or in "tribal states", they constitute the "mainstream".[24] Mainstream is such a pivotal concept in the entire discourse that its meaning cannot be left to imagination. Rather, it must be discussed threadbare, so that any misconceptions that people across the country have about it may be laid to rest. The Draft should clearly state what is meant by the term "mainstream", and if it is difficult to define it in operational terms, then it may be dropped, and we should think in terms of the institutions that should be strengthened to help tribal communities, elevating them to the level of the general population. At no step should the tribes feel that certain values and practices are being imposed upon them.

With respect to the issue regarding preserving the tribal culture, a pertinent question is: "Who is interested in preserving the culture?" Here, it is for the community to take decisions pertaining to these questions, rather than outsiders deciding which aspects of their culture should be preserved, and which changed. People might like to discard some of their practices, though these might have been central to their culture at one time. People also know, and they do not need an outsider to tell them this, that over time some of their customs and ways of behaviour become anachronistic and need to be weeded out. To assume that people are conservative and wish to cling to their past practices, or are closed to rational thinking, is blatantly wrong. In fact, this assumption has grotesquely contributed to the paternalistic attitude the outsiders (particularly, bureaucrats) have for tribespersons. In the Orientalist construction, the other is "frozen", "unmoving", and "non-rational". The Orientalists (and some anthropologists) have time and again subscribed to this image, for it has quenched the "academic romanticism" of the outsiders. The "other' is enigmatic in this discourse.

But, the reality is far from this. Tribes have themselves done a lot for their own improvement—they have led movements for environmental protection, saving their cultural and human rights, throwing the exploiters out of their territories, regaining rights over their lost land and other resources, closing liquor shops in their area, curbing practices of conspicuous consumption, and putting a full stop to all those practices that reduce their respect in the eyes of others. In other words, people are themselves capable of having a critical and introspective look at their cultures, and changing it endogenously. They know that in course of time, some strands of their culture would be lost, once and forever, and they would never regret this loss. This dynamic reality of tribal living is missing in the Draft; what it lacks is the "tribal voice"; what one hears is the discourse of the bureaucrats. Throughout the text runs the "we-they" distinction; what "we" (the outsiders) think about what "they" (the tribes) want; and what "we" think tribes should be given.

That is why the Draft may not bestow confidence to the tribal people, notwithstanding its good intentions and suggestions.

In order to improve upon it, to make it closer to the tribal heart and mind, one in which tribes discover themselves, their images, aspirations, and soul, it is imperative that their reactions and responses are sought and incorporated. The tribal issues should be made public; only then the public awareness will increase. We wish to attract private companies to invest for tribal infrastructural development, but it would only be possible if they have a sympathetic understanding of tribal societies.

It is well known that the success of a policy is dependent upon its effective implementation; therefore, the Draft proposes a periodic review of the policy, and the findings will be placed before the Tribal Advisory Councils (TACs). The Ministry of Tribal Affairs will annually undertake the review of the Policy, and the Cabinet Committee on Tribal Affairs (CCTA) would review it after every three years and redefine its objectives and the guiding principles (p. 23). The Draft is right in saying that the tribal policy is not immutable. It should be critically examined for its effectiveness.

For the task of examining the responses to the Draft that have come and will come in future, the government should constitute a committee, which should include anthropologists and other social scientists who have been associated with tribal studies for a long time. A nation-wide debate should begin. Tribal issues need to be centred and discussed at length.

ENDNOTES

1. A copy of the Draft is available on the web site—http://tribal.nic.in/national_st_policy_1.html.
2. It was in his Foreword to the first edition of *A Philosophy for NEFA* (1957) that Nehru had envisioned the approach of integration for tribal societies. Here, he had written: "...we should avoid two extreme courses: one was to treat them as anthropological specimens for study and the other was to allow them to be engulfed by the masses of Indian humanity." Integration lies between the extreme policies of isolation and assimilation, and has taken the best characteristics of each of them. For Nehru's approach to tribes, see K.S. Singh, ed. (1989); Srivastava (2007).
3. The speakers were H.S. Saksena, Virginius Xaxa, C.B. Tripathi, I.S. Marwah, A.K. Rath, Sharena Banu, and R.P. Mitra. Their respective presentations were followed by a discussion. P. Venkata Rao (of the University of Hyderabad) has informed me that his department (of anthropology) organized a session on the Draft during the course of one of its seminars in 2004, and its responses were sent to the Ministry of Tribal Affairs. Another seminars Rao attended on this Draft were held respectively in Madras University and Tribal Research Institute at Ooty. But the discussions that took place in these seminars were not published in well-known journals.

4. I lectured on and about the Draft at the Management Development Institute, Gurgaon (on 3 October 2006), Department of Anthropology, University of Delhi (on 19 November 2006), and School of Anthropological Science, Ravi Shankar Shukla University, Raipur (on 28 November 2006).
5. It was clear from the deliberations at this seminar that many speakers (especially those who spoke in Hindi) had in fact not read the Draft. They spoke from their respective general understanding of tribes and their problems. P. Venkata Rao has told me that three seminars were organised on this Draft in Hyderabad, including one at the Administrative Staff College.
6. I also published a short article in 2008 on the concept of tribe as it is presented in the Draft.
7. From now on, whenever the term Draft is used, it refers to the second version.
8. The first Draft records 67.8 million people, divided into 698 Scheduled Tribes, constituting 8.08 of India's population.
9. See Risley (1915); Ghurye (1959).
10. The Government of India has appointed a National Commission for Denotified, Nomadic and Semi-nomadic Tribes, under the chairmanship of Balkrishna Renake, for looking into the problem of these communities.
11. Some prominent examples of Primitive Tribes are Shompen, Jarawa, Sentinelese of Andaman and Nicobar Islands, Bondos of Orissa, Cholanaicken of Kerala, Abujh Maria of Chattishgarh, Birhors of Jharkhand.
12. The title of the seminar was: 'Role of Indigenous and Tribal People in Contemporary Scenario and Criteria for Determination of Scheduled Tribes'.
13. "National Plan of Action for their Survival, Protection, and Development". In Government of India, Tenth Five Year Plan, 2002–07, p. 462. (http://planningcommission.nic.in/planrel/fiveyr/10th/volume2/v2_ch4_2.pdf).
14. See Pretty et al. (1995); Kumar (2002).
15. It is the community that is scheduled under the policy of protective discrimination, and will be de-scheduled, if the need be. It should not be forgotten that each society, irrespective of the scale of its organization, whether simple or complex, is economically differentiated. It has rich as well as poor people. When a community is scheduled, all are benefited, even when many of them may not require the benefits flowing from the policy of compensatory discrimination. Similarly, when a community is de-scheduled, those who are poor and require reservation suffer. The individual is secondary in this policy.
16. I am reminded of the following words of Bhupinder Singh: "Teachers are not tribals. They have no empathy to the tribals and do not do their duty well—they are at the schools only for a week at the beginning of each month to collect their pay" ("Role of the state in the development of Scheduled Tribes". http://www.geocities.com/bororissa/tri.html).
17. "Nehru thought that the most able officers should be sent to tribal areas, since these postings were of crucial importance, posing a lot of challenges to administrators. The officers should think that they were privileged to be engaged in the great task

of working in tribal areas. For Nehru, the most significant characteristic of an officer working with tribes was that he approached the people with friendship and affection, and lived with them without feeling any sense of superiority. He might have been an uneducated fellow, having qualified no examination, but if he was prepared to live with tribes as one of them, he must be preferred over all others. For Nehru, the officer earmarked for tribal areas was a 'participant observer'; he entered tribal huts, talked to them, ate and smoked with them, and tried to live their lives without any ethnocentric bias. As a fieldworker proceeds slowly in data-collection, after having established rapport, in the same way the officer should proceed slowly after having acquired a good knowledge of local conditions and traditions, and striking the relations of trust with people" (Srivastava, 2007: 147).

18. The Draft (p. 20) also recognises the need to make tribal postings attractive through incentives, such as fast track promotions, lump sum payments, etc., for the personnel. But, material incentives would infuse only superficial commitment, unless they are coupled with moral incentives. Tribal posting should be seen as a challenge, one that would give ample opportunity to the official to introduce changes in consultation with the people. It would definitely give a lot of satisfaction to the official.
19. It in fact says so at some places. For example, in the context of schools to be opened in tribal areas, it suggests that 10 to 25 per cent students in these schools will be non-tribal; it will be done for 'encouraging integration and competition' (p. 10).
20. The role that anthropologists can play is not entirely missing in the Draft (see, p. 6), but what I am suggesting is making this work central both for study and action. Anthropologists should not only propose "actionable points" (p. 6), but also carry out the action.
21. See note 14.
22. When the UPA government expressed its concern to address the Supreme Court verdict, many thought that it was farcical because its Ministry of Tribal Affairs had already suggested a similar 'sub-categorization' among the Scheduled Tribes for government jobs and even de-scheduling of certain tribes. The headline in *The Times of India* (of 25 October 2006) was "Elite tribals were already on way out, Tribal Affairs Ministry suggested sub-categorisation of STs months before SC verdict".
23. For instance, for hill dwellers, the mainstream comprises the "plains people"; for tribals, the "non-tribals"; for lower castes, the "Brahmanical Hinduism", for south Indians, the "north Indians"; for non-Hindus, "the Hindus". See Srivastava (1990).
24. Perhaps in the context of these areas, we may use the term "tribalization", where the "minority" neighbours of the "majority" tribes emulate tribal customs and practices, and in course of time, identify themselves with the dominant tribal society.

REFERENCES

Béteille, André. 2000. Chronicles of Our Time. Penguin Books, New Delhi.
Elwin, Verrier. 1939. The Baiga. London: John Murray.

——. 1959. A Philosophy for NEFA. Shillong: Government Publications.
Ghurye, G.S. 1959. The Scheduled Tribes. Bombay: Popular Prakashan.
Kumar, Somesh. 2002. Methods for Community Participation, A Complete Guide for Practitioners. Delhi: Vistaar Publications.
Pretty, J. et al. 1995. A Trainer's Guide for Participatory Learning and Action. London: IIED Participatory Methodology Series, IIED.
Risley, H.H. 1915. The People of India. London: W. Thacker and Co.
Roy Burman, B.K. 2006. Creating consternation, Draft National Tribal Policy 2006. *Economic and Political Weekly*, 26 August, pp. 3645–7.
Singh, Bhupinder. 1990. Between two worlds, five ancient tribal groups of Andaman and Nicobar Islands. In Buddhadeb Chaudhuri (ed.), Tribal Transformation in India (Volume 1: Economy and Agrarian Issues). New Delhi: Inter-India Publications.
Singh, K.S. (ed.). 1989. Jawaharlal Nehru, Tribes and Tribal Policy, A Centennial Tribute. Calcutta: Anthropological Survey of India.
——. 1993. The problem (Statement to the Volume on Marginalized Tribals). Seminar, 412.
Srivastava, Vinay Kumar. 1990. Understanding national integration. In Vinay Kumar Srivastava, Essays in Social Anthropology. Calcutta: Institute of Social Research and Applied Anthropology (pp. 173–216).
——. 1994. Political Anthropology: Meaning and Scope. *The Toppers' India*, 1 (11): 103–7.
——. 1997. Religious Renunciation of a Pastoral People. Delhi: Oxford University Press.
——. 2007. Jawaharlal Nehru on Tribes. *Social Science Probings*, 19 (2): 135–48.
——. 2008. Concept of 'Tribe' in the Draft National Tribal Policy. *Economic and Political Weekly*, XLIII (50): 29–35 [December 13–19, 2008].

LIVELIHOOD

From Equality to Marginalization:
Women of Hunter-Food Gathering Tribes

Subhadra Mitra Channa

Introduction: Hunters Food Gatherers; Reality and Construction

Although human kind has existed as hunters and food gatherers for most of their existence, yet the present day foragers have been reduced to ignominy and not only subjected to political and economic marginalization but are ideologically devalued and constrained to be labeled as under-developed and primitive. In the western world, the stereotypical images of the hunter conjured up pictures of a brute relationship between the sexes caricatured as a club wielding cave man dragging his mate by the hair. Equally potent were the economic stereotypes of a life of want and starvation, of a lack of leisure and capacity to build "culture" and further most damning, a personality given over to laziness and brutishness. They provided a prototype of the "wild man" as opposed to the civilized. In some ways this was also an effort to understand their own past, as by the nineteenth century the notion of evolution was well entrenched in Europe and the Europeans looked upon the so called "primitives" as their cultural ancestors. In anthropological literature there has been much discussion on the construction of the "primitive". The first major anthropological work based on field-work among real hunters and gatherers, *Man the Hunter* (*1968*), *edited by Richard Lee and Irven DeVore*, laid to rest most of these speculations although the stereotypes still persist in popular imagery. Some of the most important findings listed in this seminal work and later supported by other equally scholarly researches were to establish the hunters and gatherers as quite the opposite of the monolithic construction of their image.

The greatest reversal was in the gender stereotypes, as supported by overwhelming anthropological data, the greatest equality between the sexes was found among the foragers and people at the lower end of technological development. Women contribute to the major part of the subsistence economy and have crucial decision making powers, quite often over their own sexual and reproductive aspects, a power denied to most women in so-called "developed" societies. *Marjorie Shostak* (*1981*) in her biography of Nisa, has Nisa narrating her experience of childbirth, where she is expected to go all by herself to the forest and give birth. Most such communities leave it as an exclusive right of the woman to choose to carry or not to carry her baby back to the camp. *Godelier* (*1968:142*) writes about the Baruya women, "They had the monopoly of their own initiations, and of course they alone brought new children into this world, in an area socially forbidden to men. In the few weeks following childbirth, they had the power of life and death over their child. If they accepted it they kept it, otherwise the killed it and buried it beneath the shelter in which they had given birth".

The marriage and kinship patterns of the hunters gatherers is quite similar to people at the opposite end of the scale namely urban, western countries who place importance on the individual bond between the spouses rather than on the ties between larger kin groups as among agricultural communities. Marriages are based upon mutual liking and are not binding, but totally dependent upon the continuing mutual attraction of the couple, that can and do separate as soon as this bond wears out. Women's agency in terms of her own body and sexuality thus assumes an ideal condition that is only aspired by, but hardly ever attained by urban feminists. However this is not to say that conditions are identical among all communities living under similar conditions and having the same kind of technology. The actual relationship between men and women and also their relative status varies widely across cultures and across time as well. Usually war and violence tends to undermine women's status (*Mies, 1988*) and subsistence activities fall into their domain. To the extent that they are recognized for their reproductive powers also depends upon both history and local conditions. But one can hypothesize that the tussle between men and women, where the men are not in control of too much of material resources, is one where both partners are on a relatively equal footing. Men need to have some power base, either material or supernatural in order to subjugate women. Elsewhere I have raised the same issue with respect to another category of marginalized women, those belonging to the dalit communities (*Channa, 1992, 2001, 2005*).

Sexuality and subsistence are two areas in which women have much more control while ritual and cosmology may still subordinate them. The oppression of women in such societies is therefore more ideological that material and therefore in real terms they enjoy more freedom and equality than women in say, mainstream Hindu society.

However, the very freedom enjoyed by the women and their individualism becomes a negative condition when these people come in contact with communities guided by conservative patriarchal values. This is not the place to discuss the reasons why patriarchy exists in some societies and does not in others, but the fact is that in societies which are guided by patriarchal values, the women are denied the agency that we normally find among women from forest dwelling and marginal communities. Some of the reasons relate to the existence or non-existence of property and values of hierarchy. In fact it is found that as societies become more and more divided on lines of inequality whether based on race, caste or class or the sheer force of conquest and colonization, it is the women who suffer greater and greater domination (*Etienne and Leacock, 1980*). As Victorian England established its empire over the world, women were subjected to the greatest suppression and only found liberation during the turmoil of the two world wars. Even much simpler societies with no centralized authority and little differentiation may relegate women to an inferior position if they have a warring tradition, like the Baruya studied by *Godelier* (*1982*).

The Lodhas of West Midnapore; West Bengal: Ecological Refugees?

In this article I would like to discuss the relative status of men and women among the Lodha tribe, a forest dwelling tribe branded as criminal by the colonial administration,[25] occupying forested areas of West Bengal some of whom have now been forcibly evicted from their forest habitat and settled, often under miserable conditions in small hamlets, in inhospitable terrain not claimed by the Bengali agricultural population being too dry and infertile. Several of the Lodha hamlets that I visited on a trip to Medinipore in West Bengal in the early months of 2007, exhibited a sordid story of people left to eke out a living on a land which had no water, where only a scrubby vegetation was growing and where the nearest forests, the mainstay of the Lodha traditional subsistence, were often several kilometers away. In many instances the Lodhas were deprived of the surrounding forests by the encroachment of urban populations who cut down the trees to build houses as is now seen in Jhargram, a fast growing suburban township, where the *bhadrolok* settlers from urban centers are fast marginalizing the original forest dwellers.

These settlements were nearly forty years old when these people were forced out of the forest when the forests came to be reserved, ostensibly to protect the wildlife. But today with the nexus of corrupt politicians and monetary interests, most of the forests have been destroyed and what is on official records a thickly forested area has been denuded of most of its tree cover. The Lodhas are often employed for the illegal felling of trees and if any one brings this to the notice of any relevant authority, the poor Lodha is put behind bars and the person who employed him, a local politician or big –wig goes free. The label of ex-criminal tribes reinforces this, for, "Police interests are greatly served by having a set of pre-designated offenders the moment a crime is committed in a zone where the erstwhile "Criminal Tribes" are known to move" (*Fourcade, 2003:169*). No such community in India has thus been able to shed its colonial stigmair respective of how they conduct themselves. With their original resource base denuded they are left to struggle under the harshest of conditions. Even the land on which they are situated does not belong to them and they are under constant threat of eviction, in a true sense of the term "ecological refugees" coined by *Guha and Martinez-Alier* (*1998:4*).

A Brief Ethnography of the Lodhas

The Lodhas claim that they are actually descendents of the Sabor tribes and have a higher social status than is accorded to them in this region. The Sabors are believed to be descendents of Sabari, the forest dwelling woman, who had offered berries to Lord Rama during his exile in the forest. The story goes that the innocent Sabari who had no knowledge of purity and pollution had tasted each of the berries, to make sure that they were sweet before offering them to the deity. Lord Rama was overwhelmed by her devotion and ate the berries so polluted. In the Census of 1951 there is mention of the Sabars, and that the origin of these people could be traced as far back as the Aitreya Brahmanas, where they find mention along with other aboriginal tribes who had spread all over the country form the Ganges to the Godavari. There has been some identification of the Lodhas with the Sabars, both of whom were recognized as nomadic and hunters. In some references it is also mentioned that the Kiratas or the Vyadhas described in the Mahabharata and in the Mangal Kavyas are regarded as their kin. Lord Jagganath of Puri is said to have spent time with Vishvavasu, the mythical Sabar chief and was worshipped by him as Nilmadhava in Nilachal in Orrisa.

The references to all these myths have some common threads. Firstly it is recognized that the Sabar, or Lodhas, like most other tribes in India, are actually or mythically associated with the original people of India, separate from the Aryans who were probably ethnically different. Secondly they seemed to have had a long association with the forest as nomadic hunters. But, in spite of being forest dwellers, they had contact with the non-forest dwelling people and there must have been an active exchange of rituals and culture as the folklore regarding the encounter of Rama with Sabari and the myth of Jagganath indicates. Indeed, it is believed by most scholars that Jagganath is a deity of tribal origin, who has assumed his present status by the process of "universalization".

Although the actual association of Sabar with the Lodhas is not fully established it is a fact that these names are often used interchangeably. More over tribal identities in India have not been fixed and have a dynamic nature, that has often been ignored. At present, the total number of Lodhas in West Bengal are about 8000 and they are scattered in the Northern part of the state. In Medinipore, they are found in the western jungle covered tracks. According to the Census of 1901, they had originally migrated from Central Provinces and may be linked to an agricultural tribe named, "Lodh" or "Nodh" or "Ludhi" who are found in large numbers in this region even today. But in West Bengal they have been forest dwellers and a highly marginalized people.

As of now in the Lodha hamlets most people are engaged in collecting minor forest produce, that was mainly the woman's work and doing wage labour, that was primarily man's work. But exception were to be found to both as some women also worked in the railway yard raking up coal and a few men would occasionally go to the forest to collect firewood.

The dwellings of the Lodhas that we visited, were primarily huts made of mud walls that was dug up from the village itself and made by their own people. One such huge crater was created in front of us and we were told it will fill up during the rainy season and act as catchments for rainwater. All the material used was local, including the roof that was made of bamboos and paddy shafts. The central pole of the house is its most important part, and is ritually installed by sacrificing a cock and pouring liquor into the foundation of the house, it also symbolizes the safety of the dwelling.

The families are mostly nuclear in nature, for as soon as a Lodha man gets married, they set up their own hut. They are notionally patrilineal and the woman comes to live with her husband from her parent's house. If they owned any land or a house that goes to the sons. The marriages are arranged with others of their community, not living too far away, the marriageable age for boys is around 18–20 and for girls around 12–15. The houses had fenced courtyards in which they raised chicken, goats and an occasional cow or bullock. These were usually sold in the market. The main food of the Lodhas was rice and some vegetables. They relished meat, fish, eggs and chicken and ate them as frequently as possible. Local homemade liquor, brewed in their own villages, albeit illegally, is also consumed almost by all persons, men, women, young and old. They plant useful trees like drumsticks that grow quickly and yield edible parts. Guavas and other fruit trees were also common. Attempts to make kitchen gardens were usually failures because of lack of water, however, there were several bamboo groves that served as a source of cash income for the families that owned them.

The Lodhas have their own deities that are mostly, nature deities and of these the most revered is Basumata or mother earth who is supposed to have given shelter to them. Sitala mata is a deity who is shared with the Hindu neighbours. She is supposed to be one of seven sisters, and is popularly believed to look after the health of the people and help in controlling endemic diseases like cholera, smallpox and measles; each of the sisters is associated with one version of the disease. They do not worship any idols and have their own rituals, mainly of the nature worship kind, apart from those followed by their Hindu neighbours. We were present at the time of Saraswati puja, which was celebrated with great enthusiasm by the Bengali Hindus but not by the Lodhas. In the school, too it was celebrated by the Bengali school teachers. They worship their own version of the Bengali goddess Lakshmi, as Tusu Thakur. The tutelary deity of the Lodhas is Baram devta, who is the most powerful deity, residing in a sacred grove and is the spirit of the forest. Even today, although the forest is getting destroyed and trees cut, the sacred groves of Baram still survive, for the Lodhas will never cut these sacred trees. Baram is propitiated before the commencement of any ritual or festival and offerings of terracotta elephants and horses are made at his shrine that is a tree.

The Lodhas strongly believe in ghosts and evil spirits and also in witchcraft. Here I would like to discuss the tensions in their lives particularly with respect to the incompatibility between what they believe in and what they are expected to do. The material deprivation faced by them is only outdone by the humiliation to which they are subjected and this is particularly true with respect to the exploitation and denigration of their women. In most marginalized communities, the internal status enjoyed by women is more than neutralized by the external oppression perpetuated on them (*Channa, 2001*). This was particularly true of the Lodha women, who were being exploited both for labour and for sexual favours, due to both their poverty and the responsibilities of taking care of the households. The only Lodha settlements that showed some signs of comfort were the ones where local NGOs had been working for many years and where some minor transformations in people's lifestyles had been achieved, like being more literate and able to carry on some agriculture. Some changes in dress and personal hygiene were also observed, but nowhere could one say that these people were being supported to lead a life of their choice. Even the NGO's were following the western model of development, concentrating only on formal education and agriculture. The original way of life of this tribe was almost universally condemned as backward.

When we deal with forest dwelling communities, and we talk of their coming out of the forest or getting "modernized" or falling into a settled life style pattern, the changes that are taking place are deep rooted and involve such basic values and cognitive dimensions, that it is not possible to understand the magnitude of the transformation required in the so-called process of "development" in any simple terms. Most agencies involved in such forced relocation of forest dwellers try to access the changes involved in terms of their own values and fail to comprehend what they actually expecting of these people who are being relocated, the trauma and the imperfect adjustments that such a community is forced into and the havoc that it plays with their lives. Even more insidious is the fact that few people even care as to what is happening to them, as they remain the "others" and "those people", who do not matter, as they have been dehumanized in the process of being stereotyped as dirty, lazy and worst still as criminals. In order to understand what is really happening to the Lodhas, we must first try to access the world-view and values of a forest dwelling people and then evaluate why they are as they are, on the basis of the data that we have.

World View and Values of Forest Dwellers

Firstly, we will try to understand the notion of territory as opposed to the concept of property. For forest dwellers such as the Lodhas, the forest is a place to which they belong, not something that they own and the available resources that they had been using in the forest like fruits, trees, animals and other forest produce like honey and medicinal plants were in the nature of free goods. This sense of belongingness has a primordial character to it. Almost all myths of origin vest a community with ancestral links to a territory that can never be replaced. Therefore shifting people out of their space is like uprooting a tree leaving it to die, as all meaning invested with their origin and living get eroded. Thus, while those who resettle them may feel that they are providing an alternate piece of land, to the people being uprooted, it is like losing the very meaning of their existence. Several NGOs as well as government officials pointed out to me, that many Lodhas still remain in the forests in spite of all efforts to bring them out.

"They hide and climb trees when they see outsiders. They are afraid to come out and no amount of persuasion will make them come out", I was told. To the outsiders what appears as illogical, is a matter of sheer existence for the forest dwellers who cling to the forest as it provides the only meaningful existence for them. What may appear as wilderness to the outsiders, contains all the life giving sustenance such as livelihood, spirits and gods and everything that makes their life interesting and worth living. The Lodhas know that to move around and make a living from the forest environment, is a skill, based on deep knowledge and not an easy task. It gives them a sense of worth. I was talking to one woman who was brought up in the town and never learnt to go to the forest. She told me that she did not possess the knowledge or skill. "You need to be trained to move around there. The Thakur, if annoyed, can do you great harm. One must know how to avoid them, how to deal with them. One must go to the forest with deep reverence in their hearts for the Thakurs, and must know the correct way to please them or they can crush you under their feet. Even while we are sitting here and talking they can hear us, they know everything, and therefore it is not everyone's cup of tea to go to the forest".

The Thakur, she was referring to were the elephants, which are looked upon by the Lodhas as the presiding deity of the forests. But there are other beings, both sacred and dangerous, that need to be handled and dealt with and all this is a matter of great knowledge. Those who have this knowledge prefer to use it as it gives them an edge over the so-called *babus* who do not possess their skills. Thus in addition to making a living, it is also a matter of self esteem for them to be able to do what the other wise dominant population cannot do. Even those who have been uprooted prefer to go back to the forest, even if it takes a lot of effort in order to eke out a living.

The inadequacy of the forest dwellers and foragers to adjust to a cash economy lies in their belief in sharing rather than owning anything. Ownership, in more stratified societies is an indicator of status differential. As we all know, in today's consumerist society, we have many things that we do not need but which we only covet or possess to prove that we are superior to others, or in other words our social relationships and status are informed by the consumer items. Lodhas on the other hand have little regard for material things. To them, a piece of cloth to cover their bodies is enough and they have no value for good clothes or appearance.

In the field I found, there was a distinct variation in the manner in which older men and women dressed and the younger ones, by now more exposed to the values of the outside world, dressed. The former, especially the women, were always dressed in the most ragged of clothing, the older women wore only a single piece of clothing locally referred as "*kapod*" that was quite an apology for a saree, being quite often what it literally meant, a dirty piece of cloth, worn high at about knee length with no blouse or petticoat. The older men too wore a similar piece of cloth round their waists and something to cover the upper part of the body according to seasons. In summer they would go bare bodied.

The younger people wore sarees and blouses and were a little better dressed. However, the Lodhas have still not developed the values, regarding material things that prevail in the society at large. We found, for example, that in the settlement, most people went bare footed. The obvious initial conclusion was that they did not have or could not afford to buy shoes. But a survey of the houses revealed that most of them had several pairs of foot wear, but they hardly ever wore them, simply because they were not used to them and found no need to be uncomfortable. Moreover the practical reason put forward by the women was that when they went to the forest, they could feel many things with their bare feet that warned them against dangers of being bitten by snakes or other dangerous insects or animals. The bare foot provides a sensory perception that would be killed by wearing shoes. A young man when asked if he possessed a watch said that he did, but when asked why he did not wear it said, "Why should I? Do I want to become a *babu* by wearing a watch? Women said that they did buy *sarees* but they got torn in the forest, moreover the lack of water also made washing quite difficult. The entire hamlet was served by a single well. Likewise, in the forest there would have been no need to show off their clothes, so the values of appearance are missing. However to the outsiders, this dirty and unkempt appearance is enough to brand them as "good for nothing".

Whenever people are found without much material possessions or outwards signs of having a lot of material goods, it is common to stereotype them as "backward" or lazy, the conclusion being that they are either too stupid or too lazy to acquire material goods. But the works of anthropologists have shown, that the concept of having "too much" in terms of consumable goods is dependant not upon technology, intelligence or capacity to do hard work, but on the values held by the group. The tribal people would make efforts to acquire goods beyond their subsistence needs only when they found some use for them. For example, speaking of the *Baruya*, *Godelier* (*1982:174*) makes this remark regarding their limited production of food and other consumable goods, "their production was limited because it played no essential role in the production of social relations and was confined to subsistence". This is true for the Lodhas also.

The one kind of consumption valued by them is one that is directly related to individual pleasure; l for example, they value good food above everything else. A woman I was talking to told me that most of what she earns goes into buying food items like chicken, fish, mutton and vegetables, which she buys as often as possible; "*Onge khabo*, *shonge chole jabe*" (what I eat, alone will go with me). Another woman told me that she was addicted to seeing movies. "I go to see a *boi* (movie) almost every other day. What will I get by saving fifteen rupees, it is much better to enjoy myself for a few hours".

For people used to a non-monetary barter economy and living off free goods in the forest, money *per se* has no meaning except in terms of what pleasure it can translate itself into. Hoarding, that also translates into savings in the outside world, is a value that they have not acquired to a very large extent. Thus, even though their earnings may not be too little at all times, there is absolutely no concept of keeping anything aside. The survey done on household expenditures indicated that they would drink liquor, smoke Wills cigarettes, see movies and generally spend anything they earned in a day.

While in the forest getting something to eat may not have been a problem, in the monetary economy into which they have been forced, not having any money on a particular day might mean starvation for the entire family. Since they are now part of an economy where savings are the only insurance against being left starving when there is no food, it is often likely that they are pushed to the brink of starvation. In the forest where there are plenty of free goods, such a situation may not arise, as also the value of sharing would ensure that something would come one's way. Under market conditions, even generosity and sharing may not be enough, as others too may find themselves equally deprived and living on the brink, so to say.

However, on another day they are likely blow up all their money on anything that taken their fancy, be it toys for the children or eating "*fuchka*" in the market. In the course of a Mela (fair) in the neighbourhood, I found that many children were going around playing with quite expensive toys (costing about thirty to forty rupees). One morning I found a number of little girls with no clothes but wearing a lot of imitation jewelry that they said they had got from the Mela. When inadvertently, I could not stop myself from laughing, they suddenly became conscious and ran back into their houses to put on some ragged clothes that were quite out of place with the finery they were sporting. In fact during the course of the fair I found plenty of plastic phones, guns and stuffed toys and imitation jewelry, in the hands of most of the children, all of which would be broken and thrown away in no time. Yet the Lodhas were not at all averse to taking their children, both boys and girls to the fair, feeding them all kinds of delicacies, buying them almost anything they wanted, with no thought to the future. There is absolutely no discrimination among them against the female child who are as loved and pampered as the male children. In fact they consider children their most precious resource, something that brings joy and pride to their lives.

Productivity and Labour of Lodha Women—Invisible Work?

Their semi urban neighbours, mostly upper caste Bengalis, are quick to stereotype them as lazy and good for nothing. This view is reflective both of the derogatory stereotypes held in their minds about the Lodhas, as well as the complete ignorance of the actual living conditions of these people right in their back yard. The daily routine of a middle aged Lodha woman consists of getting up at four in the morning, cooking rice and if possible some vegetables, then trekking about 7–8 kilometers to the forest, to return by about eight o'clock, carrying a huge load of firewood on their heads. They then go to the local market to sell some of the firewood for cash. They are then able to buy some vegetables and rice for the home, and return to eat a frugal meal. The women, who are located in settlements outside of the forest, prefer to walk more than five to ten kilometers a day, to collect fuel wood, some of which they use at home, and the rest they sell in the market for cash.

The upper castes who only get up by that time say "Look at these Lodha women, they are drunk in the morning and relaxing, when other people are going to work" without realizing that these women have already put in about eight hours of back breaking work and for them the day is more than half way through. Even then they are left with other tasks to perform, like getting water from the well, cleaning their houses and utensils, feeding the children and cooking the evening meal.

Women work in their kitchen gardens, weeding and tending to their vegetable patches, they work in their fields, if they have any and take care of domestic animals, like goats and calves and chicken. The goats are raised for meat and the calves are looked after till they grow up into cows and then are sold in the market. Since this is a paddy growing area, the women are also employed for transplanting the paddy saplings in the fields of landowners.

It is not that the Lodha men are idle, they too work and since they are now exposed to the market forces, most men are employed in various kinds of cash generating work. The most readily available work for them is in the railway stations, loading coal onto the wagons, a backbreaking and exhausting work in which a few women too take part, but only a very few. Some men go to the forest to collect firewood. They also do not participate in what is mostly regarded as women's work like making Sal leaf plates, a popular cottage industry. Quite a few men work as truckers, transporting bamboos and wood outside of Medinipore. But the men are not seen as being responsible for running the households which is primarily seen as a woman's work. The woman is responsible for all the work of the household ; and a woman who is middle aged with grown up children, is viewed as a pillar of her house. The following conversation that I had with a woman regarding her dead sister-in-law (brother's wife) will show us how much a woman is valued. In this household, a baby was born to a young boy and the name giving and first bath ceremony was to be held. However when we visited the household, there was no activity, one woman (the sister-in-law) came out and began to talk to me. She was lamenting the recent death of this woman, the grandmother of the child who was born. The woman who had died was the mother of three sons, the older two were married, the second son had become a new father, of the baby in question, but there was no joy in the house. The mother –in-law (now too old) is devastated by the death of her daughter-in-law of whom she was very fond of.

> "Who is there to feel happy? She was beautiful and hard working. She was a daughter-in-law of their choice, but now she is dead. She was always taking care of everything around the house. After her death everything is lying neglected. The roof is broken. There was plenty of hay from the fields to repair the roof but the men did not take care and the cows ate them. Now there is no more of it left. If she were alive, she would have repaired the roof. The paddy too is lying uncared for; she would have stored it properly, seen to everything. For the ritual today, it is customary to give a new saree to all the women who had

attended to the birth, including the midwife (from a particular caste group who come from a nearby village), But there is no one to get the sarees. The old father-in-law has gone to earn money by wage labour, the old mother-in-law is incapacitated by grief, the husband is a young boy who is trying to do as much as possible. But he is not a woman and he knows very little. He also has to do the outdoor work like getting the nai (barber) from another village. He will get some food cooked. But it is not as if the woman of the house was alive. Nothing will be done properly, just anyhow."

The most important aspect that emerged from this narrative is the status of the woman at a particular phase in her life cycle, that is when she is married and the mother of grown up children, as the most important member of this society. A woman would be around the age of thirty-five to forty, when she becomes like the central pole on which a house is built. All other members of this particular household, the two married but young sons, the two very young daughters-in-law, the old parents in law, were all rudderless without this one woman, who was a pillar of strength to them all. If the men have to do something they do it, but they are not as efficient or as responsible as women are. Thus if a man arranges for a feast or buys gifts, he will never attain the level of perfection that a woman can.

Women's Bodies: Death and Disease; Agency and Exploitation

Unfortunately, the work that we had carried on this settlement indicated through the household genealogies that quite a few women in this age category were missing. It was surprising how in many households the older women were alive, those above sixty or so, while the ones in the thirty five to forty age groups were often dead. This brings to light a very disturbing fact, that women are the worst sufferers of this disruption of their traditional life. The older women were past the age of child bearing and of doing too much hard work, moreover their youth was spent in an environment far more conducive to their own values than what existed now, as those above the age of sixty or so would have spent their childhood and youth in the forest. The younger women were still confined to the home, going out very little and therefore were still not subject to the kind of wearing away that the somewhat older women had to face when they were fully responsible for all other members of the family. In another household, when her daughter-in-law had died and her son married again, an old woman was left to look after a young girl. Untimely deaths were recorded in almost every household in the hamlet. In another household, female relatives, including married daughters had been called to thresh and clean the newly harvested grain, as the mistress of the house had died. The old mother-in-law, too weak to work, sat in one corner and complained of feeling ill and cold.

Interviews with local health care givers at the hospital and NGO workers indicated that women suffered from many diseases, most commonly, reproductive disorders, like lukeria and reproductive tract infections. According to one medical practitioner in the town, STD and Gonorrhea were common and although no AIDS tests have been conducted on these people, it was feared and anticipated that some of them may be victims of HIV infections also. It was widely reported that the Lodha women would go into the forest, in the evening with local men, especially when they were drunk, as they quite often were and would provide sexual favours for a small payment of cash or even bottles of liquor. For women pushed to the brink of survival, such practices might be the only possible means to earn a little extra money. But things cannot be explained away so simply. Most outsiders' attribute to the Lodha women and to the community in general, a lack of morals and a laxity of conduct that is a condition of their "backwardness" and of course, a "criminal past". But we have to understand two important variables to explain what is happening here. One is the traditional value system and the sexual values of these people, about which we can generalize on the basis of work done worldwide regarding forest dwellers and foragers. The other is the vulnerability of a community when they are pushed into a market economy and capitalist values with which they are not at all equipped to deal. The implications of this has been discussed with respect to Africa "African sexuality, which was formerly governed by the community and associated with the search for friendly alliances, and social means of production and reproduction, has freed itself of community social pressure only to accept that of money. Humanity's relation to itself as the first ecological dimension, has been subjected to the laws of the market place and has led countless young women into prostitution, seen as the last means of providing one's self with some form of social capability" (*Ouedraogo, 2005, 30*). With the elimination of the forests as well as the ouster of the tribes from it, they often found themselves starving, as their skills for surviving in a market economy are grossly inadequate. The following excerpt from the Indian Human Rights survey, 2007 indicates just this, "On 20 August 2006, a tribal woman identified as Anchala Pramanick died at Namopara village under Belpahari police station in West Midnapore district after going without any food for almost a week. According to the family members of the deceased, there was nothing to eat in the house and even other members of the family were surviving on water". A survey of this area had shown us, that the earlier densely forested area of Belpahari has been reduced to a desert by the subversive activities of the power holders of various descriptions in this region, leaving the original inhabitants in extreme distress.

Under such circumstances a woman may find herself forced into prostitution as the only means of getting food for her family, on a day she finds her kitchen to be empty. The brunt of poverty falls on the woman and particularly the woman in the stage of life I have already mentioned, one who is the main provider for the household. Women as subsistence providers are a value that has persisted from times immemorial. Even in the earliest known societies of hunters and gatherers, it was the food gathering activities of women that provided for most of the caloric intake of the tribe; hunting being only a supplementary activity that may have been undertaken more for ritual and prestige issues than for food (*Leacock and Lee, 1982: 3*). Thus men have always been involved in prestige enhancing practices, where there is enough differentiation to demarcate categories of men and women and men and men, but subsistence provision has always been the women's domain and therefore in times of stress and contingency it is women who have to somehow provide and therefore may resort to desperate measures.

Secondly, sexual control and monopoly on the sexuality of the wife may not be the central focus of conjugality among them. This too is often a cultural feature of those communities where "purity of blood" is not of paramount importance.

Yet women have their exclusive domains and one of the key areas controlled exclusively by women is that of child-birth. The data indicates that all births take place at home, attended to by women who belong to a caste of midwives and of course other women of family and community. Now days a doctor may be consulted or a woman may be taken to the hospital if the Dai so advises or if the situation gets out of control. But the reluctance to go to the hospital and to have a doctor attend to delivery is still very strong. The reason quite likely lies in the values attached to that view that childbirth is the exclusive area of women's agency and knowledge. The hospital, that often has male doctors, is not seen as a place conducive for childbirth and women are more likely to communicate with the female nurses than the male doctors.

The men of the community also do not think that should have anything to do with child birth. For example, a wild variety of plant with purple flowers was growing profusely in the village, however when I asked the men they said that it was only a weed and had no use. Thinking that it was very unlikely that a weed that has no use would be allowed to grow so profusely, I asked the women about it who at once told me that the leaves of the plant were used to foment the abdomen of the woman in labour to ease the delivery and that the flowers were used to ease menstrual cramps. It is also likely that the men knew what it was, but were reluctant to talk about something they considered, "feminine". Every time I observed a woman going to the hospital for pregnancy related check up etc.; it was always another woman who accompanied her. Men rarely got involved in such activities.

The resistance of women to go to the hospital for their problems is also a part of this value of dividing what is masculine from what is feminine. The hospital staffed predominantly by men, is obviously viewed as a male domain. Thus anything that has anything to do with new technology or modernity is also viewed as a male domain in almost all cultures. Thus women prefer the traditional health care practices even for childbirth. Since women have been gatherers from the very ancient times, much of herbal knowledge gathered from the forest belongs to the women. As the forests are destroyed and the indigenous dwellers pushed out, women lose their knowledge and the power that comes with it. As of now, the distrust for allopathic medicines is very strong. Few people would take the medicines even if is given to them for free. On a day when a medical team of the government hospital came visiting the village, all the children disappeared and the teacher could only catch a few wailing and screaming children for inoculation and medical check-up. Even the few medicines that were given to them were surreptitiously thrown away as "*chai pansh*" (trash). Thus, the women are caught between the non-availability or reduced availability of their own herbs and medicines and their continued distrust of "modern medicine".

Another feature that is detrimental to the health of women is because most girls are married off when they barely reach puberty, when they are around 14–16 years of age. As confirmed by the local hospital, teenage pregnancies are the rule rather than the exception, in fact this was confirmed by our observations, that showed up most first time mothers to be barely little more than children. The reason for such a practice could however be a result of their vulnerability and helplessness in the face of oppression of various kinds. I asked a young girl about sixteen years of age, who was heavily pregnant with her first child, as to why her parents got her married at such a young age, she looked at me with blank eye and replied, "I have no parents.

They died when I was very young. My brothers were even younger. My grandparents brought me up and my father's sister got me married". Further enquiry revealed that an army truck hit the father, and the mother died, as most women seem to die in this region, "just like that" of some disease. The grandparents in question were distant relatives and not directly related, but they took care of the children, as there was no one else to do so. Since sexual exploitation is a danger that looms large and also since life expectancy is very low, the only option to safeguard the girls is to get them married as early as possible, so that even if the parents are not there, especially if the mother is missing the girl does have someone to take care of her.

Thus early marriage, teenage pregnancies, lack of adequate nutrition and reluctance to adapt to modern medicines, in the absence of the indigenous medicines which used to be available earlier, all take a heavy toll of women's lives.

Conjugality: Partners in Distress

We have already mentioned that monopoly over the body of a woman, as an adjunct of conjugality, is not a core value of the Lodha society. Although a Lodha husband and wife often share a very warm relationship and recognize love to be an essential ingredient of a marital bond, sexual monopoly in the sense it is understood in conservative Hindu caste society, is not present. Men and women who are not husband and wife may share close physical proximity. For example, I once had occasion to watch a young woman massaging a middle aged man's head, in quite an intimate posture. She was sitting behind this man on a cot, putting her body weight on his back and stroking his head. The man was like her father-in-law; in fact she was his brother's daughter-in-law. The person in question was almost an invalid, t yet in no Hindu household would such physical contact be permissible under the decorum that had to be maintained between a father-in-law and daughter-in-law. In other situations, I saw men and women sitting and joking together and sharing quite intimate jokes with each other, when they may be related as affines, although such intimacy between consanguines such as brothers and sisters or mother and son was not seen. But I saw women drinking and becoming drunk, not only in front of their minor children but in front of grown up sons as well. The norms of modesty in dress too are much more liberal than among the upper caste Hindus. Grown up girls often wear knee length dresses and skirts, sarees too are worn quite high and for older women without a blouse or a petticoat. The women sit in relaxed postures, and often in not too modest body positions.

Such behaviour is to be evaluated not by upper caste standards but by the fact that Lodhas recognize equal rights of men and women in eating and drinking and even smoking. They see no reason to segregate men and women in terms of consumption and there is no such differentiation made between the boy child and the girl child too. Intimacy between husband and wife is not measured by the simple sexual relationship, but by a warm emotional bond between the couple. In this sense the Lodha husband and wife share greater warmth in emotional terms than many upper castes couples, whose intimacy is restricted due to strong joint family norms.

For example, a Lodha husband and wife often eat from the same plate after serving the elders and young ones in the family. Even a woman's sexual laxity may be viewed in this light, for love being a recognized aspect of marriage, the woman's attempts to get some money for the household may be seen in terms of "shared oppression" than a transgression of norms. The relationship of husband and wife is one of equality and sharing, as partners in everything, thus one reality of life that they are sharing is that of acute poverty and deprivation. In fact, I found husband and wife shielding each other, rather than complaining if one of them was found wanting in any respect especially by what they recognize as "outsider" (here a Bengali) standards.

One morning, while talking to a young woman with small children and a suckling baby, I discovered that she had not eaten anything since the morning. She said that she had not eaten anything because she was having fever. I was concerned about her children and the baby she was suckling and insisted that she must feed her children and also eat something herself if she wanted sufficient milk for her. To which she replied "My husband has cooked some rice in the morning before going for work and the children will eat that. He is a good cook and he cooks better than me".

However later in the day, at the time of mid-day meal in the school, where a medical team had also come for check up of the children and mothers, I found her telling a different story to the medical nurse. "I am feeding the baby so I did not want to eat *panta bhat* (stale rice soaked in water overnight) that is why I did not eat anything". I was shocked to learn that she had concocted the story about her husband having cooked rice and vegetables, as there was practically no food in the house. I suspected that what she had told the nurse too was a lie and she was probably saving the little bit of stale rice for her small children, going hungry herself. I personally made a request to the women providing the mid day meal to give this woman also some hot food along with her children, which they did. The most important fact that comes to light here is that husband and wife treat each other as a unit and not as separate entities, so a wife would cover up for her husband if she thought that by "outside" standards it would lower his prestige or that of the entire family if she admitted to having no food in the house.

The important point to be established is that the equation between the males and females is settled on a one to one basis, it may be love or hostility, caring or enmity, but there are no standards set by social values that dictate specific status for the man or the woman. It is more a relationship of one to one competition and sharing, where loving relations can turn sour, as one woman rejected by her husband told me. "My husband told me that he no longer loves me and he beat me and threw me out of the house. He does not love me because I did not have any children". However in the case of the invalid man I have mentioned, his wife came and gave him a box on the head abusing him soundly for "talking too much" and he meekly kept quiet and did not retaliate. In a third situation a woman was telling me about her passion for traveling. She says that she often went off with *michils* (rallies) organized by the party (CPI-M) and they sometimes took her to distant cities like Mumbai, Delhi, Ahmedabad etc. "I never lose a chance to travel, they give you free food and drinks and take you in a train and then in buses. You get a chance to see new places and also go to see all the gods and goddesses that live there". However when I asked her if her husband went with her, she said that he did not like travel and always stayed at home, "I do not need a husband to go anywhere. I have my own two feet and I can travel on them" was her quick retort.

The fact that women enjoy equal worth is demonstrated by the fact that the only graduate among them is a girl, and she is a teacher in a local school. She leads an independent life and is yet unmarried.

The Lodhas: Present and Future

The attempts to settle the Lodhas into some kind of a sedentary life have not been successful. They are still living uncomfortably, in poverty and in a socially marginalized existence. The high mortality rate of the women, indicates that even demographically they are not successfully adapting to life outside the forest. Their qualities, their knowledge, their capacity to do hard work and their inter-personal relations and values are neither recognized nor encouraged. A proud and independent people thus lose all meaning to their lives when made to feel inferior.

Individualism is a trait among forest dwellers that has not only been pointed out by anthropologists but also psychologists like *Barry, Bacon and*

Child (*1959*) who found that when subjected to psychological tests, the forests dwellers are more field independent, in other words when you go to the forest, you need to look after yourself and take quick decisions. Men and women live with each other often on their own terms, and there is very little that one can do that the other cannot. For example, both work equally as wage labour, say at raking up coal for the wagons that are loaded at the railway track. Again they work equally at house building and any other activity requiring physical labour. The only work exclusively done by men is that of truckers, again a work in which several men are employed, as large amounts of raw material like wood and bamboos is exported out of this region. This again points to one of the routes by which the HIV virus may have entered this population, but again there are no figures available.

The Lodhas still retain a fair degree of egalitarian values. Though there are some differences in earnings and even in possessions among them, this is not as of now, seen as a basis of social differentiation. Some persons, especially women are recognized as *daan* or witches, capable of harming others, but people keep quiet and pretend that they are not aware of this, for fear that she or he might harm them further. Despite the fear, however, there is no question of punishment or retribution, only of caution. This egalitarianism may also be viewed as a typical character of forest dwellers as a way to keep the community together against the outside enemy. In fact the only major change in value that we can see among them is that the nature of the enemy is changing, from the dangers of the forests, to the dangers of the urban invasion. While the Lodhas had knowledge to deal with the former, they increasingly find themselves ill equipped to deal with the latter. Their tutelary deities such as Baram devta, who still dwells in the forest is unable to save them from the outsiders who ravage their women, kill their children and make them mentally disabled. They would prefer to return to the safety of the forest, if they only could.

Whatever work is ostensibly being done as a welfare measure for this tribe is totally out of sync with what they would want for themselves. They are being pushed into becoming wage labourers or agricultural labourers, both of which takes them away from the knowledge that they had developed as forest dwellers and also from their beliefs and worldview. All the pride that they had in their way of life and in their myths where they are the *Sabors*, a proud people with a ancient lineage, has to do with the forest. The commercialization of the forest by planting cashew trees etc., only alienates them further as they are not allowed to touch these trees and are of not much use to them. The forest produce that they use to collect, like honey, resin and medicinal plants are hardly available any more. Had their skills and knowledge in putting the forest and its produce to judicial use, by extracting valuable resources from it been realized and developed, it would have saved both the environment and the people from being destroyed. The women are the greater sufferers, often paying with their lives and bodies in shouldering the burden of taking care of their families. Feminist ecologists like *Rocheleau and Wangari* (*1996:13*) spell out this phenomenon, "Women carry a disproportionate share of responsibilities for resource procurement and environmental maintenance, from New York city to the lower Himalayas (and limited political and economic means) to determine the future of resource availability and environmental quality"

This paper does not cover the Lodhas extensively and only a few issues have been dealt with here. The objective was to highlight the plight of a forest dwelling people forced out of the safe "womb" of the forest (*Turnbull 1982:154*). The overwhelming emotion of these people is one of fear and insecurity. Most people mentioned dark forces, "*ghurni hawa*" that comes and leaves people with mental disturbance and illness; one of the local healers, mentioned mental tension and tendency to commit suicide as one of the major afflictions in this region. They do not like to live in the houses built by the government and all the houses built under the Indira Awas Yojana, lay unoccupied and crumbling. The house built with their own hands is properly consecrated with appropriate rituals to withstand the onslaught of the dark forces, while the *pucca* houses give no such guarantee.

In the settlement several individuals were referred to as mentally disturbed, "*pagal*" or "*khapa*", significantly, more women than men fell into this category.

Whenever we discuss the relationship between men and women, it can never be done without placing this relationship in the context of a a wider network of social relationships and the environment in which the relationships are brought into practice in the first place. As already mentioned, most things in the life of this tribe have changed because of the change in environment and since not much is known of their life in the forest, we can only work with what is before us. The Lodhas were not known to be big game hunters, rather, they are skilled in catching birds and small rodents by setting traps. Even now they make beautiful bird traps to catch birds, rabbits, big rats and mongoose etc. for food. Most of this gathering from the forest, is done by both men and women and therefore, the difference in status usually associated with prestige hunting by men (hunting of big game that is regarded as culturally superior to the food collection activities of women ion some tribes), is not found among the Lodhas. In the present circumstances, however, the relationship of men and women is more of being equal partners and in the struggle to survive. Men also take on tasks as cooking and taking care of children when required.

There are no ego issues in doing any kind of work. How such a relationship could transform under other conditions is not easily predictable. In spite of all the marginalization and deprivation faced by them, they retain a joy for life and pride in their children. And lastly in spite of their notoriety as criminals, it would be surprising to note that not a single criminal case has ever been filed against the Lodha in the local police station!

REFERENCES

Etienne, Mona and Eleanor Leacock (Ed), 1980, Women and Colonization: Anthropological Perspectives, Praeger, A J.F. Bergin Publishers Book.

Barry, H, Bacon, M.K., Child, I.L., 1959, 'Relation of Child training to Subsistence economy', *American Anthropologist*, 61(I), pp. 51–63.

Channa, Subhadra Mitra 1992 "Changing Gender relations of an urban occupationary caste" In the *Eastern Anthropologist*, Vol. 45, No. 4, pp. 321–340.

Channa, Subhadra Mitra, 2001, "The Right to Selfhood: The paradox of being a dalit woman", *Social Action*, Vol. 51, No. 4, pp. 337–351.

The Lodhas, now numbering around 8000, were the original inhabitants of the forests in and around West Bengal and were designated as one of the 'criminal' tribes in 1916, under government notification, No.7022–23 dated 20th May 1916, Calcutta, a colonial prefix for all those who did not conform to the western notions of civilized or those who proved uncontrollable by centralized rule.

A crime register of Lodhas was opened on the 8th September 1916. This Act was revoked in 1952 and the Lodhas as a tribe were labeled as –ex-criminal thus retaining the colonial stigma and the attitude that went with it.

Channa, Subhadra Mitra 2005 "Metaphors of Race and Caste based discriminations against Dalits and Dalit women in India" In Resisting Racism and Xenophobia: Global Persperctives on race, Gender and Human rights, U.S.A., Altamira Pub. pp. 49–67.

Fourcade, Marie, 2003, "The so-called 'Criminal tribes' of British India: Colonial Violence and traditional Violence" In Violence/Non-Violence: Some Hindu Perspectives, Manohar, Centre De Sciences Humaines.

Guha, Ramachandra and Martinez-Alier, 1998, Varieties of Environmetalism, Delhi, Oxford University Press.

Godelier, Maurice, 1982, The Making of Great Men, Cambridge, Cambridge University Press.

Lee, Richard and Devore, Irven (eds), 1968, Man the Hunter, Chicago, Aldine.

Leacock, Eleanor and Lee, Richard, 1982, "Introduction" in Politics and history in band Societies, Cambridge, Cambridge University Press, pp. 1–21.

Mies, Maria, 1988, "Introduction" In Women the Last Colony, (ed) Maria Mies, London, Zed Books, pp. 3–10.

Rocheleau, Dianne, Barbara Thomas-Slater and Esther Wangari (eds), 1996, Feminist Political Ecology: Global issues and Local Experiences, Londona nd New York, Routledge.

Shoshtak, Marjorie, 1981, Nisa: The life and words of a !Kung woman, Harvard, Harvard University Press.

Turnbull, Colin, 1982, "The ritualization of potential conflict between the sexes among the Mbuti" in Politics and history in Band Societies (ed) Eleanor Leacock and Richard Lee, pp. 133–156.

Ouedraogo, Jean-Bernard, 2005, "Africa: human nature as historical process" in Nature, Vistaar Publications, pp. 1–37.

Migration as Means of Livelihood for the Tribals of Jharkhand

Harishwar Dayal

"Livelihood" refers to the means of gaining a living. While some of these means are available by the government or social agencies most of them are procured privately. A privately secured livelihood depends on a source of income, which in turn depends on possession of tangible and intangible assets, livelihood capabilities and on availability of employment with justified remuneration and social security provisions.

Some of the social groups in our country suffer from a deficient livelihood condition. Scheduled Tribes, one of the most marginalised sections of the country, is the most prominent among them. Most of them have neither sufficient income nor access to the government provided facilities to manage their living. They suffer from chronic mass poverty. The incidence of poverty among them is not only very high, but has also reduced very insignificantly, in comparison to other social groups. The incidence of poverty among this section is even higher than the Schedule Castes, who are also among the most deprived groups. The gap between the incidence of poverty among the tribals and other social groups including the Schedule Castes has widened over the years (*Karan, Antony and Dayal, 2005*).

There is inter-state variation in the incidence of poverty amongst the tribals too. It is extremely high (around 50 per cent) in Jharkhand, as a result of which managing a livelihood is very difficult for them in this state, and becomes even worse during the lean season, when there is not enough for them to sustain themselves from their local economy or from the forest. In order to manage their living they have to migrate-seasonally, temporarily or permanently; individually, in a group with fellow villagers or with the whole family. It has been well documented that the poor diversify their means of livelihood, in order to earn their living, reduce the risk of livelihood uncertainties and manage seasonal scarcity. Migration is one of such measure of diversification of their livelihood. This paper tries to explore the different dimensions of migration among the tribals of Jharkhand. It makes an attempt to estimate the extent of migration among the tribals of this area, the methods of doing so, the extent of livelihood support provided by it, the problems they face and how these problems can be addressed so as to improve their condition.

This paper is based on both secondary and primary information. It is based on survey of literature, related to migration from this area as well as from a survey of 16 villages of this state done by us (*Dayal and Karan, 2001*). The villages were selected randomly from the four districts of Jharkhand namely Gumla, Palamau Dumka and Ranchi. Both quantitative (pre-determined schedule) and qualitative (case study and focus group discussion) methods were used to collect relevant information. For the survey, one fourth of the households were selected randomly from each of the villages. Both tribals and non-tribals were selected. The non-tribals were selected in order to make a comparison among the two groups of migrants. All together 1,039 households were selected in the sample, out of which 336 were tribals constituting 32.34 per cent of the sample, which is almost equal to the proportion of tribal population in the total rural population of the state.

History of Migration from Jharkhand

Migration from Jharkhand is not a new phenomenon. A large part of its population has experienced survival problems from time immemorial. While some of them experienced livelihood deficiency only in lean season or during draught, others faced it throughout the year. So evidence of both seasonal and permanent migration has been found in this region. There is evidence of regular seasonal migration of tribal labourers called Dhangars from this region during the winter months, to various districts in Bengal as early as 1827. (*Mohapatra, 1985*). They were found to be employed in the early indigo factories, in the winter harvesting of the rice crops in Bengal and in the conservancy works in Calcutta (*Hunter, 1886*). Some of the tribals from this region also migrated to plantation colonies of Mauritius, West Indies, Natals and Fiji as indentured labour. Of the total North Indian male migrants to Mauritius in 1842–44, 5.8 per cent were Munda and 1.1 per cent were Oraon and of the female migrants, 9.9 per cent were Munda and 6.3 per cent were Oraon from this region who had mainly migrated from the Ranchi and Hazaribag districts; 6.0 per cent of the males and 15.8 per cent of the females migrated from Ranchi district and 4.7 per cent of the males and 3.0 per cent of the females from Hazaribag district (*Brennan, McDonald and Shlomowitz, 1998*). Very few tribals of this region however, preferred to migrate to the plantation colonies after 1850. By late 1850s the labourers from the tribal groups of Chota Nagpur were replaced by members of higher castes from the plains of south Bihar and north east districts of United Province (*Brennan, 1998*).

In the second half of the 19th century not only did the volume of emigration from this region increase on a massive scale, but their destination also changed. Emigration was now more towards the tea plantations of Assam and Dooars and after 1900, with the opening of coal mines in Jharia and Hazaribag, to the coalfields. The labour migration to Assam took place through the indentured system and was governed by various labour Emigration Acts. The labour migration to the tea gardens was of a permanent type. Usually the whole family migrated. Both husband and wife worked in the tea garden and in course of time were joined by their children. In contrast the migration to the coalfields was highly seasonal. Here, the labourers returned in time for transplanting and harvesting of the paddy crop. In July and August when it was transplanting season and in November when it was time for harvesting the crop, the mines were short of hands. This proved to be one of the reasons why a large number of non-native labourers from Gaya, Monghyr, Saran, Patna etc., districts of Bihar and Allahabad, Unnao, Pratapagarh, Balia of United province came to be recruited to the coal fields.

There was regional and ethnic variations in the migration from this region. The larger tribal groups like Munda, Oraon, Kharia, Bhumij and Ho mainly went to the tea plantations of Assam, while the "semi aboriginals" like Ghasis, Kurdmis, Goraits etc., migrated to the coalfields of Jharia, Ranigunj and Hazaribag and the mica mines of Hazaribag. Only the **Santhals** of Hazaribag and Manbhum and some of the smaller tribes were found in both coalfields and tea gardens. The regional and ethnic variations in migration were basically due to the ignorance of the avenues of employment s as also about the wages and condition of work at the coalfields and abhorrence on the part of the tribals of this area for working underground in the mines. The choice of the employer also determined the destination of the migration. The owners of the coal mines had a low opinion about the labourers from Chotanagpur. They found them irregular and non-dependable. On the other hand, the employers at tea plantation preferred the tribal labourers from this region and found these aboriginal coolies to be diligent, docile and better equipped than the other workers to survive in the malaria prone climate of Assam.

This difference in the attitude of the tribal labourers employed in these two places and the perception of these two categories of employers, were basically because of the difference in their work processes (*Mohapatra, 1985*). While the work at tea gardens was highly supervised, the work in the coalfields was dependent on the will of the workers. The workers in the coalfields were paid on piece meal basis and the aboriginal migrants of this region worked only to the extent required to meet their survival needs.

The tribal migrants working in the tea gardens now face several types of problems, as the tea industry has stagnated and employment opportunities have dwindled. The children of the migrant workers are also finding it difficult to get jobs. These migrants are not recognised as scheduled tribes in Assam and therefore do not get the advantage of facilities meant for the tribals. They are considered outsiders by the natives and suffer from their hatred, humiliation and assault.

The Present Stream of Tribal Migration

Since mass poverty, low wage and absence of perennial source of employment within the village or in the neighbourhood is still a reality, a large number of tribals of this region continue to migrate every year. The selection of the place to migrate to and the occupation taken up there depends on a large number of factors. These factors are related to several things like the characteristics of the migrant workers, of their family, village and locality, their knowledge of and familiarity with the chosen destination and the occupation at the destination, the duration for which they migrate and the arrangement/facilitating factors of migration. The old migrants, labour contractors, agents or the placement agencies facilitate migration from this region and to a large extent the kind of occupation these migrants take up, depends on the people who facilitate their migration. They entice the prospective migrants, provide them information about destination and the job, in some cases provide them with advance payment and make arrangement for the migration. At present there are three main streams of tribal migration from this region—to the brick kilns or rice mills of neighbouring states, to the agriculturally prosperous areas of Bihar, Bengal, UP or Punjab, mainly for sowing/transplanting and harvesting of paddy and wheat; and to the metropolitan towns and cities as domestic servants and maid servants. While the first two streams of migration are temporary and seasonal in nature, the third one is permanent or semi permanent.

Migrations for agricultural operations are usually for a very short period ranging from one and half months to three months to a year, usually in more than one stretch. Since most of the agricultural operations are done by women, the workers usually migrate with the whole family. The workers, who are either not willing or not capable of migrating for long period for one reason or the other, prefer this type of migration. It helps them to manage their engagements/ commitments at home, like cultivating their own land or taking care of elderly members of the family, and also get some additional income and crop share from this type of migration, to meet at least a part of their survival needs. Therefore a large number of workers migrate to harvest winter paddy, but very few go to harvest wheat. This is because wheat harvesting season coincides with the season of Mahua collection, which provides them with livelihood support locally. On the flip side, the high frequency of their visits to the destination leads to the workers developing strong bonds and acquaintances with their employers at the destination. For some, such acquaintances are a few generation old, due to which they feel safe and secure at their destination.

The migrations to brick kilns are for a slightly longer duration. Workers migrate for six to nine months. They are paid on a piece meal basis which is the reason many of them migrate with their whole family. However, there are instances of individual male and female migrations also. Usually migrations to brick kilns are arranged through labour contractors, locally known as *sardars* and *sardarnis*. They provide the labourers with advance payments and make arrangement for their transportation. The workers leave just after the harvest of the winter paddy and return before the onset of monsoon. They are mostly entrusted with the job of carrying bricks, the females carry the unbaked bricks and the males baked ones. Some of the workers are engaged in making and baking of bricks also. They live in make shift houses near the sites, where basic amenities are usually absent. Brick kilns secure additional employment and income for the migrants during a period when there are no means of livelihood in or near their village and thus helps them in their struggle for survival. One of the female respondents in a village of Gumla district told us that they are alive only because of the brick kilns in the neighbouring states. However, the migrants on return, often recount stories of under payment by the accountant or the owner, bondage of the workers, loot of their income during return and sexual harassment/ exploitation of the female workers by the owners, or the accountants or contractors of the brick kilns or by local goons.

The tribals of this region mostly considered hard working, honest and docile, are in great demand as domestic help in cities and towns. A higher wage in the metropolitan cities as opposed to what is prevalent within Jharkhand, attracts a large number of tribals to these areas, to work as domestic helps. Delhi is their most preferred destination. The areas in and around Delhi being generally prosperous, local workers have several opportunities to work. This is not the case with Mumbai, Calcutta and other metropolises where locals work as domestic help. In Delhi, however, it is the migrant workers who are employed as domestic helps, a large proportion of whom are the tribals from Jharkhand. The presence of a large number of placement agencies with their agents in Jharkhand is also responsible for the recruitment of a large number of tribal domestic help to Delhi. It is mostly children and teenagers (less than 20 years of age) and females who are employed in this kind of work.

A study conducted on the status of the workers migrating from this area to work as domestic help (*Mishra, 2005*), found out that while around 77 per cent of them were tribals, 67 per cent were of less than twenty years of age and 70 per cent were females. Around 44 per cent were found to have migrated to Delhi. They mostly migrate with people with whom they are familiar. Only 12 per cent were found to have migrated with unknown people, the rest went along with friends, relatives or fellow villagers. Around 59 per cent were paid less than Rs 1000 around 38 per cent between Rs 1000 to 2000 and around 2 per cent more than Rs 2000. Though most of the workers maintain contact with their family, some fail to do so. Around 49 per cent of the workers rarely get opportunities to talk to their family members through phone and around 10 per cent have not visited their home for a very long period of time.

Working as a domestic help has no doubt improved their economic status and enabled them to enjoy some of the facilities like a clean toilet, delicious food, watching TV and films, but it also makes them vulnerable to the excesses of their masters. Unlike the type of migration in which they live in the company of fellow workers, working as domestic help deprives them of the support of fellow workers. The incidents of being subject to harsh scolding, beating, allegations of theft and even sexual harassment, are not rare.

The Extent of Seasonal Migration among the Tribals of Jharkhand

Jharkhand is by and large a mono cropped area, where the tribals do not have an assured source of livelihood after the Kharif crop. In the lean season they depend on the forest, common property resources, and seasonal migration. As discussed earlier, the tribals of this region have been migrating in the lean season for a considerably long period of time and the incidence of high seasonal migration from this area had been reported as early as in early 19th century. A large number of tribal labourers from this area used to seasonally migrate to the Bengal Districts in the winter months of the early nineteenth century. High seasonal migration has continued and in fact has probably increased in recent years.

Our survey (*Dayal and Karan, 2001*) revealed that at least one of the members of around two fifths of the tribal households migrate for a period ranging from one and half months to nine months in a year. The incidence of seasonal migration in other category of households, on the other hand, is as low as one fifth of such households, which besides the upper castes includes the Muslims as well.

Seasonal Migration is usually considered male-centric. But in Jharkand there is seasonal migration of a large number of females as well. Around one fourth of the households reported seasonal migration of its female family members, some of them accompanying the male members, while others travelling independently, along with other male and female fellow villagers. As opposed to this, there is no similar seasonal migration of females from the other social categories. The incidence of such migration of females among the tribals is very high with more than one third of the tribal households reporting female migration and around one fourth, independent female migration. Both the male and female labourers migrate to brick kilns, agricultural fields, rice mills and for construction activities.

Table 1: Incidence of Seasonal Migration

Social Categories	Households with at least one member migrating	Household with at least one female member migrating	Household with independent female migration
ST	39.58	34.52	24.40
SC	40.10	34.01	11.68
OBC	29.15	21.61	4.02
Others	21.30	0.00	0.00
Total	33.78	25.89	11.65

Enquiry from the tribal respondents revealed that both the incidence and duration of seasonal migration has increased among them. Deterioration in their economic condition because of the increase in their population and consequent reduction in the per capita availability of their private and common property resources, land alienation, deforestation, change in composition of forest and decline in access to forest (caused both by forest department and the ultra left organizations) is mainly responsible for it. The improvement in the condition of the migrating families has also enticed some of them to migrate. The local labour contractors have also succeeded in persuading a large number of tribal families to shed their hesitation for migration. The employers usually recruit local persons as agents because they are familiar with the area and prospective migrants. Many old, experienced migrants start acting as agents and sub-agent.

The Impact of Seasonal Migration on the Livelihood of the Tribals

Migration has improved the livelihood status and opportunities of both the migrants and those who stay behind. It has improved their income, their wage rates, skills and education opportunities Though they experience a large number of hardships, inconveniences and insecurities both at destination and during their journey, and narrate some heart-rending experiences, on the whole, most of them say that migration has improved their living conditions.

Tribal Perception of Income, Employment and Wages

Income: More than half of the tribal households of Jharkhand are cultivators with mostly small holdings (More than 80 per cent of the households have less than five acres of land), on which they usually grow only one crop a year, that too with very low productivity. The wage rate is also very low in the villages. Migration, therefore is a kind of survival mechanism for them, particularly during the lean agricultural period. Around 98 per cent of the migrants reported improvement in their income because of migration (table 2). There is very little inter-district variation in the perception of the people in this regard.

Table 2: Perception of the Tribal Migrant Regarding Increase in their Income

Districts	Percentage of migrants reporting increase in income	Percentage of migrants reporting no change in income	Total
Gumla	97.3	2.7	100.0
Palamau	98.4	1.6	100.0
Dumka	98.0	2.0	100.0
Ranchi	97.6	2.4	100.0
Total	97.9	2.1	100.0

The average annual income of tribal households is, significantly higher among migrating households in comparison to that of the non-migrating households. Though the degree of difference in the income of the two categories of households depends on a large number of factors, most of the respondents attributed it to migration.

The average annual income of a migrating household is around 120 per cent higher than that of non-migrating households. It however varies from class to class. There seems to be a high positive correlation between the difference in average annual income of the migrating and non-migrating households and the economic status of the tribals. The percentage difference between the average annual income of migrating and non-migrating households increases with increase in the size of their land holding. While the average annual income of land-less migrating households is around 70 per cent higher than that of the non-migrating households of the same category, it is around 260 per cent higher for those migrating households owning 5 to 10 acres of land.

Table 3: Average Household Income of the Tribals from Seasonal Migrating

	Average annual income (Rs)		% difference
	Migrating hh*	Non-migrating hh**	
Land size (in acres)			
Nil	25125	14832	69.40
upto 1	27281	13962	95.40
1 to 3	36877	15293	141.14
3 to 5	49818	17756	180.58
5 to 10	78022	21721	259.21
Occupation of Household			
Cultivators	30255	15958	89.59
Ag. Labour	20710	9338	121.79
Non ag. Labour	23251	13190	76.28
Priv. service	42980	26300	63.42
Govt. service	91105	48060	89.57
Petty business	42122	17043	147.14
Other occupation	26180	16235	61.26
Total	35790	16335	119.10

* Households with at least one family members migrating;
** households with no family member migrating.

The difference in the average annual income of the migrant and non-migrant households is due to two reasons. Those who have a better economic status in the village usually migrate for better options than those who have an inferior economic status. They usually enjoy better relations with the agents assisting in migration and/or with the people/employers at the destination, and also have the capacity to migrate to far off places. A large number of them migrate for long periods and receive higher income. Secondly, because of their better economic condition, they invest a large part of their income from migration for productive purposes. Some of them invest it in their land and thus succeed in improving its productivity and increasing their income.

Improvement in Wage Rate in the Village

Wage rate in the villages of Jharkhand has been very low. Many of the agricultural operations are carried out on an exchange basis (*madaiti labour*) where the labourers are given only customary food and drink (*Sharan and Dayal, 1994*). Migration has changed the situation to a large extent. It has taught the migrants as well as the villagers the utility of money and has increased their expectations. When the tribals in the village realise that for the same work they are paid high wages at other places, they ask for a hike in wages. This, together with a shortage of labour in the village has forced the employers to to increase their wages in the village. The income earned through migration has increased their staying power and thus has improved their bargaining power. Table 4 reveals that 85.7 per cent of the migrants feel that increase in wages is the impact of migration. In Palamau around 93 per cent of the migrants and in the other two districts around 80 per cent of them feel that migration has resulted in increase in the wage in the village.

Table 4: Perception of the Migrants about Improvements in Wage, Skill and the Benefits of Migration

(Figures in percentage)

	Gumla	Palamau	Dumka	Ranchi
Increase in wage rate within the village	79.4	93.1	81.3	85.7
Acquisition of Skill by the Migrants	14.3	27.5	24.1	22.5
Is Migration beneficial	97.2	98.3	100.0	98.6

More than ninety per cent of the migrants, who feel that the wage rate in the village has increased because of migration, said that in the last five years it has increased up to fifty per cent only (Table 5). Around 20 per cent of them feel that it has increased only marginally, up to 10 per cent. A very small number 1.7 per cent of them feel that it has more than doubled in the last five years. Around 45 per cent of them feel that it has increased between 25 to 50 per cent. The variation in perception is because earlier the wage situation was not uniform for everybody in the village, but migration has made it uniform. Since they do not have a uniform base for comparison, they have variations in perception regarding the increase in wage rate in the last five years.

Table 5: Perception of those Migrants, Who feel that Wage has increased because of Migration about Percentage Increase in Wage in Last Five Years

(Figures in percentage)

Increase in Wage in Last Five years	Gumla	Palamau	Dumka	Ranchi	Total
Up to 10%	17.9	22.2	16.2	15.19	19.3
10 to 25%	32.1	29.6	18.9	22.78	26.9
25 to 50%	42.9	42.6	51.4	36.71	45.4
50 to 75%	3.6	3.7	10.8	10.13	5.9
75 to 100%	0.0	1.9	0.0	3.80	0.8
More than 100%	3.6	0.0	2.7	11.39	1.7

Improvement in Skill, Education and Learning

Migration motivates the migrants to acquire skills on the one hand and provides them opportunities for acquisition of skills on the other. When the migrants realise that skilled workers get a higher wage and stand a better chance of getting employment, they are motivated to acquire similar skills. In the brick-kilns, those who make the bricks are more in demand and get a higher wage than those who merely carry them. So, many of the migrants, who used to migrate for carrying bricks, gradually learnt the skill of making it and could thus increase their income. Similarly some of the migrants learnt skills necessary to work as a mason, a cook, a driver, a welder, a fitter or a factory worker, thus improving their chances of getting employment as well as higher earnings from migration. Around a fourth of the migrants from Dumka and Palamau have acquired skills because of migration. A smaller number of migrants from Gumla also reported to have acquired skills because of migration.

Migration Causing Improvement in Skill

Dukhan Singh, a young man of Chero tribe of Ghutwa village of Latehar had migrated to Deoghr for the first time in the year 1996. There he worked as construction labourer at Rs 40 a day. He started learning the masonry and in two years, became a skilled construction worker. He improved his earnings to Rs 140 to 160 a day by 2001. He has taught this skill to five more youths of his village who also migrated to different towns for this work.

Similarly Mangal Deo Oraon of Udaipura village of Latehar had migrated to Jamshedpur to become a daily wage-worker in Telco. He struck up a friendship with a truck driver and learnt driving. Now he has migrated to Patna and works as driver in Patna Municipal Corporation.

The tribal people who migrate to agriculturally prosperous areas have learnt better methods of cultivation, which they apply in their village to get better yield yeild than what they used to get earlier. Many of the residents of Baherkalan village (Chainpur village, Palamau district) migrate to Rohtas and Bhojpur for the sowing and harvesting of paddy and wheat. Some of them have started applying the new methods of cultivation they have learnet from there in their own agricultural fields. They use new variety seeds and more fertilizers and have increased their production because of it. Some of them have started growing a second crop also.

Migration has motivated the people of this state to educate their children as well. They realised the importance of education only when they ventured out from the village. "What is the use of education if one has to live and work in the village? We never faced any problem because of our illiteracy as long as we were confined in the village", said the villagers of Indravani village during Focus Group Discussion conducted among the seasonal migrants of the village. "But when we started going out for work, we realised the limitation of being illiterate. We cannot read the name of the place written on the bus stand and railway stations. We have to depend on the others for it. The employers and their managers also cheat us. Knowing that we are illiterate, they sometimes manipulate the record of our work and payment. That is why now we have become serious about the education of our children". Migration, by improving their economic condition, has made them capable of giving their children a proper education. Some of the migrants have started sending their children to tuition centres/ private schools also. The seasonal migrants of Baherakalan village told us that unlike their parents, they have become highly conscious about the need for educating their children. Some of them send their children to the private school located in the neighbouring Salhatua village.

In some cases though, migration has had some adverse impact on the education of the children of the migrants. When the seasonal migrants take their children along with them, their education gets disrupted and a long spell of absence from school de-motivates the children from studies. During a school survey, a teacher told us that during the migration season the attendance in the school drops drastically as some of the children migrate along with their parents, even those who remain in the village become irregular in absence of their guardian. On their return to school after the migration season, they fail to remember whatever they had learnt earlier and therefore do not take interest in studies.

Summing up

Seasonal migration is thus, a livelihood strategy for the tribals of Jharkhand during the agriculturally lean season. It has wide-ranging consequences on both the migrants and those who stay behind. It has caused increase in income of the migrants; the wage rate in the village has also increased because of it, which has benefited all. As a result of the income from migration, a large number of migrants have experienced an improvement in their economic condition. Migration has motivated the migrants to acquire skills and educate their children. They have learnt better methods of cultivation too because of migration. There are some adverse impacts of migration as well. The migrants are vulnerable at both the places they migrate to as well as during the journey back and forth. Therefore they usually migrate in groups, with the assistance of familiar labour contractors to known destinations and employers. They, however, require additional support from the government or the NGOs in the whole process of migration.

REFERENCES

Brennan Lance (1998): 'Across the Kala Pani: An Introduction', *South Asia*, Vol. XXI, Special Issue.

Brennan Lance, John Mc Donald and Ralph Shlomowitz (1998): 'The Geoghraphic and Social Origins of Indian Indentured Labourers in Mauritius, Natals, Fizi, Guyana and Jamaica', *South Asia*, Vol. XXI, Special Issue.

Dayal, Harishwar and Anup Karan (2001): Labour Migration from Jharkhand Institute for Human Development, New Delhi (mimeo).

Hunter, W.W. (1886): Annals of Rural Bengal, London.

Lister, E. (1917): District Gazetter of Hazaribag, Patna.

Karan, Anup, Piush Antony, and Harishwar Dayal, (2005): 'Poverty and Deprivation among the Scheduled Tribes in India.' In R. Radha Krishna and Shovan Ray Edited Handbook of Poverty in India, Oxford University Press, New Delhi.

Mishra, Sanjay Kumar (2005): A Study on present status of Migrated Domestic Workers from Jharkhand, ATSEC Jharkhand Chapter.

Mohapatra, P.P. (1985): 'Coolies and Colliers: A Study of Labour Migration from Chotanagpur, 1880–1920.' Studies in History, Sage Publications January 1885, Vol. I.

Sharan, Ramesh and Harishwar Dayal, (1994): 'Discrimination against Female Farm Labourers in the Jharkhand Region of Bihar', *The Indian Journal of Laboure Economics*, Vol. 37, No. 4.

Forest Degradation and its Impact on Livelihood:

A Study of a Tribal Village of Chhattisgarh

R.P. Mitra

The recent notification of the act recognizing forest land rights and other forest based livelihood rights of the Scheduled Tribes and other traditional forest dwellers, for the first time, attempts to address the issue of forest and sustainable development in conjunction with the rights of the forest based communities. The close associations between tribes and forest and decline in the quality of forest cover in India have raised number of issues pertaining to relationship between them. One of the synonyms for tribal communities in India is *Girijans* or forest dwellers, underlying the intimate nature of relationship which exist between them and their forest habitat. According to an estimate nearly two-third of tribal communities are forest based and are dependent upon them and there is clear overlap between the forest map of India and tribal map of India (*Prabhu 2001: 48*). They have been living in these forests for generations and are dependent upon them for their lives and livelihoods. The decline in the quality of forest cover in India in recent times and dependency of Tribal communities on them has put a question mark over the relationship between them.

According to Forest survey of India, 2001 the actual forest cover of the country is only 20.55 per cent of its total geographical area as against the recorded forest area of 23.58 per cent of the total geographical area. In terms of the quality of the forest cover, only 59 per cent of the actual forest cover of the country is in the form of dense forests. The rest of the forest cover consists of open forests and mangroves. Most of these dense forests are located in districts where substantial proportion of population constitute of communities who are scheduled as tribe. (*Kothari and Wani 1997:6*). These forests have been their homes for generations together. However, in recent years they have been displaced and forced to migrate in the name of conservation and development. The bill tries to address this issue by recognizing tribal claims to forest lands and by allowing certain forest rights to the communities. There are two views regarding the forest tribe relationship exclusionists and integrationists:

Exclusionists: On one extreme, are those conservationists, who advocate that certain species of animals (such as the tiger) cannot co-exist with humans, and there is a need to reserve at least some parts of forests to conserve these species. They also say that increased human habitation in forests will cause depletion of forest cover, resulting in significant ecological costs. Therefore forest and tribe need to be separated

Integrationists: In their approach tribal communities have lived in forests for centuries they have a relationship of reciprocity with the forest. This relationship of reciprocity is built in their institutional structure and giving them land right will be an aid to check ecological degradation of the forest. They cite the failure of the state in checking poaching and forest degradation. The myth of noble state has been exposed in limited success in protection areas devoid of human communities.

There is a third element in the equation of forest and tribe in context of India. This third element is the crippling poverty which exists among these forest dwelling communities. The scheduled tribes as such in India are the most marginalized section in terms of development indicators (*Maharatna, 2005:22*). Nearly half of them live under the official poverty line and of these many live within or near forest and are dependent upon them for their livelihood needs (*Guha, 2007:3305*).

For a very long time forest policy of government of India was oriented towards commercial exploitation of the forest or conservation at the expense of needs of local forest based communities. For example the first National forest policy Resolution 1952 clearly stated that the forest are the national property and not merely for the use of the local people. Production of industrial timber was given preference over needs of local people. In fact the needs of local people like fodder, fuel, food and forest produce was viewed as destructive practices which harm the forest. This policy continued till the 1980's for example the report of the National commission on Agricultural Forestry, 1976 clearly states that:

> "Free supply of forest produce to the rural population and their rights and privileges have brought destruction to the forest. The rural people have not contributed much towards the maintenance and regeneration of the forests. Having overexploited the forest they cannot in all fairness expect that somebody else will take the trouble of providing them with forest produce free of charge." (*GoI, 1976*).

During this time one can see a steady decline in the forest cover of India. At the time of independence the forest cover in India was 72 million hectares. Rampant deforestation that followed in the next three decade plummet the forest cover to 34 million hectares only (*Aggarwal, 1982:33*). A decline of 12 per cent of tree cover, forced the government to come out with series of measures directed towards conservation of forest and wild life.

Till the present Scheduled Tribe recognition of Forest Rights Bill, the issue was mainly seen either in terms of concern for the livelihoods of the people or protection of forest and wildlife. Policies and legislation passed since the seventies have harmed the interest of both the forest and the tribes. They turned what once was a give and take sustainable relationship into an exploitative and unsustainable relationship. Tribal communities who were culturally, spiritually and economically dependent upon it for centuries, suddenly found themselves alienated from lands and resources that are central to their survival. Since eighties there has been a realization that only through a participative approach and with the aid of local communities forest could be managed successfully. The current bill has tried to redress the problem by giving land right to all the forest dwelling communities. However, the move has generated a deep concern in the minds of conservationists who see this bill as an end of hope for the wild life in India. The focus on the forest tribe i.e., the tribal communities staying within the forest, has left in the lurch the relationship between forest and the fringe forest communities i.e. those who are not per see, living within the forest but are dependent on the forest substantially for their livelihood. These fringe forest communities find themselves in precarious situation with restriction imposed on collecting forest produce on the one hand and a underdeveloped agricultural economy on the other. This is further compounded by the external pressure to join the market economy and a rapid increase in population. All these have made it very difficult for them to retain subsistence pattern of resource use. Due to the spatial overlap between tribes and forest and decline in the quality of forest cover in India in some quarters it is suggested we should follow a policy of conservation of forest and wild life by barring the Tribal communities and their exclusion from their traditional homeland. Questions are being raised regarding sustainability of their present level of consumption in the alarming environmental situation, they find themselves in? Is the new market economy and the changing demands and aspirations of tribal communities have turned what was once a sustainable and symbiotic relationship into an unsustainable and exploitative relationship further strained the relationship between them. Is the creation of exclusive forest reserves with only wild life and no human interference the only solution possible? If so what will happen to the livelihood and existence of the tribes, already the most vulnerable community of India. The present paper is an analysis of narratives of forest degradation from one such fringe forest tribal villages of Chhattisgarh and its consequences on people's livelihood. The fieldwork for this study was conducted during in 2006–07 along with a batch 40 post-graduate and under graduate students from the Department of Anthropology, University of Delhi.

Description of the Village

The village was called Sarnatoli, named so because of abundance of tress in the area once upon a time. People believed that they have the oldest *sarna sthal*, or the sacred groove of the area, therefore the village has acquired the name Saran toli. It is located in the tribal district of Jashpur. Geographically the district is divided in two parts: the hilly belt on the northern side running from Narayanpur, Bagicha up to the Surguja district. This belt with a reserve forest, covers the Sanna, Bagicha and Narayanpur block. This part is also called upper ghat or the upland area. And the remaining southern part is called lowland or the nichoghat. The studied village is the part of the northern upland region. There are 103 households in the village, mostly belonging to Oraons with a few belonging to Nagesias. The total population of the village is around six hundred.

Sarna Toli is situated on the outskirts of Jashpurnagar, the district headquarter. The village is like a gateway to the forested region of the area. These forests were home to "primitive tribes" like the Nagesias and the Korwas. The Oraons practiced small scale agriculture of subsistence type. This is the main source of their livelihood. The agricultural productivity is low and the yield uncertain. Agricultural backwardness is primarily because of lack of any irrigation facilities and the low level of technology used for cultivation. Coupled with the growing population pressure, food security has emerged as a major livelihood issue for the people. They grow variety of paddy, maize and some families in the village have also taken to growing vegetables like chilly, tomato, and cauliflower near their homes. Agriculture is practiced without addition of any chemical fertilizer and mechanical help like tractors. Because of low productivity, the agriculture cannot fully support the livelihood requirements. Agriculture can provide household food security for only 6 to 8 months in a year and for the rest of time they have to dependent upon alternate livelihood sources to sustain themselves. They do so by working as wage labourers in the nearby town, or by keeping livestock like pig, goat, cow and hen and through relying on forest for their livelihood.

Forest and the Oraons

Any tribal culture revolves around three things Land, water and forest. Conservation of natural resources or their sustainable use has often been regarded as characteristics of tribal communities. There is a self-imposed restriction on resource use and their lifestyle is devoid of wasteful expenditure of the environment. Their relationship to the nature is described as biocentric, and priority is given to nature. Human beings perceive themselves as one of the elements of the nature, which they share with other animal, spirits and plant species. As against this, is the, anthropocentric perspective of the civilization, which is based on subordination of nature to culture. Nature is seen and contrasted with culture. Nature is characterized as wild, to be domesticated through culture. This identification with nature and living in complete harmony may not be exactly true for all the tribal communities in contemporary times. Tribes are many with great degree of ecological variability giving rise to different types of ecological adaptation. Population pressure, new lifestyles and the need for more food, energy and water have put lot of pressure on the resources and at times leading to degradation of the nature. Broadly we can classify the relationship between forest and tribes in three categories:

(a) There are tribes, to borrow a Roy Burman's phrase, who live in "oneness with nature and have a lifestyle in harmony with the nature" (Roy Burman, 1992:4). Only few tribes like the Onges, Cholanaiken and Palliyans will fall under this category.
(b) Then there are tribes who live in the small scattered settlements located within reserve or protected forest and are under transition from pure forest dependence to a mixed / agriculture/wage labour system due to resettlement and declining forest productivity.
(c) The third type of relationship is where tribes have mixed livelihood

system with a higher reliance on agriculture. Forest is mainly for seasonal subsistence and additional needs of livelihood. They have lesser access to forest as compared to the, two other categories.

Forest–Oraon Relationship

The Oraons relationship with the forest can be included in the third category. The local term for forest is *torang*. The *torang* surrounding the village was of open access nature, where generally cattle is grazed and minor forest produce is collected. Beyond the commons is the protected forest, with restricted access which is under the control of forest department directly. The Oraons are allowed only limited access to these forests. For example each household is allowed to collect maximum of 8 bamboo poles every three years for construction and house repair activities from this restricted forest. They also collect timber for making household furniture and agricultural implements. The protected forest is known as *bel* forest, due to abundance of *bel* trees in the forest. The Oraons regard *bel* as a plant of Lord Shiva and normally avoid lopping, much less felling it. The leaves and wood are used as essential items of *pooja samagri* (ritual ingredient) for worship of Lord Shiva and as fuel in *havan* (sacred fire) rituals. Half-ripe *bel* fruit is regarded as astringent, digestive, appetizer and gives relief from dysentery. The pulp of ripe fruit, being sweet, is used in marmalade. Other than the *bel*, the forest canopy consists of *sakua* or *sal* (*Shorea robusta*), *teak* (*Tectona grandis*) *bija* (*Pterocarpus marsupium*), *saja* (*Terminalia tomentosa*), *dhawra* (*Anogeissus latifolia*), *mahua* (*Madhuca indica*), *tendu* (*Diospyros melanoxylon*), *amla* (*Embilica officinalis*), *karra* (*Cleistanthus collinus*) and *bamboo* (*Dendrocalamus strictus*). Forest is used for various purposes. People collect seeds of *sal* locally known as *makka mann* as edible food. Its timber is considered most suitable for wheels and bodies of carts and other similar load carriers and for constructing super structure of house tops. People considered *sakuwa* wood as most suitable for all such applications where strength and elasticity are foremost requirements, Its fresh leaves are collected for making traditional cups and dried *sal* leaves are used for making disposal plates, bowls and cups. Sal tree when tapped, yields white opaque resin which is burnt as incense in Oraon homes during religious ceremonies. A kind of oil is also obtained from *sal* fruit which is used for burning in earthen lamps. Further, during famine poor people grind the fruit into flour and eat it to ward off starvation. From the seeds of Mahuwa known as maghdi, oil called *kachadda* is extracted and is used for lightening lamps Its bud known as *koe* and flower is used for distilling liquor locally known as *arkhi*.

Its fruit known as *doe* is consumed raw or uncooked. Fruits of *amla* and *harra* are used for medicinal purpose. They also collect certain edible mushrooms. Besides food certain other items are also collected from the forest. They graze their cattle and collect fodder from the forest. Their entire energy need is met from fuel wood collected from the forest. They make broom locally known as *calki* from grass and *jhattas* from twigs collected from forest. Need for firewood, cattle grazing, fodder, and *sal* leaves and *mahua* are met through from the open access forest.

Products collected from forest are used both for sustenance as well as selling in the open market. Money so collected from the sale of forest product is used for meeting day-to-day expenditure. Every morning and evening one could see the men lined up, with head loads of fuel wood on the main Jashpurnagar road looking for buyers. Each of these bundle cost about thirty rupees. They also sell honey, and resins in the market. Women could be seen selling cups, plates and bowls made of Sal leaves. Our household survey in the village based on income and expenditure indicates that the sale of forest product contributes nearly 10 to 30 per cent to household income. Forest food and income from the forest product help household tide over unforeseen shortfalls. This income from the forest becomes more important especially during dry spell or the years when there is a failure of annual rains. Thus forest serves two types of purposes.

(a) Forest supports current consumption like requirement of food and cash in regular seasonal pattern each year.
(b) Forest is a Safety net in lean times

Place of Forest in Oraons World View

If the forest plays such an important role in the Oraons life, it would be interesting to see how the forest is visualized by them. According to *Grim (2001:26)*, what people do about their ecology depends upon on what they think about themselves in relation to things around them. Human ecology is deeply conditioned by beliefs about our nature and destiny. that is, by religion. The Oraons called their religion as Sarna i.e. the worship of sacred groove. The term refers to the place of worship constituting of trees which are very old, supposed to be the survivals from the earliest clearing when the village was established. It has different varieties of trees. To be called as *sarna*, a groove must have at least one *sal* tree. The *sarna* in the studied village has two *sal* trees, dedicated to the supreme deity known as *Dharmesh*, and the village deity or *gram dewta*, who protect the village from the evil spirits. The Oraons believe that if a tree in the sacred groove is destroyed the village suffers from some bad luck like natural calamity. These sacred grooves are like biosphere reserve. The saran in the village was spread over a radius of 50 meters, and there were twenty six trees in them. Among these, the middle one is the oldest tree and it is selected for the altar during any religious ceremony. The Oraons believe that the land, forest and all living creatures are a gift from their high god, *Dharmesh*, the sun god. Forest for them is a sacred entity because it is home to different deities and spirits. It is imperative to inform and seek their consent, when land is used for cultivation or natural resources are used. The *Karma* and the *Sal* are considered the most sacred tress and worshipped during the festivals of Karma and Sarhul puja respectively.

The Oraons consider Sarhul as their main festival. The name Sarhul has derived from two words sar and hul. Sar comes from *sarai* (seed of Sal tree) and *hul* means to worship/pray. Along with the worship of Sal tree oraons also worship dharti mata. The sal tree is the abode of goddess sarna, who protects the village and the community from all kinds of natural calamities and disasters. There are folklores which implores how destruction and cutting down of tree are sinful activity and people should be away from it. These folklore recited during the Karma festival in the village reiterates the fact that the people should not destroy the forest. The most popular being the story of two brothers and how one of them was punished by god for destroying and cutting down trees.

Forest Landscape in Sarnatoli

The community having such a strong environment ethic should also have thick forest cover in the area. Contrary to our expectation, the nature of forest cover around the village was of more of open nature, with crown cover of less than 20 per cent. Forest landscape was dominated by trees of medium heights, which looked much younger than the grand old tree of the Sarna or the sacred groove located in the village. A large number of trees appeared to be recent growth. There were also many trees which were heavily pruned and lobbed. The dense forest only appeared in patches and in between there were stretches of grassland and barren patches. The landscape was typical example of a fragmented ecosystem, where the continuity of the landscape have been broken and the forest have shrunk into smaller patches become honey combed with grassland, and barren patches. Our first objective was to determine the process of fragmentation and who was responsible for it?

We first interviewed the forest officials about it. The forest officials laid the blame on the villagers. They said the villagers are responsible for the deforestation. They blame the Oraons for cutting down trees for selling fuel wood and forest product, and for overgrazing their cattle. But the Oraons have a very different perception of degradation. They also agree that forest in the area have been degraded but refute the fact that it was a recent phenomenon. It has been like this for many years now. They felt it was not because of them that forest area has been degraded. According to villagers of Sarna they never cut trees. The local term for cutting tree is *tarna or khotna*, which for the oraons is a prohibited term. They consider tree as sacred as something which gives them life. They use the term *Murkna* when they go to forest to cut wood for fuel known as *phara*. The term *Khoyna* is used when they go to forest to cut grass. They consider these activities as no way harmful to the health of their *torang*. They did not see why tree pruning was necessarily destructive ("don't we all prune trees in our gardens for better growth") and why the "organic" nature of their traditional leaf manuring practices was not lauded. They also said that they cut branches of karma tree for various rituals and it no way contributes to deforestation. Deforestation according to them happens when large number of tress is cut down. Cutting few trees neither contribute to deforestation nor is deforestation per se.

Encroachment of forest areas was clearly evident. The boundary of the village is constantly being expanded with new land being brought under cultivation and new houses being built by clearing forest areas. Village boundaries are considered flexible and associated with the built up area. Along with positive forces forest is also associated with menacing spirits and ghosts, who can cause various illnesses. Often the local healer diagnoses illness being caused by the forest spirit because of undue trespassing of their abode an individual. This might perhaps act as a deterrent to check people venturing in the forest. But it has a negative connotation also. As the forest is an abode of both harmful and useful spirit, therefore it may also lead to an attitude of otherness and lack of interest about the health of forest.

On the other hand they blamed the forest department for imposing restrictions on them. It needs to be mentioned that forest based communities world over have faced problems relating to intervention and destruction of their natural resources by the outsiders (*Alcorn, 1993:424*). The Oraons also expressed similar sentiments deploring the role of the outsiders and the state intervention by limiting them access to forest in the pretext of conservation. The village head Roshan Bhagat said that Oraons were forbidden from open grazing in the upland forest after the restriction imposed on them in the nineties. He further said that the collection of the fuelwood was becoming scarce and considerable time was spent on its collection. Some had taken recourse to using crops residues and cowdung for fuel purpose, thereby diverting from using them as manure. They felt helpless about it as there was no other option available to them. They blamed forest department officials for stealing timber and selling it in the market.

The Oraons feel that although they have more cash available to them than at any other time through selling of brooms, honey, fuel wood and cups and plates made from *sal* leaves in the market but they felt their poverty has worsened because the expenditures have increased. Most to suffer because of the restrictions and degradation of the forest around the village were the poorest households of the village. They were the ones who were directly depended upon the forest for the secondary source of income by selling *mahua* flowers, tendu leaves, mushroom, various types of seeds and tamarind.

The traditional Oraon culture and institutions are coming under intense pressure because of both internal and external factors. The population of the village has doubled in the last five years. Rapid increase in population with limited resources at disposal there is increased pressure on the natural resource base. The Oraons can adapt to it through two ways—either by intensification or extensification of agriculture or by extracting from the forest. The extensification of agriculture is not possible because further encroachment will cause greater deforestation. The intensification is possible and should be explored to lessen the dependence of forest on the community through greater inputs in the agriculture e.g., through provision of irrigation facilities. The linkage of the village economy with the wider regional economy is exerting a greater demand on the Oraons to conform to the consumer economy, making few of them increasingly less sensitive environmentally. The forces of modernization have further led to a situation of rising aspiration and unmet needs. Under the circumstances any control can only have negative consequences. At the same time the ecology has already been plundered to such an extent that the current level of extraction may not be sustainable. There is a need of external intervention to manage the situation with the local people. It is only by striking a balance between conservation and more sustainable approach to livelihood that future can be ensured both for our forest dwellers as well as our forests.

References

Alcorn J.B., 1993. 'Indigenous community and Conservation'. *Conservation Biology*, Vol. 7, No. 2.

Aggarwal A. et al (Ed.). 1982. The State of India's Environment 1982: A Citizen's Report. Center for Science and Environment. New Delhi.

Maharatna A. 2005. Demographic Perspectives on India's Tribe. Oxford University Press, New Delhi.

GoI (Government of India). 1976. Report of the National Commission on Agriculture: Forestry. Vol. IX. Ministry of Agriculture and Irrigation. GoI, New Delhi.

Guha, R., 2007, 'Adivasis. Naxalites and Indian Democracy'. *Economic and Political Weekly*. Vol. XLII, No. 3. Mumbai.

Poffenberger, M. and McGean, B, (Eds). 1996. Village Voices, Forest Choices. Joint Forest Management in India. Oxford University Press, New Delhi.

Prabhu, P., 2001. 'In the Eye of the Strom: The Tribal People of India. in John A. Grim (ed.) Indigenous Tradition and Ecology, Cambridge: Harvard University Press.

Roy Burman B. K., 1992. "Homage to Earth," in Indigenous Vision: People of India, Attitude to Environment', ed. Geeti Sen. Sage Publication: New Delhi.

Wani M. and Kothari A., 1997. Conservation and People's Livelihood Right in India. Kalpavriksha : New Delhi.

EDUCATION

Persistent Educational Marginalization of Scheduled Tribes:

Arguments for an Alternative

Ravi Kumar

The dominant paradigm of analysis today revolves around social identities, reifying them and making them look as substitutes of social relations. The economics of marginalization takes a backseat, and conflicts emerging from the issue of control over processes of production and distribution become "obsolete", it is nothing but natural that an analysis would emerge which denounces dialectics and the relationship of parts to the whole, as essential to understand categories of marginalization and deprivation. The case of educational marginalization is an example in point. Educational marginalization emerges through a combination of forces ranging from economic, social to cultural. However, these forces interact in a certain space. This interaction is often ignored, due to undialectical analysis and emphasis on social identities, as the sole determining factor of marginalization. Unless one understands the relationship between how the paradigms and processes of development, emerging out of the social relations and the mode of production, determine the condition of tribals, it will be impossible to analyze their current situation. This paper is a preliminary effort to locate the educational marginalization of tribal population in the political economy of neoliberal capitalism.

The Tribal Population in India

The tribal population of the country, as per the 2001 census, is 8.43 crore, constituting 8.2 per cent of the total population. During the decade of

1991–2001 the tribal population grew at the rate of 24.45 per cent (*GOI, 2007:22*). There are over 700 Scheduled Tribes notified under Article 342 of the Constitution of India. Many of the tribes are present in more than one state, Orissa reporting the highest concentration of the number of tribes scheduled (i.e., 62) (*ibid, 26*). With such a large population, it is important to note that the Government of India notifies the tribal communities as per the constitutional provisions and after following certain criteria.

The Constitution of India, in Article 366 has defined the Scheduled Tribes as follows:

> "such tribes or tribal communities or parts of or groups within such tribes or tribal communities as are deemed under article 342 to be Scheduled Tribes for the purpose of the Constitution" (*The Constitution of India, 2005:302*).

And Article 342 says that:

> "(1) The President [may with respect to any State [or Union Territory], and by public notification, specify the tribes or tribal communities or parts of or groups within tribes or tribal communities which shall for the purposes of this Constitution be deemed to be Scheduled Tribes in relation to that State [or Union Territory, as the case may be].
>
> (2) Parliament may by law include in or exclude from the list of Scheduled Tribes specified in a notification issued under clause (1) any tribe or tribal community or part of or group within any tribe or tribal community, but save as aforesaid a notification issued under the said clause shall not be varied by any subsequent notification" (ibid, 285).

The criteria followed for specification of a community as a Scheduled Tribe are:

a. Indications of primitive traits,
b. Distinctive culture,
c. Geographical isolation,
d. Shyness of contact with the community at large, and
e. Backwardness. (*GOI, 2007:32*)

Victims of Development: The Economic Status of Tribals

The tribal population has generally been considered the deprived section of population when it comes to their economic status. After the persistent effort to integrate them with the mainstream economy, their condition has only worsened. However, this need not be mistaken to be an argument in favour of or against their participation in the mainstream economic development. That is an altogether different area of debate. We find that they have the largest number of landless (around 3.6 per cent), whereas the larger segment of the tribal population (around 83 per cent) possesses land up to two hectares. In the land possession they fare slightly better than the Dalits, which also may be due to the protection that they have enjoyed till now against encroachment of their lands. The situation is now fast changing with the large scale displacement, as they get deprived of their lands (see Table 1). "The major issue affecting the tribals in India is displacement: not merely displacement by large projects but resource displacement, thus violating the basic survival rights of tribal communities. Tribal areas reveal a high degree of land alienation. Non-tribals have invaded protected tribal areas. Deforestation, mainly due to exploitation of forests for industrial purposes, is another manifestation of resource displacement. This has resulted in decreasing access to forest resources by tribal communities. With increasing globalisation and privatization, the land rights of tribal areas is under even greater threat since these are regions, which have a high natural resource base and has tremendous potential to meet multiple market demands. Added to resource displacement is project displacement, where development projects have threatened the livelihood needs of tribal communities. More than 40 per cent of displaced persons of all large development projects are tribals" (*D'Souza, 2003*).

Table 1: Per cent Distribution of Households of Different Social Groups by Size Class of Land Possessed (all-India rural)

Size of Land Holding (hectares)	ST	SC	OBC	Others	All (incl. n.r.)
0.000	3.6	2.7	1.6	2.0	2.2
0.001–0.004	12.0	17.6	11.5	9.0	12.3
0.005–0.40	30.8	54.6	42.9	41.5	43.8
0.41–1.00	23.9	14.7	19.5	18.5	18.7
1.01–2.00	16.3	6.7	12.8	13.4	12.0
2.01–4.00	10.6	2.7	7.6	9.9	7.5
4.01 & above	2.9	1.0	4.0	5.7	3.6
All	100.0	100.0	100.0	100.0	100.0

Note: The households with size of land holding of land possessed '0.000' hectares comprise households which possessed land less than 0.001 hectares as well as households which reported no information on land possessed. **Source:** GOI (2006).

If the ability to spend is taken as the indicator for enhanced economic status, then the economic condition of tribal population is worst when compared to the other social groups. Their monthly per capita consumption expenditure is only Rs 431 in rural areas (see Table 2). Of this rural tribal population, around 49 per cent live on monthly per capital consumption expenditure of less than Rs 410 (*GOI, 2006*).

Table 2: Average Monthly Per Capita Consumption Expenditure Across Social Groups

		ST	SC	OBC	Others	n.r.	All social groups
Rural	Sch. type 1*	431	487	564	678	496	565
	Sch. type 2**	482	546	608	743	540	617
Urban	Sch. type 1	954	770	868	1326	804	1060
	Sch. type 2	1088	814	983	1394	695	1150

* Schedule Type 1 uses 30 days as reference period
** Schedule Type 2 uses 7 days as reference period
Source: GOI (2005a).

Given this economic status, it is extremely difficult to categorize the tribal as capable of tackling the challenges of a neo-liberal economy, where privatization is the mantra for development. For instance, it has been repeatedly said how education which is considered free, is not free and involves a lot of hidden cost (*Tilak, 1996*; *Kumar, 2006a, 2006b*). The government is following a policy where those who remain *incapable* to purchase the facilities provided by it, are supposed to have a *different* kind of education system. The Government of India also recognized this and followed a policy of *extra care and concern* with regard to the tribal population. The problems, however, still persist. Researchers have argued that rural India, because of its infrastructural backwardness, poverty and indebtedness, reflects the starkness of educational inequality and because tribals inhabit largely the hinterlands, the most inaccessible parts where infrastructure is still the worst, the tribal India, can be termed "the least developed area" and tribals "the worst sufferers" (*Sujatha, 1999:17*). *The problem with such an analysis is that it gets caught in a time warp.* It does not look at the situation historically and locate the trajectory of tribal development in conjunction with the larger paradigms of development. Today, after 63 years of independence, independence for the tribal population as well, the question remains whether the policy of the Indian state has worked or not.

Educational Status of Tribals

The significance of tribal issues as a national priority became quite clear when the Government of India constituted the Ministry of Tribal Affairs in October 1999 after bifurcating it from the Ministry of Social Justice and Empowerment. The creation of a separate ministry has obviously been to provide a more focused attention to the integrated socio-economic development of the Scheduled Tribes. This was a major landmark in policy making and implementation because it also symbolized the seriousness of the Indian state towards tackling the problems of this population. It is an altogether different matter that post 1999 the number of reasons for displacing tribals from their lands have only increased. Earlier, various ministries have looked after the issues pertaining to the tribal population:

(i) As a Division of the Ministry of Home Affairs, known as the Tribal Division: from Independence to September 1985;
(ii) Ministry of Welfare: from September 1985 to May 1998;
(iii) Ministry of Social Justice and Empowerment: from May 1998 to September 1999 (*GOI, 2005b: p.8*).

Subsequently, various schemes were launched for the welfare of tribal children in the field of education. For instance, the scheme for Construction of Girls Hostels was started during the Third Plan period. A separate scheme for Construction of Hostels for Scheduled Tribe Boys was launched in 1989–90. Both the schemes were merged into one scheme during the 10th Five Year Plan (*GOI, 2007:54*)

The scheme of Ashram Schools was started in 1990-91 and continues. It aims at promoting and extending educational facilities in tribal areas, on the pattern of the old gurukul system. This is a centrally sponsored scheme, on cost sharing basis between the Centre and States in a 50:50 ratio. In the case of Union Territories, the Ministry provides the entire fund under the scheme (*ibid, 55*).

Apart from these, educational complexes in Low Literacy Pockets for the development of Women's Literacy have been set up. This scheme was introduced in 1993–94, for Schedule Tribe females in low literacy pockets. It is implemented through non-governmental organizations, government autonomous bodies and registered co-operative societies. This scheme aims at promoting education among tribal girls in the identified low literacy districts of the country. The scheme also aims to improve the socio-economic status of the poor and illiterate tribal population through the education of women (*ibid, 57*).

After such an apparently committed stance of the state, it is assumed that the educational status of the tribal population will improve. However, statistics do not show a very marked improvement, especially if one considers over sixty years of independence, which is a long span of time. The literacy rate among the tribes in 2004–05 has been around 52.4 per cent, as reported by the NSSO survey (see Table 3 below).

Table 3: Literacy among Persons of Age 5 Years and above for Different Social Groups

Social group	Rural + Urban		
	Male	Female	Person
ST	62.4	42.0	52.4
SC	67.9	46.1	57.3
OBC	74.9	53.7	64.5
Others	84.6	70.9	78.0
All (incl. n.r.)	75.5	56.6	66.3

Source: GOI (2006a).

The census results of 2001 reflect the starkness of the educational poverty of the tribal population in India. From the data analyzed for two age groups, 7–14 and 15–39, one finds that while in the age group of 15–39 literacy is 48.9 per cent it is 65.4 per cent for the age group of 7–14. This may imply that the number of children going to school has increased over years. But the later part of the statistics reveals that there are few children who cross the primary stage (see Table 4).

The figures from the Census point towards a high dropout rate, which is recorded across different social groups by the MHRD data (see Table 5). There are always question marks about the data being collected and the nature of compulsions that make the teachers or block levels officials to report spurious data. However, even with this assumption, the data on drop outs among Scheduled Tribes reflect their incapacity to move up the educational ladder.

The attendance rate among the tribal children is also low compared to the other social groups (see Table 6). This becomes an important indicator of the school and the community relationship, because it has been observed that due to a variety of reasons the children though enrolled in the schools do not attend.

Table 4: Education Level among Tribal Population in India (2001)

			Within Literate								
Age	Illiterate	Literate	Literate without educational level	Below primary	Primary	Middle	Secondary	Higher secondary*	Non-technical diploma**	Technical diploma***	Graduate & above
15-39	51.1	48.9	6.6	20.8	25.2	21.2	15.2	6.9	0.0	0.5	3.7
7-14	34.6	65.4	1.4	64.2	28.7	5.6	0.0	0.0	0.0	0.0	0.0

*Higher secondary/Intermediate/Pre-University/Senior secondary
**Non-technical diploma or certificate not equal to degree
***Technical diploma or certificate not equal to degree
Source: Calculated from the Census 2001 results.

Table 5: Dropout Rates of Students in Classes I–V, I–VIII and I–X in India (2002–03)

		2002-03			2003-04		
		Classes I–V	Classes I–VIII	Classes I–X	Classes I–V	Classes I–VIII	Classes I–X
General	Boys	35.85	33.72	34.89	33.66	51.74	60.97
	Girls	52.28	53.45	52.79	28.44	52.48	64.92
	Total	60.72	64.97	62.58	31.36	52.22	62.68
SC	Boys	41.13	41.91	41.47	36.83	57.33	71.41
	Girls	58.24	62.19	59.19	36.19	62.19	75.49
	Total	69.74	74.93	71.92	36.56	59.42	73.13
ST	Boys	50.82	52.1	51.37	49.13	69.04	77.92
	Girls	66.86	71.17	68.67	48.67	71.43	81.16
	Total	78.35	82.97	80.29	48.93	70.05	79.25

Source: MHRD, Selected Educational Statistics, 2002–03, pp. 102–104 and 2003–04, pp. 91-92.

Table 6: Current Attendance Rates in Educational Institutions per 1000 Persons of 5–14 Age Group and Social Groups in NSS 55th (1999–2000) and 61st (2004–05) Rounds in Rural India

Social Group		55th Round (5–14 Years)	61st Round (5–14 Years)
Rural			
ST	Male	63.2	76.7
	Female	52.7	67.8
	Person	58.2	72.6
SC	Male	70.1	80.9
	Female	58.6	73.7
	Person	64.7	77.5
OBC	Male	74.3	84.3
	Female	62.1	76.3
	Person	68.7	80.5
Others	Male	80.2	87.6
	Female	73.8	84.2
	Person	77.1	86.0
Urban			
ST	Male	80.9	87.1
	Female	74.0	85.9
	Person	77.6	86.5
SC	Male	79.2	85.0

Social Group		55th Round (5–14 Years)	61st Round (5–14 Years)
	Female	73.9	79.3
	Person	76.6	82.2
OBC	Male	82.4	88.1
	Female	78.6	87.8
	Person	80.6	88.0
Others	Male	88.0	91.5
	Female	85.4	91.4
	Person	86.8	91.4

Source: GOI (2006a).

The Indian State's Grand Betrayal—The Fallout of its Subservience to Capital

Given the above situation the recent trends within the government policy making have been quite perturbing. While on the one hand the participation of the state in providing education is on decrease, on the other hand, the high tide of privatization is engulfing whatever is left in the social sector. We find that the expenditure on education as a percentage of GDP has been decreasing (Chart 1) and this happens despite all the rhetoric and euphoria about the increasing emphasis on education. This also happens while the education cess has been imposed on the tax payers in the country. Rather than the state providing the expenditure on education, the citizens are being asked to pay for educating the educationally marginalized population. While one may find it problematic that the state is relinquishing its duty and not going by what the different committees and commissions since Kothari Commission asked it to do, others may also question the misuse of this fund, when the state institutionalizes discrimination by sending children of the under-privileged to low quality schools.

The wave of privatization which diminishes the access of the under privileged to educational facilities, is also on rise (Chart 2). On the one hand, while the state plays on the rhetoric of Right to Free Education as a constitutional right, on the other hand it has been delaying the operationalisation of the right through an appropriate legislation.

Developments such as these become important to understand the educational marginalization of tribal population because (1) education cannot be located in isolation from the larger economic and political contexts; and (2) the trajectory of educational policy is not divorced from the trajectory of capital in any society across world.

Chart 1: Expenditure on Education as Proportion of GDP

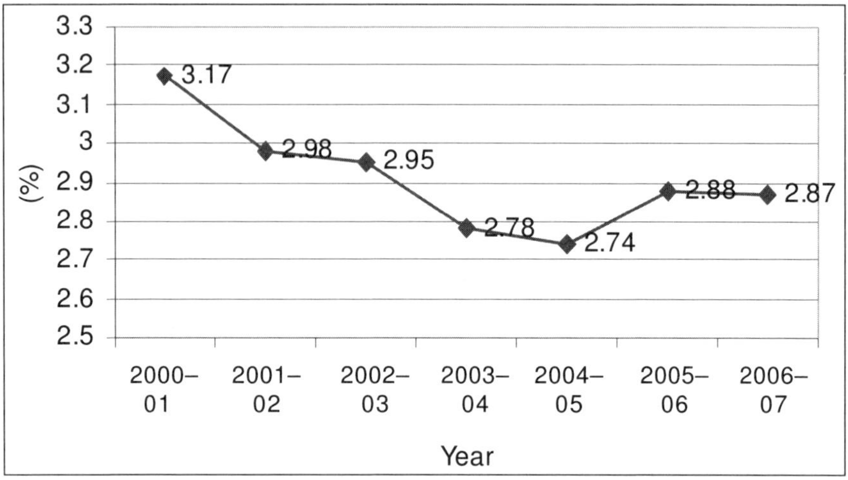

Source: *Economic Survey 2005-06 and 2006-07.*

Chart 2: Growth in Private Schools

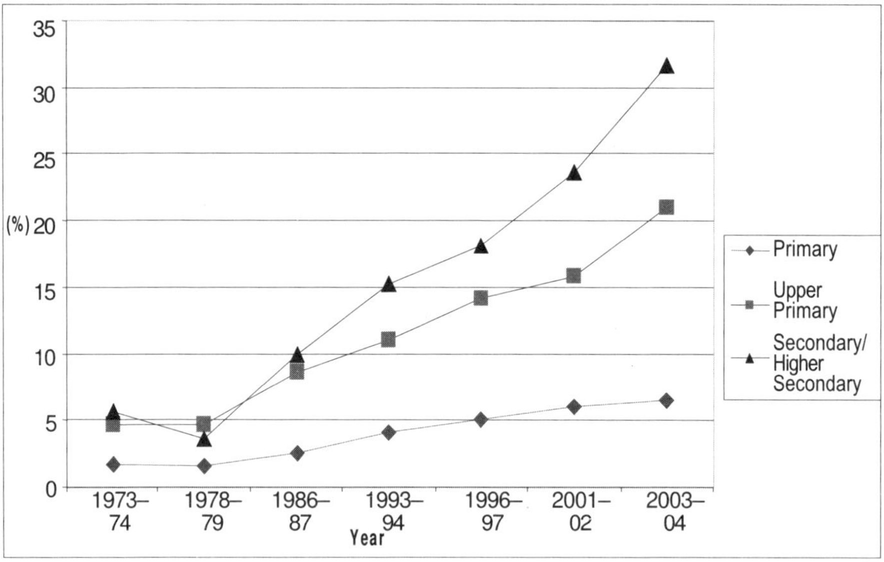

Source: *MHRD, Selected Educational Statistics, 2001–02 and 2003–04.*

One of the more serious tragedies of policy making as well as *sub-contracted development* through non-governmental organizations, etc., is that the larger political economy of development gets ignored. On the one hand, there is a large scale effort to integrate each and every section and geographical area into the rapacious capitalist development, while on the other hand the notion of serving the tribal population with a *different* kind of piece-meal reformist measures is also in vogue. Large scale displacement and pauperisation due to developmental projects is evident across the country such as in Orissa, Chhattisgarh, Jharkhand, Gujarat, Maharashtra etc. And the Indian state is implementing the designs of capital unhesitatingly and mercilessly. Use of coercion has been frequent, as shown by the killing of tribals in Orissa and elsewhere. The use of the repressive state machinery in the most callous way possible is seen in Chattisgarh by raising an army of mercenaries, namely *Salwa Judum*, to fight the organized militant resistance against the state's repression, is unleashed in collusion with private capital.

Given such a stance by the state, to deprive a large part of tribal population, the recent emphasis on public-private partnership in education or the trends towards the state's withdrawal from the education sector, will only aggravate the educational marginalization of tribals. Those who love the rule of capital, but prefer to remain humane as well, argue for a development process wherein the state needs to play a larger role. One can hardly disagree with them, but the question that one needs to ask is whether that remains even a distant possibility today, with capital being in such an offensive stance. Such being the condition, when all possible remnants of a welfare capitalist state have been shelved, even the Parliament ignored on many instances, and when the repressive state apparatuses have been used so blatantly and overtly, it would amount to being partners in such a conspiracy, if one still believes and argues that the state would reverse the process of commodification. The character of the state alters with the changes in the forms of capital accumulation and as capital tries to reach to all nooks and corners for sustaining and expanding its profit, it would be very naïve to consider anything in isolation from the larger processes of the system.

Indian Policy Making and Tribals

The development paradigm of independent India was caught in the debate on whether to adopt the approach of isolation, assimilation or integration towards the tribal population. The debate was about whether the tribals should be left to their own world, without any external interference (*Elwin, 1939*) or should be assimilated in the mainstream (*Ghurye, 1941*). Pt Nehru chose the approach of integration. Using his famous principle of "panchsheel", he talked of devising programmes and policies to integrate the tribals with the mainstream population (*Joshi, 1997:452*). This whole debate is based on the idea of locating tribals as "peculiar", living in a more or less isolated surrounding. However, scholars have challenged this idea and traced how they have been subjected to invasion by different sections of so-called "outsiders", who established their zamindaris or exploited them as traders (*ibid*). Historian D.D. Kosambi pointed out that "the entire course of Indian history shows tribal elements being fused into a general society" (*2002:27*).

Flowing from such a conceptualization is also the idea of the homogeneity of the entire tribal population, which has great impact on, for instance, the educational scenario among them. One of the problems of any collective identity conceptualization, has historically been, that it reduces an otherwise heteorgenously stratified population to a homogenous group. Hence, we do not get into the explanations of how a certain segment of the tribal population is able to make use of the government policies and programmes, while the majority cannot. Ghanshyam Shah through his field-work shows how class based stratification exists amongst the tribes. In order to understand this, he argues, two factors that influence the tribe-class dynamics must be understood. "One, India follows the path of capitalist economy, and competitive policy. Capitalist economy develops differentiations in society on class lines, and competitive policy compels politicians to widen their support structure across the narrow boundaries of kinship and caste. Secondly, political ideology and practice ignore the growing economic differentiations within and between tribes. All tribes are clustered into one group described as scheduled tribes by the Indian constitution. This practice ignores differentiations among tribes, and also legitimizes a tribe as tribe with distinct social and cultural identity" (*Shah, 1979:450*). Pradip Kumar Bose argues that the tribes are now increasingly interacting with the market (and we all know how the market brings with itself a chain reaction, creating and sharpening the social differentiation). While positing his ideas on the tribe-caste relationship he says that "in earlier times, when tribes came in contact with Hindus, the caste ideology was the dominant ideology of the economic system and, willingly or unwillingly, tribes had to assume a rank in the overall caste system. However, in modern times, caste ideology is no longer the dominant ideology, tribes are directly interacting with the market network, the regional and the national economy, without the mediation of caste, and are adopting characteristics of the commercial capitalist system" (*Bose, 1981:191*). Hence, it has been widely accepted by different scholars that tribes are not homogeneous or isolated (*Shah, 1979*; *Bose, 1981*; *Joshi, 1997*; *Nathan and Kelkar, 2003*). They are part of the larger paradigm of capitalist development.

The perceptions and debates about the tribal population could be seen as replicated in the education policy as well. The British government had an isolationist approach towards the tribes and therefore, their education was never on the agenda of the British rulers. The isolation of tribals ended when Christian Missionaries started work in many tribal areas. They established schools, among other institutions. Some of the nationalists also started a kind of "Ashram" schools, which were replicated in post-independent India (*Sujatha, 1999*).

Article 46 of the Constitution states that "the State shall promote with special care the educational and economic interests of the Scheduled Tribes and protect them from social injustice and all forms of exploitation". In this Article, the concerns flow from the possible subjection of tribals to external forces, or the lurking danger of their exploitation. The two phrases which were the rhetorical insignia of the welfare state, i.e., "protect from social injustice and all forms of exploitation", made it clear how the modern notions of the nation building project, included them in its functional sphere.

Integration of the tribals within the capitalist framework began through the planned economy—the Tribal Sub-plan and the Integrated Tribal Development Agency (ITDA) accelerated these processes. For instance, the tribals were introduced to the monetary economy through ITDA. "Replacing the barter system not only increased their exposure to the market, but also increased interaction with the non-tribal population" (*Sujatha, 1999: 36*). As with the whole of India, their integration too began with a welfarist regime of policy making and now they too are, like the rest of the country, being subjected to the callousness of neo-liberal capital accumulation. The only difference being, they have been relatively less equipped to tackle the repercussions of such a regime.

The Chimera of Equality in Education

From the beginning the rhetoric of equality and anti-discrimination has characterized education policy making in India. As discussed above, it was nowhere to be found in the British education policy and that is why Sargent Commission was completely silent regarding the education of Scheduled Castes or Tribes. Then came the path-breaking Kothari Commission or the

Education Commission 1964–66, with its idea of the Common School System. The concerns of equality were quite obvious in the commission report. In case of Scheduled Tribes, it suggested fundamental reorganization of the tribal economy through marketing, credit health and educational facilities. The effort was to "mainstream" them, with the obvious question of what would this "mainstreaming" would imply.

The report argued for five years of "effective education" for all tribal children and laid down the plans for teachers well conversant with the tribal languages. The medium of education for the first two years of school was to be the tribal language and books were to be prepared in these languages etc. Then it suggested that the tribal areas should be largely covered through the Ashram schools. It then went off to suggest how education can be imparted in harmony with the tribal culture and environment (*GOI, 1966: 125–27*).

It is relevant to recall that Kothari Commission introduced the notion of Common School System as a tool of equalizing access to education. In the paradigm of common schooling, the idea was to bring together "all schools conducted by government and local authorities and all recognized and aided private schools" (*ibid, 233*). It remained silent on the issue of private schools, whose numbers we find proliferating today. The commission could have recommended a continuation of the already existing government schooling system into the tribal areas with the pedagogic and curricular changes that it had suggested. But no such suggestion came up. Rather, another brand of government schooling was suggested, which obviously created a different identity for the education of Scheduled Tribes, which was not really required, as suggested by the ample research on their integration in the capitalist economy. They could have very well been a part of a single government schooling system, rather than a different "brand" or "layer" of schooling, with the necessary alterations in teaching learning practices, as a common school ideally calls for. This reflected the contradictions and uneasiness of the 1960s policy discourse in Indian education. It also represented the ideals that a welfare capitalism accumulation process, brings into existence.

The continuation of a similar approach is visible in the NPE, 1986. It said:

> "4.6 The following measures will be taken urgently to bring the Scheduled Tribes on par with others:
>
> (i) Priority will be accorded to opening primary schools in tribal areas.

The construction of school Buildings will be undertaken in these areas on a priority basis under the normal funds for education, as well as under the N.R.E.P., R.L.E.G.P., Tribal Welfare schemes, etc.

(ii) The socio-cultural milieu of the STs has its distinctive characteristics including, in many cases, their own spoken languages. This underlines the need to develop the curricula and devise instructional materials in tribal languages at the initial stages, with arrangements for switching over to the regional language.

(iii) Educated and promising Scheduled Tribe youths will be encouraged and trained to take up teaching in tribal areas.

(iv) Residential schools, including Ashram Schools, will be established on a large scale.

(v) Incentive schemes will be formulated for the Scheduled Tribes, keeping in view their special needs and life styles. Scholarships for higher education will emphasise technical, professional and para-professional courses. Special remedial courses and other programmes to remove psycho-social impediments will be provided to improve their performance in various courses.

(vi) Anganwadis, Non-formal and Adult Education Centres will be opened on a priority basis in areas predominantly inhabited by the Scheduled Tribes.

(vii) The curriculum at all stages of education will be designed to create an awareness of the rich cultural identity of the tribal people as also of their enormous creative talent" (Ministry of Education: 1986).

Gradually, a justification for the existence of a separate type of schools for the tribal population was created in the name of a distinctive identity of such a population. This was crystallized in form of the Ashram schools in 1990–91. The idea of cost sharing with the state as well as with the community, the appointment of under qualified and under trained teachers for the sake of cost reduction and unavailability of the required infrastructure have been some of the problems of such schools. Many of these have been pointed out by the studies as well (*Sujatha, 1999*).

Equality in Access through Quality Schooling: The Agenda for Tribal Education

In the current situation, it is important to consider how the tribal population who are largely poor and have been pauperized by the developmental projects of the Indian government, can be integrated in the educational map of the country. This integration, as in the case of other marginalized and poor sections, can be done only through enhancing participation of the Indian state in educational programmes. They need access to schooling which is of comparable quality and are not layered as the government tends to do. Such a system can be provided by the Common School System. This common school system, unlike what had been proposed by Education Commission 1964–66 and recently proposed by the Government of Bihar Commission, needs to be grounded in the idea of resistance. This resistance will pedagogically reflect the spirit of our times, the economic and political turmoil of the tribal population. The context of such a policy making has to be very clear, otherwise it will once again be an exercise in trading quality for quantity or vice-versa, without realizing that thentwo have to be complementary. The context of any education policy which promises equality in quality, as well as access to schooling, has to be defined by the neo-liberal capital accumulation processes, which has shed all traces of welfarism and gone ahead with the agenda of transforming every sphere into a commodified zone.

For a common school that promises quality, equality in access, better equipped teachers etc., the Gramscian notion of a common school becomes quite relevant for us. For Gramsci "the common school, or school of humanistic formation… or general culture, should aim to insert young men and women into social activity after bringing them to a certain level of maturity, of capacity for intellectual and practical creativity, and of autonomy of orientation and initiative". The age for compulsory school attendance should not be fixed, because it would depend on the general economic conditions, "since the latter may make it necessary to demand of young men and women, or even of children, a certain immediate productive contribution. The common school necessitates the States being able to take on the expenditure which at present falls on the family… The entire function of educating and forming the new generations ceases to be private and becomes public; for only thus can it involve them in their entirety, without divisions of group or caste" (*2004: 29–30*).

But such a system would require "an unprecedented expansion of the practical organization of the school" (*ibid, 30*). And in the Indian situation it would require the State to expand its network of schooling, an area from which it has been withdrawing. Though he explained in detail what should be taught and how, at different levels of schooling, this is not the place to dwell on that theme. Gramsci understood the contextual differences in case of children coming from different backgrounds and suggested measures of overcoming these deficiencies. The children from intellectual strata, through their family life, are prepared to go to school as they already know and develop their knowledge of literary language. The urban children enjoy this kind of advantage. But in order to universalize these gains "in the basic organization of the common school, at least the essentials of these conditions must be created—not to speak of the fact, which goes without saying, that parallel to the common school, a network of kindergartens and other institutions would develop, in which, even before the school age, children would be habituated to a certain collective discipline and acquire pre-scholastic notions and attitudes. In fact, the common school should be organized like a college, with a collective life by day and by night, freed from the present forms of hypocritical and mechanical discipline; studies should be carried on collectively, with the assistance of the teachers and the best pupils, even during periods of so-called individual study, etc." (*ibid, 2004:31*) Gramsci is stressing here on the significance of pre-primary schooling.

To conclude, we need to realize that the inequality in access and the problem of quality is universal. The tribals are also now part of the larger world and the same variables which create inequity and hamper the access to good quality education to the majority, apply to them too. Hence, it is important that they are brought into the system, which will stress on quality and equality in access in general. Till today, the initiatives of the Indian state have been nothing more than mere eyewash. The recent policies of non-formal schooling or proliferation of multi-layered schools are reflections of the Indian state shedding its welfarist skin and getting into the neo-liberal one. Under these circumstances, common schooling remains the only way out, a notion of schooling which teaches the child to dissent and understand the system with a critical outlook. It will be a system which would stand against schooling as a site of reproducing inequality.

REFERENCES

Bose, Pradip Kumar (1981, February 1), 'Stratification among Tribals in Gujarat', *Economic and Political Weekly*, pp. 191-196.

D'Souza, Nafisa Goga (2003), Empowerment and Action: Laya's Work in Tribal Education, Indigenous Education Program Case Study, Asian South Pacific Bureau of Adult Education (ASPBAE).

Elwin, Verrier (1939), The Baiga, John Murray: London.

Ghurye, G.S. (1943), The Aborigines—'so called'—and their future, Gokhale Institute of Politics and Economics: Poona.

Government of India (2007), Annual Report 2006-07, Ministry of Tribal Affairs: New Delhi.

Government of India (October 2006), Employment and unemployment situation among social groups in India, 2004-05, Report No. 516, National Sample Survey Organisation, Ministry of Statistics & Programme Implementation: New Delhi.

Government of India (November 2005a), Household Consumer Expenditure in India (NSS 60th Round) (January–June 2004), Report No. 505, National Sample Survey Organisation, Ministry of Statistics and Programme Implementation: New Delhi.

Government of India (2005b), Annual Report 2004–05, Ministry of Tribal Affairs: New Delhi.

Government of India (1966), Education and National Development: Report of the Education Commission 1964–66, Ministry of Education, New Delhi: Government of India.

Gramsci, Anotnio (2004), Selections from Prison Notebooks, New Delhi: Orient Longman.

Joshi, Vidyut (1997), 'Genesis of Tribal Problem' in Shah, Ghanshyam (ed.) Social Transformation in India, Vol. 2, Rawat Publications: New Delhi and Jaipur, pp.451–465.

Kosambi, Damodar Dharmanand (2002), An Introduction to the Study of India History, Popular Prakashan: Mumbai.

Kumar, Ravi (2006a, September), When Gandhi's Talisman No Longer Guides Policy Considerations: Market, Deprivation and Education in the Age of Globalisation, *Social Change*, 36(3), pp.1–46.

Kumar, Ravi (2006b), 'Equality, Quality and Quantity: Mapping the Challenges Before Elementary Education in India' in Kumar, Ravi (ed.) The Crisis of Elementary Education in India, New Delhi: Sage Publications, pp.13–56.

Ministry of Education, National Policy on Education (1986), downloaded from http://education.nic.in/cd50years/g/T/49/0T490401.htm on 25th October 2006

Nathan, Dev and Kelkar, Govind (2003, May 17), 'Civilisational Change: Markets and Privatisation among the Indigenous Peoples', Economic and Political Weekly, pp.1955–1968.

Shah, Ghanshyam (1979, February), 'Tribal Identity and Class Differentiations: A Case Study of the Chaudhuri Tribe', *Economic and Political Weekly*, pp.450-464.

Tilak, JBG (1996, February 3 & 10), 'How Free is 'Free' Primary Education in India?', *Economic and Political Weekly*, 31(4–5).

Sujatha, K. (1999), Education of India Scheduled Tribes: A Study of community schools in the district of Vishakhapatnam, Andhra Pradesh, International Institute for Educational Planning, UNESCO: Paris.

The Constitution of India (2005), Universal Law Publishing Company: New Delhi.

Education of the Tribes:
Role of Ashram Schools in Chhattisgarh and Orissa

B.K. Panda

The concept of establishing the Ashram schools was derived from the traditional Gurukulas and the Gandhian philosophy of basic education, in which the teacher and the students live together in the same premises. This concept is best suited in organizing the Ashram Schools due to its residential nature, closeness among the peer groups, teachers and the learning environment, the substitution by better facilities, which was otherwise not available for the children at home.

It was in 1922, an eminent social worker Thakkar Bapa, influenced heavily by the Gandhian movement, initiated an experiment of Ashram Schools in Panchmahal hills of the State of Gujarat, exclusively for the benefit of the tribal children. This experiment proved to be successful in imparting education to the tribal children. After Independence, Ashram schools were started as Gukulashrams with students and teachers living together in the same premises. Thereafter, it was decided by various state governments to establish Ashram schools in the tribal areas with residential facilities in order to provide education to the tribal children. Many of the Indian states came forward and initiated such schools in their respective states. Dhebar Commission in 1961 reviewed the tribal development programs and found the Ashram Schools in many of the states to be functioning successfully. The success stories of organizing these Ashram Schools resulted in the allocation of funds in the First Five year Plan and provision for more such schools in the subsequent plans. The Education Commission (1964–66) also recommended opening of Ashram Schools. As a result more such ashram schools were opened in the states of Andhra Pradesh, Bihar, Gujarat, Madhya Pradesh, Maharashtra, and Rajasthan. However, in addition to the school managed by the tribal welfare departments, voluntary organizations also managed the Ashram Schools in some of the states.

The Objectives and Functioning of Ashram Schools

The Ashram schools were opened with the following objectives, as envisaged by the various committees and commissions.

i. To wean the children away from an atmosphere which is generally not conducive for the development of their personality and outlook;
ii. To impart general formal education;
iii. To impart socially useful vocational/crafts along with the general education;
iv. To encourage tribal traditions like folk dances so that the schools are not only mere learning places but also centres of cultural activities;
v. To provide close interaction between the teacher and taught through increased individual attention; and
vi. To reduce the dropout rate and to improve the retention capacity of the schools.

Ashram schools in general, are residential in nature and the students are provided with facilities of board and lodging. Moreover, they function within a highly structured and systematic framework.

The broad policy guidelines for the Ashram schools as envisaged by various committees and study groups on tribal welfare programs are:

i. Ashram schools should be inter-village schools;
ii. Ashram schools should be opened in such areas where normal schools cannot be opened; and
iii. Most backward tribal groups should be covered.

The criteria for opening such schools were on the basis of concentration of scheduled tribe population and percentage of literacy among the tribals, as per census. The admission into these schools was made from the neighbouring lower primary schools of Tribal Welfare Department/Harijan and Tribal Welfare Department and other schools managed by the Education Department. However, preference was given to the children from the schools managed by the Welfare Department. The usual age limit for admission of children was between 6–14 years. In these schools, the costs of education, clothing, boarding and medical expenses were borne by the government, besides which the children were also supplied with reading and writing materials, beds and utensils etc. (*Ananda, G., 1995*; *Heredia, R.C., 1992*; *Pratap et al, 1971*; *Sujatha, K., 1983*).

Although the concept and objectives of Ashram Schools are basically common in all states, however, their planning and management varies in different states. The level of education norms of establishing schools and their activities differ and vary widely from state to state.

In some of the states like Maharashtra and Gujarat, these schools are mostly run by voluntary organizations as private aided schools. Whereas in the states of Andhra Pradesh, Chhattisgarh, Jharkhand, Orissa, Madhya Pradesh and Rajasthan, Ashram schools are exclusively under the Tribal Welfare Department of the respective state governments. Both primary and post basic levels of education are available in Maharashtra, Gujarat and Orissa. In Madhya Pradesh, Ashram schools are usually up to middle stage and at the secondary stage these are called "Model Schools". In Rajasthan, all the Ashram schools are either primary or middle stage. In Andhra Pradesh, Ashram schools have primary, upper primary and secondary stages of education. In Maharashtra, Gujarat and Andhra Pradesh, Ashram Schools are co-educational, whereas in Rajasthan, Madhya Pradesh and Orissa they are separate for girls and boys. Ashram schools in Orissa are provided at primary, upper primary and secondary levels. Vocational education is imparted in some of the secondary schools.

Scheduled Tribes of Chhattisgarh and Orissa: Population and Literacy

As per Census 2001, the Scheduled Tribe population in Chhattisgarh is 31.8 per cent of the total population of the state and it at 8th position among all the states in terms of proportion of Schedule Tribe population—there are 42 scheduled tribes in the state. The tribal dominated districts are Dantewada (78.5 per cent), Bastar 66.3 per cent) and Jashpur (63.2 per cent). Out of the 42 tribes, Gond is the most populous tribe in the state, constituting 55.3 per cent of the tribal population.

Literacy Rate	All STs (state)	Halba	Oraon	Kawar	Gond	Bhattra
Persons	52.1	74.1	62.2	61	49.2	38
Female	39.3	63.3	52	45.6	36.6	23.6

Source: Census of India, 2001.

The literacy rate of Schedule Tribes in this state is 52.1 per cent, higher than that at the national level i.e. 47.1 per cent. The male and female literacy rates at 65 per cent and 39.3 per cent, is also higher than the national level of 59.2 per cent and 34.8 per cent. The Halba, Oraon and Kawar have higher rates literacy than that of all Schedule Tribes in the state and Bhattra has the lowest literacy rate in the state.

School Age Scheduled Tribe Children in Chhattisgarh (5-14 years)

Age Group	All STs	Gond	Kawar	Oraon	Halba	Bhattra
5–14 yrs.	58.7	55.7	66.5	71.2	77.3	52.6

Source: Census of India, 2001.

In the 5–14 years age group, which has 17 lakhs tribal children, 58.7 per cent of the children attend the school which amounts to 10 lakh tribal children, while there are 41.3 per cent (7 lakh) children who don't go to school as yet. **Gonds** have the highest number of children who do not go to the Ashram school followed by the **Kawar** in the 5-14 age group. The percentage of literates who have attained education up to primary and middle levels are 26.3 per cent and 12.3 per cent respectively. Persons educated up to matric/secondary/higher secondary constitute 8.8 per cent only. While 1.9 per cent of Schedule Tribes have graduated and there is a very negligible proportion of Schedule Tribes who are non-technical and technical diploma holders.

In Orissa, the Scheduled Tribe population constitutes 22.1 per cent of the total population of the state and 9.7 per cent of the total tribal population of the country and holds 11th position in terms of Schedule Tribes population in India (*Census, 2001*) The highest tribal population is in the districts of Malkangiri with 57.4 per cent, Mayurbhanj 56.6 per cent, Rayagada 55.8 per cent and Nabarangpur 55 per cent respectively. The state has 62 Scheduled Tribes; Khond is the most populous tribe constituting 17.1 per cent of the total ST population followed by the Gond with 9.6 per cent. In addition to these two dominant tribal groups, Santal, Kolha, Munda, Saora, Shabar and Bhottada together constitute 64.2 per cent of the total Schedule Tribes population of the state. Unlike some of the tribal groups of Chhattisgarh, the tribes of Orissa have considerably lower literacy rates than the national level with 37.4 per cent in 2001. Male literacy rate has increased from 34.4 per cent to 51.5 per cent while female literacy rate has gone up from 10.2 per cent to 23.4 per cent during 1991–2001.

Literacy Rates of the Schedule Tribes: Orissa

Literacy rate	All STs (state)	Gond	Saora	Santal	Munda	Shabar	Khond	Kolha	Bhottada
Persons	37.4	47.0	41.1	40.5	39.7	35.4	31.9	27.1	24.3
Females	23.4	30.8	25.7	24.7	27.6	19.9	18.0	14.3	11.1

Source: Census of India, 2001.

The percentage of literates who have attained education up to primary and middle levels constitute 28.7 per cent and 13.7 per cent respectively. The tribal children who are educated up to matric/secondary/higher secondary etc have a share of 11 per cent only. Graduates and above constitute 1.5 per cent and non-technical and technical diploma holders constitute less than half per cent (0.4 per cent).

School Age Scheduled Tribe Children in Orissa (5–14 years)

Age Group	All STs	Khond etc.	Gond etc.	Santal	Kolha	Munda etc.	Saora etc.	Shabar	Bhjottada etc.
5–14 yrs.	45.8	41.7	56.1	46.5	31.6	42.2	51.8	44.8	36.8

Source: Census of India, 2001.

As many as 9.8 lakh children out of the 21.4 lakh children in the 5-14 age group attend the school, constituting 45.8 per cent of the total tribal children of this age group. It is alarming to note that as many as 11.6 per cent lakh children in the corresponding age group do not go to school. The Gond and Saora tribe children have more than half of the total children in the corresponding age group attending the schools.

Inception of Ashram Schools in the States of Chhattisgarh and Orissa

The Ashram schools, first started in the country during the year 1949, on the pattern of basic schools, began as Gurkulashrams, with students and teachers living together in the same premises. Thereafter, it was decided by the various states Governments to establish Ashram Schools in the tribal areas with residential facilities, in order to provide education to the children of the tribal people. To begin with, these schools were started as residential middle schools generally opened in areas with tribal concentration. These schools were known as Madhyamik Vidyalayas, consisting of four classes i.e., from class IV to class VII. During the First Plan only 28 such schools were opened, however, the number of these schools gradually increased over each plan period.

The Ashram schools also accommodated the local students as day scholars. Even the Scheduled Caste children were admitted into these schools and provided with all the facilities available for the tribal children. 10 per cent of the Scheduled Caste children in the tribal dominated areas and 10 per cent of the tribal children in the Scheduled Caste dominated areas are provided with seats in the schools located in these areas. The Welfare Department also funds the schools of the Education Department, which are located in the tribal dominated areas without duplicating and further opening schools in these areas. Instead it provides funds for food for forty children of the school. In the state of Chhattisgarh, on admission to the Ashram School every boy is paid a student scholarship of Rs 350 and girls are paid Rs 360 per month for ten months of a calendar year. Thus, there is a collaborative effort between both these departments, enabling a rationalization for opening of the schools while simultaneously serving the tribal areas.

The schools, which are managed by the Welfare Department, follow the curriculum of the Education department in the states. The inspector/ education officer of schools from the Education Department also carries out the academic inspections of these schools, in addition to the block level tribal welfare officers, who also regularly visit these schools for inspection. Presently, these schools are covered under the ambit of Sarva Shiksha Abhiyan (SSA) programme, wherein the cluster academic coordinators visit regularly and provide academic inputs to the teachers working in the schools. Provision of funds under SSA is also extended to these ashram schools, at par with the other schools. It may be mentioned here that in many of the states a certain amount of the funds, for managing these ashram schools, are provided by the Central Government i.e., Ministry of Tribal Affairs, Social Welfare and Human Resource Development.

In the state of Orissa, during the year 2007, there were as many as 112 residential ashram schools, 457 non-residential sevashrams, 143 residential sevashrams, 155 boys high schools and 91 girls high schools. All these schools are being managed by the Tribal Welfare Department. In the state of Chhattishgarh during the same year there were 887 ashram schools out of which 389 are for the boys and 247 for girls and the remaining 251 were co educational schools. About 80 per cent of these ashram schools are primary schools and the remaining 20 per cent are middle schools. Total number of seats in 887 in available were 51,785.

The strength of boarders in ashram varies with the number of students residing in the hostel. Kanyashrams and the High schools are all residential in nature. The size of the ashram schools in the state of Chhattisgarh has 30, 50, 80 and 100 seats and the classes taught are from I to V and I to VIII respectively. In the state of Orissa, the strength of the scheduled tribe and scheduled caste children residing in ashram school varies from 60 to 185 and that of high school from 60 to 250.

The various classes in each type of the schools run by the Tribal Welfare Department—Chhattisgarh/Harijan and Tribal Welfare Department (TW/HTW)—Orissa, also vary depending upon the availability of the Scheduled Tribe and Scheduled Caste children in the area.

The TW/HTW departments, from time to time, have also prescribed the staffing pattern in the various kinds of schools. In case of the state of Chhattisgarh, the schools have a head teacher, school superintendent and one or two teachers, while the other staff members are the cook, waterman and a watchman sometimes. This also again depends upon the type of the school. In the state of Orissa, the prescribed strength of staff in various types of schools varies, from 6 in upper primary to 14 in middle school and 24 in high school.

Functioning of Ashram Schools

The District Welfare Officer is delegated with the powers to supervise the academic activities in the school and to exercise administrative control over all the ashram schools in his or her district.

The ashram schools, mostly being residential in nature, they have committees to look after the various activities, functions of the mess and the hostel facilities. In some of the schools the students are also involved in these committees and in some schools, the local community members are also involved. Similarly, an Advisory committee is also constituted for each of the Ashram Schools and High Schools.

The advisory committees are expected to look after the welfare and development of the school and regular meetings are to be conducted in these schools. Any further upgradation, addition to the school building and extension work etc. are also discussed in these meetings.

Innovative Practice

During late eighties, the Tribal Welfare Department, Orissa also introduced a prize scheme on the basis of institutional evaluation, consisting of cash awards, so as to encourage the tribal students of ashram schools to perform better. This cash award is based on a comprehensive institutional evaluation carried out, covering aspects such as: (a) academic performance of the school in Higher Secondary examinations (results/performance); (b) activities of the institution in the vocational subjects like carpentry, tailoring and weaving etc.; and (c) agricultural activities of the school.

Similarly in the early seventies, the state encouraged the teachers by instituting a cash award for those teachers who came out successfully in the tribal language test, conducted every year by the state government. This was instituted in order to promote, particularly the non-tribal teachers to learn the tribal languages, in order to serve better in the tribal areas.

The organization of the school with the teacher and the taught staying together was also an innovative and noble method of improving good relations among the students and the teachers and creating a learning environment conducive to learning. The timetable of the school is also planned for the full day with a variety of activities, which is different from other schools. The concept of Ashram schools is to provide good schooling environment to the children with a healthy learning atmosphere for the overall growth and development among them.

In the state of Chhattisgarh, the tribal welfare department has instituted a "Model School Award" for the residential Ashram schools in order to improve the functioning of the school as well as to bring about improvement in the quality of education imparted in these schools. This award is given to the High Schools and Higher Secondary Schools on the basis of a comprehensive evaluation of their performance.

Special Teaching Classes in Difficult Subjects

The state of Chhattisgarh has provided for special classes for the tribal children in difficult subjects like Mathematics, Science, Geography, English, Languages and Agricultural subjects. Special classes are organised after school hours, in specified centres for the Scheduled Castes and Tribe children, residing both in the residential schools and residential hostels. The best teachers from various schools are empanelled and they are given a fixed number of periods per week, to teach in the identified centres. The government of Chhattisgarh has identified 146 such block locations, where the classes are organized. In these special coaching centres, the children come and identify the subjects which are difficult for them and the teachers accordingly clarify these difficulties and teach these children. These special coaching centres take care of the children who have difficulty in understanding some of the subjects, as well as prepare academically good students to achieve better results in the schools. This is also a step by the government towards improving the quality of education in these residential schools.

The teachers are paid remuneration of Rs 700 for 10 hours of teaching in the specified schools, every month. Teachers with a good record or teachers of higher schools with good qualifications and experience are assigned this job, where they can go to the nearby school (within a radius of 5 kms.) and teach these children after school hours.

The Organization of Ashram Schools

The conduct of any school depends upon the way it is organized both with reference to its physical infrastructure as well as to its teaching force and students. This would differ from school to school. However, the organization of a school is primarily concerned with the interaction between its members, teachers, pupils, office staff and other personnel, and these interactions produce a school climate peculiar to each school (*Dennison, 1987*). The organization of a school is one of the most important activities. The effectiveness of the school and its efficiency depends upon the proper and systematic organization of the teaching activity, enabling the learners to conceive and understand what is exactly required. It is therefore very important for the school organization to pay utmost attention to the physical setting of the school, the classes and its structure, including the learning process.

The conduct of the school also depends upon the availability of adequate facilities and provision of suitable trained and qualified teaching staff including the schooling facilities such as teaching aids, equipment, basic furniture etc. However, the common feature in all types of tribal schools is the inadequacy of these very basic amenities. In spite of the inadequacies, every school tends to function in its own way. Due to various reasons most of the goals of the schools are left unfulfilled, the reasons may be attributed to factors such as societal, pedagogical and human factors, however, if not to a great extent, even if a few of the goals of schools are fulfilled to some extent, the purpose of schooling becomes complete (*Reid, 1978*).

Earlier, the schools which were located in the tribal areas neither functioned properly nor served the needs of the tribal children by taking into account the community, their habitat, culture, language, economy, festivals and rituals. Schools need to take into account these factors which enable them to become a part of the tribal community, where the teacher could perhaps have generated interest among the children and are able to retain them in schools by reducing dropouts and attaining the minimum levels of learning (*Desai et.al., 1981*; *Kundu, M., 1994*; *Panda, B. K., 1996*; *Panda, S.C., 1983*; *Patel, S., 1991*; *Sujatha, K.,1993*). The schools as well as the teachers in actual practice need to reach down to the roots of the culture of the community and understand the background of the children, for whom education has different values and priorities. Like an anthropologist, the successful teacher should view the alien culture of the children not as a judge, but as a student, and as a part of their community and try to understand the aspirations, values placed on various achievements and home environment, so that they can make better efforts to educate them (*Harry, 1967*).

Information was collected from 10 Ashram schools each, from Chhattisgarh and Orissa, in order to understand the functioning of these residential Ashram schools. Some of the important information has been presented here, depicting the organisation and functioning of these residential schools.

Feeder Schools

The Ashram schools are located in central places, catering to many of the feeder schools in the surrounding habitations. The feeder schools may either be the government schools managed by the education department or the schools managed by the Tribal Welfare Departments, however, preference is given to the children of the schools managed by the Tribal Welfare Departments. It will be observed from the table, that each of the schools is surrounded by a minimum of 5 villages to a maximum of 50 villages. The Ashram schools cater to the children of tribal villages, which are scattered and have scanty population. The boarding facilities are provided to the children of distant villages, whereas, the local village students are provided with other freeships, but remain day scholars. The number of primary schools which serve as feeder schools, range between 3 schools to as many as 30 schools, depending upon the number of villages covered by the Ashram Schools. The middle schools range between 1 to 5 schools, which serve as feeder schools; whereas, the number of high schools which are in the surrounding villages, range between 1 to 10 schools, however the high schools do not serve as feeder schools.

Normally, the villages are very small habitations with 10 to 15 households and they are sparsely scattered. Thus the number of habitations which contribute children of school going age to the ashram schools is sometimes more in number. Even so, it is not viable to provide schools in each habitation as they have very few children; it is also not possible as in order to provide an Education Guarantee Scheme (EGS) centre requires a minimum of 20 children. The residential Ashram school becomes the only viable option for catering to the needs of the children of such scattered habitations of the scheduled tribal population.

Feeder Schools and Villages served by Ashram Schools

S. No.	No. of Habitations/ villages Served	Feeder Schools		
		Primary	Middle	Sec./others
1	20	10	05	05
2	30	20	05	05
3	05	02	02	01
4	13	03	-	-
5	20	05	01	-
6	50	10	05	-
7	08	04	-	-
8	-	-	-	-
9	50	25	05	10
10	-	-	-	-
11	25	09	-	-
12	18	05	01	01
13	10	06	-	-
14	12	08	01	-
15	12	09	-	01
16	35	22	05	-
17	18	08	-	02
18	07	03	01	-
19	30	09	02	-
20	28	14	01	02

Schooling Facilities

The Ashram schools were created with a view to provide good schooling facilities to the tribal children and in order to encourage them to enter into schooling. In order to provide better facilities and access, the Ashram schools are envisaged with better school buildings, hostels, and other incentives. On examining the information provided by the Ashram schools in the state of Orissa, it is observed that 25 per cent of the school buildings have semi-pucca buildings and 75 per cent of the schools have pucca buildings, but these buildings needed maintenance as they are not properly repaired from time to time. These schools in general had only classrooms in the school building, which ranged between 3 to 8 rooms, depending upon the number of classes in each school. There are no staff rooms in 55 per cent of the schools and 75 per cent of the schools had office rooms. 50 per cent of schools which had hostels had a maximum of 1–3 rooms, whereas, the remaining 20 per cent of the schools had 4–9 rooms in the hostel. There are some schools, which were utilizing the classrooms as student residences, as the hostel facilities are insufficient. The number of lavatories and bathrooms were found to be insufficient in many of the schools. The girls' schools (Kanyashrams) had such facilities, but they were found to be very few in number.

The state of Chhattisgarh, has made good progress in terms of providing good school buildings to the maximum possible extent in the tribal areas. There are pucca school buildings with proper class-rooms, dining halls, dormitories, kitchen and bathroom as well as toilets. The boundary walls of some of the ashram schools is yet to be constructed. The only problem which was observed is the lack of water storage facilities and over head tanks to provide continuous supply of water to the toilets and bathrooms. This led to the toilets and bathrooms being unutilized. The erratic supply of electricity is also another problem in all the tribal areas, whether it is Madhya Pradesh, Chhattisgarh or Orissa. This erratic supply of electricity has affected studies in the Ashram schools in the evenings and nights. Proper electricity could also have helped pumping water in order to store it, provided there are overhead water tanks in the hostels. This would also have made the urinals and bathrooms functional in these residential schools. The majority of the children in Ashram schools, both boys and girls, therefore prefer going to the nearby rivulets and streams for bathing and other routine chores (*Panda, 2006*).

It will be observed from the information provided by the schools, that the basic facilities of classrooms, hostel facilities and minimum facilities of bathrooms and lavatories are inadequate.

Other Facilities

In addition to the physical facilities of school buildings, the other facilities, which are essential for the school, are electricity, water, staff quarters and boundary wall etc. In the absence of such basic facilities, the schools tend to function in a state of crisis, and the objective of providing the best education with good residential facilities cannot be achieved. Unlike the non-residential schools, the Ashram schools should be in a position to provide better facilities than the tribal homes, thus attracting more children to the schools and with a capacity to retain them in the schools. Considering the economic conditions as well as the varied cultural backgrounds of the tribal families, the residential schools could have provided the tribal children with good facilities, which otherwise they could not enjoy in their homes. However, it will be observed from the data available, there are 50 per cent of schools without any boundary walls, whereas in 10 per cent of the schools the walls are under construction and 40 per cent of the schools including the Kanyashrams have been found to have boundary walls. In the absence of the boundary walls, the schools, which are residential in nature, are vulnerable to many problems such as theft, enforcing discipline among students and control over the school assets such as buildings, ground and kitchen garden etc. Water inall the schools come from tube wells, wells, water lines and nearby rivulets. In the case of Chhattisgarh, there is a provision to hire a waterman in order to fetch water for the school kitchen. Proper electricity was found to be an acute problem, 55 per cent of the schools didn't have any electricity connections, whereas 45 per cent of schools which had electricity facility faced problems of irregularity, erratic supply and repair of the electricity connections.

The school gardens and the kitchen gardens are available in a majority of the schools. The kitchen gardens are developed in order to cater to the needs of the hostel mess, some seasonal vegetables are grown in these gardens in some of the schools, however, it was not found to be sufficient in any of the school hostels.

The staff quarters are one of the most important facilities, in order to encourage teachers to reside on campus. The Ashram schools being residential in nature, in some of the older Ashram schools of Orissa, few staff quarters are provided to the teachers. It was observed that as many as 70 per cent of the schools had staff quarters with a minimum of 1 to 4 and a maximum 5 to 9 such quarters in the schools. While in the state of Chhattisgarh, the residential school has a provision of a quarter for the school superintendent.

Facilities and Incentives to the Scheduled Tribes Students

The tribal welfare department, in all the states, ensures proper and timely distribution of specified facilities to the children enrolled in the Ashram schools. Being residential in nature, in addition to the facility of providing them food in the hostel, they are also provided with uniforms and other garments and shoes, toiletteries etc. The students are also provided with the requisite textbooks, note books, pens, pencils and other stationary items for their use in their studies.

The requisite utensils, dining plates and spoons are stocked with the kitchen of the residential Ashram school. Other items such as cots, beds, blankets, bed sheets, pillows and mosquito nets etc are also provided to the residents of the hostellers of the Ashram Schools. The important facilities, which are provided to the students, are given in the table below:

Types of Facilities

1. Supply of Nationalized Text Books, Reading and Writing materials
2. Provision of school bags, uniforms and other garments
3. Provision of cots, Beds, Blankets, Mosquito nets, utensil
4. Provision of food (boarding facilities)
5. Health measures
6. Special coaching
7. Book Bank for Medical and Engineering colleges
8. Provision of sports and Games materials
9. Provision of science apparatus Library Books, Maps and Charts etc.
10. Cycles to Girls (9th & 10th Classes).

In addition to the facilities, which every child gets, once enrolled in the school, the residential schools are also provided with additional funds and provisions to maintain the schools, such as building maintenance grants, grants to procure kitchen utensils and equipment, beds, bed sheets, cots, blankets, pillows, cupboards, mosquito nets, basic furniture for the schools such as tables, chairs and basic garden equipment etc. on an annual basis. The Ashram schools are required to display the various items sanctioned and give the number of such items available with them on a painted board kept at the entrance of such schools. These grants range from Rs 20,000-40,000 depending upon the size of the school and its level. The school head is required to maintain the maintenance register and the amount spent, with requisite vouchers supporting the investments. While the school superintendent maintains the daily amount spent on the food items per child and gets it verified by the block level officer, in order to get the money released from time to time. An amount of Rs 5.0–Rs 6.00 on an average is spent per child on their breakfast and dinner, while the lunch, provided in the form of mid-day-meal, comes from a central place for a fixed number of schools, regularly, on all working days. Apart from board and lodging, the facilities provided to tribal children in Ashram schools are nationalized text books, reading and writing materials, school bags, uniforms and other garments; cots, beds, blankets, mosquito nets, utensils, etc Provision is also made for health measures, special coaching, science apparatus, library books, maps and charts etc. cycles to Girls (9th & 10th Classes) and sports and games material.

Scholarships to the Scheduled Tribes Students

Besides above facilities, the Scheduled Tribes students are also provided with scholarships in order to support their studies in the schools. Basically there are two types of scholarships, viz., the Pre-Matric and Post-Matric Scholarships. The pre-matric scholarships are given to the students studying in classes VI to VII and VIII to X. There is a provision of Merit-cum-Poverty scholarship in addition to the normal pre-matric scholarship to the children who come from poverty stricken and economically backward families. This is limited to students from classes IX and X and is given only to one student from each class.

The Post-Matric Scholarship is paid to the scheduled tribe students pursuing their higher studies, starting from classes XI-XII to various graduate courses and professional courses as well as ITI courses.

The Learning Process in the Ashram Schools

One of the important characteristics of the Ashram schools is its residential nature; this feature enables the Ashram school to function in a different way from other non-residential schools. Whether it is in the state of Andhra Pradesh, Madhya Pradesh, Orissa, or Chhattisgarh, the majority of residential schools follow a similar kind of time-table, which has been also adopted in the Jawahar Navodaya Vidyalayas and in some of the good residential schools in Andhra Pradesh and Maharashtra. Some of the schools also display their daily time table at the entrance of the school indicating time and duration of a variety of activities before and after the scheduled school time, which includes supervisory study time as well during which time teachers supervise the children and clarify their doubts as well as help them complete their homework. The morning routine begins with a morning prayer, thereafter studies begin at 05.00 a.m. or 06.00 a.m., depending upon the season and climate of the place. This is followed by some time for sports and physical activities. After that the students get ready and come for breakfast. In some of the tribal areas, the children have their lunch in the morning itself, by 08.00 a.m. or 09.00 a.m. before they leave for school. At school too, there is a timetable for the various classes and subjects according to the type of the school, with a lunch break, where they are provided a mid-day-meal and thereafter attend the afternoon classes. In the primary sections normally, multi-grade teaching is followed while for the upper classes, classes are taken up subject wise, with 35–40 minutes per period and a maximum of 6 periods per day and 36-42 periods per week.

The primary classes normally have children sitting in rows or along the walls around the classrooms, on mats provided by the school, while the upper classes have tables and benches. In majority of the schools, the teachers sit at their tables on chairs, while some schools may not have these facilities and here teachers sit along with the children and teach them. The teachers normally give a specific type of task to a particular class at the primary level and monitor their activities and also clarify their doubts while teaching them a subject matter simultaneously. The children are given tasks of group reading, reciting and practice writing etc. Basing on the competencies attained by a group of children, the next subject matter is taught. At times the teachers assign some task as homework to the children.

The teachers do not find any difficulty in teaching the tribal children now, as it has become the policy in many of the states to appoint tribal teachers in these schools. Due to appointment of educated tribal youth as teachers too, the task of teaching in the Ashram Schools is no more difficult. Such educated tribal youth are provided proper training in teaching primary classes and provided support by the cluster academic coordinators. These tribal teachers have an advantage teaching in local dialects and the children don't have any problem in conversing freely with these teachers; understanding their accent, language, local words is also not difficult for the tribal children. The problem, however, is in teaching higher classes by some of the tribal teachers. Some of the schools, which have reported a shortage of schoolteachers, have adopted a variety of measures in the schools. In addition to the multi grade teaching in the primary sections in the schools, the school superintendent and the appointed peon and watchman also take up classes in the primary section. It is interesting to note that the government policy of employing local tribal youth in various categories of jobs in the tribal areas, has enabled the local tribal youth who have completed 8th, 9th and 10th class, to get priority in employment in positions like teachers, peons, watchman and waterman in the ashram schools. These educated youth fulfill the shortage of the teacher requirements in the school and also take care of the classes whenever the regular teachers go for training and other official work. The education department also employs teachers on contract basis according to the requirements of primary, middle and high school. There are many such teachers on consolidated salary of Rs 3,000, Rs 4,000 and Rs 5,000 respectively, depending on the level of schools they have been teaching for the past four to five years. To overcome the shortage of teachers, such arrangements of multi grade teaching and appointment of contract teachers are made. Besides, the services of superintendents and other non-teaching staff are utilized. The teachers also take up additional classes if required.

In some of the states like Andhra Pradesh, Orissa and Chhattisgarh primers are being developed, particularly in order to use them in the tribal primary schools and have been successfully tried out under the Sarva Shiksha Abhiyan Programme. These primers gradually educate the tribal children and put them to the mainstream language at the primary levels, so that sudden switching over to regional languages will not affect the education of the tribal children. This is an attempt to teach the tribal children in local tribal dialect also to cover the local cultural aspects with which the children are very well versed in the textbooks.

The teachers in the Ashram schools also conduct some simple kinds of tests—both oral and written so as to understand the performance of the children from time to time, and this becomes the basis of ascertaining the learning capacity of each of the child in the class. In some of the states students of the 5th classes have to appear for public examinations and if they fail they are retained in the same class for another two to three years. Hereafter, the children either dropout or leave the school. The retention rates in the Ashram schools are found to be better compared to the other formal schools due to the very fact that they are residential institutions. Thus, providing them with a variety of facilities, and their affiliation to the schools for a long time enables these children to continue their studies for a longer time (*Sujatha, K., 1996*).

It was also observed that in general, the schools followed the time schedule provided exclusively for them. In the primary classes the teaching process involved mostly rote learning and memorizing small tasks assigned by the teachers from time to time. The most vocal and talented child in the primary levels led the group in reading exercises, followed by the other children in the class. The teachers utilized teaching aids such as charts, maps and alphabets etc. in the class. At the higher levels there are science kits, globes, charts and mathematics kits to assist in teaching. The provision made under the Sarva Shiksha Abhiyan has enabled all the Ashram schools to get some monetary support @Rs 500 per teacher and @Rs 2,000 per school, to develop independent teaching and learning material as per the requirement of the teacher. Moreover, regular visits to the nearby Cluster Resource Centres has enabled an exchange of ideas and peer interaction, to understand some of the difficult subjects taught at school. Although the teachers are required to develop lesson plans before the beginning of the year and discuss with the heads of the schools, it was mostly found that no such lesson plans are developed every year. In some of the schools the teachers of higher classes also utilized the local subject wise guide book—known as "Key", for teaching the children used in view of the public examinations, since it is easier for the students being focused on the examination. It was also observed that majority of the learning process took place inside the classrooms and very little effort was made to learn after school hours. Although there is a provision of supervisory learning in the Ashram Schools, the students utilized this time for completing their home tasks and practicing some mathematics etc. Around 90 per cent of these schools did not impart any remedial teaching to the weak learners nor identified the weak learners in the various classes (*Panda, B.K., 2000*).

Physical and Cultural Activities in the Ashram Schools

The Ashram Schools had a provision for purchasing sports accessories for the children residing in the schools. Some of the higher schools had simple sports items such as Football, Volleyball, and Carom board. Musical instruments such as Dholok and Harmonium are also available with the schools. However, the students played games such as Running Races, Khabbadi, Kho Kho and other local games. The playgrounds are not very well developed in 80 per cent of the schools. In the primary sections, children played their local games and showed an interest in practicing bow and arrow—local archery. A large number of schools (90 per cent), did not have any provision for physical education teachers and teaching games was largely left to the teachers with knowledge of some games. As such in some of the schools where there are teachers with no interest in games and cultural activities, the schools did not have any such activities.

Attention to cultural activities in the schools is also very low. The children in some schools sang their local songs and played their local music with whatever few instruments were available in the school. The local festivals and functions are observed in the school. Republic Day and Independence Day is followed in all the schools with a parade, singing of the national anthem and distribution of sweets to the children and the community members who attend the function.

In order to take care of the health related problems of the children in the Ashram schools, there are regular health check-ups conducted in each and every school once in a year. The local Primary Heath Care (PHC) centre doctors visit all the schools under their purview and make a record of it and maintain it with them; some of the schools obtain a copy of it and keep it in their records. The health record was found to have the name of each child according to the enrolment register and a "tick" against each name duly signed by the medical officer. The register does not mention any problems faced by any child. The children in the residential schools mostly suffer from the local infections during the change of seasons and are also reported to suffer from malaria, worms and scurvy etc. However, the teachers have reported that when the children are continuously residing in the school, their health conditions are better, but when they return after the vacations, they come with a variety of health related problems and takes some time to regain normal health.

On questioning the schoolteachers, it was also found that they do not maintain any first aid kits and are solely dependent on the Primary Health Care Centre (PHC) for each and every ailment; the PHC's themselves are managed only by health attendants and not the professional doctors, which is another interesting aspect that emerged in this research.

Conclusion

The effort made by both the state and central governments in providing access to schooling to the scheduled tribe children in the remote and inaccessible areas in the recent past is remarkably effective. The new and innovative approaches introducing the Education Guarantee Scheme popularly known as (EGS) and the alternative schooling (AS) provisions, enabled the governments to reach the tribal habitations, irrespective of the small habitations and sparsely distributed populations. The tribal welfare departments are also extending all facilities such as freeships, scholarships and other facilities in order to attract as well as cater to the needs of the scheduled tribe children. Various kinds of residential schools, such as Seva ashrams, Kanya ashrams, Ashram Schools and non-residential schools catering to the needs of the scheduled tribes with provision of mid-day meal facilities and scholarships have been established and upgraded continuously. Besides, the countrywide Education for all programme known as Sarva Shiksha Abhiyan (SSA) is focusing on universalization of elementary education in the entire country by 2012. The SSA programme envisages quantitative as well as qualitative improvement, primarily in the elementary education of the country—it is also focusing on the issues of the education of the disadvantaged groups, by providing equality of opportunity to these groups. More particularly, the SSA has provided monetary benefits to the

Ashram schools and also to contract teachers hired by the schools to counter teacher shortages. The visits by the cluster academic coordinators and the visit by the Ashram school teachers to the regular interactive activities in the CRC's, has provided some relief in terms of academic support to the teachers to a great extent.

Tribal people have been recognized in India's development planning as one of the most deprived and marginalized groups. Elementary education has been a priority area for their development under "Tribal Sub-Plans" for over the past 60 years. Further, the National Policy on Education-1986 accorded priority to the opening of primary schools in tribal areas and encouraged the entry of tribal youth into teaching suggested the establishment of residential schools "on a large scale". It also posited the need for development of curricula and instructional material in tribal languages for the early primary stage. In addition, it called for formulation of incentives schemes to draw tribal children to school. The issue of improving tribal children's access to schools continues to be emphasized through the Tenth Plan (2002–07) and, as noted above, is a thrust of the Sarva Shiksha Abhiyan (SSA) program.

The proportion of children out of school in remote tribal areas has remained higher than among tribal children living in non-tribal areas. The main reasons for this are the limited educational infrastructure available in tribal areas because of their remoteness; tribal hamlets being cut off from main villages or well-populated rural areas by geographic features; the difficulties faced by children living in smaller habitations in accessing existing formal schools; and so on. Other reasons, for low school enrolment among Scheduled Tribe children, include the reluctance of their families to educate them. Further, in addition to the high level of illiteracy among tribal parents, they may not value the education available, particularly in relation to its opportunity costs. Children are crucial family workers in the tribal economy, which includes working on agricultural land, grazing cattle, working as labor on work sites, collecting firewood or other minor forest produce, stone quarrying, mining, and home-based work such as processing forest produce.

Low levels of learning are found among tribal children not only because of household factors and problems with the language of instruction, where this is not their mother tongue, but also due to other school-related variables. The earlier donor-financed District Primary Education Program has shown that the achievement gap between tribal and non-tribal children can be narrowed by attention to classroom transactions and the school environment.

On meeting some of the parents in the tribal areas, they stated that they are quite satisfied with the arrangements of the residential ashram schools as the children are taken care by the schools on many fronts, in addition to the extra attention paid to them by the teachers in such schools. They also stated that in the absence of such facilities, it would not have been possible for them to send their children to the school or teach them at home, as their services would have been utilized in attending to household chores. The aspiration of these parents were also quite simple, that their children become forest officers or teachers, working in the tribal areas; they did not have in mind any professional jobs for their children, such as doctors, engineers etc.

The very concept of these residential Ashram schools has been followed in creating model residential schools for the Scheduled Tribes and Scheduled Castes in the state of Andhra Pradesh under a separate registered society act. Even the National Policy on Education—1986 and its Programme of Action—1992, has emphasized of the need for setting up more ashram schools in the tribal areas. The concept of Navodaya Vidyalyas has also emerged out of the concept of Gurukulas and Ashram schools, which are fully funded by the central government and with one being established in each rural district of the country. The Navodaya Vidyalayas have become very successful institutions, while the Ashram schools are still struggling to become institutions of importance in the tribal areas.

Some of the critical issues, which can be taken into account in improving the functioning of these Ashram schools or the residential schools in the tribal areas are:

(i) encouraging and making available tribal teachers, who can speak the local tribal language, teachers trained to deal with tribal children (attitudinal training), and administrators sensitized to tribal issues;

(ii) availability of instruction and instructional materials in the local tribal languages;

(iii) integrating the facilities and support of CRCs and BRCs in order to provide academic guidance to the teachers serving in these inaccessible areas, as well as serving the needs of tribal children;

(iv) timely sanctioning funds to the school along with necessary provisions thus enabling the schools to function smoothly;

(v) timely release of the scholarships; and

(vi) regular training of the teachers.

References

Ananda, G. (1994), Ashram Schools in Andhra Pradesh: A Case Study of Chenchus of Nallamalai Hills, Commonwealth Publishers, New Delhi.

Census of India (2001), Provisional Population Totals, Directorate of Census Operations, New Delhi.

Denison, Bill and Shenton Ken (1987), Challenges in Educational Management: Principles in to Practice, Croom Helm, New York.

Desai B, and Patel, A. (1981), Ashram Schools of Gujarat: An Evaluative Study, Tribal Research and Training Center, Gujarat Vidyapeeth, Ahmedabad.

Government of India (2005), Selected Educational Statistic, Ministry of Human Resource Development, GOI, New Delhi.

Government of Orissa (2007), Information on Ashram Schools, Web-site of Department of Harijan and Tribal Welfare Department, Bhubaneswar.

Govinda, R., (ed), (2001), India Education Report, NIEPA & Oxford Press, New Delhi.

Heredia, R.C. (1992), Tribal Education for Community Development: A Study of Schooling in the Talesaria Mission Area, Concept Publishing Company, NewDelhi.

Jha, P. (1985), An Evaluative Study of the Hostels and Ashram for Tribal Girl Students, Tribal Research Institute, Bhopal, Cit. in Buch, M.B. (ed.), Fourth Survey of Research in Education, Baroda.

Kundu, M. (1994), Tribal Education: New Perspectives, Gyan Publishing House, New Delhi.

Paisey, A. (1981), Organization and Management in Schools, Longman, London.

Panda B.K. (1996), Functions and Organization of Tribal Schools, Anamika. New Delhi.

Panda B.K. (2000), Organization of Schools in the Tribal Areas, Pariprekshya, No.7, Vols.1–2, April–August, NIEPA, New Delhi.

Panda S.C. (1983), An Empirical Study of Education of Tribals in Orissa, Buch M.B., (ed.), Fourth Survey of Research in Education, Vol. II, 1983–88, NCERT, New Delhi, p.1448.

Patel, S. (1991), Tribal Education in India, Mittal Publication, New Delhi.

Pratap, D.R. Raju, C.C. and Rao, M.V.K. (1971), Study of Ashram Schools in Tribal Areas of Andhra Pradesh, Tribal Cultural Research and Training Institute, Hyderabad, cit. in Buch, M.B. (Ed.) Third Survey of Research in Education, Baroda.

Reid, Ivan (1978), Sociologist Perspectives on School and Education, Open Books, London.

Sujatha K. (1983), An Indepth Study of Ashram Schools in Andhra Pradesh, Mimeo, NIEPA, New Delhi.

Sujatha K. (1987), Education of Forgotten Children: A Case Study of Yenadi Tribes, Konark, New Delhi.

Sujatha K. (1993), Education in Ashram Schools: A Case Study of Adilabad District of Andhra Pradesh, NIEPA, New Delhi.

Sujatha K. (1994), Education Development among Tribes: A Study of Sub-plan Areas in Andhra Pradesh, NIEPA & Asian Publishers, New Delhi.

Sujatha K. (1996), Single Teacher Schools in Tribal Areas, NIEPA, New Delhi.

HEALTH

Health Issues and Health Seeking Behaviour among Tribals of the North-Central Sub-region of India

Sutapa Bandyopadhyay Neogi

India's performance vis-à-vis human development has been mixed in the last decade. Its heterogeneous population has always provided us with a checkered growth data along the verticals that define development indices. While indicators like literacy rate, economic growth, technology know how and health indicators give us a reason to celebrate, the alarming disparity across various population groups shows us the other side of reality.

The remarkable progress that India is witnessing could do little to leave an impact on the people affected by ecologically variable niches, illiteracy, poverty, isolation, difficult terrain and superstitions. These groups constitute the tribal population of the country. About half of the world's primitive population people, comprising 635 tribal communities, including 75 primitive tribal communities, live in India. (*ICMR, 2003*)

Probing further, we find that tribal groups, and even within the tribal population, the primitive tribals, lag far behind other sections in the key health indicators. Education and economic growth are known to be the key factors that shape health seeking behaviour, thus influencing the morbidity and mortality pattern.

The present study is an attempt towards understanding the health seeking behaviour among the tribal population. However, the scope of the article is restricted to the North Central sub-region of India, primarily because they seem to accommodate a major share of tribal population in the country.

To begin with, let us look at the distribution pattern of Scheduled Tribes in the North Central sub-region of India. This sub region comprises the states of Jharkhand, Chhattisgarh, North Western parts of Bengal and northern Orissa.

As per Census 2001, as many 31.8 per cent of the population of Chhattisgarh, 26.3 per cent of Jharkhand, 22.1 per cent of Orissa is constituted by schedule tribes. Chhattisgarh has its tribal population concentrated in the southern, northern and north eastern districts. District wise distribution of Scheduled Tribes population shows that Dantewara has the highest tribal population with 79 per cent, followed by Bastar with 67 per cent, Jashpur with 65 per cent, Surguja with 57 per cent Kanker with 56 per cent, Raigarh and Raipur (*Government of Chhattisgarh, 2007*). District-wise distribution of Scheduled Tribes population in **Jharkhand** shows that Gumla district has the highest tribal population with 68.4 per cent, followed by Lohardaga and Paschimi Singhbhumwith 50 per cent each and Ranchi and Pakaur districts with 41.8–44.6 per cent respectively. (*RGI; 2001*) Orissa has the majority of its tribal population in the districts of Malkangiri with 57.4 per cent, Mayurbhanj with 56.6 per cent Rayagada with 55.8 per cent andNabarangapur and Kandhamal with 55 per cent. More than half of the total Scheduled Tribes population of West Bengal is concentrated in four districts namely Medinapur, Jalpaiguri, Purulia and Bardhhaman. Of the remaining districts, Bankura, Maldah, Uttar Dinajpur and Dakshin Dinajpur have a sizeable tribal population.

The share of Scheduled Tribes population in urban areas is less than 3 per cent across the country. Tribal population living in the states of Chhattisgarh, Jharkhand, Orissa and West Bengal are primarily rural, with more than 90 per cent of the population staying in villages.

This sizable population did not go unnoticed when the National Health Policy was drafted way back in 1983. This was reiterated in revised policy of 2002. The endeavor of the health and social sectors, however, did not pay enough dividends to bring about a palpable change in the health indicators. What we must understand at this point is that such an outcome is not merely because of health issues. Rather, it results from a complex interaction of health with literacy, education, poverty, social norms and cultural practices that finally shapes the health and treatment seeking behavior. A simplified scheme, illustrating these factors is presented in the diagram.

It can easily be concluded from this diagram that health seeking behaviour of a population is determined largely by the knowledge, attitude and beliefs of the community. The concept of lifestyle as the interplay

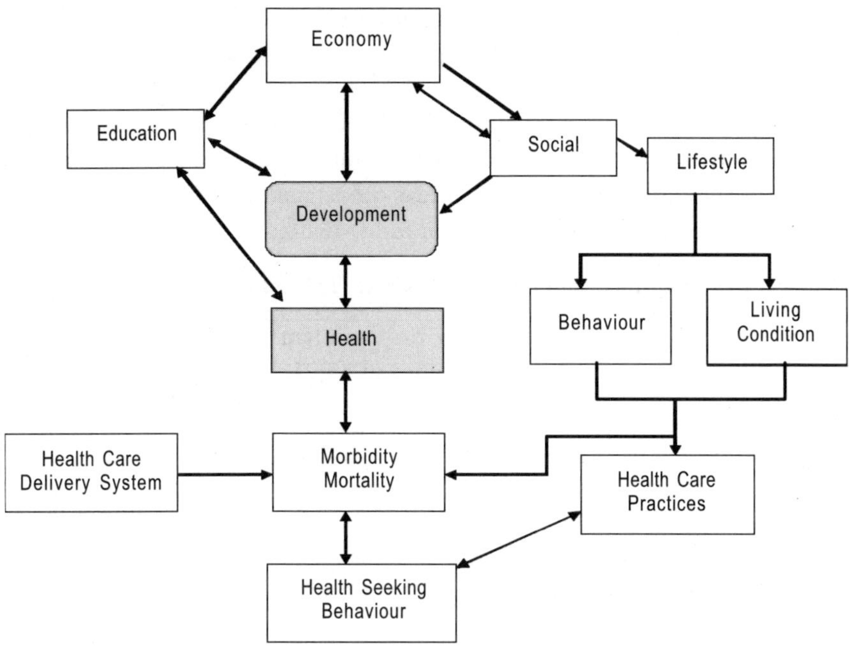

between behavioral patterns and socio cultural conditions leads one to examine specific behaviors and specific measures, as they relate to health and disease. The dynamic inter play between specific measures creates a complex and intricate system of social, economic, cultural and behavioural factors inter woven with disease risk factors and health status. This in turn is influenced by health care facility and physical environment.

Tribes are known to live in isolation, far away from civilization, with their traditional values, beliefs and customs. This is why they often fall prey to misconceptions. Added to this is the poor health infrastructure and service delivery, owing to difficult terrain. These people thus resort to some traditional practices that can be potentially harmful. The acceptability of such indigenous practices could reflect the unavailability and inaccessibility of modern health care services. In order to understand the dynamics of their health seeking behavior, it is prudent that we understand their morbidity profile and also its related knowledge, attitudes and practices.

Morbidity Profile

Common morbidities affecting the tribal population are same as those affecting the non-tribal population with a difference in the magnitude of the morbidities and some features that are peculiar to the tribes. The overall morbidity and mortality rates during infancy and childhood are higher for tribal population.

An analysis of National Family Health Survey 3 data brings out the disparity in the health status of tribal population of the country (*NFHS, 3:2007*). Scheduled tribes lag behind other castes as far as the major indicators are concerned (Table 1).

Table 1: Key Indicators from NFHS-3 by Caste /Tribe of India (Provisional data)

	ST	SC	OBC	Others
Institutional births (%)	19.6	35.1	39.6	53.2
Births assisted by skilled personnel (%)	26.9	42.3	48.5	59.2
Children below 3yrs who are stunted (%)	44.3	44.1	39.2	31.1
Children under 3yrs who are wasted (%)	25.7	20.5	18.9	16.4
Children under 3yrs who are underweight (%)	56.7	52.2	46.4	37.3
Women who Body Mass Index is below normal (%)	46.6	39.5	32.6	26.0
Children age 6-35 months who are anemic (%)	85.1	82.3	79.7	74.4

Infant mortality rates of Jharkhand, Chhattisgarh, Orissa and West Bengal have shown a decline over the years but the decline in rural areas, largely tribal population is less remarkable than for the states as a whole. The prime causes of childhood mortality are diarrhoea and acute respiratory tract infections, both of which are linked to nutritional status. The prevalence of respiratory diseases varied between 8-17 per cent among tribal population of Bondo, Diyadi, Kondha and Juanga in Orissa and Birhor in Chhattisgarh. (*ICMR, 2003*) This accounts for high mortality due to lack of early diagnosis and treatment. This is further compounded by the increased level of malnutrition.

Various studies conducted in pre-school and school children reveal a wide range of malnourishment. A study on pre-school tribal children of Chhattisgarh, Jharkhand & Orissa reveals that almost 50 per cent of the children were stunted; the figures rose to 84 per cent affecting boys in the age group of 4–12 year. [5–7] Nutritional status based on anthropometric indices reveals that almost 6 per cent of children belonging to Bondo and Diyadi tribes in the 0–14 age group, suffer from severe stunting while 20–25 per cent had severe wasting and 20 per cent were severely underweight. (*ICMR, 2002*) Wasting was found to be more frequent in girls. (*Yadav, 1999*) About 88 per cent of Oraon children living in the tea gardens of West Bengal have been reported to be suffering from moderate to severe under-nourishment, based on Body Mass Index (BMI). This deficiency could not be attributed to energy intake; rather, most of the children attended a local primary school having a midday meal program. This meal which was qualitatively deficient, replaced, rather than supplemented home meals. (*Mittal, 2006*)

An in-depth analysis of dietary patterns among Oraon tribes reveals that the energy intake of these children was almost half of the ICMR recommended allowances. Although the intake of cereals was optimal, large deficits in intake of protective foods like milk, fruits and vegetable were found. There is also a high prevalence of intestinal parasitism among the tribals. A look into the socio cultural and hygienic practices revealed that defecation in the open is the rule in tribal villages. Children often defecate in open spaces around the houses. Most of them either do not wash their hands, or use just water for washing hands before eating and after defecation.

Anaemia has been found to afflict 50 to 60 per cent of Bondo and Diyadi tribes of Orissa in the 0–14 years and more than 14 years age groups respectively. (*ICMR, 2002, 2003-4*) It is more common in women than in men. (*ICMR, 2003*) Statistical analysis has revealed a positive correlation between hookworm infestation and anemia due to indiscriminate defecation, walking bare foot and lack of health awareness. In Chhattisgarh, almost 9 out of every 10 children aged between 6–35 months are anemic and this proportion is never less than 80 per cent in any subgroup of the tribal population. (*MedInd, 2004*) It is a significant problem in women, with 54 to 86 per cent of them across various groups suffering from it.

Vitamin A deficiency in the form of night blindness, conjunctival xerosis and bitot's spot has been found in more than 40-45 per cent of tribal children in Orissa. (*ICMR, 2003–4*) This has been closely linked to nutritional disorders and diarrhea that are very prevalent among Bondo, Diyadi, Juang and Kandha tribes. Nearly 2 per cent of the children belonging to Gond tribe in central India has been found to be suffering from vitamin A deficiency in the form of Bitot's spot. (*Rao, 2005*) Prevalence of Iodine Deficiency Disorders was found in more than 1/3 population in the region. (*ICMR, 2002*) Birhor tribes have reported Vitamin A deficiency in 24.4 per cent of its population and Goitre in 3.4 per cent of them. (*ICMR, 2003*)

Worm infestation was observed among 21–35 per cent of tribal groups of Bondo, Diyadi and Kodha in Orissa in children less than 14 years old. Among adults the prevalence was around 20 per cent. (*ICMR, 2002, 2003-4*) Hookworm (19.4 per cent) was observed to be the most common helminthic infestation followed by round worm (8.8 per cent). Among protozoal infestation, E. histiolytica was the most common (10.8 per cent) followed by Giardia (3.2 per cent). (*ICMR, 2002, 2003–4*) Intestinal parasitism has been found in 46–50 per cent of the tribal population in various studies. (*Regional Medical Research, 2003*; *Rao, 2002*).

The absence of safe drinking water, poor sanitation and unhygienic conditions, subject these marginalized groups to a large array of infectious diseases. No wonder, diarrheal diseases including cholera has been found to affect about 12–13 per cent of the children and adults in a tribal population in Orissa.[ICMR;2002] More than 40 per cent of the stool samples collected were found to be culture positive with a majority being *E. Coli* (>80 per cent) and *V.Cholerae* was isolated from 10 per cent of the samples.

In a study conducted in Chhattisgarh less than 60 per cent of the children suffering from diarrhea were taken to a health care provider and 30 per cent were given oral rehydration solution. (*MedInd, 2004*) The awareness among the tribal people about treatment of diarrhea remained inadequate and many believed that children with diarrhea should be given less to drink than usual. While 59 per cent of mothers knew about Oral Rehydration Solution (ORS) packets, less than 30 per cent of children with diarrhea in the past 2 weeks received ORS in Jharkhand. These figures present a picture of the state as a whole.

Most of the childhood mortalities and morbidities can be prevented by early initiation and exclusive breast feeding of infants till 6 months of age and timely and appropriate weaning. But data from the Gond tribe reveals that only 9.1 per cent of children were breast fed within 2 hours of birth, 37.2 per cent were breast fed by the second day or third day. Colostrum was not given to 86.4 per cent of the children and supplementary feeding was started by 6 months, in a majority of the children (84.5 per cent). (*Rao, 2005*)

The delay in initiating breast feeding is accounted for by the ritual of cleansing the breasts by the aunt and discarding the colostrum, which is considered harmful. This is compounded by the belief prevalent in some parts of the country, that breast milk could be harmful to babies. There is an indigenous method which is followed to check breast milk where a few drops of breast milk are expressed and an ant dropped into it. If the ant dies, the milk is considered to be toxic and the baby is not breast fed at all. Often in cases of previous neonatal deaths/ childhood deaths or failure to gain weight, breast milk is avoided for the subsequent children. Medicines are also prescribed in some cases to purify the milk.

A potentially dangerous practice in some tribal areas of Orissa needs attention. There is a belief that a mother should not take her bath after delivery till the cord of the baby falls off. To augment the process, a custom by the name of *bhuin seka* is followed. The baby is made to lie on his abdomen over a hot surface for a few seconds and removed. This causes the cord to shrivel up and eventually fall off. Yet another harmful practice in certain tribal areas is to apply hot fomentation on the scrotum of the infant, if the size is perceived to be larger, by the mother.

Malaria is a major public health problem particularly in north central sub region, because of vast tracts of forests with tribal settlements. Malaria control in such settlements has always been unattainable due to technical and operational problems, since a large part of North central sub-region are hilly, forested and inaccessible, with poor communication facilities.

Additionally, an increase in *P.falciparum* cases has been associated with malaria resistant cases in the Bastar district of Chhattisgarh. This apparent increase in malaria infections might have been partly due to improved surveillance under Enhanced Malaria Control Project. Though the impact of chloroquine resistance has been difficult to measure because of logistics and small health budgets, studies indicate that an increasing number of patients treated with chloroquine did not clear their parasitemia. Moreover, the constant movement of people for food gathering and cultivation makes it difficult to treat individuals and the malaria gametocyte load remains high in communities.

Further, most of the malaria cases are treated with chloroquine at home, through forest guards or school teachers. The anti-malarial drugs used for such treatment is now likely to result in treatment failures, owing to drug resistance.

People have faith in traditional healers (guniya) from the same community. Only when they do not get cured, do they go to the untrained and unlicensed practitioners or quacks who may administer adulterated and insufficient dosage as treatment. These quacks prefer to give them injections for quick relief. Another point of concern is the strong misconception that malaria convulsions are due to evil spirits. This has a considerable impact on the use of anti malarial drugs.

A majority of the tribal groups still believe that malaria is caused by wrath of God, witch craft and even by drinking unhygenic water (*ICMR*; *2003–4*). Half of them said that they would prefer to obtain treatment from tribal healers (20 per cent), practice witch craft (15 per cent), use wild herbs (8 per cent), use chili (4 per cent) or turmeric powder (3 per cent). The majority of the respondents were not aware where mosquitoes breed. Almost 60 per cent were aware that spraying insecticides was intended to kill mosquitoes and 30 per cent knew that mud plastering should not be done after insecticidal spray, yet 80 per cent respondents said that they would plaster their houses within a week of such spraying. (*Sharma, 1993*) This reflects the mismatch between the malaria program and the common practice followed by the tribals to keep their homes clean. Most people even burn dry leaves to drive mosquito out of their houses.

Enhanced Malaria Control Project (EMCP) is a special initiative undertaken by the Government to address the problem of malaria. Districts covered under EMCP like Malkangiri and Mayurbhanj in Orissa and Kanker in Chhattisgarh have demonstrated a substantial decline in Annual Parasite Incidence and slide positivity rate, between 1997 and 2007. (*MOHFW, 1997, 2001*)

Malaria cases had shown a sharp decline in Chhattisgarh from late seventies to early eighties. The ratio of *P-vivax* and *P.falciparum* was to be 50:50 in 1979, while in 1985, *P.falciparum* was more than 70 per cent. Malaria in the 1980s had returned with new features like establishment of *A. Culicifacies* as a major vector, development of resistance to DDT and emergence of chloroquine resistance in *P.falciparum*. It emerged that during 1985 to 1997, the number of malaria cases increased to more than 500 per cent and number of *P. falciparum* increased more than 450 per cent. Deaths due to malaria were also on increase (>600 per cent). District wise data showed a steady rising trend in malarial incidence during 1986 to 2000, particularly in the districts of Kanker and Jagadalpur. (*ICMR Bulletin, 2004*)

Orissa contributes 23 per cent of malaria cases and 40 per cent of *P.falciparum* cases in the country. A prospective study conducted in Malkangiri and Kandhamal districts during 2002–03 showed slide positivity rate (SPR) of 14.2 per cent and 14.4 per cent in Bondo and Diyadi tribes. The *P.falciparum* rate was 93.5 per cent and 91.6 per cent respectively. Spleen rate (proportion of children with enlarged spleen mostly indicative of malaria in endemic regions) in children of 2–9 years was found in 25–35 per cent of the tribal population indicating high transmission rate in the communities (*ICMR, 2002*).

Tuberculosis is another disease afflicting this vulnerable population. Contrary to the belief that pulmonary TB is not a major health problem among primitive tribes, probably because they live in a pollution free environment, studies suggest that tribal population too are prone to this deadly disease. Evidence suggests that tribal population is in fact more prone to the infection than non-tribal counterparts. Frequent migration, socio cultural behavior, poverty and poor health care are the factors leading to its spread. Some primitive tribes are known to have a high migration rate during summer in search of employment. They could be contracting infections from the general population and spreading them in tribal areas. Moreover, the role played by environmental factors like low humidity in certain pockets of the region and dusty winds, present most of the time, could spread the infection.

A study was under taken to understand Tuberculosis related health seeking behavior in the tribal districts of Orissa. The findings revealed that blood in sputum was the main distinctive symptom of tuberculosis that inevitably leads to the death of the victim. Causes of TB were perceived to be alcohol, tobacco and hereditary predisposition, while at the same time TB could spread through direct social interaction. The first point of contact for the people with TB symptoms was the traditional healer. Though half the population knew that TB treatment was now free, but most of the patients had spent considerable amount of money on its treatment. The defaulter rate was as high as 15 per cent and the average minimum delay in diagnosis was 111 days for men and 146 days for women (*Seeberg, 2004*).

While Orissa has accomplished targets of 70 per cent case detection and 85 per cent treatment completion rates, Malkangiri district has shown a considerable decline on both indicators. Preliminary results show an insufficient number of non-health DOT (Directly observed treatment) providers (DPs), excessive distances between DPs and patients, and insufficient training of DPs were the key hurdles. On the patient side, the study revealed excessive payment by TB patients to traditional healers for ineffective treatment, distrust in the effectiveness of tablets as opposed to injection, for TB treatment and late reporting for treatment, due to stigma. While the provider generally enjoys an elevated status because of the services to the community, the patient—provider relationship is hampered in some cases, if s/he belongs to a Scheduled Tribe and the patient is seen as having a higher caste status and yet accepts medicine from the tribal DP (*Seeberg, 2004*). Case detection of tuberculosis in 50 per cent of the tribal districts of Chhattisgarh, Jharkhand, Orissa and West Bengal was less than the desired level of 70 per cent in recent years. (*MOHFW, 2004, 2006*) The cure rate, too, in half of the districts was less than the target value of 85 per cent.

A study carried out in central India suggest that more than 22 per cent of chest symptomatics were found to be sputum positive and the infection rate in children below 9 years was quite high (16.9 per cent). (*Chakma, 1996*) Prevalence of the disease among males was significantly higher than females.

The prevalence of TB among Bondo and Diyadi tribes in 2002–03 was

0.7 per cent and 3.5 per cent respectively (*Rao, 2002*). The prevalence in Chhattisgarh was 0.6 per cent and medically treated TB was 0.5 per cent, which is marginally higher than Indian figures (*ICMR, 2002*).

The tribal belts of Lohardaga and Gumla in Jharkhand are the worst affected, as 80 per cent of their population is suffering from the disease. (*Health Initiative, 2007*)

With HIV/AIDS being increasingly detected in this region, tuberculosis & HIV may result in a deadly epidemic· The spread of this combination of diseases is a concern not only in India, but in this tribal belt too. Less than 20 per cent of women are found to have heard about AIDS in Chhattisgarh and Jharkhand. (*NFHS, 1998*) Of the people who had heard about AIDS, 55 per cent did not know how to avoid infection. (*MedInd, 2004*) The prevalence of HIV among high risk and low risk population has shown an increase over the years. Chhattisgarh alone has over 2000 HIV positive cases with 383 confirmed AIDS deaths, which speaks enough about the problem. (*Kaiser, 2007*)

Skin infections are also common among the tribes. Occasional outbreaks of dermatitis and scabies are reported. The tribal people generally seek treatment from the indigenous practitioners in case of any complications like generalized dermatitis / boils etc.

In a study conducted in Orissa, 20.6 per cent and 6.9 per cent of Bondo and Diyadi tribes were found to be affected by scabies (*ICMR, 2003*). The overall prevalence of infected and non-infected scabies was 10.3 per cent and 7.6 per cent. This is comparable to the findings in Birhor tribe of Central India where 7 per cent of tribal population were found to be affected.

Cercarial dermatitis is an emerging disease worldwide, yet cases of such dermatitis often go undiagnosed, especially in communities affected by various skin infections. In an investigation that was carried out in the tribal population of Central India, the prevalence ranged between 2.1 per cent and 12.5 per cent. It was prevalent more among children, than adults. (*Rao, 2007*)

Some tribal communities show a very high incidence of hereditary diseases like hemoglobinopathies—thalassemia and other structural hemoglobinopathies. (*Balgir, 2000*) Although they are gradually becoming aware of their hereditary problems, the same is not true for the primitive tribals. For instance, the Bhuyan tribe is not aware that hemoglobinopathies is the cause for health problems like weakness, body ache and joint pains. Hence, they do not feel that it should be treated. However, if the illness persists, they go to local quacks and occasionally to Primary Health Centre (PHC) for treatment. (*ICMR, 2004*)

A higher prevalence of Beta-thalassemia has been found among other scheduled tribes in Orissa like Santhal (8.0 per cent), Lodha (6.6 per cent), Bhatra (6.6 per cent) and Kondh (6.3 per cent) (*ICMR, 2003–4*). G6PD enzyme deficiency was observed in 13.52 per cent of the Bhuyan, Jaanga and Munda tribes in Orrisa. While in the Kharia tribe hemoglobinopathies and G6PD deficiency was seen to be 13.3 per cent and 24.6 per cent respectively, 13.1 per cent of sickle hemoglobin cases was found among the Gond tribe from Central India[1] (*ICMR, 2002*; *Tribal Health Bulletin, 2003*). The usual clinical signs and symptoms like pallor, joint pains and abdominal pains were observed in these patients.

The frequency of Rhesus negative blood group is very low (1.4 per cent) in the Kharia tribe. In general, among the tribal population, the frequency of Rhesus negative blood group is low as compared to general population of India.ICMR;2002] A preponderance of blood group B over A group was found among the tribal population of Orissa. The frequency of 'O' blood group (23 per cent) is lower as compared to 'A' (31 per cent) and 'B' (33 per cent) (*ICMR, 2003-4*).

While these are the usual health issues affecting the tribal population, they too are in the grip of the burgeoning epidemic of cardiovascular diseases. Tribal societies living in isolation and now in transition to a modern life style conditions, are believed to suffer less from chronic diseases like cardiovascular diseases, diabetes and metabolic syndrome.

However, a study conducted in the Toto and Bhutia communities in Jalpaiguri district of West Bengal, shows the reverse to be true. Toto and Bhutia share a common ancestry and live in a similar ecological habitat. A section of the Bhutia tribe still lives as traditional communities, while another section had adopted modern lifestyle and lives in urban areas. The prevalence of hypertension, diabetes and metabolic syndrome was high among the Bhutia community, with no significant rural-urban differences. The Toto tribe though, had a low prevalence of metabolic syndrome and hypertension, but had an adverse lipid profile. The study indicated that these ethnic groups are genetically predisposed towards the diseases observed and that gets worse when they urban life styles (*Sarkar, 2006*). The prevalence of these diseases was also seen to be higher among the female population than the males.

A similar female predisposition was observed in a study conducted among Santhal children in Puruliya district of West Bengal (*Chowdhury, 2006*). Body fat percentage of girls was significantly higher than that of boys in the 8–9 yrs category, suggesting greater subcutaneous adiposity and a higher risk of cardiovascular disease in future.

Prevalence of hypertension was found to be 8 per cent among Lepcha tribals of Chhattisgarh district, who were neither sedentary, obese nor affluent. 30 per cent of them had very high blood pressure. The rates of mortality due to diabetes, hypertension, cancer, respiratory disease and mental illness were alarmingly high among this tribe. While significant use of alcohol and tobacco and possibly higher consumption of salt could have contributed to higher levels of hypertension, their under reported stress cannot be ignored; stress due to poverty, lack of income, lack of opportunity and lack of access to basic services. (*Bhargava, 2006*)

Infertility is yet another health problem that has recently come to the notice of researchers and policy makers. About one third couples among Khairwar tribe in central India are known to be infertile. (*ICMR, 2003–4*) Very high rate of sexual promiscuity was observed in the tribe, with positive test noted in 57 per cent males and 70 per cent females (*ICMR, 2002*). The incidence of sterility could be attributed to this. A comparative analysis of current age specific fertility rate in terms of children ever born revealed that fertility in the age group of 15-19 yrs had decreased among tribals while this was not observed among non-tribal counterparts. Although similar observations have not been reported from north central tribal population, this could be a problem because of the difference noted in the number of children desired and the number actually living. Further, the growth of the Schedule Tribe population in the states of Orissa and Jharkhand is lower than the growth of the States' total population; although the use of contraceptives in tribal districts is lower than in non-tribal districts.

It has been reported by tribal respondents that the ideal family size (3.6) exceeds their actual family size (2.7). Hence they are not concerned about contraception. Regarding causes of infertility, a sizeable number of males attributed it to divine will (37 per cent). In many of the cases, either the persons reported upon or their wives, suffered from one reproductive health problem or the other, but very few among them had ever utilized reproductive health services for treatment. (*ICMR, 2003–4*)

There were a lot of misconceptions regarding sexual problems too. About 73 per cent of the respondents belonging to Baiga tribe did not avail of any government health facilities. The main reasons mentioned were that there was "no felt need" to do so (88 per cent) and that the health posts were not conveniently located (30 per cent).

About 7 per cent of the males interviewed had availed of government health facilities during the 3 month period preceding the survey. The main reasons given for not availing of the government health services were again, the absence of a felt need to do so (76.6 per cent), due to the health centres not being conveniently located (17.9 per cent), due to non-availability of doctors or health workers (8.8 per cent) and lack of issue medicines (10.8 per cent). Further most of the people who responded harboured a wrong outlook towards sexual health mattes (*ICMR, 2003–4*).

Health Care Delivery System

Health planning in India is an integral part of national socio-economic planning. The guidelines for national health planning were provided by a number of committees dating back to the Bhore Committee in 1946. The recommendations which were reviewed by subsequent committees now read as follows:

(i) There would be one Sub Centre (SC) for every 5000 people;
(ii) There would be one Primary Health Centre (PHC) for every 30,000 population; and
(iii) There would be one Community Health Centre (CHC) for every one lakh people.

Keeping in view the difficult terrain, inability to reach out to the interior areas and backwardness of the tribal areas, it envisaged that each SC would cater to a population of 3000, each PHC to a population of 20,000 and each CHC to a population of 80,000.

But as of today, the health infrastructure in these states is far from satisfactory. In India, only 48 per cent of the PHCs are adequately staffed, while only 26 per cent is staffedin Chhattisgarh, it is 38 per cent in Jharkhand, 6 per cent in West Bengal and no such centres at all in Orissa. (Table 2) The infrastructure and logistic supply are equally poor in tribal and non-tribal areas. (*NFHS-3, 2007*)

Table 2: Percentage of Primary Health Centres Adequately (60 per cent) Equipped in Staff, Infrastructure and Logistics

State	Districts (Tribal/ non-tribal)	Staff	Infrastructure	Supply
Jharkhand		38.2	9.8	50.5
	Tribal	7.7–70.8	3.8–11.8	0–77.4
	Non-tribal	2.3–93.3	4.3 – 31.3	0–87.0
Orissa		0.2	3.2	3.5
	Tribal	0–13.8	0–10.3	0–5.6
	Non-tribal	0–18.8	0–33.3	0–20.0

(*Contd.*)

State	Districts (Tribal/ non-tribal)	Staff	Infrastructure	Supply
West Bengal		5.7	12.0	23.0
	Tribal	0–38.6	7.1–16.7	14.1–36.7
	Non-tribal	0–58.6	5–24.7	17.5–25.6
Chhattisgarh		26.3	2.8	14.1
	Tribal	13–46.7	0–8.7	0–23.3
	Non-tribal	0–36.2	0–8.5	0–33.3

Source: NFHS 3 data.

A closer look at the tribal areas of these states indicates that number of PHCs and CHCs are adequate only in Orissa and West Bengal. Though the number of sub centres is adequate in the tribal areas of Chhattisgarh, almost one-fourth are functioning without an ANM (Auxillary Nurse Midwife) There is a serious deficit of specialists working at the Community Health Centre (CHC) level. Similar data for Jharkhand, West Bengal and Orissa are not available. (Table 3). (Rural Health Statistics, 2006)

Table 3 : Health Infrastructure in the Tribal Areas

		Chhattisgarh	Jharkhand	West Bengal	Orissa
Sub-centres	Required	2088	NA	1378	2566
	Shortfall	-		**640 (46%)**	**270 (10.5%)**
PHC	Required	313	NA	206	384
	Shortfall	**33 (10.5%)**		**1**	-
CHC	Required	78	NA	51	96
	Shortfall	**14 (17.9%)**		**22 (43%)**	-
ANM	Required	2016	NA	NA	NA
	Shortfall	548			
Doctors in PHC	Required	280	NA	NA	NA
	Shortfall	26			
Physicians in CHC	Required	64	NA	NA	NA
	Shortfall	61			
Gynecologists in CHC	Required	64	NA	NA	NA
	Shortfall	58			
Pediatricians in CHC	Required	64	NA	NA	NA
	Shortfall	62			

Source: Bulletin of rural health statistics 2006.

These findings lead us to examine the following:

- **Paucity of data**: Data provides the backbone for health planning and management. Scanty vital information fails to give a direction for stakeholders and policy makers to act. Systematic and periodic documentation of ongoing health care delivery operation is necessary, to advocate r reforms and also to keep the motivation level of the peripheral workers high. Paucity of data for these areas reflects lack of priority that is accorded to the marginalized population, difficulty in collecting data, need for additional funds or even an attempt to conceal their performance. In West Bengal, the Border District Cluster Strategy (BDCS) programme, successfully used a monitoring and validation methodology to motivate workers in order to strengthen the health care delivery system.
- **Shortfall of health personnel in tribal areas**: An important reason for poor implementation and negligible impact of so many health programs, particularly in tribal areas, is the absence of health professionals. Existing recruitment, posting and transfer guidelines are poorly implemented, with the result that health centres are not fully or continuously staffed. A variety of reasons are known to contribute that include shortage of trained personnel, staff not living at their posted location, high absenteeism and political interference in posting and transfer decisions. Most doctors prefer to work in urban areas, and view postings in tribal areas as "punishment posting". Lack of basic amenities, lack of incentives and promotion and compensation packages are the other factors responsible for this state of affairs. Nearly 64 per cent of sub centres in Chhattisgarh do not have regular water supply and 76 per cent function without electricity supply. All-weather motorable approach roads do not exist in one third of the sub centers (*Rural Health Statistics, 2006*). Apart from low motivation, poor performance of the health system is generally attributed to budget limitations. Thus the reasons could be many—no public recognition, low accountability, lack of supportive supervision, absence of human resource policy and inconsistent organizational direction etc.
- **Poor utilization of health care services by the tribal population**: Though utilization of government health services is generally thought to be poor, this, does not, however, indicate the indifference of the tribals to the modern system of medicine. Quite the contrary, it is due to poor health infrastructure and inadequate staff that the tribal people generally resort to indigenous practices. Recent

evidence suggests that they are receptive to the health care system. In a study conducted in Chhattisgarh, 45 per cent households use the private medical sector for treatment when a family member falls ill (*MedInd, 2004*). However, recent reports from Bastar district of Chhattisgarh indicated that Primary Health Centre (PHC) was the highest preferred health facility. Only 25.2 per cent of them preferred the *sirha* or *gunia* (traditional healer). In Kanker district, the Sub Centre was the highest preferred (61.3 per cent) while in Dantewada, PHCs were the most preferred (63.6 per cent) health facility. The reasons for such preferences were the easy availability of treatment for various illnesses, faith in the service provider, satisfaction with the services, accessibility of the health care facility, accessibility and availability of free services (*Chopra, 2004*) In another study conducted on the Gond tribes of Central India, more than 50 per cent of the respondents expressed their satisfaction with the services of government health care functionaries and 57.8 per cent informed that they get proper treatment from government health care functionaries (*Mathiyazhagan, 2007*). They normally approach government personnel for minor ailments, immunization and contraception. However, some problems faced by the tribals in availing of government health services were mainly non-availability of medicines (14.1 per cent), non-cooperative attitude of health functionaries (11.7 per cent), time constraints (7.8 per cent), transport (5.6 per cent) etc.

- **Health care financing**: Financing of healthcare is an important determinant of the performance of health services. The general theory that the higher the expenditure on health care, the better would be the outcome, is not always true. But it is a fact that low spending on healthcare results in poor functioning of health services. The percentage of GDP that goes to health sector was 1.3 per cent in 1990 that subsequently dropped down to 0.9 per cent. Further, 70–80 per cent of the expenditure goes for salaries, leaving only a small amount for improving infrastructure. Another potential source of health expenditure is the out-of-pocket payments. It is accepted that this form of payment is very inefficient and inequitable and one of the most regressive form of health care financing. The main reason behind out-of-pocket payment is the unregulated and non-accountability of the private health sector. Besides, financial management in health sector is a major concern. On the one hand, there is a low level of government spending and the budget is less than required and on the other hand, there is inefficient and under utilization of available resources. The reasons for this could be lack of regular and timely review, unclear guidelines related to expenditure, lack of trust in subordinates, hesitation amongst technocrats in spending the money, limited funds to facilitate the work of grass root level workers.

Recommendations

In the light of shrinking public health budgets, the escalating costs of health care in private sector, increasing demand for health care services and lack of easy accessibility to proper healt care to people from the marginalized population, there is a need to examine alternative mechanisms for optimal utilization of existing resources. The lessons learnt from numerous interventional studies conducted among various tribes, over the years, have yielded successful results. These concerted efforts in short term projects had commitment and a sensitive monitoring and evaluation system. Not all efforts directed towards the difficult-to-reach areas goes futile. But in view of the existing limitations mentioned above, alternatives have to be looked into.

One answer to such inconsistencies lies in public-private partnerships (PPP), that has shown promising results in some states (*NIHFW, 2007*). NGOs and other private sectors could be brought together in a well-defined relationship with the government, to provide essential services to the people and communities could be involved, to inculcate in them a sense of ownership. Orissa government through a NGO-PPP has outsourced the management of some PHCs to NGOs. Seeing the success of this initiative, the government has handed over management of PHCs and some block level health centers to NGOs and corporate bodies.

Village level committees (VHC) have been created and those who have partnered with NGOs are found to be functioning effectively and efficiently. In Jharkhand, the Sahiyyas (Key Health Worker) operate at the village level, supported by VHCs to promote preventive health care and train community health volunteers. Villagers who are now aware of their health entitlements, demand quality health services.

A UNICEF supported strategy in Jharkhand named DULAR, involved representatives from local NGOs and Anganwadis to form VHCs, to reduce Infant and Maternal mortality rates. In Chhattisgarh, as a result of CARE's work, government is now willing to restructure and revitalize the village level committees. In West Bengal, UNICEF has helped small NGOs build rapport with district/ sub district functionaries and have made people aware of immunization and its importance.

PPP is thus a proactive tool in service delivery to low income groups. But successful collaborations require the government to emerge as a partner. Also, communities must see themselves as stakeholders in target initiatives. However, sustainability is a question, in case the private partners withdraw from PPP. As an alternative to PPP, to extend financial services, a challenge fund could be utilized for projects that have an assured social impact. Pioneered by the DFID, through Financial Deepening Challenge Fund, challenge funds have an advantage because they are capable of getting the private sector to be innovative, when financing social and economic development projects.

Pharmacists would be of great help in capacity building, as they are already working in the field and are often the first contact point in many communities. Many of them traditionally have a strong network, making them the right persons for taking forward health services. They are also known to run their own clinics. Moreover, the number of sanctioned posts of pharmacists in PHCs and CHCs in tribal areas of Chhattisgarh is 371 of which 228 are in position. It could be a potentially rewarding alternative to train them in mother and child health services. A large majority of infant deaths could be prevented by providing a package of essential services. While, for averting maternal deaths, emergency care is vital.

There have been discussions regarding setting up of delivery huts in villages, to be manned by ANMs that would function collaboratively with Panchayati Raj Institutions. These would be open round-the–clock and be equipped to conduct normal deliveries and prepare for emergencies. Additional funds to cover the costs of transportation, is a concern, but a feasible alternative would be to make the PHCs more functional.

Conclusion

While India has made significant gains in terms of health indicators, it continues to grapple with newer challenges. Tribal population living in isolation in natural and unpolluted surroundings, were once known to have enjoyed a good health status. But recent evidence indicates that they too are prone to different diseases. Not only have communicable diseases continued to persist, but some of them like malaria, have developed insecticide resistant vectors. In addition, both malaria and tuberculosis are becoming drug resistant. As a result of changing lifestyles, the tribals are also becoming susceptible to cardiovascular diseases. Other diseases, like skin infections, infertility and hemoglobinopathies, are peculiar to the tribal group. This increasing burden coupled with spiraling health costs is placing a huge financial burden on the already marginalized groups. They have originally been inclined towards indigenous practices, but this attitude is gradually undergoing a change in favor of the modern system of medicine. Unfortunately, the health care delivery system has not been able to cater to their needs. This is primarily due to poor infrastructure, non-availability of health staff and lack of political will. NGOs working in collaboration with the government have shown promising results. Public–private partnership, involving the community members would offer beneficial results. Pharmacists, if imparted adequate training, could be potential health care providers even in the remote areas. Initiatives are currently being undertaken on a pilot basis, but these should stand the test of time for us to comment on the ability to generalize.

References

Annual Report 2002, Regional Medical Research Centre (Indian Council of Medical Research), Orissa, India.

Annual Report 2002. Regional Medical Research Centre (Indian Council of Medical Research), Jabalpur, India.

Annual report 2003–4. Regional Medical Research Centre (India Council of Medical Research), Orissa, India.

Annual Report 2003–4. Regional Medical Research Centre (Indian Council of Medical Research), Jabalpur, India.

Balgir, RS, The burden of hemoglobinopathies in India and the challenges ahead. Curr Sci 2000;79:1536–47.

Bhargava, A, Jain, Y. Hypertension is falling through the gaps in primary health care. *Indian Journal of Medical Ethics*, Oct-Dec 2006; 4.

Bulletin of Rural Health Ststistics 2006.

Chakma, T, Rao, PV, Pall, S, Kaushal, LS, Datta, M, Tiwary, RS. Survey of Pulmonary tuberculosis in a primitive tribe of Madhya Pradesh. *Int J Tub* 1996;43:85–89.

Chhattisgarh Available at: *www.medind.nic.in/haa/t04/il/haat 04ilp25.pdf*

Chopra, K, Makol, N. Common Health Problems encountered by the tribal community in Bastar District. Health and Population—Perspectives and Issues 2004; 27(1):40-48.

Chowdhury, SD, Chakaraborti, T, Ghosh, T, Fat patterning of Santhal children—a tribal population of West Bengal, India. *Journal of Tropical Pediatrics* 2006 (published online on December 6, 2006)

Discussion summary—Health financing in India—challenges and opportunities. Available at: www.solutionexchange-un.net.in. (accessed on Aug 12th, 2007)

Fact sheet, Chhattisgarh & Jharkhand, National Family Health Survey, 1998–99.

Final Report of National Family Health Survey 2007 (NFHS-3 2005–2006), IIPS, Mumbai.

Health Status of Primitive Tribes of Orissa, *ICMR bulletin* 2003; 33.

Jharkhand. Data Highlights: the Scheduled Tribes, Census of India 2001. Office of the Registrar General, India.

Kaiser, E. Deadly TB-HIV Combo haunts tribal Chhattisgarh. Hindustan Times, June 28,2007. Available at: www.hindustantimes.com (accessed on July 2, 2007)

Key Indicators from NFHS-3 by Caste/Tribe of India. Available at www.nfhs.org

Mathiyazhagan, T. A pilot study on communication strategy for reaching the unreached tribal population in Mandla District of Madhya Pradesh. Available at www.nihfw.org (accessed on July 7th, 2007)

Mitra M, Kumar PV, Chakrabarty S, Bharati P., Nutritional Status of Kamar tribal children in Chhattisgarh. *India J Pediatr* 2007, 74:381–4.

Mittal PC, Srivastava S. Diet, nutritional status and food related traditions of Oraon tribes of New Mal (West Bengal), India. Rural and Remote Health 2006;6:385.

Overview of Chhattisgarh. Available at: *www.CHIPS-The IT Portal of Chhattisgarh.htm*. (Accessed on June 28, 2007).

Performance RNTCP Case Detection (2006, 2004). TB India 2006. Available at: www.tbcindia.org (accessed on Jul 1, 2007)

Poverty, hooch TB amongst tribals in Jharkhand. Available at: www.healthinitiative.org (accessed on July 2, 2007).

Rao, DH, Rao, KM, Radhaiah G, Rao, NP, Nutritional Status of tribal pre-school children in three ecological zones of Madhya Pradesh, *Indian Pediatr* 1994; 31:635-40.

Rao, VG, Dash, AP, Agarwal, MC, Yadav, RS, Anvikar, AR, Vohra, S, et al. Cercarial dermatitis in central India: an emerging health problem among tribal communities. Am Trop Med Parasitol 2007, 101:409–13.

Rao, VG, Yadav, R, Bhondeley, MK, Das, S, Agarwal, MC, Tiwari, RS, Worm infestation and anemia; a public health problem among tribal pre-school children of Madhya Pradesh, *J Commun Dis* 2002; 34:100–5.

Rao, VG, Yadav, R, Dolla, CK, Kumar, S, Bhondeley, MK, Ukey M., Under nutrition and childhood morbidities among tribal preschool children. *Indian J Med Res* 2005; July: 43–47.

Report of National Planning Workshop on public private partnerships in the Health Sector in India. Available at: www.nihfw.nic.in/seminars/summaryreport. (accessed on Aug 12th, 2007)

Sarkar, S, Das, M, Mukhopadhyay, B, Chakraborti, CS, Majumdar, PP. High prevalence of metabolic syndrome and its correlates in two tribal populations of India and the impact of urbanization. *India J Med Res* 2006;123: 679–86.

Seeberg, J. The TB Health System Research Network, Orissa, India. Presented at Global Forum 8, Mexico City, 15-19th November 2004.

Selected State/District wise number of reported Malaria cases under EMCP in India (1997 and 2001). Available at: www:indiahealthstat.com

Sharma, SK, Jaleeb, S, Kumar, K, Rahman, SJ, Knowledge, attitude and beliefs about malaria in a tribal area of Bastar district (Madhya Pradesh). Indian J Public Health 1993;37:129–32.

Tribal Health Bulletin 2003. Regional Medical Research for Tribals, Jabalpur.

Tribal Malaria, *ICMR bulletin* 2004; 34.

Yadav RJ, Singh P. Nutritional Status and dietary intake in tribal children of Bihar. *Indian Pediatr*. 1999; 36:37–42.

The Social Dimension of Health and Development in Tribal Communities of the North-Central Sub-region of India

Salil Basu

Tribal communities in India belonging to different ethnic and linguistic groups inhabit widely varying ecological and geo-linguistic conditions, in different concentration, throughout the country. They are at different stages of economic development. Though agriculture is practiced by the largest number of tribal groups, the primitive tribal communities are practically in the food gathering and hunting stage of economy.*

Through the ages, the tribal groups have retained their individual social and cultural identity by rigorously practicing different social customs. This led to the formation of biological isolates, with their specific individual socio-cultural milieu. It is an established fact that socio-economic factors, socio-cultural variants, like nutritional practices (food habits), inter-related with socio-biological norms such as mating-pattern, preferential marital alliances (Consanguineous marriages), age at marriage, all have tremendous impact on the fertility and mortality pattern. In addition, the impact of environmental and genetic factors further complicates the situation. Besides, the misconceptions, beliefs and taboos emanating from their primitive socio-religious system also have an effect on the fertility, mortality and morbidity among tribal population groups.

Tribal communities are living in difficult terrain and forest areas, in-

*There are 427 recognized scheduled tribal groups in the country of which 75 are primitive tribes (pre-agricultural level) characterized by declining/static/low growth rate (Report of the Working Group, 1989).

unsanitary conditions, which, coupled with primitive health practices perpetuate malaria and various other infectious diseases leading to higher mortality and morbidity rates.

Tribals have poor access to health services and there is reported to be under utilization of health services owing to social, cultural and economic factors. The Government of India has adopted a strategy based on the twin approach of protection of interests of tribal people, through legislative and administrative support and promotion of developmental efforts through plan schemes. Tribal areas in the country have been delineated and various projects under tribal sub-plan are being implemented.

Health Status and Health Seeking Behaviour

The overall health status of the tribal community is the outcome of the several interrelated factors which are connected with the health and health problems of a community, effects of environment in which the tribals live, behavioural pattern and life styles of the tribals, genetic characteristics, health care delivery service in tribal areas and constraints in accepting modern health care. The widely prevalent health practices, use of indigenous herbal drugs, taboos and superstitions are also responsible for determining the health behaviour and health status of the tribal groups.

Health and its Coordinates

Health is a pre-requisite for human development and is essentially concerned with the well-being of human beings. Health is a function, not only of medical care, but of the overall integrated development of society—cultural, economic, educational, social and political. The health status of a society is intimately related to its value system, its philosophical and cultural traditions, and its social, economic and political organization. Each of these aspects has a deep influence on health, which in turn influences all these aspects. Hence, it is not possible to raise the health status and quality of life of a people, unless such efforts are integrated with the wider-effort to bring about the overall transformation of a society. Health development can be integrated with the larger programme of overall development, in such a manner, that the two become mutually self-supporting. Such coordinated and simultaneous efforts to improve and change the entire social order generally yield better results because they are interdependent and mutually supportive (*ICSSR-ICMR, 1981*).

A Culture of Health

The culture of a community determines the health behaviour of the community and of its individual members. The cultural response of the community to the health problems it confronts, determines its health practices.

The complex whole, embracing the cultural perception and meaning of health problems and the health behaviour of individuals, within the context of the available and accessible health institutions is termed health culture (*Banerjee. D, 1982*).

Health culture becomes an integral component of the overall culture of a community. It is necessary to take a holistic view of all the cultural dimensions that are related to the health and health services of a community and to relate such a holistic perspective, to the overall culture of the community. The holistic concept of health culture provides a valuable framework for analyzing the work of anthropologists in the health field. However, a very few studies are available in this regard, especially among the tribal population. *Salil, Basu* with his team (1984–96), while studying in depth health status and health needs of different tribal population groups in various states of India, attempted to incorporate a holistic approach embodied in the concept of health culture.

The study of the health culture of a particular community is important because (a) the health problems and the procedure to handle such problems and other health practices are influenced by the complex interplay of socio-cultural factors, and (b) implementation of health services (health centre, immunization centre, or any kind of health programme) would be difficult without the knowledge of the community's traditional health culture (*Basu, A., 1996*). Health culture becomes an integral component of the overall culture of a community. It is necessary to take a holistic view of all the cultural dimensions that are related to the health and health services of a community and to relate such a holistic perspective to the overall culture of the community.

Health Problems

The health problems and practices of any community are profoundly influenced by the interplay of social, economic and political factors. It is necessary to take a holistic view of all the cultural dimensions of the health of the community and to relate such a holistic perspective to the overall culture of the concerned community.

The health problems need special attention in the context of tribal communities of India. Available research studies point out that the tribal populations have distinctive health problems which are mainly governed by their habitat, difficult terrain and ecologically variable niches. The health problems faced by the tribals are mostly regional health problems (*Basu, 1996*). The health, nutrition and medico-genetic problems of diverse tribal groups inhabiting widely varying geo-climatic and ecological conditions have been found to be unique and present a formidable challenge, for which appropriate solutions have to be found by planning and evolving relevant research studies, which should be need-based and problem solving in nature. Primitive tribal groups of India have special health problems and genetic abnormalities like sickle cell anaemia, G-6-PD red cell enzyme deficiency and sexually transmitted diseases (*Commissioner Report for ST and SC, 1986-87*). Insanitary conditions, lack of personal hygiene, health education and ignorance are the main factors responsible for their ill health.

Many primitive tribal communities are facing extinction like the Onges, Jarawas and Shompens in Andaman and Nicobar Islands. Possible reasons need to be explored although these may differ from population to population and are probably multiple (*Verma, 1978*). Some of the factors as indicated by investigations include (a) endemic diseases like malaria; diseases introduced from outside like tuberculosis, influenza, dysentery, high infant mortality and malnutrition; (b) Venereal diseases, induced abortion, inbreeding, addiction to opium, custom of eating tubers of dioscera (may cause sterility as they contain substances used in oral contraception); (c) Declining sex ratio (FMR), leading to shortage of women. Urgent studies are, therefore, required on different primitive tribal groups of India, which are small in size and inhabit inhospitable environment, to elicit their fertility, mortality, morbidity patterns, consanguinity status, food habits, physical growth trends, genetico-environmental disorders and factors affecting them, in order to delineate the high risk groups. These findings will ultimately help in formulating effective need-based health care strategies among these vulnerable primitive tribal groups. It is crucial that the development programmes prepared for these communities are group-specific and specially tailored to meet the problems of each small primitive tribal community (*Salil Basu, 1993*).

Eco-system and Health

Tribal people lived in harmony with the ecosystem for ages, maintaining a balanced reciprocal relationship with nature. But the eco-system has degenerated over the last century due to human interventions such as industrialization, urbanization and modernization.

The deteriorating eco-system creates a great strain on the health of those who live in close proximity to nature and are dependent on natural resources for their survival. This stress known as eco stress, eventually leads to loss of productivity, with an adverse impact on the health of the tribal population, especially women. It is a matter of great concern that the eco-stress factors are greatly affecting the regenerating capacity of the tribal people.

Health Delivery System in Tribal Areas: Problems, Issues and Bottlenecks

Despite the National Health Policy as well as the new revised 20-point programme to improve the health status of the underprivileged population, the utilization of health services is reported to be very poor. There is no significant change in so far as important indices of health, like infant mortality, maternal mortality and incidence of communicable diseases. The situation, therefore, calls for a very close and detailed analysis of the influence of special socio-cultural and economic conditions on health outcomes of these groups. Such an analysis is also necessary to find out possible modifications and improvements needed in the existing allopathic health delivery system, with a view to make it more appropriate for the under privileged groups of population.

In spite of adopting various health care measures, tribal groups are deprived of fullest benefits from the primary health care services due to inaccessible areas, difficult terrain, lack of cultivable land, extreme poverty, lack of awareness and motivation, superstition, ignorance, magico-religious beliefs and improper health care services.

Existing health machinery is designed in such a fashion that except for a few additional PHC/Sub-Centres, a more or less similar pattern of health care delivery system exists for the general as well as the tribal population in the country. In spite of the so called expansion of the health facilities and government's efforts to improve health situation of the tribals, no significant impact on the important health indices of the tribal people has been achieved. This has been corroborated by research studies carried out by the author among the tribal groups of Bastar district, Madhya Pradesh, primitive Kutia Khondhs of Phulbani district, Orissa, Jaunsaris of Jaunsar-Bawar, Dehradun (Uttar Pradesh), Santals of Mayurbhanj district and Dudh Kharias of Sundergarh district, Orissa (*Basu et al., 1989, 1992, 1993, 1994*).

The research findings among various tribal communities under different ecological settings show that simple linear expansion of the existing health care delivery system is not an appropriate answer for improving health and family welfare status of the tribal population. It has been further observed that the health facilities (i.e., PHC/Sub-centers etc) should be located as per local needs, depending on geographical and population consideration, resources and manpower availability.

Constraints and bottlenecks of the existing health and family welfare delivery system in tribal areas should be identified, specifying clearly the infrastructure required, strategies to be developed which are in consonance with the felt needs of the local tribal population.

Health functionaries manning the different health care institutions should preferably be from the tribal areas and should be knowledgeable about socio-cultural background of different tribal population groups.

To achieve operational efficiency in the health care delivery programmes, the integrated tribal development project area should be studied in the context of health services. Efforts should be made to involve local tribals, preferably girls, traditional "dais" and "traditional healers" in the health and family welfare delivery system after imparting proper training. Among the tribal population, a preventive approach, like immunization programmes, anti-infection measures and various other prophylactic programmes should be given more importance.

Constraints in Accepting Modern Health Care by Tribal Communities

Tribal groups have developed a strong magico-religious health care system. No proper and appropriate health services are available to them in any of the tribal areas of different zones of the country (*Basu, 1990*). They live in a closed social and cultural system. It is important not only to study the prevailing socio-cultural dimensions of health and family welfare among tribal communities, but also to examine the constraints in accepting modern health care facilities. The common beliefs, customs and practices connected with health and disease have been found to be intimately connected with the treatment of disease. It is necessary for health functionaries to have sufficient knowledge about their culture and society. The inadequate nature of health facilities in many tribal areas, lack of respect for indigenous culture, lack of proper facility and attention towards the patients are mainly responsible for the non-acceptance and distrust of tribal people towards modern medicine. In fact, anthropological-sociological studies covering different facets of the society are urgently necessary to understand some of the realities of health problems prevailing among the tribal population (*Chowdhury, 1986*).

Health Profile of Scheduled Tribes in North-Central Sub-Region of India

With the help of secondary data from different sources, a situational analysis of scheduled tribes has been presented with respect to distribution, demography socio-economic characteristics and health profile of four states i.e., Chhattisgarh, Madhya Pradesh, Jharkhand, and Orissa.

Emerging significant issues are highlighted below:

- As per 2001 Census, the proportion of Scheduled Tribe population to the total population is highest in Chhattisgarh with 31.8 per cent, followed by 26.3 per cent in Jharkhand and 22.1 per cent in Orissa. It is lowest in MP with 20.3 per cent.
- In terms of total Schedule Tribe population, Madhya Pradesh is observed to be the highest (12,23 million).
- Orissa state has highest number of scheduled tribes (62), including 13 primitive tribes followed by Madhya Pradesh with 46 Scheduled Tribes including 4 primitive tribes and then by Jharkhand with 30 Scheduled Tribes, including 9 primitive tribes.
- The overall sex ratio of the scheduled tribe's population in Chhattisgarh is 1013 females per 1000 males, followed by Orissa with 1002 and Jharkhand with 987. These are significantly higher than the national average of 978. Madhya Pradesh with 975 is a little lower than the national average.
- The overall literacy rates of scheduled tribes of Jharkhand (54 per cent) and Chhattisgarh (52 per cent) are relatively higher for all scheduled tribes, when compared to the national level (47 per cent).
- The work participation rate is found to be highest in Chhattisgarh with 53.4 per cent followed by 50.5 per cent in Madhya Pradesh and is higher for all scheduled tribes, when compared to the national level (49.1 per cent).
- Population below Poverty Line—Orissa with 47.15 per cent is a relatively high figure as compared to 26.10 per cent at the national level

- Female Literacy Rate—Female literacy rate is observed to be high (52.40 per cent) in Chhattisgarh, approaching the national figure of 54.28 per cent.

Table 1: Comparative Study of Demographic, Socio-economic and Health profile of North Central Sub-Region States of India as compared to India figures

S. No.	Item	Jharkhand	Orissa	Chhattis-garh	M.P.	India
1	Total population (Census 2001) (in millions)	26.9	36.80	20.83	60.35	1028.61
2	Proportion of ST Population	26.3	22.1	31.8	20.3	8.2
3	Decadal Growth (Census 2001) (%)	23.36	16.25	18.27	24.26	21.54
4	Crude Birth Rate (SRS 2005)	26.8	22.3	27.2	29.4	23.8
5	Crude Death Rate (SRS 2005)	7.9	9.5	8.1	9.0	7.6
6	Total Fertility Rate (SRS 2004)	3.5	2.7	3.3	3.7	2.9
7	Infant Mortality Rate (SRS 2005)	50	75	63	76	58
8	Maternal Mortality Ratio (SRS 2001-03)	371	358	379	379	301

The above table highlights some important features of the health profile of north central sub region of India.

- Crude Birth Rate is as high as 29.4 million in Madhya Pradesh, followed by Chhattisgarh with 27.2 million. These figures are higher than the all-India figure of 23.8 million.
- Crude Death Rate is observed to be the highest in Orissa at 9.5 million, closely followed by Madhya Pradesh with 9.0 million, as compared to 7.6 million, the all-India figure.
- Total Fertility Rate is found to be higher in MP at 3.7 million, followed by Jharkhand with 3.5 million and Chhattisgargh with 3.3million as against the national figure of 2.9 million.
- Infant Mortality Rate too is found to be highest in Madhya Pradesh at 76million, closely followed by 75million in Orissa as compared to the national figure of 58 million. However, in Jharkhand with 50 million, it is lower than the national average.
- Maternal Mortality Ratio—MMR, is observed to be as high as 379 million in Chhattisgarh and Madhya Pradesh as compared to the national figure of 301 million. Other states such as Jharhand have higher maternal mortality ratio than the national average.

Table 2: A Comparative State of different Reproductive Child Health (RCH) indicators for the SCs/STs against the rest of the population

Health Indicators	Scheduled Castes (SC)	Scheduled Tribes (ST)	Rest of Population
IMR	83.0	84.2	61.8
Under 5 Mortality	119.3	126.6	82.6
Total Fertility Rate (TFR)	3.15	3.06	2.66
% Children Under Weight	53.5	55.9	41.1
Children with anaemia (NFHS-3)	78.9	79.8	72.7
% Children with ARI	19.6	22.4	18.7
% Children with Diarrhoea	19.8	21.1	19.1
% Women with anaemia (NFHS-3, 2005-06)	58.3	68.5	51.3

Source: NHFS-2 (1998-99) and NFHS-3 (2005–06).

- It can be inferred from the above table that scheduled tribes show relatively higher figures as compared to rest of population on the infant health indicators too. Similar is the case with scheduled caste population.
- However, while comparing Scheduled Castes and Scheduled Tribe population with respect to health indicators, scheduled tribes show relatively higher values.
- Tribals have poor access to health services and there is also under utilization of health services owing to social, cultural and economic factors.
- Urgent attention needs to be given for effective coverage of tribal areas under basic health services with the help of trained health providers who are culturally and socially oriented towards tribal culture.

Disease Pattern Among Scheduled Tribes

One of the major problems of tribal society is the disease and sickness prevalent in tribal people. Responsibility for this can be attributed to both providers of health services (generally outsider—their attitude, behaviour, commitment etc.) and the tribals themselves. Their life-style —cultural practices, including subsistence, diets, occupation, habits, ceremonial/ ritualistic customs, other cultural practices and environment, make them susceptible to certain diseases.

The disease profile of the tribal population indicates that the diseases like Malaria, Tuberculosis, Veneral disease (STD) including RTI and genetical diseases (sickle cell anemia, G-6-PD red cell enzyme deficiency etc.) are most preponderant among them (*Basu S.K., 1986, 1989, 1992, 1993, 1994; Patnaik, S.M., 2002*). A recent addition to the list of fatal diseases faced by the tribal is HIV/AIDS. Further scientific research has also pointed out a close link of HIV/AIDS with TB.

A delineation of the contributing factors to any disease requires in depth investigations into the socio-cultural, socio-biological milieu of the population groups. It may include diverse factors such as the sanitation, hygiene, parasitic load, mating-pattern, preferential marital alliances, nutritional pattern, health seeking behaviour, genetic markers etc. Various factors affecting health and diseases in a particular population group, may vary from one group to another.

The principal causes of disease are: (a) Infectious and parasitic diseases (communicable diseases); (b) Nutritional Deficiencies; (c) Non-communicable diseases; (d) Diseases associated with Genetic Disorder.

Communicable Diseases

From the available studies and reports, the following communicable diseases have been found to be prevalent in high frequency in different tribal areas of India.

Yaws

Yaws is a chronic non-venereal disease caused by *Treponema Pertenue*. The disease is mostly confined to the tribals who live in the areas of Orissa and Andhra Pradesh (*Roy Burman, 1986*). It has also been reported from Tripura and Madhya Pradesh (*Saxena, Darbar and Jain, 1978*). The infectious cases for Yaws both late and early, accompanied with necrotising ulcers and bone pains etc. were observed among tribes of Jagdalpur and some other districts of erstwhile Madhya Pradesh in 1977 by a team of specialists from Pt. J.N.M. Medical College, Raipur (*Saxena, Dabar, Jain, 1978*).

Tuberculosis

It is reported that originally in tribal areas, there was either no trace of this disease or it existed only in a small degree. But later on, however, as a result of the contact with non-adivasis, incidence of this disease has increased in different tribal areas (i.e., Madhya Pradesh, Gujarat, Maharashtra, Bihar, Rajasthan, Himachal Pradesh, West Bengal, Tripura). Malnutrition has also been found to be one of the contributing factors. All tribes referred to tuberculosis as TB and none of the tribes had any extensive knowledge about it. They think that it is relatively a recent origin in tribal communities. A beneficiary social assessment study of the control of tuberculosis was carried out in tribal households from each tribal dominated district of Gujarat, Bihar, Himachal Pradesh, West Bengal (*Basu, Salil, 1995*).

Leprosy

The incidence of leprosy is high among Mikir Hills of Assam. Scheduled tribes of Jharkhand Madhya Pradesh, Orissa, Uttar Pradesh, Tripura, Laccadive and Minicoy Islands.

Malaria

As most of the tribal areas abound in forests and get heavy rainfall, malaria is widespread in these areas. As many as 40 per cent of malaria cases are reported from the tribal areas. Out of all malaria from tribal areas, 60 per cent are reported to be due to *Plasmodium Falciparum* (*NICD, 1993*).

A beneficiary social assessment study was carried out in 28 sample villages drawn from 7 tribal dominated districts which are hard core malaria prone areas(i.e. Srikakulum (AP), Dungarpur (Rajasthan), Panchmahal (Gujarat), Gadchiroli (Maharashtra), Gumla (Bihar), Surguja (MP) (now in Chattisgarh) and Mayurbhanj (Orissa) (*Basu, Salil, 1996*).

An Eco-Epidemiological Study of Drug Resistance to Anti-malarial in *Plasmodium Falciparum* (*Pf*), tribal infected areas was carried out in Mandla and Durg districts of Madhya Pradesh (*Basu, Salil, 1998*). Drug resistance to anti-malarials is becoming one of the major problems in malaria control. Drug resistance with higher percentage of *Pf* is largely confined to hard core hilly and forested areas in 100 tribal dominated districts of 7 states. About 60 per cent of the total deaths due to malaria are reported from these tribal areas. Orissa and Madhya Pradesh are at the top of the list with respect to incidence rate and *Pf* percentage.

Sexually Transmitted Diseases (STD)

The disease is generally the result of contact of tribals with non-tribals. These sexually transmitted diseases are present in various tribal groups, i.e., Andamanese, Todas of Nilgiri hills. Khasas of Jaunsar Bawar (U.P.). Kondhas of Orissa, tribal groups of Madhya Pradesh, Rajasthan, Mysore, Laccadive and Minicoy Islands.

Besides these, other common communicable diseases which are found in high frequency among various tribal groups from different tribal areas are upper respiratory infections, skin infections, gastro-enteritis, hellimenthiasis, trachoma, fevers of unknown etiology etc.

Non-Communicable Diseases

Very little information is available about the prevalence of non-communicable diseases in tribal population. Studies carried out by NIN (*Rao et al., 1986*) among the tribals of Sarguja, Jhabua and Bastar districts of Madhya Pradesh showed high incidence (53.9 per cent) of goitre (Enlarged thyroid gland) in tribals of Sarguja district. Eye conditions like cataract, corneal opacity etc. were found to be in high frequency (20.3 per cent) in Bastar district. Cases of dental caries (5.1 per cent) were noted in Jhabua. A few instances of cardiovascular diseases like hypertension, valvular heart diseases were clinically found in Jhabua, Sarguja and Bastar.

On the basis of National Family Health Survey (NFHS)-3, 2005–06 data, it can be observed that there is variation in the incidence of non-communicable diseases like diabetes, asthma, or goitre or any other thyroid disorders among men and women in the age group of 15–49 per 100,000 population.

While comparing the reported incidence of diseases among Schedule Caste and Schedule Tribe, it has been observed that:

(a) Schedule Tribes (both female and male) showed relatively much lower occurrence of diabetes as compared to Scheduled Castes.
(b) But asthma cases were reported in higher frequency both among female and male of Schedule Tribes as compared to Schedule Castes.
(c) In the case of goitre, there is not much difference among female of Schedule Tribes and Schedule Castes, whereas its incidence was observed to be much higher among male of Schedule Tribes.

Nutritional Problems/Deficiencies

The health and nutrition problems of the vast tribal population of India are as varied as the tribal groups themselves, who present a bewildering diversity and variety in their socio-economic, socio-cultural and ecological settings. The nutritional problems of different tribal communities, located at various stages of development, are full of obscurities and very little scientific information is available regarding dietary habits and nutritional status due to lack of systematic and comprehensive research investigations. Malnutrition is common and has greatly affected the general physique of the tribals.

Nutrition and Anaemia

Nutritional anaemia is a major problem for women in India and more so in

Table 3: Non-communicable Diseases in Men and Women

Background characteristic	Number of women per 100,000				Number of men per 100,000			
	Diabetes	Asthma	Goitre or other thyroid disorder	Number of women	Diabetes	Asthama	Goitre or other thyroid disorder	Number of men
Caste/tribe								
Scheduled Caste	789	1,494	754	23,125	991	1,688	348	13,188
Scheduled tribe	349	1,749	753	10,119	477	1,973	567	5,725
Other backward class	774	1,498	819	48,880	955	1,276	328	27,219
Other	1,189	2,035	1,240	41,207	1,336	1,919	424	23,214
Don't know	650	1,219	1,675	649	1,307	3,551	871	177

Source: NFHS-3 (2005–06).

the rural and tribal belt. Anaemia is characterized by a low level of haemoglobin in the blood.

This is particularly serious in view of the fact that both rural and tribal women have heavy workload and anaemia has a profound effect on psychological and physical health. Anaemia lowers resistance to fatigue, affects working capacity under conditions of stress and increases susceptibility to other diseases. Anaemia in young children is a serious concern because it can result in impaired cognitive performance, behavioural and motor development, co-ordination, language development, scholastic achievement as well as increased morbidity infectious diseases (*NFHS-3, 2005-06*). The situation has worsened over time for both women and young children i.e., the prevalence of anaemia among ever married women has increased from 52 per cent in *NFHS-2* to 56 per cent in *NFHS-3*. (See Table 2, NFHS-3, 2005–06)

Table 4: Prevalence of Anaemia in Women

Background Characteristic	Any Anaemia (<12.0g/dl)[2]	Number of Women
Caste/Tribe		
Scheduled Caste	58.3	21,921
Scheduled Tribe	68.5	9,568
Other Backward Class	54.4	46,182
Other	51.3	38,216
Don't Know	55.9	589
Total for Ever-married Women		
NFHS—3	56.2	93,316
NFHS—2	51.8	79,633

Maternal malnutrition, which is quite common among the tribal women is also a serious health problem, especially for those who have many pregnancies at close intervals; it reflects the complex socio-economic factors that affect their overall situation.

The nutritional status of pregnant women directly influences their reproductive performance and the birth weight of their children, a factor that is crucial to an infant's chances of survival and to its subsequent growth and development. Nutrition also affects lactation and breast feeding, which are key elements in the health of infants and young children and a contributory factor in proper gap between two pregnancies.

Under nutrition is much more common in children whose mothers' body mass index is below 18.5, than for children whose mothers are not underweight. Under nutrition is most pronounced in Madhya Pradesh, Bihar and Jharkhand (*NFHS-3, 2005-06*).

According to NFHS-3, 2005–06 data, children belonging to scheduled castes, scheduled tribes or other backward classes have relatively high levels of under nutrition according to all three anthropometric indices of nutritional status i.e., Height-for-age, Weight-for-height and Weight-for-age. Children from scheduled tribes have the poorest nutritional status on almost every index and the high prevalence of wasting in this group (28 per cent), is of particular concern.

A high incidence of malnutrition was observed (*Alt 1980, Basu et al., 1990; Mahapatra & Das, 1990*) in some primitive tribal groups in Phulbani, Koraput and Sundergarh districts of Orissa and also among Bhil, Garasia of Rajasthan, Padar, Rabri and Charan of Gujarat and Bonda of Orissa (*Huque, 1990*). Nutritional investigations carried out by NIN among the tribal groups of Jhabua, Bastar and Sarguja districts of Madhya Pradesh showed the following trends (*Rao et al., 1986*):

(a) Severe anaemia was very high in Bastar, followed by Jhabua and was minimal in Sarguja.
(b) The intake of foods and nutrients was more in Sarguja as compared to Bastar and Jhabua.
(c) Overt cases of PEM namely Kwashiorkor, Marasmus and vitamin deficiency signs like Bitot's spot and Angular stomatitis, were conspicuous by their near absence as compared to the general rural population.

Studies carried out by NIHFW among the Gond (Muria and Madia), Bhatra, Halba tribal groups of Bastar district, Madhya Pradesh showed the following trends (*Basu et al., 1989, 1993*):

(a) The average protein calorie intake was found to be much less in the Gond children as compared to Bhattra and Halba children.
(b) Higher frequencies of Bitot's spot, Angular stomatitis and motling of teeth were found among Gond children as compared to Bhattra and Halba children.
(c) Muscular wasting was noticed to be higher in Gond children as compared to Bhattra children.

Data on nutritional deficiency disorders among other tribal groups are scarce. Multidisciplinary and comprehensive studies providing information on habitat, local food products, determinants of malnutrition, dietary practices, economic and social system and its relationship with nutritional status are urgently required. To evolve a suitable strategy to overcome the nutritional deficiencies among the tribals and promulgate preventive and promotive health care, the various socio-economic concomitants and cultural variants have to be taken into consideration.

Flurosis (Genu Valgum) Recent available Study and Human Health

Flurosis is an important clinical and public health problem; there are several million people in India exposed to drinking water sources, with high fluoride content. In as many as 20 of the 30 States/Union Territories fluorosis is common. The presence of excessive quantities of fluoride in drinking water is accompanied by a characteristic sequence of changes in teeth, bone and periarticular tissues, leading to a variable degree of locomotor disability and neurological impairment. Studies carried out by RMRCT, Jabalpur among tribals of Mandla district of Madhya Pradesh revealed a high prevalence of *Genuvalgum* (51.1 per cent) and *Dental fluorosis* (74.4 per cent). (*Chakma, T. and Vinay Rao, P., 2004*)

Genetic Disorders

Genetic disorders have been found to occur in a high degree of frequency among various tribal groups and scheduled caste population.

There are two genetic disorders namely *sickle cell anaemia* and *G-6-PD red cell enzyme* deficiency, which have been found to occur in rather high frequencies in scheduled tribes and scheduled caste populations. Both male and females are equally affected in the case of sickling, whereas males are more affected than females in G-6-PD deficiency cases. Both these genetic disorders have profound health implications in terms of mortality for the affected persons.

Sickle Cell Disease (HbSS) and Sickle Cell Trait (HbAS)

Sickle Cell Disease is a haemolytic anaemia (shortened life span of red cell) leading to severe and often fatal anaemia. The disease is further characterized by enlarged spleen, painful crisi, organ damage, impaired mental functions, increased susceptibility to infection and ultimately death in certain conditions. The patients tend to have shorter trunk with long legs, chronic leg ulcers and an overall weak built. The sickle cell disease has been found in 72 districts of Central, Western and Southern India (*DST Technical Report,*

1990). There are more than 35 tribal population groups showing a frequency of more than 19 per cent. It is estimated that approximately a staggering 50 lakh individuals are carriers (heterozygote) among the tribals (*DST Report, 1990*). Prevalence rate upto 40 per cent of heterozygous form [sickle cell trait (HbAS), has been reported in some tribes i.e. Adiyan of Kerala, Irula, Paniyan, Mulukurumbha of Nilgiri hills, Gonds of Raipur in a protective adaptation with malaria (*Basu, 1993, 1994*).

Glucose-6-phosphate Dehydrogenase Red Cell Enzyme Deficiency

Glucose-6-phosphate dehydrogenase is an important enzyme of the red blood cells and its deficiency is inherited as an X-linked trait. Males who carry the gene show full expression, but expression in female heterozygotes varies widely. Glucose-6-phosphate dehydrogenase enzyme deficiency is one of the most common defects of inherited red cell enzyme, which renders individuals vulnerable to drug induced haemolytic anaemia. Deficiency of enzyme important in red cell metabolism, results in sensitivity to sulpha and anti-malarial drugs, such as primaquine phosphate and also by the ingestion of the broad bean *"Vicia Fava"*. More than 150 million people are known to be suffering from this defect all over the world, thus exerting a great strain on the preventive facilities of public health departments.

Investigations in India have shown that the frequency distribution of the G-6-PD enzyme deficiency is seemingly connected with the prevalence of falciparum malaria. It has been suggested that G-6-PD deficiency confers some resistance to falciparum malaria and this has stimulated surveys in various populations, under different ecological settings.

About 13 lakh G-6-PD deficient are present in the tribal population (*DST, 1990*). The prevalence is especially high among the tribes and scheduled castes of Madhya Pradesh, Chhattisgarh, Maharashtra, Tamil Nadu, Orissa, Rajasthan, Assam (more than 15 per cent), especially in the hyper endemic malaria zones.

Basu, et al, (*1989*) while carrying out intensive investigations among the different Bastar tribal groups of Madhya Pradesh/Chhattisgarh and primitive tribal group of Phulbani district of Orissa, found G-6-PD deficiency (using fluorescent spot test) in varying frequencies. Quite a high frequency of G-6-PD deficiency was found among the Bhattras (19 per cent), followed by Marias (17 per cent), Ghotul Murias (13 per cent) in males and 1.84 per cent in females was observed among primitive Kutia

Kondh tribal group of Phulbani district, Orissa.

It may be noted that the frequency distribution of G-6-PD deficiency among the tribal population, gradually increases, from South to North, North-East through Western and Central India (*Das, 1985*).

Among the Naikpod, Lambdi and Koya Southern tribes, the frequency of G-6-PD is below 5.00 per cent, while among the Western tribes like the Katkari, Bhil, Dhodia and Konkana, the percentages vary between 5-10 per cent. Central tribes like Gond, exhibit high frequency (19.0 per cent) whereas a higher frequency (23.06 per cent) of G-6-PD deficiency has been observed among the Angami Nagas (*Seth & Seth, 1971*).

Study of the genetic burden of red cell enzyme glucose-6-phosphate dehydrogenase deficiency has been conducted in two major scheduled tribes of Sundargarh district, Northwestern Orissa, India (*Balgir, 2007*).

Data on prevalence of G-6-PD deficiency in the indigenous tribal people of Orissa are limited. This study was carried out with the aim to conduct field evaluation of the incidence/prevalence of G-6-PD deficiency in two tribal populations, Bhuyan and Kharia of Orissa. It was found that the overall deficiency of the enzyme was high in both Kharia (24.9 per cent) and Bhuyan (16.9 per cent). The frequency of G-6-PD deficiency was recorded to be 22.5 per cent, 16.8 per cent and 13.7 per cent in Paraja, Paik and Paudi Bhuyans respectively, in Sundargarh District, Orissa. The deficiency was higher in Dhelki Kharia (30.4 per cent) in comparison to Dudh Kharia (20.4 per cent). The deficiency, among the Dhelki Kharia tribal community reported from Orissa, is the highest in India. The genetic burden of G-6-PD deficiency is very high in these tribal populations of Orissa, which may result in a high degree of morbidity, mortality and neonatal wastage. From a clinical point of view, anti-malarials should be administered with caution, in malaria-endemic tribal populations. (*Balgir, 2006*)

Schedule tribes in Ashram schools from eight districts of Orissa were randomly studied for five hereditary immuno-hematological disorders namely, the ABO and Rhesus (D) blood groups, sickle cell hemoglobinopathy, β–thalassemia syndrome and G-6-PD deficiency. 6-PD enzyme was found to be quite high, varying from 5.1 to 15.9 per cent among these scheduled tribes of Orissa. The frequency of sickle cell disorders was found to vary from 0 to 22.4 per cent among the major tribes, higher in Paraja (21.5 per cent), Dhelki Kharia (13.7 per cent), Gond (11.9 per cent) and Bhatra (10.5 per cent) tribes.

This situation is further complicated by the prevalence of high frequency of consanguinity found to be practised by different tribal population, e.g.,

Paniyan tribal group of Kerala shows 32 per cent of consanguinity (*Basu, S.K., 1990*).

Mortality Pattern among Scheduled Tribes

Infant Mortality: Infant mortality rate is considered to be one of the most sensitive indicators of the health status of a society. It is observed that while scheduled tribes have relatively lower infant mortality rate (62 per cent) than scheduled castes (66 per cent), the under five mortality rate is higher among scheduled tribes (96 per cent) than among scheduled castes (88 per cent). High levels of infant and child mortality are found in Chhattisgarh, Jharkhand, Orissa and Madhya Pradesh in the north central sub-region of India (*NFHS-3, 2005–06*).

Infant Mortality Rate (IMR) in Tribal Populatation: With respect to individual tribes, there is very little information about IMR and its etiological factors. Investigations carried out among the individual tribal groups of Bastar district (*Basu, 1986,*) showed a very high rate of infant mortality among Bhattras (148.56) followed by Murias (123.35) whereas Marias (85.44) and Halbas (92.78) from the same tribal area displayed relatively lesser incidence. Similar inter-tribe variation of IMR was observed in several tribes inhabiting the same area of Andhra Pradesh (range 68.00 to 213.33/1000) (*Malhotra, 1986*). These inter-tribal differences of IMR from the same geographical area need further in depth investigation. Data on reproductive wastage among tribal population are meagre. In the north central sub-region the incidence of abortion was reported to be 2.5 per cent among Muria and 0.2 per cent among Bhattra tribal mothers (*Basu et al. 1986*).

Maternal Mortality among Scheduled Tribe: Child bearing imposes additional health needs and problems on women—physically, psychologically and socially. Maternal mortality was reported to be high among various tribal groups but no exact data could be collected. The chief causes of maternal mortality were found to be unhygenic and primitive practices for parturition. For example, it was observed that among Kutia Khondhs, primitive tribes, (*Basu et al., 1990*), that the delivery was conducted by the mother herself in a half squatting position holding a rope tied down from the roof of the hut. This helped her to apply pressure to deliver the child. In a complicated labour, obviously, it might lead to maternal as well as child mortality. Similar crude birth practices were found to exist in other tribal groups like Kharias, Gonds, Santals, etc.

Perinatal Mortality: The perinatal mortality rate is the sum of the number of stillbirths and early neonatal deaths, divided by the number of pregnancies of seven or more months' duration. Although perinatal mortality is an extremely sensitive indicator of health status of the population, high quality data on perinatal mortality are difficult to obtain, because of under reporting of stillbirths and infant deaths at age 0-6 days. Chhattisgarh has the highest level of perinatal mortality (64) followed by Bihar (59), Jharkhand (58), Orissa (56), West Bengal (47), Madhya Pradesh (46) (*NFHS-3, 2005-06*).

Reduction of maternal mortality (MMR) is one of the major challenges to improve the overall quality of life. The absence of reliable estimates of MMR, particularly among scheduled tribes, makes the process both difficult and complex. There has been substantial decline in maternal mortality ratio (MMR) during 1997–2003. However, in order to achieve the target set by Millennium Development Goals (MDG), National Commission on Population (NCP) and National Rural Health Mission (NRHM), rapid expansion of institutional births with skilled attendance, especially in the EAG (Empowered Action Group) states of Bihar, Jharkhand, Orissa, Madhya Pradesh, Chhattisgarh, Rajasthan, Uttar Pradesh and Uttarachal) and in Assam would be needed. A stronger programme is required, to increase institutional delivery in low performing states and in communities having high MMR, to make a difference. States having a higher percentage of institutional deliveries generally have lower maternal mortality and vice versa.

Health Seeking Behaviour: One of the major issues in the health status measurement is the health seeking behaviour of a community, which governs the morbidity and mortality pattern. Since the concept of health occupies different meanings in different social systems, the health seeking behaviour of a community cannot be studied in isolation from the social network of a community, being deeply interwoven into every event of social, economical and biological nature of a population. This assumes greater significance in the context of underprivileged groups, where the impact of state policies and contemporary modern developmental activities has minimum, or no profound effect on its health profile. Detailed studies in terms of socio-economic, nutrition, living conditions, sanitation, hygiene, parasitic load, fertility, mortality, morbidity, health seeking pattern were carried out among Muria, Madia, Haba, Bhattra tribal families inhabiting Jagdalpur and Konta tehsils of Bastar district (erstwhile M.P.), primitive *Kutia Khonds* of Belghara, Guma and Tumdibandha Panchayat areas of Tumdibandha block of Phulbani district, Orissa and among Kharias of Sundargarh district, Orissa. (*Basu, Salil, Jindal Anil and Kshatriya, Gautam et al, 1990, 1994*)

These tribal population groups inhabit isolated and difficult terrain. The sustenance of these tribal groups depends mainly on agriculture and forest produce. Their main crops are rice, maize, kosra (cereals) and pulses. Methods of agriculture are primitive and production is oriented to subsistence requirements. They supplement their income by occasional agriculture labour, contract labour, bamboo cutting, fishing and basket weaving. The barter economy still exists in these tribal populations. These people spend a large portion of their income on social and religious ceremonies, as a result of which they are most often financially hard pressed. Their low rate of literacy further adds to their ignorance and ignorance of the surrounding environment, which continues to envelop them in deep magico-religious beliefs and taboos. Consumption of milk is considered taboo because of the superstition that a woman will not lactate, if a calf is deprived of the cow's milk. The availability of a high protein diet, therefore, is meager among these tribal groups.

Sanitation and hygiene among these tribal groups are found to be very poor. Their houses are built of mud walls with thatched roof, devoid of proper ventilation. The enclosures for animals are made within the household compound, which leads to poor environmental sanitation. They depend on ponds, ditches, wells and rivulets for drinking water, which considerably increases the chances of water borne fungal and bacterial infections.

Maternal-Child Health Care: Maternal-child care is an important aspect of health seeking behaviour, which is largely neglected among these tribal population groups. Expectant mothers to a large extent are not inoculated against tetanus. From the inception of pregnancy to its termination, no specific nutritious diet is consumed by a woman. The consumption of iron, calcium and vitamins during pregnancy is poor. More than 90 per cent of deliveries are conducted at home attended by elderly ladies of the household. No specific precautions are observed at the time of conducting deliveries, which results in an increased susceptibility to various infections. Services of paramedical staff are secured only if labour is difficult. It has been observed that a specially prepared concoction from various kinds of herbs known as "Kasa Pani", is provided to mother on the third day after delivery. "Kasa Pani" is an herbal medicine which gives soothing effect, helps in recovering the energy lost and also acts as antibiotic. Nevertheless, maternal mortality directly related to pregnancy and child birth has been found to be appreciably high among the tribal populations of Bastar district. In addition, a lot of females suffer from ill health due to pregnancy and child birth, in the absence of well defined concept of health consciousness.

Vaccination and immunization of infants and children have been inadequate among these tribal groups. Since the personal hygiene is very poor, the under 5 children are the worst sufferers and most vulnerable to infections. In addition, magico-religious beliefs and taboos tend to aggravate the problems.

Treatment of Diseases

Magico-Religious Tradition: It has been observed that there is a great difficulty in persuading the tribal people to come and avail of modern medical treatment, because they have a firm, rigid and well developed system of primitive medicine. They hold firm belief that a disease is always caused by hostile spirits, ghosts or breach of some taboo. Thus, they seek remedies through magico-religious practices to propitiate the supernatural powers.

The treatment of the disease in this method is essentially through appeasing the wrath of the Gods, evil spirits and observing some punishment in case of breach of a taboo. "*Sirha*" as is commonly known, serves as the mediator for diagnosing the diseases and the treatment plan. The "*Sirha*" or "*Gunia*" or "*Jani*", is supposed to have powers to identify the angry Gods and evil spirits. The identifications and treatment of sickness assumes the proportions of a holy ceremony among all the four tribal groups.

Indigenous/Herbal Medicines: Herbal medicines or indigenous medicines are the next preferred treatment, which is obtained through local people or from the forest. It was observed that the tribal groups perpetuate the use of "Tulsi" leaves and turmeric powder in case of fevers, and invariably in case of injuries. There is enough evidence to suggest that the tribal population groups do use the indigenous herbal concoctions to avoid pregnancies, treatment of infertility and some common ailments, although it was very difficult to get the details thereof.

Ayurvedic Medicine: The tribal population groups of Bastar district also resort to the Ayurvedic system of medicine, at times, along with traditional and indigenous system of medicine. They utilize the services of local practitioner as well as the ayurvedic dispensaries, provided by the State government.

Response to Modern Medical Care System: The attitude of tribal population towards modern medical care is not generally encouraging, because of their deep rooted belief in magico-religious practices and also because their awareness of and exposure to the outside world is little.

It has been observed that in the decision to avail of modern medical health care, the tribal people are influenced by many people, i.e. clan-chiefs, Patels, village headman, head of the hamlets/household etc. Their decision is also governed by the level of their education; women, however, are not consulted in the process of major decision making.

It has also been observed that the response of the tribals to modern health care system was better in places where the services are available close-by, such as in case of PHC and sub-centre villages. This is further substantiated by the fact that the surveillance malaria workers enjoy more respect, because they meet the tribals more often in connection with their assigned duties.

Tribals generally do not go to a PHC if it is very far off and if it the only purpose of such travel. On the other hand they do not mind travelling 8–10 kms on foot, if the PHC is located near the weekly market, combining the visit to the PHC with their market visit.

Another reason for the hesitation could be the prohibitive cost for the treatment. In case of chronic diseases, long-term treatment and the cost of drugs are important factors in non-utilization of services.

In short, it can be said that the poor health seeking behaviour among these tribal groups, is the result of their social and living conditions, malnutrition, illiteracy, ignorance, superstitions, improper and poor sanitation, unsafe drinking water, unawareness of health education, under utilization of health resources, cultural lag, poorly developed mass media, poor medical and health opportunities (variety, quality and quantity of health services) and infrastructure on the administrative side.)

Strategies of Tribal Development

A five-fold strategy needs to be adopted and actively pursued to improve the quality of life and to bring about overall development of the tribal population of India.

First is the strategy relating to Socio-cultural issues and Environment. The realistic development, holistic plans based on needs and culture of specific tribal groups need to be formulated with adequate understanding of the socio-cultural background of different tribal groups, perception of diseases, their beliefs and taboos, study of their health culture at the micro level.

There is a need to document the rich folkfore relating to health, available in different tribal communities. This may provide a model for appropriate health and sanitary practices in a given eco-system. There is also a need to identify indigenous herbs for medical use and their preservation and documentation. Efforts should be made towards developing proper sanitation, personal hygiene, and provision of safe drinking water. Efforts should also be made to dispel certain negative beliefs, taboos, and magico-religious practices, while retaining the positive beliefs.

The second strategy relates to nutrition. The development of horticulture, with emphasis on growing local fruits should be encouraged, so that nutritional needs may be solved by the tribal communities themselves. They should be encouraged tor utilize the locally available, cheap, but nutritious food. Schemes for poultry and fisheries should be initiated in the tribal areas.

Study of nutritional status and physical growth among tribal children in different ecological settings, should be carried out for an effective strategy to plan nutrition intervention programmes.

There is also a need, to evaluate the changing patterns of dependence on traditional food and dietary practices.

The third is the strategy related to Maternal and Child Health, in which hundred per cent immunisation of mothers and children, with special emphasis on measles vaccination, needs to be carried out Vitamin A should be distributed and oral rehydration therapy needs to introduced among different tribal populations, through their culturally accepted food habits.

The fourth is the startegy to tackle Genetic Disorders. Simple kits should be provided at PHC level and staff should be trained for conducting genetic disorder tests for sickling/G-6-PD enzyme deficiency, etc. Screening of villages for sicklers and G-6-PD deficient individuals andhigh risk delineated families should be given genetic advice. Effective communication on health education and health care among tribals groups in consonance with their socio-cultural characteristics, needs to be developed through distribution of leaflets and playing of audio and video cassettes, preferably in local dialects at weekly markets, ghotuls, schools, etc.

The fifth startegy relates to Training. Short term orientation courses on tribal culture for health workers at district and sub-divisional headquarters need to be organised. In tribal areas, *haats* (weekly market centres) being the focal point of activity, each *haat* should be provided with a Primary Health Centre (PHC)/Sub-centre, in order to augment the utilization of health care services. Training, on setting up cooperatives and effective marketing, needs to be introduced among the tribals, so that they can initiate income generating activities.

Need for a Holistic Study

There is a paucity of comprehensive health related holistic studies, among the tribal population of India. Most of the studies are isolated and fragmented in nature. There is an urgent need for initiating area specific, group specific, health related action research studies, in consonance with the felt needs of the tribal communities. The research should be mission oriented and directed towards improving the quality of life of the tribals. These health oriented, action research studies, will ultimately help in formulating effective, need based, health care strategies among various tribal groups and will also develop area specific/group specific health care delivery models, for areas with tribal concentration.

REFERENCES

Balgir R.S., 2006, Genetic heterogeneity of population structure in 15 major scheduled tribes: A study of immuno-hematological disorders; Division of Human Genetics, *Regional Medical Research Center* (ICMR), Vol. 12, Issue 2, pp. 86-92.

______, 2007 Current Science, Vol. 92, No. March, 2007, RMRC (ICMR) Bhubaneshwar

Baneriee, D., 1982, Poverty, Class and Health Culture in India, Vol. 1, New Delhi, Prachi Prakashan.

Bardhan, A., S.K. Sinha, K. Gopinath, A.K. Brahmbhatt, 1989, A diagnostic study of factors responsible for lesser or no utilisation of health facilities among the Bhils of Madhya Pradesh, PAC Report, Mimeo, NIHFW, New Delhi.

Basu, S.K. et. al., 1983, Socio-Cultural Dimensions, Demographic Features, Maternal and Child Health Care Practices and Sexually Transmitted Diseases n Santals of Mayurbhanj District, Orissa (Mimeo, NIHFW).

______, 1996, Need for Action Research for Health Development among Tribal Communities of India, South Asian Anthropologist, 17(2): 73–80.

______, 1994, The State of the Art—Tribal Health in India, In : Salil Basu (ed.). Tribal Health in India, Manak Publications Pvt. Ltd., Delhi.

______, 1985, Population Genetics and Environmental Studies among the tribal population of India: Consideration of Approaches for promotion of Health Care : Issues and Future Strategies, NIHFW Technical Report 8.

______, (1986, 1989, 1992, 1993 & 1994); Patnaik, S.M. (2002), Integrated Disease Surveillance Project, Tribal Development Plan (2002).

______ et al., 1993, Study of Socio-Cultural, Demographic Characteristics, Maternal and Child Health and Sexually transmitted diseases among the polyandrous Jaunsaries of Jaunsar-Bawer, Dehradun (Mimeo NIHFW).

______ and G.K. Kshatriya, 1989, Fertility and Mortality in Tribal Populations of Bastar District, Madhya Pradesh. *Biology and Society*, 6 :110-112.

______ and G.K. Kshatriya, 1993, Fertility and Mortality Trends in Dudh Kharia Tribal Population of Sundergarh district, Orissa, Paper presented at the International Symposium on Human Genetics and Variation and XVIII Annual Conference of Indian Society of Human Genetics held at Osmania University, Hyderabad, January 1993.

______ and G.K. Kshatriya and A. Jindal, 1988, Fertility and Mortality Differentials Among the Tribal Population Groups of Baster District, Madhya Pradesh. *Human Biology*, 600 :407-416.

Basu, S.K. et. al., 1994, Genetic disorders and Health Care. Shri Kala Prakashan Publishers, Delhi.

______, 1994, Tribal Health in India. Manak Publishers, Delhi.

Basu, Salil, 1993, Health Scenario and Health Problems of the Tribal Population in India. In Mrinal Miri (ed.). Continuity and Change in Tribal Society. Indian Institute of Advanced Study, Shimla.

______, 1996, Malaria Control Project—Beneficiary Social Assessment, (World Bank Aided Project Report).

______, 1996, 'Health Status of Tribal Women in India', (In) Amar Kumar Singh and M.K. Jabbi (edited). Status of Tribal in India, Health, Education and Employment, Council for Social Development, Har Anand Publications, New Delhi.

______, 1996, 'Health and Socio Cultural Correlates in Tribal Communities', (In) R.S. Mann (edited) Tribes of India : Ongoing Challenges, M.D. Publications Pvt. Ltd., New Delhi.

______, 1995, Social Assessment Study: Perception, Attitude, Experience of Tribal Communities vis-a-vis the Role of Health Providers for the Acceptability and Demand for tuberculosis Treatment in Tribal Areas (World Bank Aided Project Report).

______, 1986, Genetics, Socio-Cultural and Health Care among.Tribal Groups ofJagdalpur and Konta Tehsils of Bastar District, Madhya Pradesh (In) A.K. Kalla and K.S. Singh (eds.), Anthropology, Development and Nation Building, Concept Publishing Company, New Delhi.

______, 1998, supported by Pfizer Limited and DGHS, Govt. of India

______, 1992, Health and Culture of the Underprivileged Group of India, In: Alok Mukhopadhyay (ed.). State of India's Health, Voluntary Health Association of India, New Delhi.

______ and G.K. Kshatriya, 1989, Fertility and Mortality in Tribal Populations of Bastar District, Madhya Pradesh, India Biology and Society, 6,100–112.

______ and A. Jindal, 1990, Genetic and Socio-Cultural Determinants of Tribal Health: A primitive Kutia Khondhs Tribal Group ofPhulbani District, Orissa. ICMR Final Report, NIHFW, NewDelhi.

Chakma, T and Vinay Rao, P., 2004, *Biannual Newsletter*, Vol. 1(2), October, ICMR, Jabalpur.

Chetlapalli et al., 1991, 'Estimates of Fertility and Mortality in Kutia Khondhs of Phulbani District, Orissa, *Journal of Human Ecology*, 2(1), 117–20.

Chaudhuri, B., 1986, Medical Anthropology in India with special reference to tribal population, in: B. Chaudhuri (ed.). Tribal Health, Socio-Cultural Dimensions. Inter-India Publications, New Delhi.

Continuity and Change in Tribal Society, Edited by Mrinal Miri, 1993: Health Scenario and Health Problems of Tribal Population in India by Salil Basu pp. 259-284.

D/H&FW [M] Govt. of Rajasthan (2003); Bhasin, V. (2004), Gupta, N.; Pal, P.; Bhargava, M.; Daga, M. (1992): Naik et al (2005); Mamta Report (2005).

DST Expert Committee (1990), Health, Drinking Water and Management of Genetic Disorders.

DST Technical Report Series, Department of Science and Technology, New Delhi.

Elwin, V., 1961, Nagaland Research Department, Advisors Secretariat, Shillong.

Guha, B.S., 1935, The Racial Affinities of People of India. Census of India 1931, Vol. 1, Part III B, Government Press, Shimla.

Haque, M., 1990, Height weight and nutrition among the six tribes of India. In L.B. Chaudhury (ed.). Cultural and Environmental Dimension on Health, pp. 192–206. Inter-India Publications, New Delhi.

Indira Gandhi National Open University, 1990, School of Social Sciences, ESO-02, Block 6, Society in India.

Jindal, A and Kshatriya, G.K., 1990, The Determinants of Health Seeking Behavior Among Tribal Populations of Bastar District, Madhya Pradesh, South Asian Anthropologist 11, 1–6.

Mukherjee, D.P. and S.K. Nandy, 1986, Anthropology of tribal health—The Case of the Asur in Netarhat Plateau. In : B. Chaudhury (ed.). Tribal Health: Soco-Cultural Dimensions, pp. 247–258. Inter-India Publications, New Delhi.

Nahonal Sample Survey Organisation, Government of India, 1991, A Report on Living Conditions on Tribals and Non-Tribals of Tribal Areas No. 380.

Prasad, R.R., 1988, Tribal Development in India—Strategies and Programmes, *Journal of Rural Development*, Vol. 7(1), 81–103.

Registrar General, India, New Delhi in Collaboration with Centre for Global Health Research, University of Toronto, Canada.

Report of a Study Group of Health for All—An Alternative Strategy.

Report of a DST Expert Committee, 1990, Health, Drinking Water and Management of Genetic Disorders, DST Technical Report Series, Department of Science and Technology, New Delhi.

Report of the Commissioner for Scheduled Castes and Schedulated Tribes, Twenty Eighth Report, 1986–87.

Rizvi, S.N.H., 1986, Health Practices of theJaunsars—A Socio-cultural analysis. In : B. Chaudhuri (ed.) Tribal Health: Socio-Cultural Dimensions, pp. 223–246, Inter-India Publications, New Delhi.

Roy Burman, B.K., 1986, Morbidity and Nutritional Status of the Scheduled Tribes of India, In : B. Chaudhuri (ed.) Tribal Health, Socio-Cultural Dimensions, pp. 85–98, Inter-India Publications, New Delhi.

Report of the Working Group on Development and Welfare of Scheduled Tribes during Eighth Five Year Plan, Government of India, Ministry of Welfare, 1989 MN, New Delhi.

Registrar General of India, 1979, Survey of Infant and Child Mortality, Ministry of Home Affairs, New Delhi.

Registrar General, Ministry of Home Affairs, 1973, cited from Malhotra, 1986.

Registrar General, India, New Delhi in Collaboration with Centre for Global Health Research, University of Toronto, Canada, 2006.

Swain, S., S.C. Jena, P. Singh, 1990, Morbidity Status of the Kondha Tribes of Phulbani (Orissa), In: B. Chaudhury (ed.). Cultural and Environmental Dimension of Health, pp. 177–191, Inter-India Publications, New Delhi.

Survekshana, 1995, Round 44th, 5th Issue.

Sahu, S.K., 1991, Health Culture in Transition: A Case Study of Oraon Tribe in Rural and Industrial Nexus, Khana Publishers, New Delhi.

Saxena V.B., Darbar B.S. and Jain M.K., June 1978; Resurgence of Yaws, A Preliminary Report from Jagdalpur District, Madhya Pradesh, India, *Indian Journal Preventive Social Medicine*, Vol. 9, No. 2.

Vidyarthi, L.P., 1983, Tribals of India, In: People of India : Some Genetical Aspects, XV International Congress of Genetics, December 12–21, ICMR, New Delhi.

——— and Rai, 1979, The Tribal Culture of India, Concept Publishing House, New Delhi.

Challenges of Health Care in Central Indian Tribal Areas

P.C. Joshi

As discussed in the previous articles, the challenges of health care in tribal areas are many and varied. Again, this is because the tribal areas are relatively inaccessible, unfamiliar and at times un-friendly, economically poor and above all have distinct culture, which includes the traditional knowledge and practices pertaining to health issues, which more often than not, comes in the way of any organized efforts at public health care delivery. The difficulties are also because there is wide variation in the cultures, livelihood technologies, attitude and ecosystem of the tribal areas giving rise to area-specific morbidity, necessitating area or tribe-specific health care strategies in planning. What may work in one context or tribal area may not work in another. The knowledge and practices enshrined in the traditional medical systems of the tribal areas are, likewise, posing a tough challenge in the path of organized health care efforts. Since people have strong faith and believe in their customary ways, they often are reluctant to use new methods and procedures. Consequently, highly ambitious programmes like universal immunization, safe motherhood, child nutrition, water and sanitation improvement, vector control, etc., always face the danger of failure. And many times, these programmes do fail or meet with a lukewarm response.

Against this backdrop, the very serious question confronting us is, whether it is sufficient that we have earmarked special norms for tribal areas in the health care policy and, will doing this alone be sufficient to bring quality health care to the tribal areas in our country?

Besides the above mentioned internal constraints, the situation on the external public health effort front is also worth examining. The excessive and alarming disease burden and nutritional abnormalities in the tribal areas are also indicative of the failure of the public health care delivery system. What kind of health care is actually being received by the tribal areas? Are doctors, nurses and para-medical persons physically present at the place of their posting? Even if some of them are present, do they have adequate medicines and infrastructure? Do they treat tribal patients, who are poor, illiterate and often unsophisticated with care, sympathy and dignity? The challenges, of health care in central Indian tribal areas, need to be seen and examined in the backdrop of above-mentioned situation.

Contrary to the vast range of eco-cultural distribution and differences, there are only a few studies on tribal communities dealing with health, disease and treatment. The available studies are generally anthropological in nature, with very few clinically sound studies. With the establishment of the ICMR centre on tribal health, there have been some studies undertaken in tribal area, but the main emphasis of such studies has been on bio-genetic dimension, such as sickle cell anaemia study. The available, relatively scanty studies reveal that the tribal-health maintenance system is attached with a lot of complexity, intertwined with socio-cultural beliefs and practices. The concept of health of the tribal groups of India has not yet been properly defined. General conclusions on tribal health indicate that their health care system pays more emphasis on the magico-religious model, to explain disease etiology and treatment. *Sachchidananda* (*1994*) sees the field of tribal health as a cultural concept, as well as a part of its social structure and organization which is continuously changing and adapting itself to changes in the wider society. Additionally, the concept of health in the context of tribal societies is as much a moral concept, as it is physical or materialistic. In the absence of external law enforcement, the tribal beliefs and practices related to health and illness perform a very important function of social control and sudden disbelief in these customary behaviours may lead to serious consequences in the form of crime and exploitation. *Choudhary* (*1994*) and *Lewis* (*1958*) believes that the study of tribal health should be with reference to their distinctive notions regarding different aspects of diseases, health, food, human anatomy and faiths, as well as in the process of interaction with modern world. Thus, the health of the tribal populations and their morbidity pattern should be seen in relation to the public health indicators as well as their customs, traditions and beliefs.

Tribal concept of health, disease, treatment, life and death, is as varied as their culture (*Majumdar, 1933*; *Basu, A., 1990*; *Basu, S.K., 1994*).

Accordingly, the tribal society is guided by traditionally laid down customs and every member of the society is expected to conform to it. In the tribal context, the fate of individual and the community at large depends on their relationship with unseen forces, which intervene in human affairs. If men offend them, the mystical powers punish by sickness, death or other natural calamities (*Chaudhuri, 1967*; *Ratlam, 1955*). The distinctive cultural rootedness of tribal ethos has immense implications for the delivery of health care services in these areas and many times the tribal ethos acts as a barrier in proper patient care and drug compliance.

The general view is that diseases in tribal communities are caused by bad spirits and the spirits are bad, either because one has not properly propitiated them or one has disturbed them (*Lal, 1925*; *Bharathi, 1993*). Thus, to the tribal ethos, the real enemies of human health and prosperity are the supernatural and the dead (*Sinha and Banerjee, 2004*). Accordingly, they pay special emphasis upon appeasement, prayers, taboos, exorcism, divination, shamanism and sundry other means in events of sickness (*Joshi, 2004*).

The present paper is an appraisal of the health situation of the scheduled tribes concentrated in the areas of Jharkhand and Chhattisgarh. The main focus of the paper is on examining the public health care delivery and its impact on the tribal populations. The impact of health care policy and planning as it is implemented on the ground, where the tribal societies live, has been bracketed out of the health care services, indicators and utilizations data. There are some positive as well as s negative aspects underlying the health sector, among the tribes. These are being highlighted so as to know the grey areas in the health sector that need to be taken care of.

The nearly 80 per cent of the scheduled tribe population in India is largely concentrated in the central and north-eastern India. The general location of this population is in remote and inaccessible areas and as a result it suffers from the ill-effects of backwardness in education, employment and health care. These areas further show low population density, poor urbanization and poor access to basic amenities. The cash generating activities are generally monopolized by the non-tribals, who exploit the scheduled tribes and appropriate their resources. As a result, the tribal people have low employment opportunities which force them to seasonally migrate for unskilled work in cities and towns. The physical infrastructure is also very poor and miserably maintained. This incapacitates the economy to absorb funds including institutional finances.

Some positive points with respect to tribal areas are the favourable sex ratio and cultural traditions of relatively better gender relations, than the caste societies, which represents good potential for their development. The scheduled tribe areas are also rich in biodiversity and as such are rich in medicinal plants and indigenous knowledge, the true potential of which, unfortunately, has not been realized as yet in spite of the health policy emphasizing promotion of indigenous systems of medicines.

Government of India, from the very beginning has been formulating and implementing special programmes for the scheduled tribes so that their life may be improved. The main objective of the National Health Policy 2002 is to achieve an acceptable standard of good health amongst the general population of the country. The approach was to increase access to the decentralized public health system, by establishing the infrastructure in deficient areas such as tribal, hilly and forested areas, and by upgrading infrastructure in the existing institutions. Primacy would be given to preventive and first line curative initiatives at the primary health level, through increased sectoral share of the allocation. The increased outlay would be utilized for strengthening the existing facilities and opening additional public health services outlets consistent with the norms for such facilities. The recommendation of this policy would attempt to maximize the broad based availability of health services to the citizens of the country, on the basis of realistic consideration of capacity. Under the broad macro policy prescriptions contained in this policy, state governments would have the flexibility to design separate schemes, tailor-made to the health needs of different socio-economic sections of society, including the tribals.

The central Indian tribal areas have now come under the newly formed states of Jharkhand and Chhattisgarh and as a result, the tribal areas in central Indian are under the care of the newly formed political leadership and the administrative machinery. The delivery of accessible, affordable and quality health care to tribal areas remains a big challenge even today. Although the National Health Policy has assured special norms for tribal areas, yet, people continue to die in large numbers in the absence of quality health care in tribal areas.

The central Indian states of Jharkhand and Chhattisgarh are home to a large number of scheduled tribes. As against the all-India average of nearly 8 per cent Scheduled Tribe population, the states of Chhattisgarh and Jharkhand have 31 per cent and 28 per cent of Scheduled Tribe population respectively. Barring the central district of Chhattisgarh and the northern district adjoining the state of Bihar in Jharkhand, the remaining districts of these states are dominated by Scheduled Tribe population. Districts of

Simdega, Gumla, West Singhbhum and Lohardagga in Jharkhand and districts of Dantewada, Bastar, Kanker, Surguja and Jashpur in Chhattisgarh have more than 50 per cent of the Scheduled Tribe population. (Table 1).

Table 1: District-wise Percentage of Scheduled Tribe Population in Jharkhand and Chhattisgarh

S.No.	Jharkhand Districts	% of ST Population	Chhattisgarh District	% of ST Population
1.	Simdega	72.4	Dantewada	78.5
2.	Gumla	69.8	Bastar	66.3
3.	West Singhbhum	66.4	Jashpur	63.2
4.	Lohardagga	56.4	Kanker	56.1
5.	Pakur	49.3	Surguja	54.6
6.	Latehar	49.3	Koriya	44.4
7.	Dumka	46.6	Korba	41.5
8.	Ranchi	43.6	Raigarh	35.4
9.	Saraikela Kharswan	36.8	Mahasamund	27.0
10.	Jamtara	32.7	Rajnandgaon	26.6
11.	Sahebganj	30.1	Dhamtari	26.3
12.	East Singhbhum	29.0	Kawardha	20.9
13.	Godda	25.1	Bilaspur	19.9
14.	Garhwa	15.7	Durg	12.4
15.	Deoghar	12.8	Raipur	12.1
16.	Bokaro	12.2	Jajgir Champa	11.6
17.	Hazaribag	12.2		
18.	Giridih	9.9		
19.	Palamu	9.0		
20.	Dhanbad	8.8		
21.	Chatra	3.8		
22.	Koderma	0.9		

Source: As per the Census of India 2001 and SRS 2000.

It is observed that the sex ratio in the scheduled tribe dominated districts in Chhattisgarh and Jharkhand is 1000 and 989, respectively as against the state average of 990 (for Chhattisgarh) and 941 (for Jharkhand). The scheduled tribe dominated districts score lower in terms of literacy than the state as a whole. The average literacy rate for the scheduled tribe dominated districts in Chhattisgarh is 53.9 per cent against the state average of 65.2 per cent. The average literacy rate for the scheduled tribe dominated districts in Jharkhand is however slightly less than the state average (52.3 per cent against 54.1 per cent of the state average). Female literacy is a very crucial development indicator having immense relevance for health of a population. The disparities in female literacy are quite marked, for the state of Chhattisgarh. The scheduled tribe dominated districts in Chhattisgarh show 44.1 per cent as the average female literacy rate against the state average of 52.4. The disparities in the state of Jharkhand are however, not so marked.

The scheduled tribe population is primarily located in the rural and forested areas. Besides disadvantages in terms of accessibility, there is immense diversity in terms of their language, economy, education, eco-system, ethnicity and customs. There are tribes like Gonds, Oraons and Mundas, which are present in large number and are educationally, politically and economically progressive. On the other hand, there are tribes like Kamar, Birhor, Baiga, Hill Korwa, which are still lagging behind and require meticulous planning and sensitivity in the implementation of health care programmes. The inter-tribal disparity in terms of economic status, educational achievement and health indicators needs to be considered and incorporated in the health care programme implementation.

Then there is big developmental hiatus between the tribal and non-tribals. In general, the business activities are controlled by the non-tribals in entire central India. The tribal people are thus placed in an unequal position vis-à-vis the outside traders. Money lending and heavy profit making by the traders, is a very common feature in these regions. For example, in the district headquarter of Jashpur Nagar of Chhattisgarh state where the Oraons reside and Gariyaband, where the Gonds and Kamars reside, nearly 95 per cent of the business is controlled by the non-tribals. In such a situation, the tribal communities are caught in the vicious cycle of exploitation by the better off outside traders. The economic dependence and poverty, has an adverse impact on health seeking and acceptance of the health care programmes.

Table 2: Development and Health Indicators of Jharkhand and Chhattisgarh States

S.No.	Development and Health Indicators	Jharkhand	Chhattisgarh	India
1	Population (2001)	26.9 m.	20.8 m.	1027 m.
2.	Population Density	338	154	324
3.	Decadal Pop. Growth (1991–2001)	21.4%	18.1%	21.3%
4.	Sex Raio	941	990	933
5.	Child Sex Ratio (0-6 years)	966	927	975
6.	Literacy Rate	54.1	65.2	65.4
7.	Female Literacy Rate	49.4	52.4	52.4
8.	Composite Index (Rank)	34	23	-
9.	Birth Rate (per 1000)	26.5	26.7	24.8
10.	Birth Rate Rural(per 1000)	28.8	29.2	26.4

S.No.	Development and Health Indicators	Jharkhand	Chhattisgarh	India
11.	Death Rate (per 1000)	9.0	9.6	8.0
12.	Death Rate Rural (per 1000)	9.8	11.2	8.7
13.	Infant Mortality Rate (per 1000)	70	79	60
14.	Infant Mortality Rate Rural (per 1000)	74	95	66

Sources: Census of India 2001 and SRS 2000.
National commission on Population, district wise Indicators 2001, p. 98.
Registrar General India Sample Registration General Bulletin Vol. 35, No. 2, October 2001.

The development and health indicators confirm the poor performance of these two tribal dominant states. The composite index calculated for assessment of social and economic development by the National Commission on Population, taking cognizance of health, fertility, family planning and literacy ranks Jharkhand as the 34th among all states and UTs in India, while the Chhattisgarh is ranked 23rd. Interestingly, while Chhattisgarh has climbed four steps up from its erstwhile parent state Madhya Pradesh, Jharkhand has slid down one step, from the parent state Bihar.

Compared with the all-India average, both states perform quite poorly in the development and health indicators. Be it birth rate, death rate, infant mortality rate, the states of Jharkhand and Chhattisgarh appear to be in bad shape. What alarms is the condition in rural areas, where most of the tribal populations lives. In such places, the delivery of health care and health education has not reached the masses. The situation of Chhattisgarh is worse than Jharkhand and there is an urgent need for the health bureaucracy in Chhattisgarh to look into this aspect quite seriously.

Table 3: Health Infrastructure for the States of Jharkhand and Chhattisgarh

S.No.	Particulars	Jharkhand		Chhattisgarh	
		In Position	Shortfall	In Position	Shortfall
1.	Primary Health Centres	330	476	516	143
2.	Community Health Centres	194	7	116	48
3.	Sub Centres	3958	1099	3818	346
4.	MPW (Female)/ANM	4392	-	3667	667
5.	MPW (Male)	4311	-	2940	878
6.	Doctors at PHCs	2332	-	817	-
7.	Gynecologists	61	133	NA	NA
8.	Physicians	22	172	12	104
9.	Pediatricians	22	172	9	107
10.	Total Specialists	146	630	31	433
11.	Nurse/Midwives	451	1237	590	174
12.	Lab. Technicians	239	285	219	413

Source: *Bulletin of Rural Health Statistics in India 2005, Ministry of HFW, Department of Family Welfare.*

Health problems and health practices of any community are profoundly influenced by interplay of a complex of social, economic and political factors (*Bose, 1980*). These factors have also had considerable influence, not only on the development of medical technology, but also in determining the access of different social strata of a community to such technology. The situation of health infrastructure, in the two tribal states, is dismally poor. Only non-specialist doctors at the PHCs are sufficiently recruited in both the states. Except for the Multi Purpose Workers/Auxillary Nurse Midwives (Female) and Multi Purpose Workers (male) in Jharkhand, the states show considerable shortfall of health care personnel in the states. It is well known that the Primary Health Centre is the backbone of public health care delivery system. In Jharkhand, much less than half the sanctioned PHCs are functioning, while in Chhattisgarh, there is a shortfall of 143 PHCs. What makes matters worse, is the acute shortfall in the category of specialists; be it gynecologists, pediatricians or physicians. This situation compromises quality access to mother and child health care and consequently, we see a high proportion of mother and children dying in these areas.

The schedule tribe populated districts in Jharkhand and Chhattisgarh have been identified as the districts, where the percentage population of the scheduled tribe is more than the state average. The preference for institution delivery does not seem to be the norm in these areas. More than 90 per cent of pregnant mothers do not consider it worthwhile to go for institutional delivery, in the districts of Sahebganj in Jharkhand and district of Koriya in Chhattisgarh. This proportion is lower than 20 per cent in many of the districts (W. Singhbhum, Dumka, Gumla and Lohardagga in Jharkhand and Korba and Sarguja in Chhattisgarh). The overall condition of tribal areas in Chhattisgarh is slightly better than in Jharkhand. The figures for pregnant women going for complete ante natal check-up, however, are quite impressive in districts like Korba, Raigarh and Dantewada, with more than 80 per cent pregnant women going for full ante natal check-up. In the state of Jharkhand however, only the districts of East Singhbhum and Ranchi have good coverage for ante natal check-up while the rest of districts are lagging behind.

The familiarity of mothers with the health facility, generally converts itself into good childhood care. However, the full immunization of the children is much lower than the ante natal check-up, indicating lack of persuasion by the health staff. The very low percentage of full immunization for the districts of Sahebganj (7.2), Dumka (18.5) and West Singhbhum (23.6) in Jharkhand is detrimental for the future health of the children.

Table 4: Key Indicators in ST Dominated Districts of Jharkhand and Chhattisgarh

S. No.	Districts	% Safe deliveries	Contraceptive Prevalence Rate	% of 3+ Births	% of Girls Marrying < 18 years	% of Children with complete Immunization	% of Pregnant Women with full ANC
	Jharkhand						
1	Sahebganj	9.5	14.4	57.9	62.6	7.2	28.4
2.	W. Singhbhum	19.6	20.0	54.3	28.5	23.6	37.4
3.	Dumka	11.7	26.4	54.3	49.5	18.5	24.9
4.	Gumla	17.2	18.1	59.4	27.2	35.6	40.5
5.	Lohardagga	14.9	20.3	66.2	43.2	48.4	41.7
6.	E. Singhbhum	43.9	47.9	40.5	33	71.3	68.9
7.	Ranchi	24.6	34.4	56.1	39	64.1	58.4
	Chhattisgarh						
1.	Bastar	25.1	37.3	45.3	24.1	44.9	65.3
2.	Koriya	9.2	39.1	50.5	55.3	61.9	65.2
3.	Korba	18.3	44.5	48.9	35.6	73.9	88.2
4.	Surguja	19.5	46.8	45.8	55.9	54.8	71.8
6.	Jashpur	20.1	47.4	49.5	23.9	62.7	72.1
7.	Raigarh	24.3	49.1	37.3	13.0	66.9	83.9
8.	Kanker	28.9	51.7	42.1	8.8	73.0	71.9
9.	Dantewada	38.5	54.7	42.7	5.9	76.5	86.7

Source: Rapid Household survey (RHS-RCH Project) Phase II, 1998-99 (Jharkhand). RCH-DLHS. 2002-04 (Chhattisgarh).

The state of Chhattisgarh fares better than the Jharkhand, which needs to take up immunization coverage in mission mode.

Health care utilization in Bastar and Raigarh in Chhattisgarh and Ranchi, East Singhbhum and Gumla districts of Jharkhand is presented in the Table 5. In most districts, except Gumla, nearly one third of the eligible tribal population was found to be using any family planning methods. However, when it comes to surgical methods of birth control, contrasting gender divide is evident in all the tribal districts.

Female sterilization is far higher than male sterilization. In fact, male sterilization is almost absent in Jharkhand districts. Another aspect worth a mention here, is the quality of surgical method of birth control. A very high percentage of women in Chhattisgarh (above 70 per cent) reported side effects of sterilization, which indicates low quality of surgical interventions and this issue needs to be addressed by the health administration, particularly in Chhattisgarh. The situation of immunization

Table 5: Health Care Utilization in Selected ST Dominated Districts of Jharkhand and Chhattisgarh (in percentage)

S.No.	Key Indicator	Bastar	Raigarh	Ranchi	East Singhbhum	Gumla
1.	Currently using any family planning method	36.3	34.3	34.4	30.2	18.1
2.	Female Sterilization	26.4	24.5	26.8	23.5	13.4
3.	Male Sterilization	7.1	7.8	0.0	0.0	0.5
4.	Seeking Treatment for side effect of Female Sterilization	72.7	70.5	28.5	22.2	40.0
5.	% of Institutional Deliveries Total	11.8	8.1	18.5	10.8	4.9
6.	% of children 12-36 months receiving complete immunization	54.6	52.7	64.1	60.7	35.6
7.	% of mother used ORS for treating their children with diarrhea	9.6	8.8	25.0	21.9	15.9
8.	% of mothers using Government facility for breathing problem to their children	38.4	35.3	13.5	11.5	9.3

Source: *RHS-RCH Survey 1998-99.*

is also not good in both the states. The highest immunization is only 64.1 per cent and it is as low as 35.4 per cent in Gumla district of Jharkhand. The immunization coverage needs to be above 90 per cent as then only can we ensure a safe childhood in these areas.

The utilization of services for diarrhea and acute respiratory tract infection (ARI) also varies across both the states. It appears that utilization of services for diarrhea is comparatively better in Jharkhand with Chhattisgarh lagging behind, while reverse is true for ARI. But the overall low proportion of mothers using government facilities for diarrhea and ARI, seems to suggest that these activities should be taken up on war footing in order to reduce infant and child mortality instances.

On the basis of available records from Chhattisgarh for select diseases causing epidemic for the year 2005 (Table 6), it can be observed that both preventive and promotional health activities are not effective in the tribal areas. Consequently, the water borne diseases namely, gastroenteritis, diarrhea, dysentery and jaundice tend to show excess morbidity burden for the tribal areas. Although, the figures suggest that there is partial mortality burden associated with these water borne diseases, we need to treat such a conclusion with caution. The water borne disease control measures need to be strengthened in the tribal areas with multi-sectoral cooperation. The experience of water sanitation projects in north India needs to be extended to the central Indian tribal regions, involving multi-sectoral collaboration and as a culturally suitable and socially acceptable implementation strategy.

Table 6: Morbidity Profile on Select Epidemic Diseases in Chhattisgarh for the year 2005

S.No.	District	Gastroen-teritis	Diarrhea & Dysentry	Jaundice	Cholera	Meningitis	Measles
1.	Bastar	2739	10956	20	0	0	0
2.	Koriya	1077	4301	10	0	0	0
3.	Korba	168	14177	0	0	0	0
4.	Surguja	1250	7711	34	0	10	6
5.	Jashpur	1382	21921	210	0	0	31
6.	Raigarh	4276	19595	126	0	0	0
7.	Kanker	0	8587	0	0	0	0
8.	Dantewara	65	22376	0	0	0	4
	Total	10957	109624	400	0	10	41
	% of State Total	37.0	48.0	76.0	0.0	22.0	90.0
	Excess Burden in%*	6.0	17.0	45.0	(–) ve	(–) ve	59.0

* Excess burden has been calculated by deducing percentage of tribal population in the state.

Source: Directorate of Health Services; Chhattisgarh; Annual Report on Epidemic situation.

Conclusion

The tribal areas in the central Indian states of Chhattisgarh and Jharkhand are marked by poor health care coverage, poorly maintained health infrastructure, specific pattern of bio-genetic diseases, high concentration of infectious diseases, lack of health education, inadequate health care staff and prevalaence of cultural practices that adversely affect health seeking. Special provisions in the health care programmes have made some impact, but in many remote areas which are far off from the road and rail link, the impact of new knowledge and technology remains a distant dream.

There are currently two contradictory objectives that need to be simultaneously met in respect of improving the health status of the scheduled tribes in these states. The primary focus on health education, nutrition, immunization, hygienic living and sanitation besides meticulously improving the health care infrastructure, health care personnel, supplies and approach can greatly reduce the burden of diseases such as childhood diarrhea, acute respiratory tract infections, chicken pox, measles, night blindness, marasmus, skin infections, orthopedic fractures, high risk pregnancies, malaria, etc. It means going beyond the paper and target driven approach towards a more participatory, transparent, flexible and friendly health care delivery.

It is common knowledge that providing adequate health personnel in the tribal areas is generally a neglected area. In a visit to Kachharpara, a Kamar tribal hemlet in Chhattisgarh, the villagers requested that the malaria health worker should visit them at least once a week. The villagers complained that he is the only person who visits them from the health department and his visits to are rare. To say that tribals' participation in the health care programmes is poor is far from true, as there have been almost negligible attempts to involve them seriously in the programme itself. The primary level health posts are either un-manned or are served by de-motivated staff. The tribal and other marginalized people are thus left to the mercy of the quacks or greedy private practitioners.

In one instance, for a case of complicated pregnancy, the Kamar villagers had called a nurse from Gariyaband town. But by the time she could arrive, the child was already born. Even then, the nurse charged them 700 rupees as her fee, for visiting them. The poor Kamar were really surprised and said, "Thank God, she did not do anything. Otherwise, we might have been asked to pay may be 7,000 rupees". In the context of the poor reach of public health care services to the scheduled tribes, their dependence on the baiga local healer for treatment needs to be understood and should not be viewed as their aversion to the scientific medicines.

The second objective is the utilization of indigenous knowledge. Since time immemorial, the tribal communities have been using herbs, minerals and other substances in treating their sick. They also have physiotherapeutic knowledge, used in treatment of fractures, sprains, spasms and other internal conditions, besides an immense knowledge about child birth, gyneacology and snake bite. The entire medicinal heritage of tribal society can also be seen as alternative system of therapy. The challenge on this front is two-fold. The first is to examine the therapeutic efficacy of tribal medicines and its re-introduction for health promotion, prevention and cure. Anthropologists and botanists have amassed vast amount of data on ethnomedicines, on medicinal herbs being used in scheduled tribe areas. Many of these herbs are claimed to be effective. There is not much known beyond the verbal testimony of the people. There is thus an urgent need to verify tribal claims regarding the efficacy of the plant medicines. The second major challenge confronting us today is to obtain the intellectual property rights of the tribal medicines and to propagate this therapeutic heritage, of course, after ascertaining its benevolent properties. The fruits of intellectual property have to be returned to its rightful custodians too. This will require interdisciplinary efforts by anthropologists, biotechnologists, lawyers, pharmacologists, botanists, social activists and above all the alert and aware tribals.

In recent times, insurgency activities, primarily in the scheduled tribe dominated districts of Chhattisgarh and Jharkhand is another area of serious concern. While the causes for this emergence may be the failure of development and exploitation of the tribal population by the non-tribals, but, it is equally true that the insurgency greatly hampers the pace of development, especially health care development. The poor scheduled tribals are in a catch 22 situation. There was already reluctance on part of the doctors and other health staff to serve these areas and now their reluctance is justified, in the light of poor security scenario in the tribal areas. It is therefore the duty of the state government to provide adequate security to the health personnel and also win back the heart of the scheduled tribes by sincerely implementing and monitoring their health care development.

The idea of the creation of a new state was based on the sound principles of better governance and administration. It is nearly a decade since these two states were formed and this is the right time to take stock of the progress and to address the core issues hindering overall development of the states. Tribal aspirations were sufficiently met with the election of a tribal as the chief minister of Jharkhand and many ministers in both the states, being from among them. The overall picture that emerges from an evaluation of the health care infrastructure and its management is that it is not sufficiently geared, to fulfill the aspirations of the people.

It seems that the states have been paying more attention to economic development than to hitherto soft areas like health, social security, education, etc. There appears to be a shortfall in PHCs and specialist doctors. Although the general doctors in both the states are in excess supply, it has to be empirically established that they are also available at their place of posting and not running after the health ministry for transfer. Once this is ensured, the PHC, CHC, health sub-centres need to be strengthened with auxiliary staff and a functional supply chain of medicines, equipments and referrals. The available morbidity data tend to suggest that the primary health infrastructure is deficient in both the states, though in some districts, the mother and child health services are functioning adequately.

The high morbidity due to water born diseases suggests that the preventive health services require a major boost. Improvement in water supply and better disposal of water and other waste would go a long way in bringing down the morbidity. The simple messages of diarrhea prevention, ARI precautions, immunization, and sanitation need to reach the hinterland. The traditional IEC approach of distribution of pamphlets, pasting of posters is not going to be sufficient. A more proactive, behaviour changing, communication strategy needs to be aggressively taken up for the tribal areas. The tribe-specific local traditions, customs and folklores should be studied and then the health education drive should communicate health messages in consonance with local culture and traditions.

Medical anthropological knowledge to identify traditionally nutritious diets and their preparation can be mainstreamed through adequate health education campaigns. The two states, though appear to be small, are home to a very rich cultural and biological diversity. This immensely rich diversity should be taken up as a positive indicator for opening up possibilities, in defining nutritional and health supplements. The tribal people in India have been objects of occasional research and study for many decades, both before and after independence. A few have romanticized them—painting idyllic pictures of primitive and native simplicity, a life of dance and song, of ritual and colour. Yet others have looked upon them as curious psychological, anthropological phenomena, as exotic museum pieces tied to institutions like ghotul, dhumkuria, rarung, shaminism, witchcraft, etc. (*Chaudhuri, 1986*).

Researchers have, of course, not been able to close their eyes to the abject poverty, ignorance, disease and vicious exploitation in which the tribal masses wallow. The process of change within the tribal societies had consequently operated at a low key, perpetuating the older mode far too long, and thus, leading to the socio-economic stagnation of a high order. The traditional knowledge of the tribal in the use of wild fruits, nuts, roots, leaves, etc. can be and should be incorporated in health care. The tribal system of medicines should not be seen as a parallel and competing system, but as associate and complementary system to the public health care delivery. In this context, establishment of a network of health services by the government and other agencies (e.g., missionaries), represents a purposeful intervention to bring about changes in the health culture, not only by making available and accessible the medical care to population, but also by actively promoting the use of some aspects of the services (e.g., family planning, vaccination, etc.) within the population (*Basu, S. and Mitra, K. 2001*; *Government of M.P. 1988*). Health culture, therefore, becomes an integral component of the overall culture of the community. The culture of a community also indirectly influences its health culture, because certain cultural practices such as child birth practices, food and drinking habits, and pregnancy practices are directly related to the generation of some community health problems (*Babu, B.V. et al. 2001*).

The holistic concept of health culture provides a valuable framework for analyzing the interaction of the pre-existing health culture of a community with that of the recently introduced health institutions (i.e. dispensary and hospitals) (*Kakar, 1977*; *Singh, B. 1995*).

REFERENCES

Babu, B.V., Hazra, G.P., and Satyanarayan, K. (2001), Community Perception of a District Health System, *Journal of Health Management*, 3:1: 109–116.

Basu, A. (1990), Anthropological Approach to Tribal Health. In Tribal Demography and Development in North-East India.ed by. Ashish Bose, Tiplut Nangbri and Nikhlesh Kumar. pp. 131–142. Delhi. B.R. Publishing Corporation.

Basu, S. and Mitra, K. (2001), Health Development of Tribal Communities in India: Need for Action Research, *Indian Journal of Social Development*, 1:1: 134–156.

Basu, S.K. (1994), The State of The Art of Tribal Health in India In Tribal Health in India. Ed by. S. Basu, pp. 312–349, New Delhi, Manak Publication Pvt. Ltd.

Bharathi, B.S. (1993), Spirit Possession and Healing Practices in a South Indian Fishing Community, *Man In India*, 73(4): 343–352.

Bose, S. (1980), Health situation and problems of health development. ICSSR. Research Abstract. Quarterly. Volume-XI.

Chandra, R. (2004), "Tribal Health and Medicine" in Tribal Health and Medicine edited by Kalla, A.K. and Joshi, P.C. New Delhi. Concept Publishing Company.

Chaudhary, B. (1994), Tribal Health and Medicine Socio-cultural and Environmental: Dimensions. In Tribal Economy, Health and Wasteland Development. Ed. Mahanti, N., New Delhi, Inter-India Publications.

Chaudhari, B. (ed). (1986), Tribal Health: Socio-Cultural Dimensiòn, New Delhi, Inter India Publication.

Chaudhuri, B. (1967), Magic vs Medicine in a tribal village. Adibasi. ix. 3-9.

Government of M.P. (1988), Madhya Pradesh Ke Adivasi Kshetron Mein Parivar Niyojan/Pratibandha (Ek Mulyankan). Tribal Research Institute. Bhopal.

Hira Lal. (1925), Rows to propitiate the goddess of small pox, *Man in India*, 5:258–260.

http://mohfw.nic.in/kk/95/ic/toc.htm

Joshi, P. C. (2004), The World of Tribal Healers. In Tribal Health and Medicine edited by Kalla, A.K. and Joshi, P.C. New Delhi. Concept Publishing Company, pp. 202–241.

Joshi, P. C. (2004), Issues in Tribal Health and Medicines. In Tribal Health and Medicine edited by Kalla, A.K. and Joshi, P.C. New Delhi. Concept Publishing Company, pp. 404–407.

Kakar, D.N. (1977), Folk and Modern Medicine: A North Indian Case Study. Delhi, New Asian Publishers.

Lewis, O. (1958), Village Life in Northern India. New York. Random House

Majumdar, D.N. (1933), Disease, Death and Divination in certain primitive societies in India, *Man In India*, 13: 115–149.

Ratlam, R. (1955), A study in magic and medicine. *Vanyajati*. 3(2). 67–72.

Sachchidananda (1994), Socio-cultural Dimension of Tribal Health. In Tribal Health in India, Ed. Basu, S. Delhi, Manak Publication.

Singh, B. (1995), An Overview of Tribal Health. In Tribal Health in India. Ed by. Bhupinder Singh and Neety Mohanty, New Delhi, Inter-India Publication, pp. 17–32.

Sinha, A.K. and Banerjee, B.G. (2004), "Tribal Witchcraft and Personalistic Disease Theory: Concepts and Issues" in Tribal Health and Medicine edited by Kalla, A.K. and Joshi, P.C. New Delhi. Concept Publishing Company, pp. 179–201.

ENVIRONMENTAL ISSUES

Environmental Degradation and Social Injustice in Tribal Areas

Deficit of Governance and Failure of Democracy

K.B. Saxena

"Environmental degradation and social injustice are two sides of the same coin. The human conditions and the state of the environment are closely related to each other" so runs the "Statement of Shared Concern" of the contributors to the First Citizen's Report on the State of India's Environment (*CSE, 1985*). The truth of the statement is nowhere better reflected than in the region with tribal concentration because the tribes, more than any other social group, are crucially affected on environment for their survival. The paradigm of "development" pursued by the state triggers processes which cause both extensive environmental degradation and social injustice to the people. The tribals are victims of this double whammy but powerless to stem this tide.

Social Injustice

This social injustice arises from the fact that besides polluting air and water bodies and affecting the productivity of land, environmental degrading development activities also cause economic deprivation. They threaten rural livelihoods, deprive the tribals of fuel-wood, fodder, material for making, income generating product and house construction, tubers and roots for food, medicinal plants, destroy their crops and cause numerous health problems. The injustice to the tribes is greater because their longstanding, traditional and culturally rooted access to the resources involved—land, water, forest, fishery is extinguished with curtailed to benefiting profit making entities. This happens with the backing of the government, which takes up projects and grants necessary authorization and concessions to the agencies for this purpose. The affected people feel hurt that their own government has let them down (*Guha, 2001*). The tribals have also a deep sense of awareness about their symbiotic relationship with the environment. Therefore, the damage caused to the latter through multifarious polluting activities is perceived as a direct assault on their survival since the eternal bond embedded in the relationship gets ruptured. The injustice is greater to the tribal women, who by virtue of the division of labour in the household are required to do most of the collection work—fuel, fodder, water, edible roots and fruits. They end up losing their vital economic role and its concomitant social autonomy and status within the family. The abuse of nature which causes the socio-environmental degradation is thus both an ecological as well as a human disaster. It destroys productivity of people's assets, deprives access to livelihood and lowers the quality of life. It is responsible for their increased vulnerability to exploitation and destitution. They are pushed further into the abyss of poverty and lose even their physical capacity to cope with this catastrophe. But it affects the poor and the marginalized more than the better off sections who have the resources to escape from impact of these adverse externalities. The injustice increases further when the government ignores environmental dimensions in its frenzied zeal for accelerated growth and totally disregarding its negative externalities for the people. Evidently, in government's view, the affected poor and the tribals do not matter powerless and marginalized as they are within the system. Rather, the injustice to them is rationalized as a necessary sacrifice for development which is claimed to serve the "larger good". The tribals have seen the hollowness of this claim because they do not derive any benefits from this development its process is loaded against them (*Pandey, 1998*). They have, therefore, been questioning the ethical foundation of this development and resisting its imposition on them. This resistance has pushed the issue of social justice center-stage in the agenda of development and governance. The tribals are speaking truth to power (*Guha, 2001*).

Fatal Overlap

Tribal areas constitute the most pronounced site of this environmental degradation and social injustice. Most of the minerals of the country are located in the areas which contain the largest and the most dense forest cover and sources of numerous river systems. These are also the regions which have concentration of the tribal population, the poorest and the most marginalized sections of society who depend upon the over-ground resources for their survival. Jharkhand, Orissa and Chhattisgarh are the richest and the largest mine bearing states with 70 per cent of coal, 80 per cent high grade iron ore, 60 per cent of bauxite, 40 per cent of manganese and most of the chromite (*CSE, 2008*). The mineral producing regions are also covered by large forest cover with 43 per cent in Chhattisgarh, 30 per cent in Jharkhand, 27 per cent in Orissa and 26 per cent in Madhya Pradesh. The districts with large tribal population carry an average forest cover of 37 per cent which exceeds the national average by 85 per cent. The "fatal overlap" lies in this co-existence which assumes poignancy when industrial mining and other development projects degrade, deplete and destroy these resources making the tribal even more vulnerable than they already are with the highest levels of poverty and the lowest indices of human development. This situation is progressively worsening with the unprecedented pace of mineral extraction and industrial expansion pursuant to the shift to the globalised neo-liberal economy with virtually no protection for the environment and little ameliorative action for the tribals built into it. This explains why the naxalite movement has emerged in 40 per cent of the mineral rich districts in six major mineral producing states (*CSE, 2008*).

Environmental degradation can be caused both by nature and human action. In the case of tribal heartland, the centre of naxalite movement, it is overwhelmingly the latter which contributes to it. These areas are rich in resources which the modern civilization considers of huge value for economic growth. The resources in demand are land, forests, water, and bio-diversity. All have been targeted for accelerated exploitation-land for extraction of minerals, fossil fuels, metallic and non-metallic ores and setting up of industries based on them, infrastructure and residential colonies; forests for its diverse produce from the existing species and their conversion into consumer and industrial goods, cultivation of new species of commercial value; water resources for sustaining industries, conversion into electricity and building reservoirs for irrigation and supply of drinking water to urban areas, and biodiversity for mass tourism. Development activities in respect of each one of them, besides displacing people on a large scale1, cause extensive damage to the environment which in turn severely jeopardizes the livelihood and quality of life of the people but fails to evoke the needed response from the Government. The various dimensions of these adverse effects, resource wise, are discussed in brief here.

Land

Land is targeted primarily for mineral extraction. Geographical distribution of fossil fuels, metallic and non-metallic mineral reserves have a high degree of concentration in central and north eastern India. The forty contiguous districts in this belt produce more than half of all national mining output. The new economic policy opened up the area to facilitate intensive extraction of these resources for accelerated industrialization and export in the 1990s, removed controls and allowed private/foreign investment for this purpose. The amendment of Mining Policy in 2006 to allow 100 per cent direct foreign investment created a rush for multi-national mining companies to exploit the reserves of key minerals which have a built-in market for them. A huge number of MOUs with foreign investors have been signed by the governments of Orissa, Chhattisgarh, Jharkhand and MP for rapid exploitation of mineral resources (*Perspectives, 2007*) notwithstanding the fact that some of these foreign companies have unsavoury record of environmental degradation practices and human rights violations (*Acharya, 2008*). This has pushed up demand for land for the primary purpose of extraction and manufacturing and the secondary purpose of creating infrastructure providing power, transport, storage, processing and office and residential colonies. This implies drastic changes in the existing land use from agriculture and forestry to industrial and infrasturutral development. This change in land use degrades the environment around these activities and adversely affects the people dependent on it for their day to day existence.

Factors of Land Degradation

Mining activity has an all round devastating effect on the environment of the area where it is undertaken which few other economic activities can match. It is carried out in two ways—open cast and underground. The choice is determined by the nature and economic value of reserves and the level of technology required to produce the output for the desired purpose. Either way, the extraction of ore releases extensive dust which spreads all around and spoils all elements of environment. It makes agricultural lands barren, pollutes water resources, denudes forests, defiles air and lowers quality of life for the people who live and work in this area. The dust spreads both in the process of extraction of ore (particularly in the open cast mines) transport of ore and its beneficiation as also through the mining dumps. The land is damaged by mineral activity in different ways. Firstly, the area directly involved in extraction of ores and fossil fuels becomes totally unproductive, and virtually turns into wasteland unless properly restored through extensive efforts. Since mineral reserves extend over a large area, the degradation involved is also extensive. The land in the area is also degraded by different forms of erosion. Nearly two-thirds of land of upper Damodar Valley falls in this category. This land is lost for agriculture and forestry. Further, the mining wastes are stacked on productive land or dumped along the roadside or thrown into the river course. The circulation of dust from mining activity and waste dumps on the neighbouring land in areas not involved in extraction reduces its productive potential wherever it settles down. This results in the decline of agricultural productivity and the valuation of the affected land. This is a collateral damage the social cost of which is not even accounted for let alone compensated. This type of damage has been reported from several areas in Jharkhand, Orissa, M.P., Chhattisgarh. For example, in west Singhbhum district of Jharkhand, farm lands in a 10 mile radius of Jhinkpani cement factory have turned barren. The paddy production per acre has reportedly declined by two-thirds. The trees are withering away (*Viegas and Menon, 1989*). Similar effect has been reported from iron ore mining area of Keonjhar district, sponge iron plants of Sundergarh districts, and sukhinda block of Jaspur district in Orissa where chromium mines are located.

Land is also damaged by underground and stockyard fires in coal mining areas which can also lead to subsidence. Jharia coal fields in Dhanbad district of Jharkhand and Jhasurgrah Colliery area in Madhya Pradesh are some of the sites from where such fires have been reported. The underground fires raging in Jharia coal fields of Jharkhand extending to an area of 17.32 sq.km has made living in the area unsafe. Cracks have appeared in houses and temperature has risen alarmingly. In terms of social impact, 78 villages and around 22000 persons are affected (the number would be larger as there is a lot of floating population in the area). No effort has been made to shift them to safer location. (*Tiwari and Mahapatra, 2000*). This makes the area unfit for habitation, agriculture and grazing. The underground mining operations also use timber for supporting the roof of mine galleries to prevent them from collapsing during the process of extraction. This leads to deforestation of the nearby forest for getting this timber. The mineral based industries require a lot of land both for setting up of industrial plants as well as supportive infrastructure such as engineering units, rail and road network, sidings and stock yard. In addition, office space, residential colonies and urban amenities for these industries also need land. This change in land use degrades the environment of the area and deprives people living in the vicinity of their traditional sources of livelihood and other life supporting benefits.

No Action for Restoration

The extensive damage to the environment and the people could be reduced to some extent if agencies involved in mineral extraction simultaneously undertake the following measures:

- Filling the used mines with bags of mine waste.
- Reclamation of land through soil and water conservation measures.
- Construction of check dams with water-filter beds at the base and covering the dam with vegetation to stabilize the structure.
- Extensive a forestation.
- Location of waste dumps away from human settlements, agricultural land and water bodies/sources.
- Strong pollution control measures with people's participation.
- Necessary facilities to monitor the effects on people and to provide needed services to neutralize the adverse effects.

  The mining agencies are aware of the need for these technological and sociological interventions and are expected to carry them out in terms of the existing regulations. The enforcement of pollution control measures is however, weak despite the existence of dedicated organizations for discharging this responsibility. The enabling provisions for this purpose, relating to the restoration of degraded land in the Mines and Minerals (Regulation and Development) Act remain unimplemented. With the accent of the Government on fast growth, the enforcement agencies turn a blind eye to the violation of regulatory provisions and compromise their professional ethics. There are no strong civil society organizations to put pressure on the Government. The affected people are too poor and weak to mount sustained protest. On the other hand, polluting agencies (public and private) have a strong clout with the enforcement agencies and political leaders and are able to ignore the local protests, if any.

Impact on People

Peoples are adversely affected by mineral development activities in the following ways:

- Extensive acquisition of land leading to large scale displacement of persons from their land, habitat and environment without their rehabilitation and restoration of their environment.
- Loss of livelihood with no provision of viable alternatives for those who are totally dependent upon land.
- Deprivation of access to forest resources with change in land use and consequents loss of several life supporting benefits.
- Degradation of land in the vicinity of mines and waste dumps leading to infertility, decline in productivity and devaluation in market transactions with no compensatory mechanism in place to undo this loss.
- Dust particles get deposited on surrounding vegetation and over a period of time produce a suffocating effect. The plants eventually die.

Water

Patterns of Contamination

Mining activity not only affects land and forests but also water resources (rivers and waterways). It affects availability of, access to and the quality of water. Hard rocks which usually contain a lot of minerals are located in hilly terrain covered by forests. Both forests and hills are sources where our rivers came from. Substantial mineral reserves are located in areas close to the origins or in the catchments of rivers as for example, iron ore reserves in the water courses of Indravati in Chhattisgarh, Baitarni in Orissa, Tungabhadra in Karnataka. Most of the coal reserves in Jharkhand and West Bengal are to be found within the Damodar river basin, and coal deposits of Orissa in Mahanadi-Brahmani basin. Mining activity has the effect of degrading the catchments and changing the courses of rivers besides affecting the quantum of flow of water and its quality. Mining of riverbeds erodes their banks (*CSE, 2008*). The degradation of water resources takes place in the following ways:

- Opencast mining particularly on the mountain top reduces and dries up perennial streams. It also increases surface run off and decreases infiltration causing floods and droughts in the region. The opposition of tribals to mining in POSCO, Niyamgiri and Vedanta Projects is on account of this apprehension besides other reasons.

- Underground aquifers are breached in the course of mining activity thereby altering hydrological regime and depleting ground water. This deprives the people of underground water streams for drinking and agricultural purposes.
- In and around Talcher coal fields of Orissa, wells are sinking and water tables have gone down so much that even deep tube wells do not yield water. Talcher region has become a living desert (*Tiwari and Mahapatra, 2000*). Captive limestone mines of major cement plants have bleached the groundwater in their area.
- Increased sedimentation and mining waste choke and contaminate water courses in rivers, streams, ponds and water channels.
- Huge quantities of water are consumed for mining operations such as wet drilling, cooling the machinery, dust suppression, washing ore and its beneficiation which affects access of people of the area to this water. Dewatering of underground mines also shrink ground water reserves which deprives availability of drinking water to people in the area from this source. The extent of resource diversion from social to industrial use can be gauged from the fact that ten billion liters of ground water is pumped out every day from the Talcher coal fields which have dried up aquifers in an area of 1000 sq. km. (*Tiwari and Mahapatra, 2000*).
- Untreated effluents from industrial and beneficiation plants are released into the nearby streams making water unfit for drinking or domestic use.
- Washings from waste heaps and slimes from beneficiation plants cause silting of water courses leading to floods in the area and shortage of water in downstream areas.
- Groundwater is polluted by underground tunnels when it enters the exposed areas.
- In the process of clearing mines for extraction, accumulated water from underground mines is released into the nearby water courses, which cause floods and water logging in some areas and reduce availability of ground water in other areas. Also, such water from mines carries silt with it, which contaminates the quality of water. This practice adversely affects agriculture and availability of water for drinking. The people are forced to use this very water for drinking in the absence of an alternative. There is no effort by the polluting agency to treat this water. One example of this callousness is the action of Mahanadi coal fields, a public sector

undertaking organization, which supplies this water without treatment for drinking to the villagers. The water is highly carcinogenic as it contains heavy metals and is a continuing source of poison.

- Mineral based industries also consume a lot of water which again reduces its availability to the people in the area. It pushes wastewater into the rivers and streams which contaminates water used by the people. In Jamshedupur steel city, Subarnarekha river is drying up due to the industrial consumption of water. Aluminum plants are also water intensive. In Orissa, water is proposed to be diverted from Hirakud dam to feed the Vedanta Aluminium plant in Jharsuguda, which has irked the locals as it would deprive them of water for drinking and irrigation which was the reason for construction of the Hirakud dam. Water from Sardar Sarovar is diverted to meet the industrial needs rather than the drinking water demand in various regions of Gujarat (*TISS, 2008*).
- The quality of water is affected by "acid mine drainage" besides pollution from heavy metals, leaching, processing chemicals and erosion and siltation. This acid is drained out by rainwater from mine site to water bodies contaminating them. This source of pollution is most pronounced in coal fields in Meghalaya. AMD contains toxic metals (*CSE, 2008*).

Hotspots of Water Pollution

One of the hottest spots of acute pollution of water sources resulting from mining and industrial activities is Damodar river flowing through the coal mining belt of Jharkhand it One of the most polluted rivers in the country it has been termed as "the river of sorrow". Due to the excessive pollution load it carries, its water is unfit for use even for agriculture. The pollution is caused by an extensive discharge of industrial effluents and mining waste, unchecked by the enforcement agencies, into the river creating a visible oily substance in some stretches. The river continues to be the main source of drinking water for a large populace in the rural and urban areas of the region. The other highly polluted river is the Subarnarekha flowing through the mineral—industrial belt of Jharkhand, West Bengal and Orissa. The third such river is Sankini in Bastar district located downstream of NMDC's (National Mineral Development Corporation) iron ore mines in Bailadila which is the drinking water sources for people in 51 neighboring villages.

Heavy pollution to water courses is also reported from villages in Joda block of Keonjhar district, Koida block of Sundergarh district where 142 mines are located. Brahmini river in stretches is polluted by steel plants in the area. The chromite mines discharge in Talcher-Angul area discharge 29,434 kilo liters of heavy metal laden water into the Brahmani river (*Tiwari and Mahapatra, 2000*). Many villages in Rajgangapur block are also affected due to the pollution of water streams from more than 47 sponge iron plants in Sundergarh district of Orissa.

Impact on People

This contamination of water sources affects people in several ways.

- They are forced to consume water from those very polluted sources for drinking, domestic use and also use it for agriculture. The drinking of this water causes gastroenteritis and associated ailments while use of this water for agriculture affects the fertility and productivity of land and the quality and value of output from it.
- The agencies which cause this pollution and degrade the quality of life of people take no responsibility for treating this water, attending to health problems caused by its consumption and compensating for the damage to the land and produce.
- Floods and water-logging affect agricultural activity in the area. The scarcity of water downstream causes hardship due to the reduced access to drinking water.
- The death of livestock has also been reported from these areas due to the consumption of contaminated water and vegetation.

Air

Mining and industrial activities also produce immense air pollution in an atmosphere which was clean, fresh and healthy. Large-scale mining generates huge quantity of waste, a major source of air pollution at the mine site. The quantum of waste generated by mining of major minerals approximates 1.8 billion tones (*CSE, 2008*). The crushers, smelters and ore concentrators release a thick layer of silica dust. The blasting of rock for exposing location of ores releases noxious fumes in the atmosphere. The fine dust particles from the mining dumps spill over from ore carrying trucks and contaminate air. Thousands of trucks plying in the mining areas and releasing diesel and petroleum fumes in a day also worsen the quality of air. Jharkhand, Chhattisgarh and Orissa have seen indiscriminate mushrooming of sponge iron plants during the last 10 years which are highly resource inefficient and polluting. The area has already more than 250 plants many of which are expanding. Around 100 TDP sponge iron plants can emit as high as 230–250 tonnes of pollution load. The air in the area is thick with smoke and coal dust (*Down to Earth, 2006*). Korba, Bhillai, Satna (MP) and Dhanbad (Jharkhand) are hotbeds of air pollution. Similar is the case with Angul-Talcher coalfields in Orissa. All these cause numerous health problems when the polluted air is inhaled. Mineral based industry also generates toxins such as mercury, arsenic, lead, zinc, chromium and cadmium. Some mining waste may also contain salts and radioactive contents (*CSE, 2008*). The problem is compounded by very poor overburden management. As a result, rainwater carries them to watercourses and lands. Similar problem occurs with regard to the tailings which pollute air when their particles become airborne and water courses during monsoon.

Noise

Noise pollution is another consequence of drilling, blasting and excavating of mineral ores, grinding and refining processes involved in metal extraction and continuous operation of heavy earthmoving machinery. It has adverse Impact on the health of the workers engaged in these operations as well as the people living in the nearby areas.

Health Effects

Environmental degradation resulting from industrial, mining and other development activities has created serious health problems for the local population and the fauna in the forests. A large number of occupational diseases are caused by dust from mines and polluted air from industrial units. Workers in mines, smelters and crushers suffer greater affliction being directly exposed to the impact of dust, contaminated fumes and noise. One NGO working among the unorganized mines workers in Jharkhand, an area which has a long history of mining, has estimated that around 25-30 lakh people are suffering from pneumonocosis. A number of deaths have occurred on this account (*OSHAJ, 2008*). The workers are not given any protective devices to reduce its intensity. The water pumped out of mines for supply of drinking water to coal mine townships causes numerous disorders of the digestive tract. The workers in open cast mines also report skin diseases and sunstrokes due to atmospheric conditions. Abandoned mines also threaten life and property due to the danger of subsidence besides health related problems caused by pollution of water courses.

Tailings from uranium mining and processing near the Subernrekha river has even caused radioactive pollution which causes cancer, leukemia, malformation in foetuses. Drops of uranium waste spill into the nearby stream, the life line of residents of Dungridih tribal village in east Singhbhum district of Jharkhand. Frogs and fish die within a few hours. This happens every now and then due to leak in pipes that carry the uranium slurry to the tailing ponds located around 15–20 villages. The leak, if not immediately plugged, causes fall of toxic waste into the nearby stream and Digrih dam that joins Subarnrekha river downstream. Rubber pipes that carry uranium slurry to tailing ponds are old and leakages are a common occurrence. This has caused death, devastation and misery in the tribal villages surrounding them and the Jaduguda mines. The water quality in the upstream of uranium mine is unfit for use by the people. The contaminated sand removed from the river bed and uranium waste is not stored in a safe place. The trucks that carry ore to the mills are often left uncovered leading to falling of ore off the vehicles which severely harms the nearby tribal population. People living in the uraninum mining belt are victims of serious diseases like the-lassemia, TB, silicosis, rheumatoid arthritis, kidney disorder and cancer. High incidence of reproductive disorders such as congenital deformities, miscarriages, early mortality of children have been detected near Jaduguda mining belt and tailing ponds. The mortality rate is high and the average life expectancy is low. The local activists of a NGO called Anumukti have produced a damning report on these dimensions. Jharkhand organization against Radiation (JOAR) also narrates these disturbing facts. Bihar legislative Assembly, when Jharkhand was a part of the Bihar State, even demanded closure of the Jaduguda mine. But the Uranium Corporation of India, a PSU of the Government of India, refuses to even own the responsibility for these dreadful effects of its activities. It dismisses allegations of negligence or violation of safety norms. Even Supreme Court failed to give any relief when approached by JOAR (*CSE, 2008*). The uranium mining is now being expanded to new areas in Jharkhand A.P. and Meghalaya leading to agitation by the local people. (*TOI, N.D., May 13, 2007*; *Mukherjee, 2007*).

Threat to Safety

There is a great deal of laxity in the observance of safety rules in most mines and factories. The resultant death and injuries to the workers do not get correctly reflected in official records. Private sector units are more culpable in this regard. Even in public sector establishments, the number of deaths and injuries is quite large. The Supreme Court directives regarding workers' safety and welfare remain unimplemented. The level of supervision and monitoring is weak, to say the least. The affected families do not receive the required rehabilitation. As a large number of workers facing these hazards are excluded from the purview of labour laws such as the Factories Act, 1948, Employees State Insurance Act, 1948 and Workmen Compensation Act, 1923 they do not receive even entitlements these laws provide in such cases. Their exclusion from the applicability of these laws is on account of the definition of "establishment" contained in them. The small number of workers below the level defining an "establishment" in these laws provides the convenient loophole to the employers to ignore their provisions on account of their non-applicability. It is not uncommon for employers to deliberately fragment establishments or to outsource hazardous work to smaller units to escape the legal obligations. The poorer implementation of laws compounds the problem. The management, both private and public sector, is indifferent to workers' health and safety with greater accountability deficit in the former. The enforcement machinery and medical establishments also show a tilt towards management. Those who are not workers and yet are affected by environmental degradation are nobody's responsibility. This segment constitutes a huge area of local population which remains uncared both by polluting agencies as well as the concerned state governments.

Illegal Mining

In addition to the damage caused to the environment and its consequential effects, illegal mining and illegal practices in legal mining compound the misery of the people. Slaughter mining reminiscent of pre-coal nationalization days become more rampant now. This will lead to subsidence on a large scale leading to the enlargement of the degraded area. BCCL, a PSU of the Government of India, has an area of around 632.96 sq.km of degraded land in the Jharia coal field of Jharkhand alone. In Raniganj coal field of West Bengal, the subsided area is around 30 sq.km. Some of these areas have been declared unsafe for human habitation and are, therefore, potential areas of disaster to happen (*Down to Earth, 2000*). These areas are environmental traps where disaster can strike any time since no tangible preventive plan in place.

The local tribals and other poor in the absence of any regular and dignified employment are forced to engage in illegal mining (rat mining) usually carried out in the abandoned mines for a living or unskilled temporary work with very low wages as contract labourers for short episodes outside the mines. In the Hazaibagh district of Jharkhand, nearly 500 bags of coal is illegally mined everyday (*Down to Earth, 2000*). The conditions of local people, particularly tribals, far from improving have worsened. This is the uniform experience from all mining areas.

While poor living conditions in mining areas adversely affect longevity and labour productivity, the economic conditions of people taken as a whole also do not improve as their incomes and prospects of livelihood do not increase. The mining and industrial activities absorb very few local people when compared to the number who lose livelihood on account of the displacement from land and work. If the cost of environmental degradation, loss/decline of productive potential of land and Impoverishment produced by lack of rehabilitation of the displaced persons is added, the balance sheet would turn out to be negative (*CSE, 1985*). In fact, there is a strong co-relation between poverty and mining. Government policies have pushed the affected people in mining areas "deeper into poverty and destitution" (*CSE, 2008*).

Forest

Forest Policy and Social Injustice: Environmental degradation is also caused by exploitation of forests in diverse ways. The most prominent of them is diversion of forest land for non-forest use. Mining and industrial activities take up a large area of forest land leading to deforestation. Around 1.64 lakh hectare of forest land has been diverted for mining in the country. The dense forests in some districts of tribal areas have been completely denuded of forest cover (*CSE, 2008*). This diversion is progressively increasing due to spurt in mining and industrial activities resulting from globalisation of economy, notwithstanding the forest conservation Act, 1980 which disallows use of forest land for non-forest purposes. This concern led the Supreme Court to direct that in case of such diversion compensatory on aforestation non-forest land would have to be carried out financed by the project authority and net present value of existing forest would be realized from it. The people dependent upon forests are severely affected by this change in land use as they are deprived of access to livelihood and other benefits from it. The impoverishing effect becomes more pronounced when the affected persons are compelled to access more distant forests to obtain such produce but are unable to do so as they would lose the day's wage.

Commercialization of Forest Resources: Historically, forest resources had a social orientation. They served the diverse needs of the people living in the vicinity. The colonial government made the first break with this policy to generate revenue for the government. They rapidly reclaimed forest land for agricultural purposes. Subsequently, they used forest resources for meeting industrial and commercial needs. In the earlier phase of their rule, they used forest resources to provide timber for railways, defense and raw material for the industry. This resulted in massive deforestation which necessitated a shift in the policy towards conservation. The latter consideration included them to appropriate forest and manage it with a view to have total control over its resources. This measure extinguished/curtailed rights of the local communities in them. After independence, the Government continued with the same policy and intensified exploitation of forest for industrial and commercial use, curtailing access of the people further.

Timber and Bamboo are among the major resources of Forest. The wood based industries, paper and paper products are their largest consumers. With the increase in the demand for these products, there was progressive depletion of bamboo resources. As a result, exploitation of these resources shifted from peripheral areas to virgin forests due to the exhaustion of resources in the former—a trend described by Madhav Gadgil as "Sequential Exhaustion" (*Gadgil, 1989*). The social injustice inherent in this policy arose from the deprivation of access of the tribal communities to the forest resources and giving priority to industrial requirement of raw material over people's survival needs. Even greater injustice lay in giving lease of forest areas to the industry at low rates of royalty and subsidizing price of bamboo made available to it from the forest. Orissa for example, supplied bamboo at 10 paisa per bamboo to the industry while it was available to the needy people at Rs 2.00 (*Viegas and Menon, 1989*). There have been protests in some places against the discriminatory price policy and restrictions in supply of bamboo to the local people. In several areas, wood is not available for making ploughs or house construction whereas it is supplied to the industry without any interruption (*Gadgil and Guha, 1995*). The pressures to generate revenue also led to faster exploitation of forests for meeting domestic commercial demand. This over exploitation deforested a large area and led to depletion of food resources accessed by the tribals particularly in the lean season which has adverse impact on their nutritional status and make them vulnerable to ill health. The denudation of forest, also resulted in climatic change reflected in the frequency of droughts in Orissa and Jharkhand (*Viegas and Menon, 1989*). The adverse effects on the women are even greater. They have to spend larger number of hours traversing 6–8 km. each way, even longer distance in some places, to collect fuel, minor forest produce and make do with less food in the intra-family distribution. This gender dimension emerges from the limited rights enjoyed by the tribal women mediated by "dependency relationship" on adult males in private property (*Aggarwal, 2007*). The access to common property resources not only provides a source of subsistence. The tribal women but also confers a distinct economic role in the family which bestows social autonomy and status.

Conservation Policy

The massive deforestation resulting from forest policy pursued by the Government was counteracted by conservation policy for greater protection of forest and increase in the forest cover. This had even more deleterious consequences for the tribes. The thrust of this policy was to further reduce forest areas accessible to the tribals by expansion of the area of the reserve forests and setting up wild life sanctuaries and national parks. This measure implied a decrease in forest area unaffected by protection and closure. Where the tribals and other forest dwellers enjoyed some rights and curtailment/ denial of access to forests resources. Still worse, the policy involved relocation of the tribes living in the expanded reserve forests and their consequent displacement from land and habitat located in them. Their occupation of forest land for cultivation was treated as encroachment and they began to be forcibly evicted. Even the tribals settled in forest villages since the colonial period to provide services to the forest officials were denied ownership rights on land they occupied and cultivated. In respect of non-reserve forest areas, where access of the tribals was permitted, restrictions were imposed on the collection and disposal of minor forest produce.

The conservation policy had another facet which extended to non-forest areas. This involved forestry activities on public and private land through social forestry programmes. These programmes had broadly three type of schemes: farm forestry carried out on individual farm land; development of wood lots by the forest department for meeting community needs along roadside, canal banks and on public land and wood lots developed by the community on common land for their own use. These schemes ostensibly promoted to meet the fodder and fuel needs of the community and to reduce pressure on forests have been turned into production forestry to meet the increasing commercial demand (*Viegas and Menon, 1989*). The evaluation of these programmes has brought out several adverse effects on the poor, particularly the tribals.

Farm Forestry

The farm forestry programme has prompted many farmers to convert rich agricultural land for tree farming for commercial gains and for reducing labour requirement. This has benefited affluent farmers as they alone are in a position to do so, not being dependent upon such land for food security. The programme has not met the energy needs of the poorer sections, lost on account of forest closure, which was one of its objectives. Tree farming on irrigated land also Impacted on the food security of the local population when subsistence farmers took to it or when agricultural labourers working on the land lost employment. The latter effect has been produced by the decline in demand for labour as tree farming requires considerably reduced labour input when compared to crop farming. The trend towards transfer of land to the absentee landowners/companies was also observed. This shift in the cropping pattern created/aggravated fodder crisis as well. The farm labourers lost their source of agriculture waste from crop farming which served as fuel since the weeds that grow in tree farming do not yield any fodder. Overall, the balance sheet of the programme has been unfavorable to the local poor. The beneficiaries of the programme are the urban and industrial consumers who got increased supply of wood besides the large farmers who increased their income. Due to the predominantly commercial orientation of the programme with accent on marketable forestry output to the increase income, meeting the fuel and fodder needs of the poor never acquired any seriousness in its objectives. As the programme was implemented with assistance from the World Bank in many places, this bias towards marketable tree farming was heavily influenced by the World Bank conditionalities for financing such projects.

The landless people are particularly distrustful of social forestry programmes because the woodlots undertaken on village commons reduce availability of grazing land for the poor landless households owning some cattle. They also lose their rights over such lands as also their only source of brushwood used as fuel. In the distribution of output of wood lots, the poorest sections fail to get any benefit. The poor farmers are even reluctant to accept free distribution of saplings for homestead plantation promoted under the programme fearing that the Forest department may take over their land for management which they may never be able to get back. The protection of such woodlots was also a serious problem where the tribals had developed them. They had to suffer depredations of the armed wood cutters from outside who forcibly cut tree crop and took it away in daylight. This phenomenon has been observed, for example, in Rajmahal hills inhabited by the primitive Paharia tribe of Jharkhand whose crops are forcibly taken away by the non-tribals living in the foothills. These gangs engaged in taking away tree crops are often instigated by sawmill owners and timber contractors in the area. The tribals developing these woodlots have no strength to resist them and get no help from the local administration. They suffer a double whammy. They not only lose fruits of their labour but also face the wrath of the forest officials who accuse them for the loss of tree crops and harass them.

Social Forestry

Social forestry programmes also came in for adverse publicity on account of the choice of species promoted therein. The most favoured species of the forest officials was eucalyptus selected for its fast growing nature and its unsuitability for grazing by animals. The promotion of eucalyptus plantation has been involved in controversy on account of its perceived adverse ecological effects which include exhaustion of water resources around the area of plantation, chemical contamination of the fields, degradation of top soil, spread of root formation etc. There are also reports of increased water runoff and soil loss when eucalyptus replaces natural forests. In the case of the tribals, food security was affected due to the reduced area of land available for shifting cultivation and the loss of edible wild roots which could be obtained from local vegetation. They were also deprived of the availability of thatching grass for housing and firewood for cooking. The programme had no relevance to the needs of the tribals. This is the reason why in several areas of the country people agitated against these plantations and, in some cases, also uprooted them. One example of it was the removal of teak plantation in sal forests of Jharkhand.

Plantation Policy

Commercial orientation in the forest policy is also reflected in the choice of species for plantation. There was a shift in the existing pattern of plantation with diversity of natural species to mono-cultures of fast growing species signaling primacy of market demand over conservation. This has environmental as well as social implications. The density of forest and bio-diversity subsisting on natural growth with a variety of species is lost. The social injustice evident in this change is the diversion of nature from its traditional role of meeting household and community needs to the one which commodities it to meet the demand of the market. The local tribals are deprived of fuel, fodder, tubers, roots and sundry other benefits. There have been violent protests of the affected persons against this change in different parts of the country.

The other shift in forest policy from its social orientation is the decision of state governments to transfer degraded land to industry for producing its raw material needs by relaxing land ceiling laws and Forest Conservation Act (*CSE, 1985*). This measure is justified on the ground that these lands would be more efficiently managed by the industry. On the other hand, the government have consistently declined to allot such land to the poor local tribals and cooperatives/self-help groups of landless persons for growing trees despite advocacy of this measure by civil society organizations and progressive sections of the policy makers. When confronted with strong opposition to the move to lease land to industry, a subterfuge has been adopted which does not attract the land ceiling laws and the Forest Conservation Act. One state government is reported to have leased out degraded forest land to its State Forest Corporation which virtually resorts to the same arrangement through the backdoor. The corporation assigns the "management" of land to a private agency through a long term agreement to produce raw material for the industry. This measure, whatever be its operational structure, virtually transfers control over large areas of forest land to the companies which has serious problems for the local population. Needless to repeat this leads to loss of access to the transferred/leased lands and employment available to the local tribal population of the area from the works undertaken by the forest department for routine maintenance. Besides being deprived of access to fuel, fodder and other critical benefits, the employment opportunities for them also get reduced both on account of capital intensive technologies used for plantations as also the tendency of the management to bring cheap labour from outside. The state governments have shown no inclination to protect the interests of the local population by obligating the industry/private management to guarantee employment to the local people and make them partners in their enterprise. Worse, they are greatly inconvenienced in their day to day movements as the private managing agencies close these areas and fence them to protect their crop.

Control Over Trade

Nationalization of trade in respect of several items of minor forest produce constitutes another dimension of the forest policy. This measure results in lower returns from sale of produce to the tribals who collect them because of the low prices fixed by the forest agencies for its procurement. Greater hardship is caused by the inability of the agencies to buy all the produce collected. In the circumstances, the tribals have to sell the produce to private traders illegally and get an even lower price. The policy to exercise monopoly control over MFP is guided by the consideration of revenue generation though the intervention is purportedly justified to protect the tribals from exploitation by traders in the market.

The changes in the forest policy are also leading to the disappearance of many crafts due to non-availability of raw material from the forest. The most affected by this loss of traditional skill and income earning opportunities are the tribals and the dalits. The dalits earn their livelihood by making bamboo baskets, boxes, brooms, mats, pottery and several other artifacts. The tribals also make a number of hand crafted items. The tribal women collect wild cocoons and roll silk yarn out of them for weaving cloth or use lac drawn from forest to make bangles. Making leaf cups from tree leaves is another income generating actively of the poor tribal women. It is evident that the shifts observed in forest policy benefitted, the urban consumer and the industrialists but failed to projects the interests of the tribals. It is evident that the shifts observed in forest policy benefitted but failed to project the in forests of the tribals.

Joint Forest Management

Faced with a crisis situation characterized by rapid forest degradation, scarcity of bio-mass to meet people's needs and its inability to guard the forests, a major initiative for institutional change was taken by the Central government in the 1990s. Drawing upon the revised National Forest Policy, 1988, it introduced a new institutional structure for forestry management. The innovative feature of the programme was the involvement of the village communities as partner with the forest department in the management, protection and regeneration of degraded forests. This programme was named as the Joint Forest Management. The conceptual frame of the programme envisaged certain entitlements by way of usufruct benefits to the communities in return for their efforts to guard the forests, check grazing and encroachment and to undertake plantation to meet the needs of the community. Guidelines were issued by the Central Ministry of Forest and Environment in 1990 on the design of the programme and its operational details. Twenty two state governments have adopted JFM including states in central India affected by the naxalite movement. Besides using government funds, substantial financial assistance has been obtained from the international donor agencies for executing this programme. These donors have introduced non-government organizations as a bridge between the forest officials and the local communities to facilitate greater participation of the latter. As for the impact of the programme, it is claimed to have succeeded in increasing forest cover, improving livelihood conditions of the forest communities in some places and even weaned away some of the tribal sympathizers of the naxalites (*Jodha, 2000*).

Over a period of more than 15 years (the programme is still in place) a large number of critical but basic issues have come up, which touch upon equity, voluntary character of participation, legal tenability of the management structure, sustainability and the skewed power relations between the parties involved in the JFM. Leaving aside the claim regarding its contribution to income generation of the participating tribals through work opportunities, these issues cast serious doubts on whether the programme has even empowered local communities in the management of forests or given them matching gains for a variety sacrifices made by way of putting in free labour and making vigorous efforts for collective mobilization to fulfill their role. Forest has long been a major site of conflict between the tribes and the government. The policies in respect of the forest area have caused tremendous hardships and immiserisation which has contributed to their alienation from the government and the growth of naxalism in the tribal heartland.

Some situation specific cases of better performance notwithstanding, (*D'Silva and Nagnath, 2002*; *Corebridge and Jewitt, 2004*; *Jewitt, 1999*) the programme has failed to transform the power relationship between the foresters and the local communities by way of the former sharing decision making powers with the latter or promoting genuine devolution to them or showing any radical change in their characteristic authoritarian attitude (*Dhanagre, 2000*). JFM agreements do not operate on a clean slate. They are "superimposed" on the existing complex patterns of village rights and obligations which are ignored. Forest bureaucracy usually does not have the orientation to create enabling environment for participation in such a situation (*Jeffery, 1999*). The forest bureaucracy through this programme still determines they access of the participating tribals to forest albeit in a different manner from the old one. This determines the benefits which could be derived by them from this programme. In the circumstances, the net gains obtained by the communities who provide free labour and commitment for forest protection and regeneration would hardly induce them to continue with this effort voluntarily. This is because the structure and processes of this arrangement are overwhelmingly loaded in favour of forest officials who retain the authority to design and alter the terms of the "understanding" (agreement) arrived at with the communities (*Upadhyay, 2003*). The latter have no secure entitlements or even legal basis to challenge the arbitrary or iniquitous decisions. The JFMCs (joint forest management committees) are embedded in the executive order of the forest officials and do not constitute a legal entity (*Upadhyay, 2003*). Besides, they are assigned degraded forest lands which yield poor economic returns when compared to the efforts required to regenerate and protect them. The benefit sharing mechanism envisaged in JFM also cheats the communities of their labour in different ways. It counts the usufruct from a specified area protected by them which, in any case, they were taking traditionally as part of their customary rights. There is very little by way of additional benefits to them proportionate to the labour put in. The methodology of calculation of percentage of benefit share (by excluding the operational cost of harvesting, staff, maintenance and ancillary expenditure) as well as determining incremental benefits reduce even the meager entitlement conceded to them in the agreement (*Upadhyay, 2003*). The market oriented plantation decisions at the behest of forest officials' views destabilize the existing contours of the programme and jeopardize community entitlements and autonomy even further.

Besides, the entire JFM concept privileges only the JFMC members with sharing of benefits. As a result, the non-members become disentitled of their customary rights and traditional income earning opportunities with the introduction of the community participating in JFM thereby creating inequity and division within the community (*Upadhyay, 2003*). Even the poorer members of the community participating in JFM are at a disadvantage due to the differentiation within the community. Squeezed between the state and the market, the differentiated community cannot effectively promote conservation of the forest and ensure that the rights of the community are restored (*Kumar, 2004*; *Corebridge and Jewitt, 2004*). There is a conflict of interests and unequal distribution of power within the JFM membership which does not facilitate equal participation of all members or promotion of gender, ethnic or class equity. Operationally also, JFM failed to ease the work burden of women since the forest protection restricts their gathering activities. Structurally, it ignored the constraints and issues of gender in the participation of women in JFM despite recognizing their role in programme management (*Jewitt and Kumar, 2004*).

The tasks which JFM performs have also created jurisdictional problems. The programme encroaches upon the powers of the PRIs (Panchayati Raj

Institutions) with no institutional linkage to iron out the conflict involved. In schedule V areas, it violates provisions of PESA Panchyats (Extension to scheduled areas) Act, 1996 where control over natural resources and ownership of MFP (Minor Forest Produce) has been conferred on the *Gram Sabha* (*Upadhyay, 2003*). Inter-village conflicts also arise from the inflexibility over the "unit" which forms the protection committee—there being no sync between the members constituting the unit (i.e., the village) and the users of the forest plot (which may be a single hamlet or more than one village in certain situations) (*Jeffery, 1999*). JFM also fails to harmonize with local tradition, knowledge and efforts. It neither builds upon this rich heritage nor concedes necessary flexibility by building upon peoples' voluntary and more committed efforts towards protection and regeneration of forests by the existing village social institutions. In fact, JFM agreements constitute the biggest threat to the functioning of these institutions (*Jeffery, 1999*). Its standardized and uniform conceptual formulation, programme structure and operational guidelines do not even take into account let alone accommodate bio-physical, socio cultural and institutional diversities (*Jodha, 2000*). No participation of people can be built in a programme frame where the design, structures and terms of cooperation are unilaterally determined by the more powerful of the two parties (*Balooni et al, 2007*). This type of guided and centralized mode of participatory management of forests with varying degree of commitment by the officials of the forest department, bias towards conservation and regeneration and reluctance to share power and alter iniquitous distribution arrangements provides little hope that it would meet the grievances and aspirations of the tribal communities.

Water

The huge potential for diverse use of water resources in the tribal areas is also targeted for economic growth. These resources are required for generating electricity, supplying drinking water to urban and industrial population, meeting the needs of the industry and for extending irrigation facilities to agriculture. Ecologically sensitive areas in the hilly terrain present suitable sites for tapping this potential through construction of large dams. These activities for exploitation of water resources directly create conflict with the local population. As these activities multiply with the induction of foreign capital and the pressure generated by the industry and the urban population, the conflict also intensifies. The multiple adverse effects experienced on account of displacement of the people, loss of their livelihood, destabilization of their community organizations and cultural networks as well as the degradation of the environment on which the people critically depend, are the cause for this conflict.

Dams

Dams constitute the most pronounced and the widely used form of exploitation of water resources. Large dams, by changing the course of natural flow of water, cause severe damage to the natural environment and rich biodiversity as they are located in ecologically sensitive regions. A large number of such dams have been constructed in the tribal area and more of them are proposed. The tribals are among the social groups worst affected by this activity. The adverse externalities from large dams for the affected people are evident from the agitations carried out by them wherever such dams are taken up for construction (Narmada, Koel Karo, Polavaram are among the numerous such movements.) The agitations are primarily focused on large scale displacement caused by this programme with no prospects of meaningful rehabilitation. But the projects of dam construction affect even those not displaced due to the deprivation of access to forest resources on account of deforestation. Besides leading to the loss of forest actually involved in construction and submergence area, the forest is also cleared for building approach roads, residential quarters and storage structures for construction materials. Also, the contractors indiscriminately cut trees from outside the project area. In the cost-benefit calculations made for such projects, loss of forest is undervalued and the social cost of degradation of environment and displacement of people (not the financial cost involved in acquisition of land and resettlement) is not even taken into account. The productive potential considerable areas of land in the vicinity of such dams get deteriorated due to water logging and salinity. The resultant rising water table affects production and productivity of many crops. The rich bio-diversity in terms of rare wild flora is also lost. The deforestation and change in land use cause loss of several benefits which the tribals access from the forest. They are, therefore, forced to depend on the remaining forests which leads to severe competition with other communities accessing them giving rise to conflicts. There is an extensive literature on large dams which highlights various adverse consequences both for people and environment. The latest scientific evidence shows that large dams contribute around 24 per cent of methane emissions from their reservoirs and, therefore, to global warming as well. Indian dams contribute 35.5 million tones of emissions per year from its reservoirs—the largest share of global warming compared to other countries from this source (*Parsai, 2007*).

Bio-diversity

Mass Tourism

Not merely the land, water and forests, even the bio-diversity is being exploited for economic growth. This is done through massive expansion of tourism which is seemingly projected as a people-friendly development activity with considerable distributive benefits. The areas inhabited by the tribal communities present an attractive destination for rich foreign tourists because of the pristine natural beauty and even lifestyle products and livelihood practices of tribal groups. A visit to these areas is projected as an "exotic" experience. Tourism has been promoted by relaxation the existing legal and regulatory restrictions relating to the entry into ecologically sensitive areas and financial policies to attract private investment. Globalisation has intensified these efforts. The Nature Tourism called "Eco-tourism" is touted as the fastest growing form of tourism which even poorer states are advised to promote for accelerating "development". The tribal areas which were till recently excluded from mass tourism activities, are now targeted specifically. Like the other three (land, water and forests), use of bio-diversity for economic growth too has adverse implications both for ecology and local communities which are ignored. International year of Eco-Tourism 2002 gave boost to this activity in India which has already raised concerns followed by protests from the local people and civil society organizations.

The national policy and guidelines on eco-tourism in India, 1998 has outlined all geographic areas comprising eight eco-systems as eco-tourism resources. The National Tourism Policy 2002 has laid greater emphasis on eco-tourism. The policies make astounding presumption that eco-tourism would eliminate poverty, preserve cultural heritage and improve overall environment. They have identified ecologically sensitive areas for promotion of tourism. The civil society critique of this policy raises several issues of vital concern to the local communities. One of them relates to its non-participatory character and the other to its orientation to the global market. The Policy and guidelines on eco-tourism seek to ensure its regulated growth with positive impact on environment and community development and lay down role and responsibilities of the government, the operators, the developers and even the non-governmental organization. Local communities are not enlisted as stake holders and partnership with them is not envisaged as one of the key objectives of the policy and structures of tourism development despite conceding that the failure to involve communities in decision making process is one of the main internal threats (*MoTC, 2002*). Their role is conceived merely in terms of duties to have friendly relations with tourists and observance of conservation practices but no rights or expectations (*MoT, 1998*). Though the Government is expected to prepare the tourism management plan for each area in consultation with the local community, this has nowhere happened. The environmental and social carrying capacities of the selected areas have also not been weighed in developing state policies despite being so envisaged in the guidelines. The two policies are patterned on international guidelines geared to the interests of the global companies. Several State governments with large tribal populations have formulated their own policies on these lines. The relaxation of regulatory restrictions for promoting tourism include liberalization/ removal of permits of entry and other rules, creation of infrastructure for tourists prohibited by the Forest Conservation Act, 1980 in the Protected Areas, construction of accommodation and other facilities, designating tourism zones inside the Protected Areas. Ministry of Environment and Forests has also excluded tourism projects from the requirement of EIA (Environment Impact Assessment) Notification, 2006. Government of India has already liberalized market access to foreign capital by re-including "scheduled areas", which had earlier been excluded, in its latest offer on "services" negotiations under WTO (*Equations, Jan, 2007*).

Impact on the Tribals

This commercialization of bio-diversity has also other adverse effects on the tribal communities which generate conflict. Tourism emerges as a new agenda of environmental degradation and destabilization of tribal society. It disturbs their existing cultural-economy- governance matrix as tribal life is inseparably woven with ecology. Creation of tourism zones inside the Protected Areas also exposes contradictions in the government policy and intensifies conflicts between the forest establishment and the tribal communities. It permits presence of large number of people and global industry in an ecological sensitive region from where tribal communities have been aggressively displaced on grounds of conservation. While such areas had few tribal settlements with minimum infrastructure, tourism brings in larger number of people and creates infrastructure for them. The government permits tourism industry to use forest resources for earning profit but restricts the access of tribals to them even for livelihood options. (*Equations, March, 2007*). That no conservation prescriptions can neutralize the degradation of bio-diversity resulting from commercialization of nature under the impact of mass tourism is borne out by the manner in which the natural beauty of several tourist locations in hill areas and near coastal beaches in non-tribal areas has been spoiled. The isolated tribal areas and ecologically sensitive zones had hitherto been spared of this but this restriction has now been removed. Mass tourism would involve construction of metalled roads, bridges, culverts, picnic spots, trekking circuits, treetop houses, watch towers and accommodation for tourists and tourism providers in project areas at the periphery of the Protected Areas. These areas are not even covered by any regulations but would bear a more damaging impact. The greatest threat to the local communities lies in the severe competition for limited forest resources. They would be deprived of the several life supporting benefits resulting from the scarcity such competition would generate. The competition would create conflict in access to resources—water, edible products, and ingredients for economic activities. The accent on commercialization of biodiversity would also undermine the regulatory role of the Forest department. It would unmistakably lead to deforestation and increase in poaching besides other forms of degradation. The past experience shows that the local tribal communities would be blamed for these adverse developments which they never sought in the first place and over which they would have little control. They would have no capacity to stem this adverse impact against powerful forces unleashed by commercialized tourism. The situation so created would lead also to conflicts of the local communities with the tourists.

Impact on Wild Life

The mass tourism would also impact on the behaviour of wild animals. As it is, people in the vicinity of forests face the wrath of the wild animals resulting from change in behaviour due to deforestation, increased movement of vehicles, human activity and organized shows for tourists in sanctuaries and national parks. These wild animals stray into habitations and ransack houses and crops besides causing injury and death to the inhabitants. There are many areas where this is happening creating panic and insecurity in the affected population.

Lack of Participation

The commercialized mass tourism and the resultant foreign influences would cause the worst impact on the tribals. It would trigger the process of disintegration of tribal society and its cultural ethos leading to social degradation. The much touted income benefits from tourism would also not accrue to the tribals because they have no capacity, wherewithal and support to take advantage of the opportunities that may came up nor such a capacity building has been integrated into the design of the policy, guidelines and the strategy of implementation. Neither the Centre nor the states have made efforts to seek consent of the local community while making the policy. The local communities have been given no role in regulating tourism activities which the framework and spirit of PESA, 1996 requires. Tourism has not even been incorporated as a subject over which the *Gram Sabha* has jurisdiction under this law. The constructive initiatives taken by the tribal civil society groups for participation in the policy making exercise have also been spurned. A group of people representing the tribal communities from different districts in Jharkhand presented a "Jharkhand peoples' policy on sustainable tourism" which include benefit sharing, access to natural resources and provision of a core team formed by the local community which should be actively involved in planning, implementing and monitoring of tourism activities. No action has been taken to incorporate these suggestions by the state government (*Equations, January, 2007*).

Protective Instruments

There is no dearth of regulatory arrangements to check environmental degradation. Starting with the mandate provided by the Constitution, Article 48 A obligates the state to protect and improve the environment and to safeguard the forests and the wild life of the country. Article 51 (A)(g) creates a duty in individuals to obey the mandate of the environment. Article48(A) and Article 51A(g) read with Article 14 (social and economic equality) and Article 21 (right to life) imply that activities which destroy environment and disturb life of the people dependent on it should not be promoted (*Iyer, 2007*). The criminal and civil laws of the country also have some relevance. Sections 268 to 290 of the Indian Penal Code deal with public nuisance which apply to the pollution of air, water and unhygienic environment created by smoke, filth etc. The Law of Torts can be used for seeking damage from person/agency responsible for environmental pollution. There are regulatory instruments to deal with the specific environmental issues thrown up by different sectoral activities. On the mining side, the Mines and Minerals (Development and Regulation) Act, 1957 and Mines Act, 1952 along with the rules framed under them operate as the basic laws. The rules which deserve mention in this connection include the Mineral Concession Rules, 1960 and the Mineral Conservation and Development

Rules, 1988 and the Granite Conservation and Development Rules, 1999. The levy of cess and other taxes on minerals are governed by the Cess and Other Taxes on Minerals (Validation) Act, 1992 which has been made applicable by some states only. In the case of coal, the provisions of the Coal Mines (Conservation and Development) Act, 1974 apply. On the environmental side, the regulatory framework includes, the Water (Prevention and Control of Pollution) Act, 1974, the Environment Protection Act, 1986, Forest Conservation Act, 1980, Environment Impact Assessment Notification, 2006, Wild Life (Protection) Act, 1972, the Air (Prevention and Control of Pollution) Act, 1981 which address specific sectors of polluted resources. The Prevention of Cruelty to Animals Act, 1960, National Environment Tribunal Act, 1995, Water (Prevention and Control of Pollution) Cess Act, 1977 tie up operational aspects of enforcement.

The Supreme Court has made some significant judgments for protecting the environment by liberally interpreting Article 21 dealing with Right to Life to include citizen's right to live in eco-friendly atmosphere as the basic right guaranteed under Article 21. "Green Benches" have been constituted in many High courts to dispose of environment related cases expeditiously. Several landmark judgments were delivered directing closure of factories, industries, mining activities which were polluting environment (*Legal Service, 2008*). The constitutional mandate, however, is defeated by policies of the Government. With its accent on capital driven fast rate of economic growth, it is promoting a pattern of development which would involve grievous injury to all that is of lasting value in nature and injustice to the affected people and tribal communities particularly. The social cost of such "development" is too high and would not be compensated by the national wealth it may generate. The social conflict it would cause has the potential to imperil economic growth as well as social stability unless corrective measures are taken in time.

People's Resistance

The access to and use of natural resources has been the site of intense struggles—a "cauldron of conflicts" on variety of scales and relating to different natural resources—land, water, forests, minerals, fisheries (*Gadgil and Guha, 1995*). Victims of environmental degradation have not taken the social injustice of development quietly. They have increasingly struggled against this "pattern of development" which produces such enormity of ill-effects. Chipko movement, Narmada Bachao Andolan and struggle of Bhopal victims of gas leak are some of the outstanding examples. But in rural areas, the resistance has been most prominent on forest issues revolving around deprivation of access to forest resources, eviction from forest habitat and land, plantation policies, subsidization and preferential allocation of forest resources to industry, allotment of forest and pasture land to industry, increase in collection wages of tendu leaf etc., which led to some changes in the forest policy.

The resistance to the construction of dams and displacement from land and habitat have had a long history rooted in the colonial times (Mulshi Satyagrah) and is widespread across the country. The degradation of environment caused by mining activity provoked people's resistance in the non-tribal areas like Doon valley and Kumaon and has also been witnessed in the Gandhamardhan hills of Sambalpur (Orissa), Niyamgiri hills (Orissa), Jaduguda (Jharkhand) in the tribals areas. Industrial pollution has provoked movements against Harihar Poly fibres (Karnataka), Gwalior Rayons (Kerala), MIDC, (Raigad, Maharashtra) and Gwalior Rayons, (Nagda, MP), Soil salinity (North Arcot, Tamil Nadu), Industrial pollution (Chaibasa, Jharkhand) etc. These movements have focused on iniquitous access to natural resources resulting in displacement of settled communities and deterioration of environment affecting livelihood and quality of life both of which are rooted in the paradigm of development. Most of these movements have occurred outside the domain of party politics and have, therefore, signified failure of the representative democracy to articulate people's suffering. The institutions of politics and democracy have supported the current pattern of development responsible for this situation (*Gadgil and Guha, 2007*). The governance is also seen as collusive and unable to provide any relief against the negative policies. These movements have also strongly conveyed the message that the environmental agenda of the poor is different from that of the elite. As the democratic traditions do provide sme space for resistance and policy change (*Jewitt, 2004*), there is need fr greater pressure for such movements for a paradigm shift in policy engineering and institutions and structures of politics.

Locating Responsibility

The foregoing analysis bring out evidence of how villages/areas surrounding prestigious "development projects" have turned into killing fields. The reality on the ground is even more devastating than what has been portrayed here. The more painful feature of the situation is the virtual silence of those who should have been in the forefront of action to prevent activities which caused such horrendous environmental degradation, to punish those responsible for it and to restore the environment and peoples' faith in democracy and governance. The occurrence of these environmental externalities has been attributed to three important failures: market failure, policy failure and institutional failure. Market failure arises on account of failure to internalize the externalities, affecting the rural communities, absence of a compensatory pricing mechanism for industrial pollution between the victims and the polluters, more particularly, where property rights are not well defined and enforced. Such as the common property resources. Policy failure is on account of ineffective state intervention in designing a strong regulatory system and a competent and proactive enforcement mechanism due to the political interference and legal impediments. Institutional failure underlines the insensitivity of institutions (public and private) to respond even to the collective mobilization, pressure and protest which can be attributed to the insensitive attitude of those involved (*Behera and Reddy, 2002*). But all the three failures are subsumed in the deficit of governance. This deficit arises from the serious constraints imposed by the paradigm of development adopted by the Government which gives primacy to economic growth and its concomitant imperative of the supremacy of market and its autonomy from regulatory intervention, ignoring its social-cost, immediate and long term, both to the people and the environment.

Governance Deficit

At the base of this governance deficit lies a glaring apathy towards the impact of industrialization and other economic activities on people and their environment. This is nowhere better reflected than in the deficiency afflicting the laws relating to mining. Besides the acute inadequacy of regulatory arrangements to address the social and environmental impact of mining, the existing laws are ambiguous, loose in formulations, hedged by caveats, lack clarity and definitiveness in fixing responsibility and seeking compliance. This permits the mining agencies to disregard legal obligations. The large scale violations observed during official inspections corroborate this phenomenon. This deficiency is exacerbated by multiplicity of agencies for enforcement of laws and regulations with no clear demarcation of responsibility and inadequate personnel to manage their tasks. Very few establishments, therefore, get inspected and those which are covered reveal high incidence of violations. The compliance of remedial/punitive action with regard to violations is tardy and produces little impact (*CSE, 2008*). The same situation operates in respect of environmental regulations which are oriented towards giving clearance for mining operations than ensuring compliance of the prescribed standards of safeguards. Lacking in monitoring and enforcing capacity, these provisions create no deterrence for non-compliance by willful defaulters or incentive for compliance by others. The structure of environmental impact assessment is designed as a technocratic exercise lacking in objectivity and participation of the affected people. The consultancy agencies chosen to prepare these reports can be clearly accused of a conflict of interest. The public hearing process intended to elicit peoples' views is manipulated, carried out under coercion and threat to produce "manufactured consent". The views expressed by the participating people carry no weight in the decision on clearance of the project. "Environmental impact" itself is narrowly conceived and excludes social and economic dimensions of impact. The stringent provisions of the forest laws to prevent non-forest use are compromised and clearance for mining and industrial projects given without serious scrutiny. Even provisions of wild life protection laws have been relaxed to permit mining inside the reserve forests despite stringent Supreme Court guidelines. The compliance of forest laws is effected merely in terms of seeking an equivalent area of non-forest land with sufficient funds for compensatory aforestation to be carried out by the forest agencies. On the Supreme court directive, recovery of net present value of forest lost in addition to compensatory aforestation would also be realized apportion higher cost for non-forest use. There is no better indication of the indifference of the Government towards environmental issues than the Hoda Committee Report of the Planning Commission which recommends a more liberal process of clearing mining projects in the forest areas. The changes suggested for this purpose include a single-window clearance outpost for processing clearance of mining lease, obtaining forest and environmental concurrence parallely rather than sequentially, routine approvals for renewals of lease and doing away with public hearings for mining leases involving an area of less than 50 ha. (*CSE, 2008*). The most notable governance deficit is to be found in the absence of a regulatory arrangement for mine closure until 2003 which has been responsible for hundreds of exploited mines and thousands of abandoned holes near them which are a health and safety hazard. The existing legal provisions on mine closure like all others are also weak. They donor force companies to undertake pollution control and proper restoration of sustainable eco-system, and socio-economic rehabilitation of the affected people with severe penalties for non-compliance (*CSE, 2008*). The failure to strengthen laws to make them more stringent and enforcement institutions more effective appears intentional so as not to slow down the "pace of development". Environmental issues almost invariably lose out when in conflict with development projects.

Failure of Democracy

But the disinterestedness of political institutions and processes to highlight the devastating consequences, short-term and long-term, faced by the affected people and mobilize them for exerting pressure on the government to protect their interests represents a serious failure of democracy. No interest has been shown by the mainstream political parties or the elected representatives of the people to take up issues such as effective enforcement of existing regulations and monitoring of their compliance, putting in place more stringent regulatory provisions, holding the government accountable for non-performance on this account and above all humanizing the pattern of development responsible for this situation. Even at the time of elections, issues of environmental degradation do not get included in the manifestoes of political parties or the rhetoric of contesting candidates. The democracy has shown to be bereft of any sensitivity towards the misery of a large section of the people for it provides no outlet for redressing their grievances. The political vacuum is filled up by non-governmental organizations and localized social movements who rally round the affected communities. These efforts are, however, frustrated by their fragmented nature, divisive tactics of the polluting agents, expensive, dilatory and often ineffective judicial interventions and indifference of state agencies. The resistance movements and non-governmental advocacy eventually die out. It should, therefore, cause no surprise that naxalism has presented itself as an alternative to democracy in this area. If this challenge to democracy has to be neutralized, environmental degradation should be brought center-stage in the agenda of politics. This would force the institutions of democracy to take note of and exert pressure on the structures of governance. Environmental degradation should be linked with. with other issues affecting the tribal communities—land alienation, displacement etc., for networked agencies concerned to words this end. Simultaneous action is needed to deepen democracy by enhancing the bargaining position of the tribal communities with the industry through environmental information (*Kathuria and Haripriya, 2000*). This is potential waiting to be tapped for sustained work and mobilization of the people at the grassroots by political workers and civil society activists.

REFERENCES

Acharya, Keya (2008): 'India: Mining Boom Affecting Tribals, Environment', Iner-Press Service News Agency, November 11, 2008. Htt://ipsnews.net/print.asp?idnews=43654

Aggarwal, Bina (2007): 'The Gender and Environment Debate: Lessons from India', in Rangarajan (ed).

Balooni, Kulbhushan, Ballabh, Vishwa and Inque, Makoto (2007): 'Declining Instituted Collective Management Practices and Forest Quality in Central Himalayas', *Economic and Political Weekly*, April 21, 2007.

Behera Bhagirah and Reddy, Ratna V (2002): 'Environment and Accountability: Impact of Industrial Pollution on Rural Communities', *Economic and Political Weekly*, January, 19, 2002.

Centre for Science and Environment (1985): Second Citizen's Report on State of India's Environment, New Delhi.

Centre for Science and Environment (1999): Fifth Citizen's Report on State of India's Environment, New Delhi.

Centre for Science and Environment (2008): Sixth Citizen's Report on State of India's Environment, New Delhi.

Corebridge, Stuart, Jewitt, Sarah, and Kumar, Sanjay (2004): Jharkhand: Environment, Development and Ethnicity, Oxford, New Delhi.

Corebridge, Stuart, Jewitt, Sarah, (2004): 'From Forest Struggles to Forest citizens'? in Corebridge, Jewitt and Kumar.

Dhamagre, D.N. (2000): 'Joint Forest Management in UP: People, Panchayat and Women', *Economic and Political Weekly*, September 9, 2000.

Down to Earth online (2006): 'Sponge iron industries are killing fields', Vol. 15, November. 8, Tuesday, September 5, 2006, accessed on august 29, 2008.

D'silve, Emmanuet and Nagnath, B (2003): 'Behroonguda: A Rare Success Story in Joint Forest Management', *Economic and Political Weekly*, December 9, 2000.

Equations (2007): Tourism and Indigenous Communities' Concerns, Bangalore, January, 2007.

Equations (2007): Eco-tourism Impacts on eco systems and indigenous communities rights, Bangalore, March, 2007.

Gadgil, Madhav (1989): 'Forest Management, Deforestation and Peoples' Impoverishment', *Social Action* 39 No. 4. Oct–Dec.

Gadgil, Madhav and Guha, Ram Chandra (1995): 'Ecology and Equity', Penguin, New Delhi.

Gadgil, Madhav and Guha, Ram Chandra (2007): 'Ecological Conflicts and the Environmental Movement in India', in Rangarajan (ed.), Pearson Longman, New Delhi.

Guha, Ramachandra (2001): Environments: A Global History, Oxford, New Delhi.

Iyer, V.R. Krishna (2007): *Hindu*, May 3, 2007.

Jeffery, Roger (ed) (1999): The Social Construction of Forests—Introduction, Manohar, New Delhi.

Jewitt, Sarah (1999): 'Autonomous and Joint Forest Management in India's Jharkhand: Lessons for the Future' in Jeffery (ed).

Jewitt, Sarah (2004): 'Mothering Earth? Gender and Environmental Protection in Jharkhand, India', in Corebridge, Jewitt and Kumar.

Jodha, N.S. (2000): 'Joint Management of Forests: Small gains', *Economic and Political Weekly*, December 9, 2000.

Kathuria, Vinish and Haripriya, G.S. (2000): 'Industrial Pollution Control – Choosing the Right option', *Economic and Political Weekly*, October 28.

Kumar, Sanjay (2004): 'Forest Dwellers' Knowledge of Local Ecological Services', in Corebridge, Jewitt and Kumar, Oxford University Press, New Delhi.

Legal Service India (2008): 'Environmental Degradation and its protection',—A legal perspective, http:www.legalserviceindia.com, November 11.

Ministry of Tourism (1998): Eco-tourism in INDIA, Policy and Guidelines.

Ministry of Tourism and Culture (2002): National Tourism Policy.

Mukherjee Reena (2007): 'Protest against Uranium Mine', Civil Society, April, 2007.

Occupational Safety and Health Association of Jharkhand (OSHAJ) (2008): Letter addressed to Minister in charge, Health and Labour, Government of Jharkhand on Sillicosis Death in Jharkhand, March, 15, 2008 by Secretary General Samit Kumar Carr, Jamshedpur.

Parsai, Gargi (2007): *The Hindu*, May 20.

Perspectives (2007): Abandoned: Development & Displacement, The Perspective Team, Delhi University.

Rangarajan, Mahesh (ed) (2007): 'Environmental Issues in India': A Reader, Pearson Longman.

Tiwari, Manish and Mahapatra, Richard (2000): 'A Nationalised Nightmare', Down to Earth, July 15.

Tiwari, Manish (2003): 'NGOs in Joint Forest Management and Rural Development —Case Study of Jharkhand and West Bengal', *Economic and Political Weekly*, December 27.

Upadhyay, Sanjay (2003): 'JFM in India: Some Legal Concerns', *Economic and Political Weekly*, August 30.

Viegas, Philip and Menon, Geeta (1989): 'The Impact of Environmental Degradation on People', ISI, New Delhi.

Index